QUEEN VICTORIA'S MATCHMAKING

QUEEN VICTORIA'S MATCHMAKING

THE ROYAL MARRIAGES
THAT SHAPED EUROPE

DEBORAH CADBURY

PUBLICAFFAIRS

New York

PublicAffairs
Hachette Book Group
1290 Avenue of the Americas, New York, NY 10104
www.publicaffairsbooks.com
@Public_Affairs

Printed in the United States of America
Originally published in hardcover and ebook by Bloomsbury Publishing in September 2017
First US Edition: November 2017

Published by PublicAffairs, an imprint of Perseus Books, LLC, a subsidiary of Hachette Book Group, Inc.

The Hachette Speakers Bureau provides a wide range of authors for speaking events. To find out more, go to www.hachettespeakersbureau.com or call (866) 376-6591.

The publisher is not responsible for websites (or their content) that are not owned by the publisher.

Photographs are from the author's personal collection except where credited otherwise.

Print book interior design by Integra Software Services Pvt. Ltd.

Library of Congress Control Number: 2017952726
ISBNs: 978-1-61039-846-6 (hardcover); 978-1-61039-847-3 (ebook)

LSC-C

10 9 8 7 6 5 4 3 2

To Pete, Jo and Julia,

with love

Contents

Photo inserts between pages 94–95 and 244–245

PART ONE

Vain the Ambition of Kings
1887–1891

Vain the ambition of kings
Who seek by trophies and dead things
To leave a living name behind,
And weave but nets to catch the wind.

> John Webster, 'Vanitas Vanitatum', originally
> published in *The Devil's Law Case* (1623)

Prologue

It was early afternoon on Sunday 13 March 1881. A young blonde woman standing on Malaya Sadovaya Street in the heart of St Petersburg in Russia saw the gendarmes on horseback leave the street. That told her all she needed to know: the target would not be returning by this route. Weeks of secretive and dangerous work tunnelling under Malaya Sadovaya Street, culminating in planting a mine the previous night, had been wasted. She gave the signal, raising her handkerchief as though to blow her nose. On cue, four further terrorists armed with home-made bombs hurriedly left to take up their prearranged positions on the alternative course by the Catherine Canal, a white sheet of ice that threaded through St Petersburg towards the Baltic Sea.

These were the final moments of a two-year campaign during which the assassins had hunted their target. He had been sentenced to death in June 1879 at a private meeting in the forests near Lipetsk, about 250 miles south-east of Moscow. The gathering had had a holiday air, as though they were picnickers with their bottles of wine, vodka and food. But they had formed a terrorist group called *Narodnaya Volya*, the 'People's Will', and reached a unanimous verdict. Only regicide would make the world take notice and tremble. Emperor Alexander II, the mighty autocrat and 'tsar of all the Russias', must die.

The sound of the horses was heard first, then the closed carriage of the condemned man was easily recognised, accompanied by his guard of seven Cossacks. The carriage was followed by two sleighs, one of which bore the Chief of Police. It was a short journey from the riding academy at the Mikhailovsky Manege where Alexander II had been reviewing the troops, through the fairy-tale setting of Peter the Great's magnificent imperial city, its domes and minarets still laden with winter snow. Shortly after 2.15 p.m. the carriage suddenly swung into the view of those waiting for the tsar by the Catherine Canal.[1] The moment was almost at hand.

For the bomb throwers there was still time to re-think the actions that would almost certainly cost them their lives. One of them did flee the scene. But nineteen-year-old Nicholas Rysakov did not hesitate. The bomb in his hand was concealed by a white cloth. As the tsar's carriage was almost upon him he lifted up his arm, eyes fixed on the fast-approaching horses' hooves, and took aim.

The detonation tore through the cold air and the smothering snow. The horses reeled and fell. There was a shattering crash of breaking glass and wood. Smoke drifted to reveal a Cossack guard, a policeman and two members of the public lying in the snow, bleeding heavily. Security guards seized Rysakov.

The imposing figure of Alexander II emerged from the damaged carriage, apparently unharmed. The bomb had been a split second too late, catching the rear of the carriage. The tsar asked a Cossack for a handkerchief to wipe the blood from his face.[2]

'Thank God I'm fine,' he said, 'but look ...' A guard had died, a boy was dying.

'It is too early to thank God,' cried Rysakov.[3]

Alexander did not seem to hear those who were urging him back into the carriage. He may have imagined the danger was over, he may have been too shaken, or perhaps this was just his moment of defiance. He paused briefly, crucial seconds of hesitation ...

The next bomb landed directly at the tsar's feet, hurling him into the air with the force of the blast. As he landed he found he was still alive, yet he struggled without success to lift himself from the ground. Around him a pool of blood grew ominously, bright red in the white snow. Close by, twenty others lay injured or dying. The tsar suddenly felt very cold. The guards gathered up his broken body and placed him on a sleigh.

They took him to the Winter Palace, a magnificent Baroque icon of the tsar's imperial rule. By divine right, Alexander II, like his Romanov forebears, held absolute power over the lives of his subjects and there was no institutional framework to challenge his will. The colossal Winter Palace was like a majestic stage on which to project his wealth and strength: its fabled interiors included a white marbled ballroom, a dining room where feasts were held for 1,000 guests, and galleries that could accommodate 10,000 people. From this opulent proclamation of autocratic Russian power, Alexander II ruled almost one-sixth of the earth's surface.

None of this could help him now. His family followed the trail of blood across the marbled floors, up the sweeping wide stairway to his study, among them his twelve-year-old grandson, Nicholas. Dressed for an afternoon of ice-skating, the frightened boy stood at the foot of the modest bed where his grandfather lay covered by an old army cloak. The tsar's face was horribly mutilated, transforming him into something not quite human. One familiar eye stared out unmoving and unseeing with an almost hypnotic effect. Under the blood-soaked cloak, the hollowed-out shape of his grandfather was evident: the right leg appeared to be missing, the left was misshapen, a fast-accumulating pool of blood obscuring the exact nature of the trauma.[4] The cloak sagged where his stomach should be. A priest was attending to his immortal soul, murmuring the last rites.

Nicholas witnessed this terrifying spectacle at close hand. This was all that was left of his grandfather, the acclaimed Alexander the Liberator, the man who had pioneered reform in Russia, freed the serfs in 1861, modernised the judiciary, expanded the education system, and was about to take those first, faltering steps towards constitutional reform of the world's largest autocracy. It seemed ironic that the most liberal tsar in generations, who had been drawing up proposals for a national assembly with wider participation, should suffer such a terrible fate. There had been many attempts on his life by the People's Will – and now finally, their will had prevailed.

Nothing could quite prepare Queen Victoria for the 'ineffable horror' she felt later that day when a series of telegrams arrived from St Petersburg. Reading them in the sanctuary of Windsor Castle, the light fading over the peaceful English home counties beyond, the crime that had been committed in Russia opened a vista onto a very different landscape, one which heralded a new phase in Europe and marked the birth of a modern form of political terrorism.[5]

The first 'very alarming' telegram to arrive at Windsor indicated that Alexander II had been shot and injured. Just before 6 p.m. came a full account from the British ambassador in Russia, Lord Dufferin, of the 'dreadful & never to be forgotten event'. The bomb exploded 'between his legs, shattering and wounding them frightfully, as well as the lower part of the body', the queen recorded in her journal.[6] Soon Dufferin had further particulars. 'All the clothes were blown off as far as the chest, one leg had almost disappeared and the rest of the body was most frightfully mangled.'[7] Nonetheless surgeons thought they might be able to save the tsar by amputating his limbs, and the instruments were being prepared in readiness until they realised he was beyond rescue.[8] Queen Victoria felt 'quite shaken and stunned by this awful news. May God protect all dear ones! Poor, poor Emperor, in spite of his failings, he was a kind & amiable man.'[9]

The queen knew the tsar personally. The horrific picture of his death evoked in the telegrams contrasted with a very different memory of the man she had met over forty years earlier at the beginning of her reign. In the spring of 1839, when he was the young heir to the Russian throne, Grand Duke Alexander had paid a visit to Windsor. The twenty-year-old queen had been still unmarried; the twenty-one-year-old tsarevich had come to Europe in search of a consort.

Seen through Victorian eyes, the land from which the grand duke came was a place of violent contradictions and unfathomable dangers. The very name of 'Russia' conjured up a tempestuous history of raging Mongol hordes, bloodthirsty emperors, religious wars hatched beneath the gleaming oriental domes of the Russian church and conditions of near slavery or 'serfdom' for millions of its inhabitants. But when the heir to the Russian throne had arrived at Windsor in late May 1839, he had defied Queen Victoria's expectations. Strikingly tall – a Romanov trait – with a commanding presence, Grand Duke Alexander seemed to her 'a dear, delightful young man', so frank and merry, 'with a sweet smile, and such a manly fine figure'.[10] The young British queen had appeared to him clever, high-spirited and stylish. They dined, danced and went riding together; there had been a sudden, unexpected intimacy.

'I really am quite in love with the Grand-duke,' the queen wrote in her journal on 27 May 1839. He led her into the dining room, St George's Hall, and afterwards into the red drawing room, 'I danced 1st a quadrille with the Grand-duke, then followed a Valse … (of course I and also the Grand-duke sitting down during the Valse) …' When it came to the Mazurka, 'the Grand Duke asked me to take a turn which I did (never having done it before) … the Grand-Duke is so very strong, that in running around, you must follow quickly, and after that you are whisked around like in a Valse … We had such fun and laughter … I never enjoyed myself more,' wrote the queen. She was so excited she could not sleep until 5 a.m.[11] The light-hearted mood continued at Ascot the next day. The Grand Duke proved to be impetuous and 'imprudent'. The excitement she felt at the dance that evening when he put his arm round her waist just a little too far and lifted her from the ground prompted her to admit to her diary, 'I really love this amiable and dear young man'. She turned to the man she trusted most, her devoted Whig prime minister and mentor, the charming Lord Melbourne. It was very fatiguing, she explained, 'my liking the Grand Duke so much'.[12] Queen Victoria asked her Russian guest to stay.

The Grand Duke, in turn, sounded out his father, Tsar Nicholas I, over the question of marriage to the British queen. His father refused. The heir to the Russian throne could not possibly be a satellite to the British throne.[13] Grand Duke Alexander was obliged to leave. The queen felt 'quite <u>unhappy</u>' (underlined twice). He kissed her goodbye in such 'a very warm affectionate manner' that the queen felt more as though 'I was taking leave of a relation than of a stranger'. He said he 'never would forget' their time together, 'and I shall never also' (double underlined), the young queen vowed solemnly.[14]

Now he was gone. The brutal manner of his death in 1881 undermined the fragile facade of security of European royalty; perhaps it challenged its very existence. 'It makes one shudder and tremble,' wrote Queen Victoria's beloved oldest daughter, Vicky, the Crown Princess of Germany, to her mother on 14 March 1881. 'One is so horror struck that one really does not know what to say! Poor dear Emperor Alexander! ... To be destroyed in so horrible a manner! ... The saddest part is that it should be one so well intentioned and kind who was not the tyrant others had been before him, though he had a little of it in him as mostly all the Tsars have. The state of all grades of society there is so bad and too sad! How will they get into a civilised state of liberty and order? When will all that cruel oppression, that sending to Siberia & slowly killing families wholesale – will cease ... I am so sorry for Sasha and Minny [the new emperor and empress] to take up a murdered father's crown is too dreadful ... I have not closed my eyes all night I was so shaken with horror!'[15]

The royal family knew that this was the culmination of six attempts on the life of Alexander II. 'The poor emperor always expected such a death & for years has felt like a hunted hare,' Vicky added to her mother. 'Safe nowhere. What is life at such a price!'[16] In recent years the all-powerful tsar had at times felt little more than an animal, 'a wolf tracked by hunters', as he put it, with a tangible feeling that his life was measured out in small quantities.[17]

Alexander had narrowly escaped death in the autumn of 1879 when the People's Will had tunnelled under a railway track where the imperial train was due to pass and planted a mine. This plan had been foiled by a fortuitous change to the tsar's travel arrangements. In February 1880 the terrorists had smuggled a staggering 300 pounds of dynamite into the Winter Palace itself, targeting the dining room most frequently used by the tsar. This plot, too, had failed by chance. The tsar's guest was delayed and dinner was served late, sparing the Romanov family but killing twelve guards.

'How too dreadful!' Queen Victoria had written when she heard the news. 'Such a thing to happen in one's own house! Hardly credible! ... Every day there seems to be some fresh dreadful event! What times we live in!'[18]

As the terrorists had intended, the gruesome Russian regicide captured headlines across the world. Queen Victoria pored over the newspapers at Windsor and found she could 'think of nothing else'.[19] There were sobering assessments of the prospects for European peace on the accession of a new tsar and the shifting allegiances between Europe's Great Powers: the mighty empires of Britain, Russia and Austria-Hungary, the recently unified Germany and the republic of France. Peace in Europe rested on the balance of power between these countries to ensure that no one state could dominate the others. The *Standard* on 15 March 1881 saw shadows begin to fall across Europe since 'the jealousy, not to say quarrel ... between Russia on the one hand and Germany and Austria on the other are neither few nor slight'. Russia had recently lost ground in the unstable Balkan region of south-east Europe, and 'it would not take much', the *Standard* forecast with remarkable prescience, for trouble in Serbia in the Balkans 'to cause a collision at any time' pitting Russia against Austria and Hungary. This problem was entwined with the longstanding and seemingly irresolvable 'Eastern Question' provoked by the steady decline of the Ottoman Empire, which heightened tensions between Europe's Great Powers as they jostled for territorial gains. The *Standard* predicted that new European alliances would develop such as 'a friendly understanding between Russia and France'.[20]

Apart from their analysis of Europe's Great Powers, the British press were unanimous in their condemnation of terrorism. Queen Victoria had suffered several attempts on her life, her attackers invariably working alone and often mentally unstable. Alexander II's assassination, however, was entirely different – the culmination of years of effort by an organised terrorist group specifically targeting royalty to bring down the state. 'The most monstrous and revolting of regicides', which undermined 'the central foundation of authority, order, society and law', declared the *Morning*

Post, summing up the British perspective.[21] But amongst the headlines, the queen was appalled to come across one publication that adopted a very different tone. 'Triumph! Triumph! One of the most abominable tyrants of Europe whose downfall has long been sworn – the emperor of Russia is no more', gloated Johann Most, in a German periodical published in London on 19 March called *Freiheit*, or *Freedom*. The tsar died 'as a dog dies', Most continued, and news of his death had 'plunged into princely palaces around the world ... like a thunderbolt', reaching those 'who have a thousand times deserved a like fate ... Truly it may happen again here.'[22]

The queen turned at once to her most faithful correspondent, her daughter Vicky, in Germany. It was a 'monstrous' article that 'openly preaches assassination' in the name of freedom, the queen wrote, 'and the language is beyond anything I ever saw'.[23] Johann Most, a German anarchist who believed in the destruction of the state, argued for regicides and assassinations as the best means of recruiting converts and igniting revolt. Royalty was a key target of the revolutionaries, a visible symbol of the authority of the state. Where would it all stop? Lord Dufferin soon reported news of a fresh threat. A 'Nihilist Manifesto' was posted on the walls of St Petersburg University, 'triumphing in the assassination and giving the new Russian emperor three months to introduce a new regime'. If Alexander III failed to do so, or if he executed his father's assassins, 'they will not give him 24 hours'.[24] Could Europe be on the cusp of violent change? The assassin's creed in barbarous Russia might precipitate revolution or inspire mass uprisings throughout civilised Europe. The queen felt 'quite bewildered and shaken by this shocking tragedy' and found the accounts in the newspapers 'most harrowing'.

A generation had elapsed since the late tsar had once walked the halls of Windsor as a handsome Grand Duke with his future before him and led her onto the dance floor. Within months of that memorable visit the queen had found her cousin, Prince Albert of Saxe-Coburg-Gotha, quite outshone any Russian Grand Duke. When the German prince had arrived at Windsor on 10 October 1839 she had found him 'beautiful' and beheld him 'with some emotion'. Within days, with her heart 'quite going', the queen made up her mind. She summoned 'dearest Albert whom I <u>adore</u>' to a private meeting on 15 October 1839 and proposed. 'We embraced each other over and over again ... oh! To <u>feel</u> I was, and am, loved by <u>such</u> an <u>Angel</u>.'[25]

Their union had defined the intervening forty years of her reign. Queen Victoria and Prince Albert had had nine children and by the 1880s their family was a British institution that was shaping the future of Europe. Eight of their nine children had married into Europe's royal houses. Queen Victoria's oldest daughter, Vicky, led the way, marrying the heir to the Prussian throne, the first of six of the queen's children to marry into German royal houses. Her oldest son, the wayward Prince Albert Edward, or 'Bertie', had married a Danish princess, Alexandra, bringing connections to the royal houses in Denmark, Greece and Russia. For Prince Albert, these marriages were part of a remarkable vision that he hoped would contribute to the peace and stability of Europe.

The ravages of Europe during the Napoleonic Wars at the beginning of the nineteenth century, in which up to six million people lost their lives, had influenced British policy. To achieve a balance of power, no one continental country should become sufficiently dominant to unleash such destruction across Europe again. Prince Albert and Queen Victoria saw the creation of dynastic marriages between their children and European royalty as a further safeguard. This was not just about extending royal power and prestige, but a means of contributing to 'British Peace' or *Pax Britannica*. Each marriage was a form of soft power: a path to spreading British liberal values across the continent, perhaps even a push back against the destabilising forces of republican-ism, revolution and war.[26] Albert saw the prospect of a federal Europe in which a series of strong, independent countries, stable under their own constitutional monarchies – ideally modelled as closely as possible on the British constitution – were united by the common goal of achieving European peace and prosperity. As the entwined flags of every country so joined in royal matrimony fluttered over the nuptials they seemed to hold great promise, each royal union a potential statement of allied national interests and ideas, bringing hope to the cheering masses – well before there was any concept of a 'European Union'.

Victoria and Albert had no fewer than forty-two grandchildren and for years the queen was the recipient of correspondence from grandsons and granddaughters growing up in Europe's palaces. Letters arrived with unvarying regularity, marking birthdays and anniversaries from the Neues Palais in Potsdam, the Palais Edinburg in Coburg, Fredensborg Palace near Copenhagen, Eastwell Park, Cumberland Lodge, Sandringham, Marlborough House, Birkhall and others. From the first scrawls carefully supervised on pencil-drawn lines thanking 'Grandmama queen' for presents or telling her about pets, to letters that conveyed their growing experience of their courts or travels, she had watched the progress of the next generation flourish into a cousinhood so large that it formed a unique network or club occupying a singular place at the top of European society. Her union with her beloved Albert had even greater significance as royal connections could be extended and secured still further. The queen had a markedly European outlook and with her trusty *Almanac de Gotha*, a *Who's Who* of European royalty, at her side, she took an informed interest in the prospective marriages of her grandchildren.

Queen Victoria's grandchildren gained automatic entry into what amounted to the world's most exclusive dating agency, where one good-looking princess might find herself sought after by the heirs to several thrones. The queen knew that a constellation of judgements had to be called upon when weighing up any hopeful bride or groom. It was not just a question of their country's prospects and the stability of their throne, but also their religion, moral character, education and looks as well as their ability – perhaps not voiced – to produce strong, healthy heirs. She felt uniquely placed to orchestrate the selection process and help her grandchildren navigate the mysteries of the royal marriage market where young dreams of romance and power often needed realistic guidance.

The birth of a modern form of terrorism with the appalling Russian regicide did not dampen her enthusiasm for matchmaking. As the weeks passed and the queen had a chance to appraise the situation, she saw the Russian murder as a confirmation of her long-held views on the 'horror of Russia & Russians!' rather than an assault on all royal power.[27] The assassin's creed in barbarous Russia reflected harsh extremes of tsarist rule that had persisted despite Alexander II's reforms. Lord Dufferin appeared to confirm this view when he told Queen Victoria that the late tsar's reforms were good but had been introduced 'so precipitously as to derange the social fabric', creating conditions in which 'the nihilistic conspiracy was born and bred'.[28]

The queen saw no reason to change her views on other European royal alliances and her grandchildren were expected to play their part in this royal stage production and live up to Prince Albert's vision. This book explores how seven of Queen Victoria's grandchildren were elevated to the thrones of Europe at a critical time in Europe's history and the influence of her matchmaking on the remarkable rise of the royal dynasty.

DRAMATIS PERSONAE

This is not a complete list of Queen Victoria's grandchildren, but highlights her seven crowned grandchildren (in bold), along with siblings who played a key role in their story.

Victoria, Queen Victoria's oldest daughter, known as 'Vicky'

Children of Vicky and her husband Frederick III,
German Emperor (r. March–June 1888)
Wilhelm II, who became Emperor of Germany (r. 1888–1918)
Victoria of Prussia, known as 'Moretta'
Sophie, who became Queen of Greece (r. 1913–17; 1920–22)

*

Edward, Queen Victoria's oldest son, known as 'Bertie'

Children of Bertie and his Danish wife,
Princess Alexandra
Prince Albert Victor, known as 'Eddy'
Prince George, who became George V (r. 1910–36)
Princess Maud, who became Queen of Norway (r. 1905–38)

*

Alice, Queen Victoria's second daughter

Children of Alice and her husband, Grand Duke Louis of Hesse
Victoria of Hesse (later Battenberg)
Elisabeth of Hesse or 'Ella', who became Grand Duchess
Elisabeth
Alix, or 'Alicky', who became Empress of Russia (r. 1894–1917)

✻

Alfred, Queen Victoria's second son

Children of Alfred and his Russian wife, Marie of Edinburgh
Marie or 'Missy', who became Queen of Romania (r. 1914–27)
Victoria Melita or 'Ducky'

✻

Beatrice, Queen Victoria's youngest daughter

Children of Beatrice and Prince Henry of Battenberg
Victoria Eugenie or 'Ena', who became Queen of Spain
(r. 1906–31)

NOTE ON NAMES AND DATES

Since many of Victoria and Albert's descendants are themselves called 'Victoria' and 'Albert', it is perhaps not surprising that the royal family made use of nicknames, and I have adopted these family names where it helps to distinguish younger generations of 'Victorias' and 'Alberts'. For example, Queen Victoria's oldest daughter, Victoria, later the Empress of Germany, was widely known as 'Vicky'. In turn, Vicky's second daughter, Victoria, or 'young Vicky', was nicknamed 'Moretta' by her family and I have named her accordingly. Prince Albert's oldest son, Albert Edward, became best known by the name of 'Bertie'; in turn, Bertie's oldest son, Albert Victor, was nicknamed 'Eddy'. I have also adopted the anglicised spellings of names, such as Margaret instead of 'Margarethe' and Victoria instead of 'Viktoria', with the exception of names where the foreign spellings are very familiar such as Kaiser Wilhelm.

In the nineteenth century, Russia and other parts of eastern Europe followed the Julian or 'Old Style' calendar, which was twelve days behind the Gregorian or 'New Style' calendar widely used in the West. In the early twentieth century the Julian calendar was thirteen days behind the Gregorian calendar, which was not adopted in Russia until 1918, and later still in Romania and Greece. For consistency I have dated events according to the Gregorian calendar of the West. The (Old Style) Julian calendar dates are indicated by [OS] in my notes on sources.

1

'A Good Sensible Wife'

'A good sensible Wife is what Eddy needs most...'
Bertie to Queen Victoria, December 1891

In the spring of 1887, as preparations began for Queen Victoria's Golden Jubilee to mark her fifty years on the throne, an unwelcome altercation arose between the queen and those closest to her. The difference of opinion began over the seemingly trivial matter of the crown she would wear to the forthcoming Jubilee parade through central London. For Victoria's children this was an occasion for their sixty-eight-year-old mother to abandon her black widow's weeds and white cap and emerge resplendent from her years in retreat. At her Golden Jubilee she should be highly visible, every inch of her 4 foot 11 inch frame an icon, crowned with many splendid diamonds, indisputably proclaiming her as the great queen and empress of a glorious empire.

Queen Victoria took a different view. No need for a crown; a bonnet would suffice. This would highlight her role as mother, grandmother and even great-grandmother. How could it diminish her authority as queen, she reasoned, to emphasise her position as mother? More than a mother: Europe's great matriarch? The dynastic unions of her children were a powerful reminder of her unique status in Europe. With a stubborn and counter-intuitive shrewdness Victoria saw that to emphasise her maternal role was to underline her power. Not only this but the symbolism of the 'universal mother' forged a link between herself and all her subjects.

Her children were dismayed. Fifty kings and princes from across the world had been invited, who were bound to form a colourful and regal contrast to Queen Victoria's plain dowdiness topped with a mere bonnet. Indian Maharajas and their suites, flamboyantly attired in brightly coloured tunics, turbans studded with jewels and distinctive white salwars: such exotic company might eclipse the queen altogether. Ten miles of scaffolding were being erected; hundreds of thousands of people would witness the event. How could the British queen-empress, the world-famous monarch of this most envied nation, parade among such distinguished company in a humble bonnet? As one former minister, Lord Charles Halifax, had reminded the queen on an earlier occasion, the people 'want the gilding for their money ... They want to see a Crown and Sceptre and all that sort of thing'.[1] His view was widely shared. The year before, the foreign secretary, Lord Rosebery, had written to Queen Victoria's private secretary, Henry Ponsonby, but without success: 'The symbol that unites this vast Empire is a crown and not a bonnet.'[2] Now the queen's daughter-in-law, Princess Alexandra, was dispatched to bring her to her senses and press the case once again for a crown. The exchange between the queen and her daughter-in-law did not last long. Alexandra emerged from Queen Victoria's apartments in a matter of moments, 'quaking' according to the queen's biographer, Elizabeth Longford.[3] The bonnet had the day.

Such displays of unwillingness to bend to the will of others were adeptly judged by the queen. There was a certain paradox in her position. The monarchy was by no means universally popular. The queen had recently been jeered in the East End of London. Just a few weeks before her Golden Jubilee, one leaflet in circulation drew attention to 'extreme Radical and Socialistic ideas' that 'poured ridicule' on the very idea of a national celebration in the queen's honour since the monarchy was a 'costly and useless luxury'.[4] Ever since the death of her husband, Prince Albert, in 1861, Queen Victoria's retreat into a life of seclusion dominated by her grief had drawn criticism of royalty and its purpose from all quarters. Growing anger at her continued invisibility was captured by one wag who pinned an advertisement to the gates of

Buckingham Palace in 1864: 'These commanding premises to be let or sold in consequence of the late occupant's declining business.' By the 1870s the queen's prolonged 'over indulgence' in the 'luxury of woe', in the words of one observer, had resulted in widespread anti-monarchical feeling.[5] The Liberal politician, Sir Charles Dilke, highlighted the cost of the monarchy in 1871 and called for its abolition. There was talk of abdication as he gained the support of radicals, such as Charles Bradlaugh, member of parliament for Nottingham, and many republican clubs were founded.[6]

This was a time when radical new ideas were challenging Britain's class-ridden status quo. The emerging socialist movement was exposing social inequalities and demanding a fairer distribution of wealth and opportunity. Fledgling trade unions were giving a voice to industrial workers and arguing for reform. Karl Marx and Friedrich Engels had urged 'Workers of the world, unite!' as early as 1848 in their *Communist Manifesto* and highlighted the exploitation of the masses by the few. In exile in England, Marx had laboured in the British Museum to produce his seminal work, *Das Kapital*, in which he expounded his dream of a communist state and exposed the failings of capitalism with its privileged elites. 'Let the ruling classes tremble,' cried the communists and Marxists who gathered en masse to protest in Hyde Park in 1871. Meanwhile the anarchist movement had already given birth to modern terrorism on the continent.[7] Although the horror of the tsar's assassination in 1881 had not been repeated by the time of the queen's Golden Jubilee, different branches of anarchist thinking had deep roots in Europe and raised a whole raft of far-reaching ideas of which the abolition of the state – and the monarchy – was just a prelude.

But Queen Victoria was not for trembling. She rose above the ferment of ideas, impervious, obdurate, gradually imbued with her own unique authority. Ministers may have buckled over her continuing seclusion and the frustration of having to travel 600 miles to her favourite residence, Balmoral, in Scotland, but they invariably – and usually deferentially – complied. She became 'saturated with an instinctive … consciousness of the supremacy of her position', observed her private secretary's biographer, his son Arthur Ponsonby. She had a 'habit of dominating' in which her imperiousness conveyed such 'complete assurance and self-confidence' that even the most forceful minister could find her presence disconcerting.[8] Whatever was said about her, she felt her position to be unassailable. An entire entourage revolved around the queen's wishes. She saw nothing odd, if she felt so inclined, in communicating 'by means of messages through footmen'. Those who were ushered into her presence often felt overawed. The fact that she could be exasperating, interfering or stubborn was often excused or perhaps blamed on her sex and politely accommodated by the gentlemen running the government. Her prestige increased with Britain's rising imperial and industrial supremacy until she came to occupy a singular position apparently unequalled by any other sovereign, known across the world as simply 'the Queen'.[9] And as a flood of telegrams of congratulations began to pour into the queen's office in the weeks approaching her Golden Jubilee, all appeared to augur well for the great event: from ruling chiefs in India, governors of far-flung outposts of empire, from schools, clubs, guilds, unions, city halls, choirs and Sunday schools.[10]

Queen Victoria marked the opening of the festivities on 20 June 1887 in the manner of her choosing, as near as she could get to her late husband. The queen had built an imposing mausoleum for Prince Albert at Frogmore, near Windsor, and on the opening morning of her jubilee she took breakfast, as she so often did at Windsor, on the lawn close to his tomb, still feeling the great aching, unfillable space in her life. 'The day has come and I am alone,' she wrote in her journal.[11] At Buckingham Palace later that afternoon she received the many royal figures who had gathered from across the world. The supper-room, she noted, 'looked splendid', the many lights on the large horseshoe table casting a warm hue over the uniformed princes and the 'beautifully dressed' princesses. But she was old enough for memory to play havoc with her feelings. When she woke the next day the sounds of loud cheering outside took her straight back to that glorious day thirty-six years earlier, opening the Great Exhibition in 1851 with Prince Albert at her side. Even surrounded by her family she felt 'alone, oh! without my beloved husband for whom this would have been such a proud day!'[12]

Preserved in the royal archives for over 100 years, the fading *Ceremonial of Her Majesty's Jubilee Service*, gives a vivid glimpse of the extraordinary pageant, a sight like no other, that wound its way through the packed London streets on 21 June 1887 to Westminster Abbey. The first procession streamed out of Hyde Park Corner at 10 a.m. and brought an exciting glimpse of the Empire to Victorian England: bejewelled and be-turbaned Indian princes, deputations from the Raja of Kapurthala, the Maharaja of Bhurtpore, the Maharaja of Jodhpore and many other Indian dynasties. Half an hour later foreign sovereigns and their colourful suites proceeded from the Alexandra Hotel: the Sultan of Persia, the Prince of Siam, Prince Komatsu of Japan, Queen Kapiolani of Hawaii, and key ambassadors such as the envoy from the Ottoman Empire. At 10.45 a third procession of European royalty departed from the Pimlico entrance of Buckingham Palace: Archduke Rudolf, heir to the throne of the Austro-Hungarian Empire, the crown princes of Sweden and Portugal, the kings of Belgium, Greece and Denmark. The world, it seemed, had come to pay tribute to 'the Queen'. For one American writer, Mark Twain, watching among the throng, the processions merged and 'stretched to the limit of sight in both directions', and still they kept coming, the potentates, the dignitaries, the riders in colourful uniforms, their helmets and breastplates burning gold in the bright sunlight.[13]

Finally at 11.30 a.m. the queen's own procession started from Buckingham Palace and as the long line of carriages emerged from the gates, no one could be left in any doubt as to the size and glory of her dynasty. First out were the Prince of Wales Hussars and the Household Cavalry, followed by carriages for senior members of the royal household. Six more carriages conveyed the queen's granddaughters, one granddaughter-in-law, three daughters-in-law and three of her daughters. 'Princes of the blood' came next, riding in order of their relationship to the queen: nine grandsons and grandsons-in-law, five sons-in-law and then three of the queen's sons. Then twelve Indian officers on horse-back heralded the queen's own handsome landau drawn by six horses, the Royal Hanoverian Creams.[14] At the sight of the queen the cheers of the crowd rose into one long continuous roar that sustained along the length of the route and was quite deafening. Packed onto the pavements, the balconies, terraces and rooftops, even clinging to the chimneys, at that moment the great mass of people seemed in love with their queen, so soberly dressed and self-contained. She wore a long dress and her bonnet, fashion-ably trimmed with white Point d'Alençon, diamond ornaments and pearls around her neck. Her one concession was to wear her exquisite small diamond crown later for her official photographs. She was accompanied in her carriage by her oldest daughter, Vicky, a future German empress, and her Danish daughter-in-law, Alexandra, a future British queen.[15]

Queen Victoria was most gratified by the great press of people all the way from the palace gates to Westminster Abbey and 'such an extraordinary outburst of enthusiasm as I had hardly ever seen in London before'. When she arrived at the abbey, state trumpeters high up on the roodscreen played a fanfare and the congregation rose for the national anthem. From the entrance the queen could see the cavernous space inside glowing with colour, the military in different shades of uniform, the crimson robes of the judiciary, the many splendid costumes of princes from across the world. As she proceeded down the long nave to the coronation chair, escorted by her family, a march from Handel's *Occasional Oratorio* filled the air, adding to the solemnity of the occasion. This was the moment: Queen Victoria, elderly and modestly attired, appeared to be the shining symbol of prosper-ity and peace in an uncertain world. Those around her may have outshone her in their magnificence, but, as she walked through the abbey, there was no doubt who was queen and empress of the mightiest empire in the world.

Whatever his opinion on her bonnet, the Liberal statesman Lord Rosebery later humbly conceded that few 'could view unmoved ... that touching and majestic moment in the Abbey when your Majesty appeared alone and aloft – symbolising so truly your Majesty's true position'. As the service concluded, the many members of the queen's family advanced forward to bow or curtsy before her and kiss her hand, some with tears in their eyes as she embraced them warmly; sons and daughters, grandsons and granddaughters, grandsons-in-law and grand-daughters-in-law. Queen Victoria felt it to be 'a very moving moment' and she was not alone. Her role as mother of the large royal dynasty merged with her role as the mother of the mother country and the symbolism stirred Lord Rosebery. 'When later your Majesty passed from the Sovereign to the Mother, the touch of nature which has brought your Majesty into sympathy with the humblest of your subjects added the supreme emotion to a matchless scene.'[16]

However glorious her role and however flattering her ministers, the queen had to act within the limits of her powers as head of state. In contrast to the immense power of the sovereigns of three of Europe's great empires, autocratic Russia and semi-autocratic Austria-Hungary and Germany, according to Britain's constitutional monarchy the queen could not dictate policy, raise taxes or lead the country to war. The last British monarch to veto a bill had been Queen Anne, 180 years previously. No matter how much Queen Victoria preferred one prime minister over another, she learned to put up with her least favourites, even Gladstone who she loathed and often attempted to oppose. Her progress was part of Prince Albert's achievement; his vision had been to fashion a new role for the monarchy that rose above party politics, although even he believed the sovereign should have powers over the executive.[17] Nonetheless he had helped Victoria to understand her most critical mistakes, notably in 1839 during the 'Bedchamber Crisis': the young queen had refused to relinquish any of her Whig ladies-in-waiting when the Conservatives had tried to form a government, in order to engineer that her Whig favourite, Lord Melbourne, stayed in power.[18] In Victoria's later years her private secretary, Ponsonby, noted that she still occasionally chafed against her inability to dictate policy and showed an increasing desire to interfere, which was often thwarted. Either she could not quite comprehend or it was convenient for her not to comprehend the exact limits of her power. But there remained one sphere of activity over which she exercised more than a symbolic control and it arose through her role as a grandmother.

Proceeding through the London streets on that hot day in June 1887 were key players in the royal family's future success: her grandchildren. The queen had long understood the importance of their marital alliances to extend royal power and influence, and in this particular sphere it was within her unique power to shape the political landscape of Europe. Thirty-four of her grandchildren survived to adulthood, and as they came of age she could turn Prince Albert's vision into reality. But by the time of her Golden Jubilee, Queen Victoria had to acknowledge that an indefinable human element had entered Prince Albert's plans. The varying abilities of their descendants and the extraordinarily complex political situations in which they sometimes found themselves had not proved conducive to achieving the grand vision. Central to her concern was the future of the British monarchy.

For many years Queen Victoria had been troubled that her oldest son, Bertie, would not make a good king. Far from having that air of a Sunday school teacher about him that Prince Albert would have approved of, Bertie's prodigious appetite for life's little pleasures, especially with the opposite sex, had not diminished with his steady progress through middle age and the inconvenient widening of his girth. Ever since the queen's beloved husband had been snatched from her in his prime, so reduced, she thought, by the revelations of Bertie's adventures with an actress called 'Nellie' that Albert had succumbed to typhoid, their wayward oldest son had elevated philandering to an art form. With painful frankness, she blamed Bertie unfairly for the death of her husband. 'Oh! That boy ... I never can or shall look at him without a shudder', she had confided to Vicky in Germany.[19] Over the years there was gossip of Bertie's liaisons with some fifty women, at least one of whom had landed him in the divorce courts, not to mention exciting goings-on in the most luxurious of Parisian brothels, *Le Chabanais*. No doubt Bertie was at pains to conceal from his mother that he had even had a contraption custom-made, promisingly called 'a seat of love', which aimed to provide sublime little extras for his possibly fading libido to help jolly things along.[20] For Queen Victoria, whose sober life revolved around her duties, the seasons marking the transitions to Balmoral, Windsor or Osborne House with almost unvarying predictability, even without knowledge of *Le Chabanais*, her oldest son's reckless impropriety with women was shaming and made her 'very sad and angry', she told Vicky. It overturned the Albertine ideal that required a monarch to meet the highest standards of mental, physical and moral attainment. 'Oh what will become of the poor country when I die!' she lamented.[21]

The queen's continuing disappointment in her first heir apparent prompted her to look to her second, Bertie's oldest son, Prince Albert Victor, or 'Eddy' as he was known in the family. For the public watching the spectacle of the Golden Jubilee on that hot day in June, Prince Eddy was easily recognisable among the seventeen princes on horseback: a twenty-three-year-old of pleasing appearance whose even features bore a resemblance to his mother. But whereas Princess Alexandra was an acknowledged beauty, he was not quite handsome, and lacked her vivacity and his father's air of confidence. Nevertheless he cut an impressive figure dressed in his naval uniform, the heavy fabric and decorations masking his natural delicacy. Years of cavalry training enabled him to ride well, his bearing dignified, his youthful air full of promise. Standing amongst the press of people with his programme sheet, the American journalist Ralph Blumenfeld noted the cheers of the crowd as he passed; the young prince was a 'popular feature' of the procession.[22]

As Queen Victoria's oldest British grandson, Eddy's prospects were brilliant as arguably the most eligible young prince in history: the second in line to the British throne at the height of the empire's power. His inheritance assured him of his position in the world as a future ruler of the largest empire the world had ever seen, approaching a quarter of the surface of the globe. He could offer his future consort the first position in Europe. In the words of his Aunt Vicky, of all the princes, Eddy was 'first prize'.

His grandmother knew otherwise. Rumours of a most indelicate and unwelcome nature were beginning to wend their way down the corridors of Balmoral and Windsor. Although Eddy knew how to charm the queen, she was not fooled. Her investigations revealed a young prince who was very far removed from being anything like his namesake, *the* illustrious Prince Albert. The young man on whom the whole great edifice would eventually rest had to be taken in hand.

———

The high expectations required of the young prince were enshrined in his very name, purposefully chosen by Queen Victoria shortly after his birth in January 1864: Prince Albert Victor. In her eyes, her late husband embodied all the shining attributes that this new prince required for his passage through life. It was the queen who proclaimed the baby's illustrious name at his baptism in the chapel at Buckingham Palace, having given his mother, Alexandra, and father, Bertie, little choice in the matter.[23]

From the very beginning the newborn prince fell short of the most exacting standards of physical perfection the queen looked for, through no fault of his own since he was born two months prematurely and weighed only three and three-quarter pounds. The queen blamed his father, Bertie, once again. Her oldest son's pleasure-seeking and raffish 'whirl of amusements' continued after his marriage and she believed had exhausted his pretty young wife as she had struggled to hold his interest.[24] Prince Eddy remained weak and 'very fairy like' at a year old, the queen observed. 'What is not pretty is his very narrow chest (rather pigeon chested)', which she felt took after his mother's slender frame, rather than the sturdier build of his father.[25]

Prince Eddy was joined in the nursery after eighteen months by a younger brother, George, who was more robust, and over time by three sisters, Louise, Victoria and finally Maud, born in 1869. Queen Victoria was never completely at ease with the apparently chaotic lifestyle of their parents, whose hectic social round formed a marked contrast to her own wholesome routine.

Bertie was often absent and Alexandra, a devoted and indulgent mother, loved to take her children on prolonged trips to her home country of Denmark. She placed a firm emphasis on fun; boisterous and unruly behaviour was rarely chastised. Victoria was concerned that this approach was not conducive to raising future monarchs. Bertie and Alexandra's children seemed to her 'puny and pale ... wild as hawks' and worryingly 'ill-bred' and 'ill-trained'.[26]

Discipline entered Prince Eddy's life when he was almost six in the shape of a nursery governess called Miss Brown, who began to teach him and George the rudiments of reading and writing. Sensing a certain lack of progress, Queen Victoria intervened in 1871, personally selecting a tutor for the two boys. The Reverend John Dalton, a liturgical scholar equipped with a First Class degree from Cambridge, appeared to be blessed with all the right attributes to bring out the best in the two princes. Dalton was industrious, learned and suitably deferential whilst also full of advice that happily coincided with Queen Victoria's own views. He subjected the boys to a strict regime that began at 7 a.m. each morning and was designed to instil an appreciation of languages, the arts, history, mathematics – Euclid as well as algebra – and of course, the Bible.[27]

Unfortunately, five years of this intense instruction appeared to leave Prince Eddy lacking the same appetite for study as his famous namesake. *The* Prince Albert was said to have displayed a keen attention to his lessons from a young age, but the Reverend Dalton reported with concern in 1876 that Prince Eddy could scarcely be made 'to work at all' without the presence of his younger brother, George. The following year Dalton was obliged to admit that his young charge was 'somewhat deficient' in habits 'of promptitude and method, of manliness and self-reliance'.[28]

In an attempt to remedy such blemishes, in 1877 after consultation with the queen, thirteen-year-old Eddy was enlisted with his brother, George, as a cadet in the Royal Navy on HMS *Britannia*. Despite rigorous supervision, as the months passed Dalton was sufficiently confounded by Eddy's lack of progress to advise his parents to consider removing him from the *Britannia*. Alexandra was 'dreadfully distressed' at this news and favoured keeping her sons together rather than educating Eddy 'at home alone'.[29] The other cadets continued to outshine the heir to the throne and after two years Dalton admitted that his charge was still unable 'to fix his attention to any given subject for more than a few minutes consecutively'.[30]

Such undesirable news provoked much deliberation in elevated circles. The queen, the prince's parents and even members of the cabinet became drawn into discussions over the next steps in the edification of the young princes. Bertie favoured sending his sons overseas, but the queen was not satisfied that a continued absence from home was the solution. On the other hand, she and her long-suffering daughter-in-law were united in a desire to shield Eddy and George from any knowledge of their father's rakish pursuits. Eventually, all were agreed that fifteen-year-old Eddy and fourteen-year-old George should be sent for a prolonged tour of the British Empire on HMS *Bacchante*. As ever they were accompanied by Reverend Dalton, who took steps to screen the princes from exposure to any tittle-tattle about their father that found its way into the newspapers.

Every care went into creating the kind of moral upright-ness exhibited by the boys' grandfather. Just to be sure, Queen Victoria's homilies on virtue reached her grandsons in all corners of the empire. 'Be always good, simple, pure of heart and mind, honest, dutiful, unselfish, honourable and kind to all ...' she 'most earnestly' instructed Eddy on his sixteenth birthday.[31] Such advice arrived with unsolicited regularity. 'May God bless you and give you strength to resist all evil and all temptations and be good, honest, God-fearing, unselfish, unfrivolous (which is very neces-sary in these days) dutiful, & affectionate to your grandmother and sovereign ...', she counselled in January 1883.[32] Eddy's polite replies to his grandmother show he had at least learned tact. Her 'good advice gave me much pleasure', he wrote. 'If I follow out all you have said I could not do better.' He reassured his grand-mamma that the days he had spent with her in Balmoral were the 'happiest days I have had in Scotland'.[33]

His studious grandfather, as a young nineteen-year-old, had ventured to correct no less an authority than the pope on the finer points of Egyptian influences on Greek art. Eddy's letters to his grandmamma faithfully charted his course across the world but failed to provide comparable evidence of an emerging scholar. He had climbed the pyramids, seen a cattle farm in a desolate spot in Cape Verde off the west coast of Africa, and visited his Uncle William, the king of Greece, where he found 'the drive out from Athens was very pretty'.[34] Although Eddy was 'endowed with natural good feeling', Dalton reported to Bertie from Singapore, 'he will not exert himself enough ... he is still more fond of animal than mental gratification, of eating, idling and play than of work and duty', and he had developed 'little stratagems and excuses for shirking what is disagreeable, but these are readily seen through'.[35] Perhaps finding the need to defend himself, Dalton suggested 'this weakness of brain, this feebleness and lack of power to grasp almost anything put before him ... is a fault of nature'.[36]

How was it possible that Prince Eddy, heir to the enriching heritage of his grandpapa, sprung from the same seed, could be in possession of such a fault of nature? After much deliberation it was decided to separate the two brothers and send Eddy up to Cambridge. This did draw a response from the allegedly 'listless and vacant' prince. 'I can't tell you how strange it seems to be without you and how much I miss you in everything all day long,' Eddy confided to George in June 1883.[37] All their lives the brothers had been treated like inseparable twins and now even bedtime felt strange. 'I can hardly realise yet that you are not there, as I miss you more when I go to bed, more than at any other time,' Eddy wrote in his next letter to George just five days later.[38] The princes' lives were now directed along different lines and partings remained painful: 'I can't tell you how much I felt for you on Sunday night when we had the unpleasant business of saying good bye,' wrote twenty-two-year-old Eddy to George in February 1886, 'and I know well what your feelings were and how wretched you must have felt at going away'.[39]

Queen Victoria invited Eddy for a short stay at Balmoral on 3 September 1883 before he went up to Cambridge. He arrived after luncheon and went straight up to her rooms. As he entered she could see at once 'he was looking rather pale and languid

from having grown so fast'.[40] Over the years she had learned to
be more circumspect about expressing her forthright views and
was far more forgiving with her grandchildren than she had been
with her own children. The interview went well. Eddy may not
have natural ability but that was hardly his fault. The 'dear good
boy' appeared to be doing his best; he had a charm of his own
and was gentle, kind and polite. The queen may not have seen
the report of his mentor, James Stephen, who was appointed to
coach Eddy for university over the summer. Stephen reported
bluntly to Dalton that there was little point in sending the prince
to Cambridge, since 'he hardly knows the meaning of the words
to read'.[41] He had experimented with several different approaches
to teaching, Stephen told Dalton, but whether reading aloud,
lecturing, straight dictation or written question-and-answer
sessions, he was confounded. The prince's 'one great difficulty is
in keeping his attention fixed ... sometimes he attends pretty well
for a time, and then suddenly, for no apparent reason, his mind
relapses almost into a state of torpor'.[42]

The prince was nonetheless despatched to Cambridge in the
autumn of 1883 accompanied by the ever-hopeful Dalton. Eddy
reassured his grandmother that he hoped 'to get on as well as
possible', although he admitted that at first he found university
life 'rather dull'.[43] By now Dalton himself was coming in for
criticism. Too late, questions were being asked about whether
Dalton's belief that knowledge had to be 'drilled' or 'instilled'
into the young prince was so heavy handed that it had killed off
any tender shoots of interest.[44] 'What on earth has stupid Dalton
been about all these years,' protested one courtier, Lady Geraldine
Somerset. 'He has taught him nothing!'[45]

The twenty-one-year-old prince was at last freed from Dalton's
close scrutiny in 1885 when he embarked on a military career,
enrolling for training at Aldershot. Those who hoped that Eddy
would come into his own once freed from Dalton's all-embracing
influence were to be disappointed. Once again the prince tried to
reassure his grandmother. He was working hard and began 'to
find the life there very pleasant', although he admitted 'Aldershot
is a very cold and exposed place in winter and especially as our

barracks are on the top of a hill.'[46] Privately, he considered the general was 'a lunatic' and objected strongly to cavalry training regimes that involved jogging around in circles in restrictive clothing until well past the point of discomfort.[47] Nonetheless after six months' training Eddy joined the distinguished cavalry regiment, the 10th Royal Hussars, and was stationed at York.

For so long a disappointment to his own mother, Bertie, too, struggled to conceal his own frustration when his son, in turn, failed to live up to expectations during his first public duties. At one formal ceremony in Dublin the prince forgot his instructions and loud whispers directing him when to stand or kneel were painfully audible to the crowd. Under provocations such as these his father lost patience. 'Eddy, you are a d------d fool,' he once snapped.[48] Exasperatingly for Bertie there are no indications that Eddy fought back against such fatherly reproaches. Instead Bertie's anger or frustration is more likely to have been greeted with the vulnerability of a scolded puppy, looking out from beneath heavy-lidded eyes, his soft chin gently sloping, his expression sometimes vacant. Eddy was invariably polite and gentle, his good nature unruffled, his sisters and mother lavish in their encouragement. He was still so coltishly tall and slight that his mother encouraged him to use extended collars and cuffs to help conceal his swan-like neck and delicate wrists, which earned him the nickname 'Collars-and-Cuffs'. Many who saw him, such as Henry Ponsonby, attested to his pleasing personal attributes. Eddy was sharp enough to put himself out for the queen, delighting her on one occasion by dancing a quadrille that prompted several exclamation marks in her journal. The prince continued to be the tactful recipient of counsel from his grandmamma. 'Thank you a thousand times for your kind letter full of good advice, which I appreciate so much,' he wrote to her in 1888 on his twenty-fourth birthday.[49]

Whether he was actually following the queen's advice was another matter. The prince found his own way of dealing with the extreme watchfulness of his elders as he endeavoured to make his rite of passage from awkward youth to man of the world and he was less than forthcoming about what he was up to. Most of

the records of this period of Prince Eddy's life were destroyed
by Queen Victoria's youngest daughter and companion, Princess
Beatrice, who edited her mother's papers after her death. As a
result it is only possible to get glimpses of the prince's alleged
transgressions and what his family knew of them.

However, two revealing letters have recently surfaced that
survived Beatrice's labours. They are written in Prince Eddy's
hand and addressed to his doctor in the army, known as Roche.
Dating from December 1885 these letters reveal that within
months of being released from Dalton's sphere of influence, the
overprotected prince had acquired a sexually transmitted disease.
'I have felt well all the time I have been away from Aldershot,' he
told Roche, after taking his prescribed capsules four times a day.
'There is still a slight sign of glete [discharge] but so slight that
it is hardly perceptive.' The prince was frustrated to find that it
was not so easy to clear up his infection. A year later he asked for
more capsules. 'I still continue to have this tiresome glete ... It is
very annoying,' he wrote to his doctor on 18 December 1886. The
most likely cause of his 'glete' or discharge is gonorrhoea, which
at the time was difficult to treat.[50]

Given that these letters were written from Marlborough
House and Sandringham, it is possible that the concerned prince
had taken his father into his confidence. He could not confide in
his beautiful mother; she was an irreproachable figure in his life,
a standard-bearer of virtue who was admired across the country
for her loyalty to her erring husband. Eddy adored her and to
disappoint her would be distressing. Although Eddy found his
father intimidating, he may have hoped that Bertie, a man of the
world, would be in a position to help him. It was around this time
that Bertie appears to have confided concerns about his oldest son
to a couple of friends, outlining a matter so secret that years later
one would write, 'I may not even hint at the nature of the advice
asked for, given, and acted on ...'[51]

Family letters began to refer to Eddy's 'gout', and it is possible
that Bertie sought to shield his wife from the shock of knowing about their oldest son's indiscretions by letting her believe
Eddy suffered from no more than this. But if 'gout' was the code

for Eddy's sexual infection, his younger brother George sailed provocatively close to giving the game away in one letter to Queen Victoria: 'Poor Eddy has been laid up with gout in his foot, how very unfortunate, he is really much too young to get that; I never heard of anybody getting it at 24 before,' he wrote incredulously.[52] The symptoms of his 'tiresome gout' on this occasion included a painful inflammation of his toe, Eddy told his brother. 'I could not do anything and could only hobble up and down stairs.'[53] This would appear to be a different ailment in addition to his sexual infection, although for both illnesses Eddy was required to pay close attention to his diet as advised by his army doctor, Roche.

Whatever the code word for Eddy's sexual infection and who was in the know, there remains the question of how he caught it. Despite strenuous efforts to make him as unlike his father as possible, the young prince enjoyed the company of pretty women and his letters to George show he took a keen interest in the opposite sex. 'There were two or three new girls who have just come out,' he reported to his brother after one May Ball in London, which was 'one of the best I have ever been to'. He studied them closely enough to conclude that 'none of them were strikingly beautiful', but he did take time to talk to George's childhood friend, Julie Stonor. Eddy could be charming and flirtatious and on another occasion he told George of 'some amusing American ladies staying [at Glen Muich] who kept us awake', including 'a Miss Colt who is decidedly pretty and very nice'.[54] But he had no long-term relationships in his early twenties and it has been argued that Eddy discovered a more exciting side to army life with plenty of diversions in towns near his barracks. The innocent prince could be easily led and might have found his way to the local clubs and brothels. If so, his mother had no idea, assuring the queen that when it came to clubs and races, 'he really has no inclination that way'.[55]

Eddy's biographer, Theo Aronson, has speculated that the young prince was homosexual or bisexual – a theory that would help to explain why Princess Beatrice went to such lengths to destroy his records. At the time society operated under an appalling double standard. Bertie's numerous affairs with women did not help his reputation, but did not prove disastrous for the monarchy. When it came to homosexuality, however, Victorian sensibilities were shocked. This was seen as an unnatural practice that was against the will of God and judged punitively. As late as 1861 the sentence for buggery could be hanging and long after this punishments involved lengthy prison sentences and fines. Eighteen years after the queen's Golden Jubilee, Oscar Wilde was imprisoned and ruined socially for 'the love that dare not speak its name'. But after examining Eddy's relationships with his alleged lovers, such as his mentor at Cambridge, James Stephen, and others, Aronson concedes the evidence is 'circumstantial'.[56] The claim remains unproven.

Whatever the truth about how Eddy acquired his sexual infection, one thing was plain: Queen Victoria must not find out. Despite her seclusion, the queen had an uncanny knack of uncovering just what was going on; those who excited the queen's interest often felt certain that, like the oracle at Delphi, she knew all. Keeping indelicate matters from her was no slight undertaking, but invoking her displeasure was almost unthinkable. She had repeatedly lamented Bertie's way of life. On no account was Eddy to copy his father. She had constantly advised him to keep his grandfather's name before him. Her homilies on the ills of society had followed Eddy across the world. She herself had come to encapsulate all the moral virtues of middle-class family life in Great Britain. The very sight of her plump figure swathed in black and her unsmiling face, fleshed out with age, summoned up highly prized Victorian family values: purity, fidelity and avoidance of the sins of the flesh. News that her second heir, like her first, might be corrupted by a playboy world could only make her shudder.

At the time of her jubilee in 1887, even without an intimate acquaintance of her grandson's private problems, the queen had cause enough for concern about Eddy. His knowledge remained woefully inadequate. He knew little of Europe, spoke no language other than English, and did he not profess a complete ignorance of the Crimean Battle of Alma at a recent dinner? His listlessness and lack of drive were worrying. Rather than dedicating himself to the

army he was keeping late hours in London. For a man in the prime
of life, he managed to look thin and wan. Ill-discipline, intemper-
ance, over-indulgence, these were words the queen was more used
to applying to her son than her grandson. There were formidable
duties ahead for the prince as a future heir to the throne. How
would he hold his own on a European stage among emperors and
kings? They included men like Emperor Franz Joseph, the authoritarian ruler of the Austro-Hungarian Empire that stretched across
a swathe of central Europe from northern Italy to the Ukraine. Or
Eddy's 'Uncle Sasha', the new emperor of Russia, Alexander III, a
giant of a man whose mere physical presence inspired confidence
and who had brought order to autocratic Russia after the assassination of Alexander II. The queen knew that Eddy needed taking
in hand and that his adoring mother, Alexandra, and wayward
father, Bertie, were unequal to the task.

There was for her one very obvious solution. The queen was
coming to the view that to help the young prince accomplish his
formidable duties he was in need of a suitable consort: a princess of redoubtable qualities like her own, who would be able to
bring out the very best in him. Queen Victoria was looking for
a very exceptional bride; a consort whose high principles, sound
education and shrewd judgement could compensate for Eddy's
deficiencies of character and be the making of him; whose virtue
and common sense would triumph over Eddy's weaknesses. As
Europe's great matriarch she had a bird's-eye view of the most
eligible and blue-blooded brides in Europe.

Traditionally, she had long favoured Germany as a suitable
source of royal consorts. The country that had given her the
beloved Prince Albert was also a land of rich culture and learning;
of Goethe, Bach and Beethoven, and most importantly, when it
came to choosing a spouse, the Protestant faith. For the queen,
Germany was a natural ally, the place from which the British
royal line had deep roots that stretched back to the early eighteenth century and the reign of George I, who was also a ruler of
the German House of Hanover.

But at the time of her Golden Jubilee in 1887 the queen was
troubled by unexpected news from Vicky of upheavals in the

German court. Her sensible oldest daughter appeared to be 'half distracted', the intrigues around her were 'dreadful', her news 'distressing and disturbing'.[57] Vicky's letters home bound mother and daughter together in a tragedy that was not just devastating for Vicky but marked a turning point in their long-shared vision for the future of Germany formed thirty years earlier when Prince Albert was alive. Its outcome had the potential to destroy the entire purpose of Vicky's brilliant dynastic marriage and undermine the Albertine vision of royal alliances; perhaps even to have troubling consequences for the stability of Europe. This made it all the more important to find the perfect consort for Eddy, one whose presence alone could allay any doubts about his credibility as the premier prince of Europe.

2

Vicky and Frederick

'I wish he could get a good "skelping" [flogging] as
the Scotch say ...'
Queen Victoria on her oldest grandson, the
future Kaiser Wilhelm II, February 1885

The crisis in the German court first surfaced in the weeks before
the Golden Jubilee celebrations in London. The ninety-year-
old German emperor, Wilhelm I, was in failing health. Queen
Victoria's 'beloved' son-in-law, Crown Prince Frederick, was
next in line to the German throne, but during the spring of 1887
Vicky became worried that her husband was unable to shake
off a seemingly innocuous symptom: a persistent hoarseness
in his throat. In May the prince's German doctors identified a
tumour on his vocal cord and fearing it was malignant, recommended an immediate operation to cut out the swelling. This
was life-threatening surgery but also his best hope of a cure.

Excruciating possibilities now opened up before Vicky and
Frederick. 'I wish I could fly to you and be with you to cheer
you up, darling child, and encourage Fritz,' the queen wrote
from London. But when a British doctor was summoned, Dr
Morell Mackenzie, he advised against any surgery unless cancer
was confirmed. To Vicky and Frederick's immense relief the
pathological report found no evidence of malignancy. While the
German doctors were uneasy that Mackenzie was too optimistic,
the Crown Princess was sure the British doctor was right. 'I am
<u>convinced</u> of it!' she wrote to her mother.[1] 'Darling and Beloved

Child, Truly, earnestly and most gratefully do I thank God that the … alarm about our precious Fritz has been dispelled,' the queen replied on 27 May, three weeks before her Golden Jubilee. Queen Victoria was determined that her daughter and son-in-law should now come to England for the celebrations. 'You both must not be absent on this day which will move me deeply …'[2]

Mother and daughter, always close, were reunited for the great pageant through London, Vicky sharing Queen Victoria's landau. In middle age, Vicky resembled her mother more closely, the fullness of her face softening her features, her figure filled out with repeated pregnancies. The crowd was especially interested in her husband. Newspapers had warned of a life-threatening illness; but Prince Frederick defied them. Riding ahead with the princes, tall and good-looking, wearing the impressive uniform of the Prussian Cuirassiers, he appeared to have the invincibility of a warrior-king about to claim his inheritance. The American journalist, Ralph Blumenfeld, considered him 'the most striking figure in the procession'.[3]

Summer weeks of rest in Scotland and then in Italy raised hopes of recovery, but during the autumn of 1887 the prince's symptoms returned. Vicky found it hard to hear his voice. In the second week of November the German heir to the throne was examined by six doctors, who were now united in their conclusions. Frederick was suffering from an incurable cancer. The choices before him were stark. His life might be prolonged with surgery to remove his larynx, but this would render him mute as a future emperor – if he survived the hazardous operation. Or he could put the matter in God's hands.

The news spread alarm across Europe. The old German emperor did not have long to live and his son, Frederick, the heir to the throne, was almost certainly dying too. Queen Victoria and her daughter were consumed by each hope, fear and renewed uncertainty. If Crown Prince Frederick died, the German throne would pass to Vicky's oldest son, the queen's oldest grandson: twenty-eight-year-old Prince Wilhelm. For both mother and daughter this would be an unmitigated tragedy that would undermine – perhaps destroy completely – the entire purpose of

Vicky's great marital alliance to the Prussian heir to the throne almost thirty years earlier.

In those seemingly halcyon days when her husband was still alive, Queen Victoria had supported Prince Albert in his vision for the marriages of their children. His remarkable plan had its roots in Coburg in Germany, birthplace of Queen Victoria's mother, Princess Victoria of Saxe-Coburg-Saalfeld and later Duchess of Kent, her uncle Leopold, king of the Belgians, and her beloved husband, Albert. In the first half of the nineteenth century, Germany as a state did not yet exist. Coburg was one of thirty-eight independent German kingdoms, dukedoms and other principalities that became loosely bound together under the leadership of the Austrian Empire as the 'German Confederation'.

The 'Coburg vision', articulated by Albert and his close advisor and friend, Baron Christian von Stockmar, had two political aims: to see the unification of Germany and then to 'establish unity of purpose between Germany and England'. For Prince Albert and Baron Stockmar this was a 'noble purpose' that would bring stability to Europe. They believed 'the peace of the world, the social, intellectual and political progress of Europe' depended on a political understanding between Britain and a newly unified Germany. After the trauma of the Napoleonic Wars, Stockmar believed that such an alliance would create a 'natural equilibrium' in Europe, making 'the Teutonic nations strong enough to enforce respect for public law, and to prevent every breach of the peace whether it came from East or West'.[4]

In September 1855 when Queen Victoria and Prince Albert sought an engagement between their much-loved fourteen-year-old daughter, Vicky, and the second heir to the Prussian throne, Prince Frederick, the romantic feelings of their daughter obligingly developed over a two-week courtship to mirror this political and strategic vision of Europe.[5] Vicky's match was a veritable template of the centuries-old tradition of royal marriages that were a key part of diplomacy and a means of 'sealing the deal'.

Prussia was then the largest and most dynamic of the German states, and by marrying into its royal house, Vicky hoped to fulfil her father's dream and play her part in shaping the political direction of the continent, inspired by his ideal of a liberal, unified Germany bringing peace to Europe.

Britain's perceived role as an international peacekeeper had largely grown throughout the nineteenth century along with her empire and her navy. Although her dominion over the waves advanced British self-interest, it also assisted other countries as world trade routes were safeguarded and the slave trade was blocked. But the supremacy that facilitated *Pax Britannica* did not just reside in the strength of her navy; it was interwoven into many facets of British culture. Britain was the industrial workshop of the world, the world's banker, a leader in the arts, science and humanitarian reform, and above all, home to the mother of all parliaments: a constitutional monarchy that strictly limited the powers of the sovereign and was gradually extending the electoral franchise. The British model was pointing the way: enlightened, liberal democratic reform was a means of keeping at bay the unstable forces of revolution and war.

In the 1850s, with perhaps greater clarity than the queen's ministers, Prince Albert grasped the potential of Protestant Prussia to unite all the German states under its banner and understood the power that this new country would wield in Europe. He could not imagine that a unified Germany under Prussian domination would exert its influence as a military dictatorship or autocracy. Vicky's brilliant marriage to a future Prussian heir to the throne aimed at nothing less than to fashion the political development of Prussia-Germany along British lines. The young princess would nurture this seed of enlightened, liberal thinking on Prussian soil and help steer the new state towards a parliamentary constitutional monarchy.[6] Her marriage was the first in a series of royal dynastic marriages that aimed to forge closer ties across Europe and facilitate peace.

Vicky and her father had always shared a special bond; her precocious intelligence and willingness to learn delighted her principled father, and formed a marked contrast to her lazy brother,

Bertie. On her marriage to Prince Frederick in St James's Palace in January 1858, Vicky became nothing less than a 'royal missioner [sic] to Prussia' to propagate the exalted ideals of her 'adored Papa's faith'.[7] Prince Albert had not only mentored Frederick for many years but also personally coached his gifted daughter in politics to prepare Vicky for her future role, and he left her in no doubt about the seriousness of the task ahead.[8] Fortunately, Vicky had strong feelings for her Prussian prince, but her marriage was not just a question of her health and happiness, Albert warned. At stake was 'the future of your country and people and thereby one might almost say, the welfare of Europe'.[9] British people shared the high hopes, lining the streets despite heavy snow to cheer as the 'Daughter of England' departed for Prussia: 'God Save the Prince and Bride! God keep their lands allied.'[10]

However high-minded the aspirations for the foreign alliance, nothing could mitigate the pain of parting. For Albert, his oldest daughter's marriage was a personal sacrifice to his ideals; nothing could replace her presence. He loved Vicky with an intensity that appeared to go beyond the usual father-daughter relationship. In the coming months the demands of his unending workload, which appeared increasingly self-inflicted, failed to provide relief. Vicky was gone and there was nothing in this world that could fill the dark void created by her absence. The seventeen-year-old bride in the militaristic Prussian court also suffered. 'I think it will kill me to take leave of dear papa,' Vicky had told the queen. Now she kept his picture close, as though the very sight of him could bring comfort. 'I treasure your words up in my heart,' she told her father, assuring him they would influence 'the whole of my life'.[11]

When Prince Albert died on 14 December 1861, three years after his daughter left home, Queen Victoria's desolation overwhelmed her family. Her first letter was to Vicky, 'I am crushed, bowed down! ... I feel I am living with Him [Albert] – as much as before – that He will yet guide and lead me.' She could see nothing ahead but 'an everlasting blank!'[12] Weeks later it was as though she, too, had died: her life was 'utterly extinguished', she told her daughter. This second life was just a shadow, nothing less than 'death in life'.[13] But Vicky also felt 'the future is gone'. Everything she had done was 'in hopes of pleasing Papa'. She had trusted in his 'unerring judgement' and now felt stranded, adrift in Prussia, without her inspiration, the architect of her marital alliance and career.[14] When Vicky returned to Osborne House there was little to bring her comfort. Grief was institutionalised in the daily routine of the household. Her father's personal belongings were laid out for him each day, water was brought to his private rooms. Inwardly, 'it is nothing but a great vault', she told her husband. 'The old life, the old customs have gone ...' Vicky found her mother 'cries a lot ... she always sleeps with Papa's coat over her and his dear red dressing gown beside her and some of his clothes in the bed! ... I keep asking myself involuntarily where he has gone, and always think that he will come back.'[15]

Both Vicky and her mother felt charged with a renewed mission to carry out Prince Albert's wishes. 'His views about everything are to be my law!' wrote Queen Victoria. 'No human power will make me swerve from what he decided and wished.'[16] Vicky felt no less strongly. In one respect the women were able to achieve this aim. Suitable dynastic matches had already been identified for Albert and Victoria's next two children. Vicky in Berlin was well placed to advise on the short list and discreetly appraise the most eligible German royals. The next to be married was Queen Victoria's second daughter, Alice, whose union to Prince Louis of the Grand Duchy of Hesse and by Rhine in July 1862, six months after Albert's death, was 'more like a funeral than a wedding', observed the queen.[17] It was Vicky who identified the stunningly beautiful Danish princess, Alexandra, as the most likely spouse to hold her brother Bertie's interest and stop his errant behaviour. Bertie's marriage in March 1863 still felt for the queen 'far worse than a funeral to witness!' without Albert at her side.[18] This union rapidly extended British royal connections when, in the same year, Alexandra's father became King Christian IX of Denmark and her brother became King George of Greece, while in 1866 her sister, Dagmar, married the future Tsar Alexander III. Four more of Queen Victoria's younger children would marry German royals.

Despite these close ties of marriage, when it came to German politics, over the coming years the hopes of mother and daughter to fulfil Prince Albert's goals withered in turn, each painful setback charted in Vicky's letters home. 'Your dear letters', and the anticipation of them, 'are one of the few things I care for now ...', the queen told her daughter.[19] But these letters gave rise to increasing concern as the next crisis gradually took on an ominous shape in the form of Vicky's formidable adversary: the reactionary Prussian firebrand, Otto von Bismarck.

In 1862 Vicky's father-in-law, King Wilhelm I of Prussia, faced with a liberal majority in the Prussian *Landtag*, or representative assembly, failed to win approval for the budget to pay for the reforms of the army that he wished. Seeing this as a direct challenge to the authority of the Crown, Wilhelm I threatened abdication in September, only agreeing to stay if Otto von Bismarck, then Prussian ambassador to Paris, became prime minister. Vicky was appalled. Bismarck was an adventurer, she told her mother, 'a most unprincipled and unrespectable character ... a wicked man'. The idea of 'that wretch' governing the country 'makes my hair stand on end!'[20] At stake was the crucial idea of parliamentary government for Prussia. Bismarck was determined to preserve the principle of personal monarchy whereby the Crown retained control over both the executive and, crucially, the army.

Vicky felt the isolation of her position, 'now we no longer have Papa who always wrote to us. I now feel completely cut off!' Her father had always appeared to understand the context of Prussian politics. When her husband wavered, Vicky rushed in with the idealism of youth, failing to see the complexities, slowly enmeshing herself in Bismarck's web. 'Your success in future days rests solely on your firm insistence on the constitutional, liberal ... principle,' the queen guided her daughter in March 1862. Vicky remained unswerving in her commitment to these ideals: 'Our only duty is to make this dear country so perfect, strong and mighty by means of liberal practical constitution and by orderly and legal methods,' she wrote.[21] She hoped Prussia could become an example to other countries and win the confidence of Europe. But Bismarck soon outmanoeuvred the liberal-leaning heir to the throne and his wife. This was his moment and he seized it. In his eyes, an all-powerful, militaristic Crown was the key to Prussian strength, rather than a clique of civilian ministers. He promised his total allegiance to Wilhelm I and saw his own power as chief advisor to the Crown. It was not 'Prussia's liberalism' but 'Prussia's might' that would assure the country's future, he famously announced on 30 September 1862 to the Chamber of Deputies. 'The great questions of the times will not be solved by speeches and majority decisions, but by iron and blood.'

As Prince Albert had foreseen, Germany was indeed unified by 1871, not peacefully as he had wished through diplomacy and the moral force of an enlightened Prussia, but through wars engineered by the 'iron and blood' Chancellor Bismarck. As late as 1866 the *New York Times* commented, 'there is, in political geography, no proper Germany to speak of. There are Kingdoms and Grand Duchies and Duchies and Principalities ... each separately ruled by an independent sovereign.'[22] But in just a few years, Europe bent to the iron will of Bismarck, its boundaries re-drawn as a unified Germany had emerged, fashioned in blood, steel and astute diplomacy.

In 1864, under the scheming Bismarck, Prussia and Austria fought a war against Denmark, jointly gaining the duchies of Schleswig and Holstein in the Jutland Peninsula (now part of northern Germany). This war sharply divided the British royal family and tested new marriage ties. Vicky and the queen supported Prussia, but Bertie and his wife backed Denmark, which had an ancient claim to these two duchies. Princess Alexandra was in despair, crying and unable to sleep as her recently crowned father, Christian IX of Denmark, lost almost half of his country. Bertie was so vocal in his support for his wife that the queen felt obliged to remind her son and heir that he was bound to Germany 'by so many ties of blood'.[23] Nonetheless, this war began to undermine Queen Victoria's faith in great foreign marriages. 'Great alliances ... are only a source of worry,' she confided to Augusta, the Queen of Prussia, and she claimed to attribute 'little political importance to them'.[24]

The war of Prussia and Austria against Denmark did not settle Bismarck's ambitions. Two years later, the all-obliterating machine of the Prussian army was at war again, this time joining forces with Italy *against* the Austrians. Europe took note of advances in Prussian weapons technology as their army, now fully equipped with breech-loading needle guns, turned their firepower on their former ally. These guns, precursors of modern automatic rifles, could fire at a much faster rate than the traditional muzzle-loading muskets. The Prussians rapidly wrested exclusive control of Schleswig and Holstein from the Austrians in the north and annexed a swathe of territory including the kingdom of Hanover, the electorate of Hesse-Kassel, Nassau and the city of Frankfurt (areas of central Germany today). Four years later, Prussia fought a third war, this time against France, leading to the annexation of the Catholic South German states. Bismarck's ill-judged land grab of Alsace and Lorraine, a part of northern France for almost 200 years, left a lasting legacy of French resentment. The Franco-Prussian War of 1870–1 finally sealed German unity as the many separate states of the Germanic peoples of northern Europe united under the banner of the Prussian House of Hohenzollern while retaining their individual monarchies, governments and parliaments.

Bismarck ensured that the vigorous new country of the German *Reich* would be dominated by a strong, authoritarian ruler at its helm. He turned his back on the Albertine vision, and in January 1871 Vicky's father-in-law the king of Prussia was proclaimed Germany's first emperor, Kaiser Wilhelm I. Although Wilhelm could not wield the absolute authority of the Russian tsar, his powers were remarkable. The emperor could appoint and dismiss ministers, including Germany's chancellor, and control foreign policy and the army. There was a German imperial parliament, the *Reichstag*, whose members were elected by universal male suffrage, but in practice this had no executive authority since it could not initiate legislation or hold government ministers to account. For Vicky this parliament was little more than a fig leaf. But in the magnificent gilded palace of Versailles, a building that seemed to embody the very soul of humiliated France, the deed was immortalised at a ceremony in the Hall of Mirrors. The Hohenzollerns, the royal house of Prussia, became the imperial house of Germany, raised above the other royal and princely German dynasties. Bismarck's *Reich* was now the leading power on the continent, an empire to respect, even fear.

Through Vicky's British eyes, it was as though newly united Germany had been thoroughly 'Prussified'. Her husband, Crown Prince Frederick, was now heir to a highly militarised semi-autocracy in which their liberal ideals were sidelined. Army chiefs operated largely independently of parliament and reported directly to the king-emperor. Bismarck and the military elite, rather than elected members of the *Reichstag*, held favoured positions. The Hohenzollerns' friend, Alfred Krupp, 'the Canon King', ran the Krupp steel works in Essen whose improvements in the design of canon and weaponry had helped secure these victories and continued to supply the military on an industrial scale.

Vicky may have had 'a man's head' in her father's estimation, but a great deal more was required to stand up to Europe's pre-eminent statesman. Even before he came to power, Bismarck had the measure of her English views and her powerful influence over Crown Prince Frederick, and he took steps to isolate them both. When her husband was sometimes torn between his loyalty to his authoritarian Prussian father and his liberal English wife, Vicky urged him to challenge Wilhelm I and Bismarck. This only served to compound their difficulties and they were isolated, even ridiculed at court. Vicky lacked the guile to navigate the quicksands of German politics and could be dogmatic and outspoken. 'Never were we untrue to our sacred flag,' she wrote later.[25] Her opinionated candour prompted one British minister to warn that the Crown Princess of Germany was 'always clever, never wise'. Seeing her cherished papa's vision pushed ever further out of reach, she poured out her frustrations privately to her mother. The scheming and all-powerful Bismarck was 'the most mischievous and dangerous person alive'. His policies at times were 'disgraceful' and the German people 'so blind and so short sighted as not to see the ruin and mischief which is being worked'.[26] As her mission floundered, she lamented 'I always feel like a fly struggling in a very tangled web and feelings of weariness and depression, often of disgust and hopelessness take possession of me'.[27]

It was not just in court politics that Vicky was outmanoeuvred. The impotence of her position in fulfilling her beloved father's vision was underlined in deeply personal terms through the disturbing development of her oldest son, Prince Wilhelm. The arrival of a son in January 1859 within a year of her marriage appeared to seal the success of the alliance between Prussia and Great Britain. Hopes ran high, the flags of both countries dancing enthusiastically over the celebrations proclaiming the arrival of a child who would surely inherit the best of each kingdom. The British queen's first grandson was a future heir to the German throne, the unity between the two countries embodied in his very name: 'Friedrich Wilhelm' after his Prussian forebears and 'Albert Victor' after his British grandparents. At the outset the young prince shouldered great expectations, but with each painful step through childhood he frustrated his parents' vision, his faults charted in voluminous correspondence between his British mother and grandmother. The women's doubts focused on the young prince's character about which mother and daughter shared for many years an intimate understanding in a no-holds-barred exchange.

Vicky was dismayed to observe her son's wild streak from an early age. Wilhelm was 'too lively and violent' to apply himself to walking and talking, she confided to her mother in early 1860.[28] Shortly after his second birthday she noted that he got so 'violent and passionate that it makes me quite nervous sometimes'.[29] Six months later, when Vicky visited Osborne House, the queen observed for herself that her German grandson was 'so violent' that her own youngest daughter, Beatrice (then aged four) was 'rather afraid' of him.[30]

Both Vicky and her mother made allowances for the fact that the young prince had suffered trauma at birth. Too late, the doctors had discovered that the baby was in a dangerous breech position and applied such force to free him that they caused permanent damage to a nexus of nerves in his neck, shoulder and arm. As the months passed it became clear that the prince's left arm was not growing normally and was resistant to treatment no matter what fearsome cures were applied. The baby's good arm was strapped to his side to encourage the use of his palsied arm. Another gruesome treatment was to plunge his damaged arm into a freshly slaughtered hare in the belief that the blood and heat of the animal might impart some rejuvenating quality. Electrical stimulation was tried, and most loathed of all by Prince Wilhelm, at the age of four, 'a head stretching machine' was used to counter the effect of his head being dragged downwards. All these approaches failed and eventually surgery was required to minimise the effects of the birth trauma. The various well-meant treatments were sufficiently traumatic that they may well have prepared the ground for the psychological problems that would plague the prince later in his life. Historians have not ruled out the possibility that the Prussian prince may have suffered slight brain damage at birth as well.[31]

Vicky continued to have concerns about Wilhelm's development as he was followed in the nursery by a succession of younger siblings: Charlotte, Henry, Sigismund, Victoria, Waldemar, Sophie and Margaret. Unlike his British cousin Eddy, Wilhelm applied himself with tremendous self-discipline and after years of patient struggle, he mastered all the physical skills he would need as a future emperor, even becoming an accomplished horseman and an excellent shot despite his handicap. Nevertheless he continued to exhibit troubling character flaws. Vicky felt her son displayed an undue sense of self-importance and could be opinionated and arrogant. At times he could be 'a most destructive little person' who 'flies into most violent passions', she told her mother.[32] Vicky was convinced he was spoiled by others and she applied the most exacting standards herself.

Queen Victoria was sympathetic, but viewed from a distance at first could not be certain that her daughter's high expectations were exacerbating the problem. Wilhelm took pains with his grandmother. His letters marking the birthdays and anniversaries were invariably well written in English and eloquent in his gratitude for presents received. Her oldest grandson was bright and willing to apply himself at high school, the Friedrichgymnasium in Kassel, and later at the University of Bonn. The queen tried to reassure her daughter and calm her concerns about her oldest son. 'I think Willie does not mean to be unfeeling,' she wrote in August 1879.[33] A few months later, acknowledging that Wilhelm was 'quite tiresome and provoking' in his *esprit de contradiction*', she still felt that this was common in young people and 'it very likely will get better if no notice is taken of that'.[34]

Wilhelm became adept at slipping into his letters to his grandmother comments that she might want to hear, as though defending himself against criticism that he suspected must have been aired by his mother. In an apparent show of unity with his mother he wrote, 'she and I, we both agree wholly in loving and adoring everything that is in England or English, especially the lovely service of the Church of England'.[35] Such sentiments conflicted with letters from Vicky, who remained distressed at his opposition to her 'English' liberal ideas and his marked preference for the militarism of his grandfather, Wilhelm I, and Bismarck. In 1880 Vicky returned to her theme. 'Willy is chauvinistic and ultra-Prussian to a degree and with a violence that is often very painful to me.' Aware that her mother thought that she could be provoking confrontation, Vicky added, 'I avoid all discussions ... and remain silent', even when his 'bigotry and narrow-mindedness' gave grounds for concern.[36] Two weeks later her mother replied, again gently chiding her daughter to be less critical. Acknowledging her daughter's grief over her favourite son, eleven-year-old Prince Waldemar, who had died of diphtheria in March 1879, she added, 'I only tremble when I hear too great lamentation over the deficiencies of those left.'[37] Within a few years, however, even Queen Victoria conceded the special difficulties Vicky faced and – in private at least – put her view without hesitation: her German grandson 'often needed a good smacking'.[38]

Vicky hoped to ease her difficulties with her son by finding him a suitable wife. In 1878 the nineteen-year-old prince suddenly expressed strong feelings for the very princess she had recommended, Augusta Victoria of Schleswig-Holstein, or 'Dona'. For a brief period relations with his mother improved as Wilhelm felt grateful to his parents for their help in enlisting the emperor's

permission for him to ask for Dona's hand. Vicky had an unexpected ally in Bismarck, who believed that an alliance between the
imposing Hohenzollerns of Prussia and the aggrieved Schleswig-
Holsteins, who had lost out in the German fight with Denmark,
would strengthen German unity. But to Vicky's surprise, given
that she and her mother had liaised so closely over the matches of
her siblings, Queen Victoria would not lend her support, shrewdly
pointing out that she must keep out of such an important German
matter and 'behave quite passively'. It would be a mistake for the
British queen to be seen meddling in the prospective match of
the German heir.[39] Queen Victoria waited until Kaiser Wilhelm
I finally approved the alliance in January 1880 before meeting
Dona and her sister, Calma, at Windsor, who struck her as 'dear
nice girls, tall, pretty figures, very fair with blue eyes'.[40] Vicky had
persuaded herself that Dona would be 'an angel of peace & Love
and comfort for us all', and the queen agreed that gentle Dona 'is
well calculated to be an element of peace in ruffled waters'.[41]

Their hopes were soon frustrated. After his wedding on 27
February 1881, Wilhelm had independence and his own household, almost entirely staffed by those who supported the emperor
and Bismarck's point of view. Dona worshipped her volatile
husband and was exceedingly anxious to please. Gradually her
docile nature moulded around his, and Vicky soon found her
daughter-in-law as narrow-minded, reactionary and Prussian
in her thinking as her son. In December 1886 Wilhelm proudly
reported to Queen Victoria that on his grandfather's orders he
was now working at the Foreign Ministry, 'to learn from and
under the guidance of Prince Bismarck how to do politics and
how to manage to steer the ship of the state between the shoals
and intricate channels of treaties, foreign susceptibilities etc'.[42]
He cut his political teeth on two important missions to Russia in
1884 and 1886. But his initial success was undermined when he
wrote secretly to the new Russian tsar, Alexander III, contemp-
tuously badmouthing his parents and alleging they were under
the control of Queen Victoria. Vicky found her son's outbursts of
aggression against her unbearable and soon realised that he was
being coached by Bismarck against his liberal parents.

By the mid-1880s one long-running feud within the German royal house developed into open warfare between mother and son. Vicky wanted her second daughter, Victoria, known as 'Moretta' in the family, to marry a handsome German prince who had been elevated to the Bulgarian throne, Prince Alexander of Battenberg. Queen Victoria lent her support to the plan, and spurred on by Vicky, Moretta and Alexander became secretly engaged in 1883, subject to approval from Kaiser Wilhelm I. But the prospective marriage sharply divided the German court and once again Prince Wilhelm aligned himself with Bismarck and his German grandparents against his British mother. At stake were two very different visions of Germany's foreign policy and future role in Europe.

Bismarck believed that any strengthening of German influence in eastern Europe on the Black Sea through a German-Bulgarian marriage would appear threatening to Alexander III. For the tsar, Bulgaria was tantamount to an outlying region of Russia and no other power should meddle with it. Bismarck argued that Vicky's proposed alliance for Moretta would harm Germany's relationship with Russia, perhaps nudge Russia into an unwelcome alliance with France or even provoke war. Seen through the eyes of her antagonistic son, Vicky's passionate support for the match could be construed as a British 'plot' to weaken Germany. But nothing was further from her mind.

For Vicky the match promised a far-reaching extension of her father's vision for Germany and its place in Europe. Not only did she want to play a role in liberalising Germany when her husband came to power but also to spread these enlightened values to eastern Europe. She glimpsed the possibility of her three younger daughters, Moretta, Sophie and Margaret, marrying into the Crowns of Bulgaria, Greece and Romania. They in turn might plant the seed of liberalism in the Balkan region of south-east Europe and build ties between a liberal Germany and Britain, which would cooperate in pushing back the destabilising influence of barbarous Russia in eastern Europe. Moretta's match to the Bulgarian prince was the first stage in a visionary expansion of the Albertine plan.[43]

Prince Wilhelm railed at his mother, behaving like a man provoked beyond all reason. Quite apart from the implications of the match for Germany's relations with Russia, he and others in his family believed there was another insuperable obstacle to the handsome Battenberg prince: his pedigree. Alexander of Battenberg's line was 'contaminated' by the presence of non-royal blood; there was at least one count in the family tree, not to mention a valet too. This issue struck at the quintessential essence of royalty. For Wilhelm, the Hohenzollerns stood apart, inviolable, blessed with some indefinable royal quality that came with being princes of the blood, which entitled them to their position as Prussia's and Germany's ruling house. With one of the outbursts of violent temper for which he would become known, he threatened to 'club the Battenberger [Prince Alexander] to death' if Vicky and Moretta persisted with the match.[44] Such was the fury vented by Wilhelm and his family on this particular issue that Vicky, who reported everything faithfully to her mother, asked the queen to burn her letters. 'That very foolish, undutiful and – I must add – unfeeling boy I have no patience with, and I wish he could get a good "skelping" [flogging] as the Scotch say and seriously a good setting down,' Queen Victoria replied sympathetically to her daughter in February 1885.[45] Vicky appears to have been so fearful about what she had disclosed that the queen wrote a couple of days later to reassure her daughter that her letters 'are burned and I burn many a one which speaks of people which might be disagreeable hereafter'. A large number of Vicky's letters in 1885 have not survived.[46]

During the jubilee year of 1887, Wilhelm continued to cause his parents immense distress during each alarming phase of his father Crown Prince Frederick's illness. His thirst for power was undisguised, with open criticism of his parents circulating in Berlin. Vicky felt hunted by the press. Her son's contempt for her was barely disguised and she was also tainted by the failings of the English doctor, Mackenzie, whose overly optimistic advice earlier in the year appeared to have denied her husband, the German heir to the throne, a chance of long-term survival. Queen Victoria was much troubled by the way Vicky and Frederick 'are both tormented ... it makes my blood boil'.[47] An order from the ailing old emperor enabling his grandson to sign documents on his behalf was handled with great insensitivity by Wilhelm, as though he had power already. The queen felt obliged to remind Prince Wilhelm of the need to consider the 'dear Patient – no one can over rate the value of that precious life to dear Mama, and you all, – to Germany, Europe, if not the whole world'.[48] Wilhelm assured his grandmother that he was doing all he could, an assurance that conflicted with Vicky's own account. The warring tone of Wilhelm's reply was hardly reassuring. 'Politically the outlook is rather cloudy ... Providence alone knows what is in store for us all; may it be Peace! If not, well then let Lord Nelson's signal fly at the mast head of every nation which is willing to keep Europe from harm'.[49]

The close ties that a British-German grandson was intended to symbolise appeared to have turned into the reverse. Wilhelm was unstable; blown this way and that by his latest enthusiasm, alternating between an overweening confidence and crushing defeat when that buoyant mood evaporated. All the imagined insults and pricks to the wounded vanity of the German prince gradually coalesced into intensely conflicting feelings towards Britain and his British relatives: admiration and resentment, goodwill and hatred. Vicky knew that schooled in a 'poisonous atmosphere' by Bismarck and his allies, her son confused demonstrating a 'hatred against England ... as patriotism'.[50] It was a short step in his mind to merge his mother's Englishness and her liberal values: liberalism was not quite German and would weaken his country. German might and glory had been born out of Prussian militarism. Even Bismarck himself, who had done so much to encourage Prince Wilhelm's alienation from his parents, began to foresee trouble if Crown Prince Frederick was unable to become the next emperor. Wilhelm 'is impetuous ... cannot keep silent, is susceptible to flattery and could plunge Germany into war without foreseeing or wishing it'.[51]

The final collapse of Vicky's hopes for fulfilling the wider mission of her marriage was at hand. After months of decline, the ageing Kaiser Wilhelm I died on 9 March 1888 and Vicky's husband became Frederick III, German emperor and king of Prussia. The great moment for which Vicky and Frederick had worked for thirty years was upon them. This was their hour, their chance to shape the future of the country, perhaps even to dismantle the apparatus of autocratic power and steer German governance towards a more liberal system under a constitutional monarch. The queen was overwhelmed. 'My own dear Empress Victoria,' she wrote to Vicky. 'I am thankful and proud that dear Fritz and you should have come to the throne.'[52] There was a blizzard of snow in Berlin as the failing new emperor, with an unmistakeable look of death about him and with great effort, struggled to seize his hour. He issued a manifesto: 'my whole endeavour will be … to make Germany a protector of peace and to care for the wellbeing of the country'.[53]

Their chance was painfully denied them. Bertie attended the funeral of Emperor Wilhelm I and was shocked at the change in his brother-in-law, Emperor Frederick. The apparently invincible prince of nine months earlier at the Golden Jubilee was wasted and had 'a hunted, anxious expression, which was very distressing to see', Bertie wrote to the queen.[54] The speechless emperor could communicate only by means of a pad of paper and pencil.[55] Vicky felt wrecked, as though she was on 'a sinking ship'. Her father's dream, her sacred flag, was now in shreds. Thirty years of discussions about how she and her husband would bring Britain and Germany closer together were now irrelevant.

Even if Emperor Frederick had had the strength to implement the reforms, he was unable to do so. Bismarck's supporters were watching for any attempt by the new emperor to rush through liberal English ideas. Such was the deep suspicion in Berlin at the prospect of any interference by the empress that the British prime minister, the Conservative statesman Lord Salisbury, sent a warning. On no account could Britain be seen to meddle in Germany's affairs, he advised the British ambassador. Vicky would 'incur most serious risk' if she attempted to do so; she must appear 'mildly Bismarckian'.[56] Every aspect of Vicky's life appeared to be coloured by the bitter conflict over her Britishness. Even her older children, Charlotte and Henry, joined Wilhelm in open support of her enemies. Already Wilhelm 'fancies himself completely the emperor and an absolute and an autocratic one', Vicky warned her mother.[57] Queen Victoria was outraged at her grandson's behaviour to his mother and father.

When Lord Salisbury heard that Queen Victoria had ventured forth from her holiday in the Mediterranean with Beatrice to visit her family in Berlin he sensed trouble. Recognising that Queen Victoria's approach to dealing with her grandson might stray some way from Foreign Office diplomacy, he felt the need, once again, to send a warning. 'Most unhappily,' he wrote, all her grandson's 'impulses' would soon have political consequences 'of enormous potency'. Germany and Britain 'are so necessary to each other' that anything said to him 'must be carefully weighed'.[58] The prime minister made his private views plain to his friend, the Duke of Rutland, who was to accompany Victoria in Germany. The queen was 'very unmanageable about her conduct to her relations', wrote the prime minister. 'She will persist in considering William only as her grandson. But the matter has become political and very grave and she must listen to advice.'[59] The queen was no longer at liberty to speak her mind and any family row could harm Anglo-German relations.

However affronted Queen Victoria may have felt on receiving instructions from the prime minister about how to manage her grandson, she did not grace him with a reply. Nonetheless, as she approached the outskirts of Berlin on the morning of 24 April 1888, noting from the train window the increasingly flat landscape and glimpses of soldiers drilling, she was preparing to be her dignified best. She and Beatrice arrived at the small station of Charlottenburg and there to greet her on the platform was Wilhelm, with Vicky and all her other children. Vicky stepped briefly into her mother's carriage for a moment's privacy. 'I clasped her in my arms and kissed her warmly,' the queen wrote in her journal.[60] Both women were determined not to give way before the other. Wilhelm was all smiles and courteous respect for his grandmother. He escorted her through the station to their waiting barouche and travelled with her to the Charlottenburg Palace. Vicky took her mother to a suite of rooms once occupied by Frederick the Great and could not restrain her tears once they were private. In her mother's eyes, she seemed 'so good and brave'.[61] The queen's most painful encounter was with her son-in-law, Frederick. Both knew he had not long to live. The emperor, true to character, tried to make some gesture of gallantry, raising his skeletal frame in bed as best he could to give his mother-in-law a small bouquet. Victoria tried to find words of comfort but in her heart she 'was wrung with grief and pity'.[62]

The queen hoped to be of use and her chance came on 25 April when Bismarck came to see her. It was their first meeting for more than thirty years and the queen found Vicky's great enemy did not live up to her expectations. 'An immense man ... in full uniform' entered the room, but to the queen's surprise he adopted a 'gentleness of manner and very agreeable tone'. Germany's Iron Chancellor and Britain's imperious Queen-Empress soon found much on which to agree. Bismarck's 'great object was to prevent war upon which I observed that this was also our great desire', the queen recorded. As they discussed Europe's Great Powers both shared 'a great distrust' of Russia. Bismarck explained his fears that Russia and France would unite against Germany or that Russia might attack Austria, in which case Germany would be obliged by treaty to assist Austria. When it came to family matters, Bismarck and the queen found they were in agreement over Wilhelm's inexperience. With tears in his eyes, Bismarck acknowledged Emperor Frederick's 'hard fate' to have waited for so long 'and not be able to do what he could for his Country', and he promised the queen he would 'stand by' Vicky.[63] Bismarck had expected Queen Victoria to support Vicky in her continued insistence that Moretta should marry Prince Alexander of Battenberg and so he was relieved to find that she had concluded the match was unworkable. 'That was a woman!' he said afterwards in admiration.

As the emperor's health declined, 'the gaze of Europe concentrated on one sick room', observed the *Daily Telegraph*. For the British press it was as though Germany hovered at a crucial fork in the road, one path leading towards increased autocracy with all its dangers, the other towards greater liberalism and peace.

'The heroic and much loved Emperor Frederick ... has ever been a lover of liberty and progress', who aimed to 'gradually democratise the institutions of the fatherland', claimed the *Telegraph*. His life was considered to be 'the one guarantee still existing for the continuance of European peace'. Fearsome accounts of an increasingly skeletal emperor gasping for breath appeared to symbolise something more: the dying struggles of the fight for a liberal Germany.[64]

In June 1888 the emperor moved to the Neues Palais at Potsdam – now renamed Friedrichskron – and anxious crowds gathered outside waiting for news. A reporter for *The Times* recorded the strange events of the night of 14 June. The little telegraph office at the station was open all night, the light streaming from its windows gradually 'restricted to little more than that emitted by a few solitary lamps and tapers'. There was no sudden improvement in the emperor's condition to report. Shortly after eleven o'clock the next morning the imperial standard 'floating in the balmy morning breeze' was suddenly lowered to half mast. 'If it had been the blade of a guillotine' its fall could not have been a more 'painful shock' to the grieving onlookers, continued *The Times*. 'Now cracks a noble heart. Good night sweet prince.'[65] Almost immediately the mourners were disturbed by the noise of fast-approaching horses. A squadron of the Hussars of the Guard in bright scarlet jackets rode up and 'rapidly dispersed like the leaves of a fan to take possession of all the points of access to the huge palace area'. On the orders of the new Kaiser, Wilhelm II, soldiers surrounded his mother's palace. They had been waiting behind a colonnade near the palace even while his father lay dying. Just to be sure every point of access or exit was sealed up 'hermetically', the cavalry was soon reinforced by 'a splendid company of infantry, pouring with perspiration', which came 'at the double ... the ground almost shaking beneath the swift tramp of their feet'.[66]

Inside the palace, Vicky fled to her apartments, 'utterly broken hearted'.[67] In her eyes, 'Germany's good angel – her guardian angel – her star of hope – has gone', and with him the last vestiges of the Albertine dream for Germany. Her fleeting moment of power, for which she had been preparing all her life, perished with her husband. Not one piece of liberal reform had been enacted during her husband's short reign. Her vision of a bright new Europe aspiring to the very best in human nature no longer existed. 'Power now belongs to brute force – and to cunning,' she predicted. Even so, it was a shock as she glanced through the windows that very morning to see furtive movements everywhere in the grounds. Fully armed soldiers emerged 'from behind every tree and every statue!' she wrote.[68]

Wilhelm's first act of absolute power was to make sure his mother understood that there was no tie of love to entrap him. Grieving and alone, she was the enemy now. In the eyes of the new emperor, his mother had shamed the House of Hohenzollern and brought the *Reich* 'to the brink of ruin'.[69] Insisting she was plotting against him, Wilhelm was convinced there would be documents in the palace that would incriminate his mother as a spy. 'Of all that went on in our house I will not speak!' Vicky wrote. She turned away 'from the miserable spectacle with pride and disgust'.[70]

———

For all the high hopes that Vicky's marriage had once embodied, the accession of her twenty-nine-year-old son as Emperor Wilhelm II marked a turning point in Anglo-German relations. Feeling persecuted by his treatment, Vicky left the home she had shared with her husband and settled at their farmhouse nearby at Bornstedt, joined by their youngest daughters, Moretta, Sophie and Margaret, who remained loyal to her. Her political power vanished almost overnight. Queen Victoria, too, found her ties with the German court diminished. In a matter of weeks she lost the intimate links she had enjoyed through her daughter, her son-in-law Frederick, and his mother, Augusta, who was seriously ill.[71] Instead the new German emperor found reason to take offence at his British relatives. While he was in Berlin for Emperor Frederick's funeral, Bertie had rashly raised the highly charged issue of whether the Germans would return the provinces of Alsace-Lorraine, won in the Franco-Prussian War, back to the French. Wilhelm found a way to vent his fury in a pointed snub to his uncle a few months later. Bertie arrived in Vienna only to be told he must leave at once because the German emperor was also expected and had priority. Wilhelm delighted in asserting his new-found seniority over his uncle and other British relatives, who he felt still treated him 'like a little boy' and not as a mighty German emperor.

In a throwback to the past, the new Kaiser grandly imagined himself as a guardian of the ancient notion of the divine right of kings with a duty to protect Germany by strengthening his own powers. Not for him a constitutional monarchy with a sovereign who reigned but did not rule. Emperor Wilhelm II wanted to increase his hold on power and Bismarck was soon worried by his disturbing 'lust for war'.[72]

After unifying Germany in 'blood and iron' during the 1860s, Bismarck had used diplomacy to maintain peace in Europe through an elaborate network of treaties. The most significant of these was the powerful 'Triple Alliance' forged in 1882 between Germany, Austria-Hungary and Italy, a military alliance uniting the countries of central Europe. If a Triple Alliance country was attacked by another Great Power, the others would come to its aid. Recognising that Germany's strong position in central Europe left it exposed to attack from Russia in the east and France in the west, Bismarck had skilfully navigated a path to court Russia and isolate France. After years of diplomacy to maintain the balance of power, he was appalled to discover the new Kaiser was behaving as though war was inevitable, claiming that Russia was looking for 'a favourable moment to fall upon us and the armed forces of France now threaten us'.[73] In his first speech as Kaiser, Wilhelm underlined his control of the army: 'we belong to each other – I and the army – we were born for each other and will cleave indissolubly to each other ...'[74]

Wilhelm was not only quick to assert his power as emperor but also as the new head of the German family. Within days of coming to power, he intervened in the marriage plans of his sisters, starting with Moretta. Emperor Frederick had amended his will to support Moretta's match to Alexander of Battenberg, but Wilhelm ignored this, saying his father had been coerced by his mother. Indeed, he claimed his German father had been placed under such unreasonable pressure by his English mother that on one occasion he witnessed his father's gruesome protest to his wife as he 'banged with his fists on the table' and started to suffocate resulting in such violent coughing 'he ripped open all things at his throat'.[75] Such scenes have not been verified, but undoubtedly Vicky persisted with the match, even against Queen Victoria's advice. It was almost as though she was trying to replace her son with her prospective son-in-law, hoping that Alexander of Battenberg would support her vision, take her side, and help her curb her son's excesses. These hopes now evaporated as the new emperor ordered Prince Alexander to renounce his sister. Vicky and Moretta's six-year dream came to a sudden end. Moretta was so distraught at the outcome and anxious about her much discussed marital prospects that her obsessive dieting appears to have started around this time. 'Her one craze is to be thin,' Vicky told her mother. 'She starves completely, touches no milk, no sugar, no bread ... nothing but a scrap of meat and apples.'[76]

The new emperor also took action over the marriage prospects of another of his sisters. Princess Sophie had first met Constantine, the Crown Prince of Greece, at Queen Victoria's Golden Jubilee in 1887, and the attraction was mutual. This time Wilhelm could see the benefits to Germany of extending ties to the Mediterranean with his sister as a future queen of Greece. When Prince Constantine formally asked Wilhelm for Sophie's hand in marriage, he received the Kaiser's enthusiastic support.

Although this match had once been a part of Vicky's grand vision of a liberal Germany spreading its enlightened influence across south-east Europe, now that the other parts of her plan had failed, Sophie appeared isolated. Vicky began to worry about sending her daughter so far away at a young age and the potential for conflict between Greece and its neighbours in the volatile Balkans. The Ottoman Empire, which had controlled the region for over 500 years, was weakening. Sophie risked being caught up in the 'unsolved and dangerous eastern question!' she told her mother. Queen Victoria saw no reason to oppose her grandson. The engagement was 'a ray of sunshine in this sad time'.[77] She believed 'Tino's' good family was 'a priceless blessing' and his own 'good heart and good character ... go far beyond great cleverness ...'[78]

Queen Victoria took care not to thwart her German grandson's views on matchmaking but she continued to feel deeply distressed by his behaviour and privately did not mince her words. 'It is too dreadful for us all to think of Willy & Bismarck & Dona – being the supreme head of all now! Two so unfit and one so wicked,' she confided to one granddaughter.[79] Germany had fallen to 'that dreadful tyrant Wilhelm', who 'makes rows about anything'.[80]

The bonny little boy who had once adored his grandmother had become an intimidating bully, beyond control, bloated with aggressive ambitions. Even Bismarck, who had done most to fashion the semi-autocratic powers of the mighty emperor of late nineteenth-century Germany, now privately conceded the danger. Too late he understood 'the young man seemed bent on war' and the magnificent edifice of German governance he had built was unstable. 'Woe unto my poor grandchildren,' he said.[81] The great marital alliance that ensured Queen Victoria's grandson should become the German emperor appeared to have become the exact opposite of what was intended: a liability, even a danger.

3

Ella and Sergei

'Russia I could not wish for any of you ...'
Queen Victoria to Victoria of Hesse, January 1883

The momentous events in the German court frustrated Queen Victoria's ability to implement Albert's grand vision of match-making that she had faithfully followed as she guided six of their children into alliances with German royal houses. She had trusted in the wisdom of her late husband and felt his ideals to be her 'law'. But twenty-five years after his death, as she now looked to the marriages of their grandchildren, her ability to fulfil his grand plan for the dynasty was more uncertain, her faith in foreign matches less sure.

Queen Victoria reacted with pragmatism, guided almost by instinct and convention rather than a carefully worked-out master plan. As her influence in the German court waned, her attention turned to the future of the British throne. The search to find the right consort for her British grandson, Albert Victor, known to his family as 'Eddy', was a delicate undertaking. The future British heir to the throne formed a marked contrast to the new German emperor. For all his flaws, Kaiser Wilhelm highlighted the youthful vigour and strength of the German regime. By the time he came to the throne in 1888, Dona had already given him four sons; a fifth was on the way, the virility and succession of the mighty Hohenzollerns proved beyond doubt. In press photographs the new German emperor invariably struck a defiant pose: the warrior dressed in full military regalia, eyes fixed, full-grown moustache stiff and upturned, the whole crowned with the distinctive *Pickelhaube*, or spiked helmet, a symbol of military success complete with eagle frontplate. Next to this, Wilhelm's British cousin, 'drawing-room Eddy', with his swan-like neck, delicate physique, and that look he had of not being quite awake even in the most martial pose, appeared immature and enfeebled.

Queen Victoria hoped to bring out Eddy's more regal attributes. She did not require a spouse for her British grandson who would help to shape the future of Europe like her daughter, Vicky. This spouse needed only to shape Eddy, to mould his lethargic, unformed character into something more traditionally kingly. There was not a great deal of choice because in the queen's eyes it was essential that an heir to the British throne should marry from within the elite circle of European royalty. The queen did not have to search long for a suitable bride. Amongst her thirty-four grandchildren, there was one candidate who appeared to fit the post perfectly.

Discreetly bypassing Vicky's two unmarried daughters in the warring German ruling house, Queen Victoria looked to the children of her second daughter, Princess Alice, the Grand Duchess of Hesse. The queen had strongly protective feelings towards her Hessian grandchildren that were intimately bound up with the misfortunes of their mother. Alice had followed her older sister, Vicky, to Germany in 1862, after marrying Prince Louis of Hesse, the heir to the small German Grand Duchy of Hesse and by Rhine centred around the town of Darmstadt. Alice and Louis had had a large family but their happiness had been destroyed in a few short weeks in 1878 when a diphtheria epidemic swept through central Germany. Their beloved youngest daughter, four-year-old May, succumbed to the disease, followed swiftly by thirty-five-year-old Alice. She died on exactly the same day – 14 December – as her father, Albert, seventeen years before; this coincidence chilled the queen as though it were an enigmatic portent.

Alice was survived by one son, Ernest, and four beautiful daughters. The oldest, Victoria of Hesse, named after her grandmother, was followed by Elisabeth, Irene and lastly Alexandra or Alix. At the time of Kaiser Wilhelm's accession in 1888, only the youngest daughter remained unattached: Queen Victoria's favourite, Alix, who was still free and available for Eddy. 'My heart & mind are bent on securing dear Alicky for either Eddie or Georgie,' the queen wrote on 2 March 1887 to the oldest daughter, Victoria of Hesse. 'I hope to <u>live</u> to <u>see</u> one of darling Mama's girls here.'[1] Such a view, from Queen Victoria herself, whether expressed as a wish, an expectation or a demand, undoubtedly carried weight. The queen 'was a tremendous, sometimes almost a fearful force', observed another granddaughter, Princess Marie of Edinburgh. Members of the family 'had to count with Queen Victoria, had to listen to her, and if ... not exactly to *obey*, had anyhow to argue out all differences of opinion'.[2]

As Princess Alix of Hesse turned sixteen in June 1888 she certainly looked the part of a future queen. There was widespread agreement on her uncommon beauty. She was tall and elegant and on the cusp of maturity, her even features were finely chiselled, the rich colouring of her red-gold hair and blue eyes a striking combination. Her personality, too, seemed to fit. There was nothing gushing or trivial about Alix. She had an air of self-possession that made her appear slightly older than she was; at heart she was serious-minded, even intense. While Alix herself felt held back by her shyness, to the casual observer her reserve appeared to add to her regal manner. Occasionally her nervousness overwhelmed her, such as when the queen asked her to play the piano in front of a large gathering at Windsor. Alix's flawless complexion coloured as she endured the unwelcome attention of being centre stage; she felt as though her 'clammy hands' were literally 'glued to the keys'.[3] But such youthful awkwardness did not seem out of the ordinary. Alix had many attributes in common with her grandmother; she could be self-willed, independent, and she came into her own in the close-knit family circle where she could let down her guard. From Queen Victoria's point of view, Alix possessed many admirable qualities that formed something of a contrast to Eddy's immaturity.

First among these was her sound education, which Queen Victoria had personally supervised. At the time of her mother's death, six-year-old Alix was still too young to join her older sisters in the schoolroom. She remained in the nursery under the care of the devoted Mary Orchard, or 'Orchie', who endeavoured to fill the void, but Alix sometimes found her 'silently crying'.[4] The little girl once nicknamed 'Sunny' by her mother on account of her *joie de vivre* now understood that something fundamental in her life was missing. She described that period in her life later as 'perpetual sunshine, then of a great cloud'.[5] Queen Victoria tried at a distance to be the mother that her Hessian granddaughters had lost, especially for the youngest. '<u>How</u> I love you darling children, how <u>dear</u> you are to me & how I look on you as <u>my own</u> I can hardly say,' she wrote in July 1880 to Victoria of Hesse. '<u>You</u> are so doubly dear as the children of my <u>own</u> darling Child ...'[6] Queen Victoria was not noted for being motherly when her own children were born, but as a grandmother the tragedy of the motherless family far from maternal help was hard to bear, and Alix became her special favourite.

From an early age Alix was encouraged to write regularly to her grandmother. Her letters bearing news of birthdays or pets were neatly written out on pencil-drawn lines with scrupulous attention to such details as large loops on the 'G' and 'd' of 'Grandmama'.[7] Unlike her sisters, Alix invariably signed herself 'your loving and grateful *child*', rather than grandchild, with a generous scattering of circles and crosses for hugs and kisses, underlining the closeness of the bond.[8] As she progressed to the schoolroom, accounts of her progress contained much to please her grandmother. Under her English governess, Margaret Jackson, she applied herself energetically, perhaps aware of the thorough monthly reports demanded by the queen. With her serious approach, her retentive memory and a natural fluency in both English and German, Alix made good progress. Lessons started as early as 7 a.m. and covered a wide range of academic subjects including history, mathematics and literature, as well as all the expected accomplishments including painting and the piano – for which Alix had an instinctive flair. The Hesse children were exposed to a wide range of ideas; their intellectual mother had studied such controversial works as the French Enlightenment philosopher, Voltaire, the German theologian, David Strauss, and the English art critic, John Ruskin, whose essay *Unto This Last* challenged the inequalities of capitalism.[9] Alix's oldest sister, Victoria, remembered once lecturing bemused relatives on 'the advantages of socialism'.[10] As a child Alix was taught to think of others and proudly told her grandmother at Christmas 1879 that she was 'learning to knit mittens for poor people'.[11] In the schoolroom she wrestled with such texts as François Guizot's *History of the Republic of England and of Cromwell* and John Milton's *Paradise Lost*.

Queen Victoria enlisted the help of her oldest Hessian granddaughter, Victoria, to help her supervise the others at a distance. There was no danger of spoiling the children. Victoria of Hesse by her own admission ruled 'with a rod of iron' and could be relied upon to give the queen a full account of progress.[12] After her own studies in French and German, she would help Alix with her lessons and drawing. She encouraged her younger siblings to turn to their grandmother for advice. Her tactful letters repeatedly expressed her gratitude to the queen 'for all your love and kindness' and her desire 'to please you in all I do & by teaching the others the same & by looking up to you as I would to dear Mama were she still with us'.[13] Victoria of Hesse did her best to ensure her grandmother's wishes over matters of discipline were also met. 'I am very sorry to hear that the others were lazy at Balmoral,' she wrote after one visit. Her sisters 'are very sorry to have vexed you about their lessons and wish me to tell you ... that they will work hard now'.[14]

Alix grew up with a love of all things British. Portraits of British forebears, of kings and queens and Grandpapa Albert hung on the walls of the Neues Palais in Darmstadt. Aunts and uncles frequently visited from Britain, and presents from the queen arrived with unfailing regularity to mark each passing birthday and Christmas: dresses, jewellery, lace, pretty items for her dressing table, a dolls' tea service. Alix in turn drew pictures, knitted comforters and painted frames for the queen. She looked forward to her visits to see the 'best and dearest of grandmamas' who appeared to her both 'a very august person and ... a Santa Claus'.[15]

Leisurely holidays with her beloved grandmother enjoying the pleasures of life at Osborne House, Windsor and Balmoral were a key part of her childhood; they were perfect little kingdoms, apparently untouched by calamity, seemingly in a time of their own. The Hesse children played with their Wales cousins who were close to them in age. 'We formed a regular scale,' recalled Victoria of Hesse. She was the oldest, followed by her cousin, Eddy, her sister, Ella, and cousin George. The 'nursery party' consisted of the two younger Hesse girls, Irene and Alix, and the younger Wales girls, Louise, Victoria and Maud.[16] Adventures exploring the Highlands invariably ended with a visit to 'the merchants', the children's name for a little shop near Balmoral filled with essentials such as sweets and notepaper. The two elderly women who ran the shop took a particular delight in the motherless Hesse children, and the bounty that emerged from such visits in the form of mouth-watering scones or sweets appeared to Alix years later to capture the essence of her holidays with 'Grand-mama Queen'. It was an enchanted world ruled by benign influences presenting a picture of long-held peace.[17]

In the summer of 1888 Queen Victoria invited her favourite granddaughter to join her at Osborne and then Balmoral in Scotland. Opportunities were planned for Alix to see a great deal of her British cousin, Prince Eddy. The queen was hopeful about the possibilities for her favourite granddaughter. Might she fall in love – or at least, form an attachment – to her British cousin? 'A good long stay with us here wh wld be delightful wld do her the gst good …' she insisted in June 1888 to Alix's oldest sister Victoria.[18] The magic of Balmoral in summertime was the perfect background for Eddy and Alix to spend some time together. Alix could not fail to see the desirability of the British throne and the young prince who would inherit it one day.

But in seeking Alix for Eddy, Queen Victoria unexpectedly found herself opposed by another of Alix's older sisters, Elisabeth or 'Ella'. Alix's future was intimately bound up with the choices already made by Ella, who had the temerity to act expressly against the advice of 'Grandmama Queen' when it came to matters of the heart. The conflict between Ella and her grandmother had run for almost a decade and was charged with their differences over that great empire rivalling Britain's power in the east: Russia. The outcome of this clash would have a decisive impact on Europe's history – and on Eddy's choice of bride.

———

Ten years earlier when Queen Victoria's second daughter, Alice, died, the older Hessian granddaughters were unmarried and on the point of coming out into society. In 1878 Victoria of Hesse was fifteen, Ella was fourteen and Irene was twelve: all 'fast growing out of a Child' in the queen's words. This was a critical time in the life of a Victorian princess, and the queen had been most anxious to guide her older granddaughters in Germany. 'Dear Papa will, I know, be teazed & pressed to make you marry,' she warned. But they should not marry too young, and above all, not seek '<u>to be married</u> for <u>marrying's sake</u> & to have a <u>position</u>'. The oldest, Victoria, she knew, had far too much sense to fall into such a trap but, she warned, this was a 'very <u>German</u> view of things' and she wanted her granddaughters to be '<u>prepared</u> & on your <u>guard</u> when such things are brought before Papa'.[19]

The queen's struggles to influence her Hessian granddaughters at a distance were compounded by the fact that the second Hessian daughter, Elisabeth, or 'Ella', was widely regarded as the most eligible princess in Europe. She combined perfect beauty with a composed and guileless manner and was seldom in opposition to anyone. In the 1870s Ella had inspired Germany's highest-ranking prince, her cousin, Wilhelm. He regarded his Hessian cousin as 'the most beautiful girl I ever saw'. In the years before Wilhelm began his sudden pursuit of Dona in 1878 he had been besotted with Ella and reached the point where he told his mother 'I shall make her my bride'.[20] He was not alone in his admiration for Ella. 'One could never take one's eyes off her,' wrote her infatuated younger cousin, Marie of Edinburgh. She regarded Ella's beauty as almost mystical, 'a marvellous revelation', her features all 'exquisite beyond words, it almost brought tears to your eyes'.[21] Even the queen was prompted to observe in

her correspondence with her daughter Vicky that 'Ella is lovely –
beyond all expression and so sweet and gentle'.[22]

While a student at Bonn University, Prince Wilhelm had found
his feelings for his cousin Ella overpowering. Personal attributes
that he had taken for granted, his willpower and ability to concen-
trate, became dissipated under the affliction of this uncontrollable
new emotion. He was lost, obsessed, and *'liebte sie wirklich'* –
he 'really loved her' – observed Ella's sensitive younger brother,
Ernest.[23] Wilhelm himself appears to have made a less favourable
impression on his pretty Hesse cousins. He could disrupt the
games they were playing on a whim and dominate them to the
point of bullying. Whatever Ella's feelings about him, she was
invariably discreet in her letters to her grandmother. 'We enjoyed
his stay very much,' she told the queen after one visit. She had
been riding with him, 'which was so nice', and he 'read to us all a
very nice book'.[24] By the spring of 1878, Wilhelm's grandparents,
the Kaiser and Kaiserin, his parents and Queen Victoria all understood that the future German heir 'wished to marry Ella'.[25]

It has long been thought that Ella disliked Wilhelm's attentions, possibly she was even repelled by her cousin, and turned
him down. Almost certainly to save his pride, years later Wilhelm
blamed his parents, claiming that he never actually proposed to
her since his parents refused permission. Surviving letters reveal
that Wilhelm's switch to pursue Dona instead was so swift that it
prompted concerns from his father, Frederick, who felt uncomfortable with his son's 'sudden changing of the saddle', especially
given that 'he had already declared himself' to Ella.[26] An alternative reason for the dramatic change in Wilhelm's feelings has
been put forward by his biographer, John Röhl. It is known that
the prince's mother, Vicky, was opposed to the match, and Röhl
speculates that her anxieties went well beyond a general dislike of
first-cousin marriages.

Vicky knew that her youngest brother, Leopold, suffered from
haemophilia, a life-threatening disease in which the slightest
injury can cause severe bleeding owing to the body's inability to
form blood clots. She had also witnessed at first hand the suffering of her sister Alice's youngest son, Friedrich, who was also a

haemophiliac and had died at the age of two in 1873 in a tragic accident. It is possible that Vicky consulted medical experts to understand how both her brother and her nephew suffered from the same inherited disease although they had different parents. At the time the specific mechanism of inheritance through the gene was not yet understood, but enough had been observed about the transmission of haemophilia through the female line for Vicky to piece together the possibility that her enchanting Hesse nieces might be carriers of the disease, like their mother Alice. If Vicky explained this to Wilhelm, this could account for his dramatic change of heart. The prospect that his own Hohenzollern heirs might be sickly or die would be enough to stop his courtship of Ella in its tracks. However, there is no proof that Vicky consulted medical experts or if she did, whether they were in a position to give this advice. It is also intriguing that if she did have suspicions she failed to pass them on to her mother, who remained unaware of the risk. When Wilhelm married Dona in 1881, the queen was still thinking of Ella and did not consider the possibility that her beautiful Hessian granddaughters might be carriers of the disease. 'I could not think with regret of what <u>might</u> have been,' she wrote to Vicky. Unlike the submissive Dona, she believed her granddaughter Ella had more spirit and might have held some influence for the good over Wilhelm. 'But I will say no more about that painful past. That is over.'[27]

After Wilhelm's courtship, beautiful Ella continued to turn the heads of Europe's princes. Queen Victoria found it 'very unfortunate' that her Hessian granddaughter turned down 'good Fritz of Baden', an 'excellent' prince 'so good & steady, with such a safe, happy position'.[28] Two Danish dukes also failed to win Ella's hand. Yet all was not lost; the queen began plotting in favour of Prince Charles of Sweden. But before long, Queen Victoria heard that Ella was to be paid the compliment of a visit from one of her dashing Russian cousins: twenty-five-year-old Sergei, the younger brother of the tsar, Alexander III. The fact that Sergei was a Russian grand duke, with all the associated glamour and power, was the most damning thing Queen Victoria had against him. He was very tall – a Romanov trait – and his photograph revealed his even, chiselled features, and his arresting eyes gazing at the camera giving nothing away. It was said that he had a sensitive nature like Ella and took a keen interest in Russian and Italian art.

Queen Victoria may have been shrouded in black and many years a widow but she did know what it felt like to receive the attentions of a Russian grand duke. Sergei was the fifth son of Tsar Alexander II, the very Romanov who forty years earlier had come to England and led the queen onto the dance floor for a mazurka. After those memorable few days at Windsor in the spring of 1839 the Russian tsarevich had left Windsor for Darmstadt and chosen a Hessian princess, Marie, as his bride (who years later became Sergei's mother and Ella's great-aunt). Even at a distance of 1,000 miles Queen Victoria sensed trouble. Would Ella align herself with the very country that the queen most feared, Russia?

Of all the warnings Queen Victoria had issued since the death of their mother Alice, she had taken particular care to alert her Hessian granddaughters to the dangers of Russia, and her fear about a Russian marriage for any one of them almost amounted to an obsession. Long before the assassination of Sergei's father, Alexander II, she pointed out that their 'dear mama ... had such a horror of Russia & Russians'. She urged them not to 'get at all Russian' from the inevitable social engagements that arose through their Russian relatives.[29] Victoria of Hesse had replied by return that there was no chance of that. Even if her Russian cousins 'were a hundred times more kind they would not make us a bit Russian, they have such odd manners and say such odd things to each other and even once about the English that it made one quite angry'. Apart from 'considering themselves perfect', Victoria of Hesse found her Russian cousins to be 'lazy', with no clue 'how to amuse themselves' and totally ignorant of 'what to say'.[30]

Queen Victoria would not let the matter rest. Her objections to the Russians were zealously woven into her correspondence with Victoria of Hesse, to be passed around the family in the hopes of instilling into the innocent unmarried princesses the dangers of marrying into Russian royalty. For the queen had long viewed Russia as 'our real enemy & totally antagonistic to England'.[31]

Ever since the Romanovs came to power in the seventeenth century, Russia had expanded at an average rate of 20,000 square miles a year, becoming the world's largest country two centuries later. To the east, Russian borders reached across the Bering Straits to Alaska. In Europe, the imperial bear had swallowed up Poland and Finland, and to the south-east it menaced the Ottoman Empire, while along its southern border, Russia's expansion in Asia threatened the Persian Empire and Britain's 'Jewel in the Crown': India.

This expansionism brought imperial Russia and the British Empire repeatedly into conflict and fuelled the queen's concerns about Russian aggression. One key battleground arose from the weakness of the Ottoman Empire, 'the Sick Man of Europe', which for six centuries had ruled lands around the eastern Mediterranean, at its greatest extent dominating the peoples of south-east Europe and the Balkans, north Africa and west Asia, who now questioned Turkish rule. This gave rise to 'the eastern question', which flared up in different forms across the nineteenth century. A cartoon in *Harper's Weekly* captured British fears, showing a large Russian bear sporting an imperial crown, licking its lips in contemplation of a sickly and sleepy-looking Turkey, with an Islamic crescent moon on its head. 'Which is the gobbler?' read the caption.[32]

In the first half of the nineteenth century Tsar Nicholas I had built up the largest army in the world numbering one million men, and when he crossed the Danube in 1853 into Romania, which was under Ottoman rule, he stumbled into the Crimean War. 'The power and encroachment of Russia must be resisted,' the queen urged her cautious prime minister, Lord Aberdeen, in March 1854.[33] Two days later Britain joined the Turks, the French and the Sardinians against the Russians. For the first time the bloodthirsty horrors of the battles of the Crimean War such as at Alma and Balaklava were reported by the mass media and they shaped perceptions at home of a heroic British lion standing up to a tyrannical Russian bear. The queen was 'in the greatest anxiety' as Britain and her allies advanced on Sevastopol, a Russian stronghold and naval base on the Black Sea.[34] But the long siege in fact exposed Russian weaknesses. The health of Tsar Nicholas I went into decline and he died of pneumonia in March 1855.

When Alexander II became tsar, he aimed to recover his father's losses and in 1871 regained access for his fleet in the Crimea. A few years later the troubled 'eastern question' resurfaced yet again when Slavic Christian minorities in Serbia and Bulgaria, which were part of the Ottoman Empire, rose up against their Turkish masters. Alexander II backed the Slavs against the Turks whereas British allegiance lay with the Turks, who supported their interests in the Mediterranean. Queen Victoria believed Britain must 'remove from Russia the pretext for constantly threatening the peace of Europe on the Eastern or Oriental question' by creating an independent buffer state out of the rebellious Turkish-ruled principalities of eastern Europe.[35]

War broke out in April 1877 when Russia joined the Serbs in the fight against the Ottoman Empire. In less than a year Alexander II's troops were advancing on Constantinople, which many in Britain, including the queen (but not her prime minister, Disraeli), saw as grounds for war. Whoever controlled this ancient city, sited so strategically between east and west, controlled Britain's short cut to India through the eastern Mediterranean. The queen's obsessive hatred of the Russians was well known to the tsar through her second son, Alfred, who shared her letters with his wife, Marie, the tsar's daughter. Incensed, Alexander, the man who had once led her round the dance floor, now saw her as that 'old madwoman the Queen, that tramp!' The tsarina joined in his condemnation, seeing Queen Victoria's remarks as 'worthy of a fish-wife'.[36] Britain sent battleships to the region. Europe was catapulted to the brink of war. The crisis was resolved in 1878 at the Congress of Berlin where, despite Russia's victory over the Turks, its control in the Balkans was checked by other European powers. Amongst the agreements reached, Romania, Serbia and

Montenegro were recognised as newly independent countries in the Balkans, liberated from years of Turkish rule. The Principality of Bulgaria was also established with the tsar's nephew, Alexander of Battenberg, on its throne.

A second key area of conflict between imperial Russia and the British Empire was in central Asia. The struggle for control from Constantinople eastwards, across the deserts and mountain ranges to Afghanistan and the mountain passes of the Himalayas, became known as the 'Great Game', and it captured the imagination of the Victorian public with tales of spectacular derring-do in unmapped and hostile lands. But Russia's continued expansion overland brought them gradually to within twenty miles of British India. The queen who rarely left the confines of Windsor, Osborne and Balmoral was in thrall to her 'Jewel in the Crown'. She pressured her prime minister, Disraeli, to pass the Royal Titles Act, making her 'Empress of India' in 1876, dismissing opposition to her claim in her usual grand manner. 'I am all for it, as it is so important for India,' she wrote in her journal on 17 March 1876.[37] She feared Russian encroachment. 'How can we ever trust the Russians?' was her continual lament.[38]

It was not just Russia's expansionism that worried the queen, but its autocracy. The tsar's absolute power was deemed ordained by God and as integral to the order of things as the stars in the heavens. The tsar chose ministerial appointments and wielded power over all aspects of policy including war. Although Alexander II had been in the process of introducing reform and he emancipated the serfs in 1861, a vast peasant underclass continued to subsist in harsh conditions on the land, their ranks swollen by another type of worker in the factories and mills of Russia's newly industrialising cities, whose plight was equally desperate. A great gulf remained between the working masses and the elite. The glaring injustices of Russian society brought in their wake the terrifying spectre of terrorism.

New ideas opposing autocracy were in ferment; students, radicals, Marxists, anarchists and nihilists loathed the absolute power of the tsar and the extremes of social injustice thriving in his kingdom. One Russian anarchist, Mikhail Bakunin, met Karl Marx and Friedrich Engels in London, and believed their communist ideal of a 'state of the proletariat' did not go far enough. For Bakunin, any state – whether capitalist or communist – should be abolished altogether in favour of 'collective anarchism', which aimed for equality by diffusing power through local independent assemblies or 'communes'.[39] Bakunin's vision called for a revolution so total – starting in Russia and spreading across Europe – that all of civilisation must go up in flames before a new society, phoenix-like, could spring from its ashes. Russia's university towns of St Petersburg, Moscow and Kiev became home to a secret, subterranean network of radical anarchist groups fired with such far-reaching ideals.

The Congress of Berlin, in which a hard-won victory appeared to have been snatched from Alexander II, proved to be a flashpoint for discontent. A wave of attacks came in quick succession in the late 1870s. The governor of St Petersburg, General Feodor Trepov, and the district prosecutor in Kiev, M. Kotlyarevsky, were shot at point-blank range; both survived. Not so lucky was the police spy, A. Nikonov, and the governor general of Kharkov, Prince Kropotkin, and the Chief of the Third Department in charge of political security, General N. V. Mezentsov. The tsar, who had already suffered two attacks on his life in 1866 and 1867, was targeted again in April 1879, directly in front of the Winter Palace in St Petersburg. Humiliated in front of a large crowd in Palace Square, the tsar was forced to duck and dive to dodge the five bullets that rang out in broad daylight.

Alexander II proclaimed a war on terror. The most reforming tsar in generations now extended police powers. In his efforts to restore order he, in turn, was increasingly held responsible for 'tsarist terror' as radicals were hunted down and punished, invariably paying with their lives. In this febrile atmosphere in June 1879, the secret court of the terrorist group People's Will met at Lipetsk and condemned the tsar to death. Alexander II was an 'enemy of the people' and revolutionaries aimed to destroy his rule with terror: 'propaganda of the deed'. The astonishing scale of their attacks highlights the level of pre-planning and organisation that miraculously took place right in front of the police.

When the People's Will set out to blow up the imperial train in November 1879, they prepared attacks on three possible sites through which the tsar might pass from the Crimea. For the fifth attempt on the tsar's life a terrorist posing as a carpenter secretly smuggled enough dynamite into the Winter Palace to fill an entire trunk. On 13 March 1881 the sixth attempt on his life finally succeeded, ironically just at a time when the tsar had committed to introducing constitutional reform.

The golden lives of the Romanovs were now ruled by fear, their beautiful palaces invaded by unknown terrors. Yet this was the very family into which Queen Victoria feared her pretty grand-daughter, Ella, might be tempted to marry. The queen knew that the older Hessian princesses were fully aware of the horror of Alexander II's death. The truth of her warnings must have been clear to them. When their father, Louis of Hesse, had set out for St Petersburg to comfort his Russian relatives, the princesses had turned to their grandmother. The tsar's death was 'too dread-ful – how I pity poor Aunt Marie & the present tsar who can never feel sure of his life', sixteen-year-old Ella had written to her grandmother. 'I will be so glad when he [papa] is back from this dreadful Petersburg.'[40]

Their father had returned with news of the changed lives of the Russian royal family. St Petersburg was a city in fear. Rumours ran wild of further attacks and bombs or torpedoes embed-ded in the ice. The new emperor, Alexander III, and his Danish wife, Dagmar, now the Empress Maria Feodorovna (the sister of Princess Alexandra), were almost imprisoned by the exten-sive security of their Anichkov Palace, which was being further fortified against mines with a trench. Queen Victoria had learned further details from her British ambassador. 'The poor emperor is scarcely allowed out and his only exercise is to walk round a not very large walled garden,' Lord Dufferin reported to her in March 1881. He found it hard to see 'any end to these fearful uncer-tainties'.[41] Dufferin was convinced that a reactionary policy 'was impossible … some kind of constitution must be introduced', a view that was widely shared.[42] Sir Henry Eliot, the British ambas-sador to Vienna, told the queen that the Russian Empire was 'diseased to the core, financially and politically'. The only thing that could save Russia from revolution was 'the granting of some sort of constitution'.[43]

Alexander III disagreed. He was not listening to the foreign ambassadors. Nor to the nihilists who warned him to 'beware the fate that has befallen his late father' and granted him a mere three months to introduce a new constitution.[44] The first conspirators arrested cockily 'boasted that though the heads of the conspiracy were taken, the tail would accomplish the object in view'.[45] Their chance was swiftly denied them. The new tsar was no intellectual; he saw things clearly and simply and was forceful in getting things done. He deplored the reforms introduced by his father. This had only served to raise expectations that could not be met. Instinctively, he felt it was time to put the genie back in the bottle, dismiss imported foreign notions of a constitution, and re-establish the Russian way of doing things. Autocracy had made Russia great for 300 years. It was time to reassert tsarist control with a vengeance.

Those responsible for his father's murder were hunted down and hanged. Liberals were dismissed or took their leave from the new tsar's government. Anti-Semitism was rife; the Jews were wrongly blamed for Alexander II's death, prompting a wave of pogroms. Far from curbing the violence, Alexander III tacitly supported it, introducing tough restrictions on the Jewish community. He also created a new instrument of state security, the notorious Security Bureau, 'the Okhrana', a secret police force whose covert operations and double dealings were of such labyrinthine complexity and secrecy that many came to fear its reach. Undercover agents and agents provocateurs sought to infiltrate terrorist and revolutionary groups, and offices were dedicated to perlustration – intercepting the mail of suspects.

Although the tough stance adopted by Alexander III created a semblance of order, Queen Victoria recognised this had required punitive repressive measures. She continued to warn the Hesse princesses of the 'dreadful state Russia is in'. This was no place for her granddaughter. In her cautionary missives the queen highlighted the 'very depressed bad state of Society' and the fears that swirled around the Russian throne and the Romanovs' stupendous wealth, which she saw as provocative, incendiary, and bound to lead to trouble.[46] From grand dukes down, she believed the society was corrupt. 'Russia, I cd not wish for any of you & dear Mama always said she wd never hear of it,' she declared to Victoria of Hesse in January 1883.[47] By now Ella had turned down several suitors and the queen remained concerned that her granddaughter might fall for one of her Russian cousins, Sergei or Paul, sons of the murdered tsar. Victoria of Hesse tried to abate the queen's fears. 'I do not think she cares for one of the Russian cousins,' she replied disingenuously.[48]

But during the spring of 1883 Ella succumbed to the attentions of the imposing Russian grand duke and accepted Sergei's proposal of marriage. Queen Victoria was shocked. Ella was revealing a will of steel behind her apparently compliant manner. It was hard for the queen to settle her mind to the match. She decided on a plan and invited her headstrong granddaughter to come and stay. In the relaxing privacy of the Scottish Highlands, far from worldly pressures, the queen intended to use all her powers of persuasion to turn the young, inexperienced Ella away from this dangerous path.

Elisabeth of Hesse arrived at Windsor Castle on 22 May 1883 and the queen found the very sight of her granddaughter brought back 'endless dear recollections'.[49] It was not long before they were speeding by train towards Balmoral, the queen lifted into her carriage on account of a swollen foot.

This was an unsettling time for Queen Victoria. It was her first return to Balmoral since the death of her special favourite, John Brown, earlier in the year. Ironically, while the queen was seeking considerable control over her granddaughters' choice of suitors, she herself had refused to listen to anyone's objections over the unconventional relationship that had developed between her and John Brown since Prince Albert's death. Queen Victoria's biographer, Lytton Strachey, has described this relationship as an extension of her own control. A relationship with her servant, no matter how dominating, never cost her independence. When she succumbed to Mr Brown's instructions to wear her wrap or step down from the carriage, 'was she not displaying, and in the highest degree, the force of her volition?'[50] Now he, too, had died. His arm was no longer there to support her, the visceral relief of his physical presence close at hand was gone. She had lost 'the dearest, most devoted and invaluable friend I ever had', she admitted to Victoria of Hesse. She felt quite 'deranged' by his loss, 'we were so devoted to each other'.[51] Although tired from her journey on that very first evening, the queen insisted on visiting John Brown's grave. Sensitive Ella obliged her grandmother. She understood that his presence had brought her closer to Albert, as though the proximity of his gillie inexplicably reconnected her to the dead, and now it was as if two ghosts walked with them around Balmoral, the queen leaning on two sticks to ease her lameness.

Ella had a secret that challenged her grandmother's control and that she rather dreaded to disclose: news of yet another marriage. Her oldest sister, Victoria of Hesse, was planning to accept Prince Louis of Battenberg, a brother of Alexander, Prince of Bulgaria. The queen was indeed offended. She felt herself to be a mother to her Hessian granddaughters, but she was not being consulted like a mother. 'Darling Victoria, I cannot be silent,' the queen began in protest on 19 June 1883. But her protest was muted. It was hard to object to the charismatic Louis. The queen did not share the arrogance of the Hohenzollerns, who dismissed all the handsome Battenberg princes for not being of royal blood 'a little like animals'.[52] Quite the reverse, the queen decided that her oldest Hessian granddaughter had 'done well to choose a Husband who is quite of your way of thinking & who in many respects is as English as you are'. The only drawback was the want of 'the fortune', she wrote, but 'I don't think that riches make happiness, or that they are necessary'.[53] While she came round rapidly to Victoria of Hesse's choice in marriage, when it came to Ella's grand duke, the queen's emotions were powerfully engaged.

Alone with her all-powerful grandmother, dressed in forbidding black, projecting, as always, an air of unfathomable wisdom, Ella's confidence in her choice did indeed begin to waver. Her grandmother's diminutive height and evident discomfort on account of her foot was no indication of her strength. Her throne was safe; her empire the envy of the world; her advice almost universally respected. Perhaps the state of Russia was too uncertain? Perhaps Grand Duke Sergei was not what he seemed? Days turned into weeks at Balmoral, Ella slowly absorbing her grandmother's views as they took drives out in the open carriage and turns around the estate, the queen in her pony chair. Inevitably, some of the foreign news that breached the sanctuary of Balmoral created openings to discuss Ella's future, such as accounts of the coronation of the new Russian tsar, Alexander III, a forceful reminder of the murder of his father. The queen lost no opportunity to reiterate her concerns and Ella was left in no doubt of her grandmother's astute perceptions.

Windsor was 'in all its summer glory', observed the queen when she and Ella returned there in June.[54] The queen's favoured spot was beside Albert's tomb in the royal mausoleum at Frogmore. She loved to take breakfast under the trees in the grounds with Ella and Beatrice, and long hours could be spent there talking and writing. When the inevitable showers fell, Queen Victoria was carried into the mausoleum, followed by her two companions, where the conversations continued under the nearby influence of the revered Prince Albert. In the third week of July, Ella travelled with the queen to Osborne and it was mid-August before she prepared to return to Germany. 'Dear Ella, who had been 3 months with me, seemed quite distressed to leave,' the queen noted on 16 August.[55] Within a week of her departure, the visit had the desired effect. Ella broke off her engagement.

Queen Victoria was jubilant. It was not the kind of triumph that she could broadcast too loudly, but nonetheless she wrote at once to Victoria of Hesse. She and Auntie Beatrice, 'for no one else shall know abt it, are delighted ... at Ella's refusal of Serge ... Anything is better than making an unhappy marriage.'[56] Two days later it was still on her mind. 'I rejoice that she has acted as she has done abt Serge,' she wrote. Realising that she was blamed by her Russian daughter-in-law, the Duchess of Edinburgh, who was Sergei's sister, for this 'insult', the queen was at pains to deny her role in the matter. 'I did not set her [Ella] agst Serge,' the queen protested. 'But I did tell her to reflect well before she accepted him & to remember the climate and the state of the Country & that (contrary to what she wished ...) her living out of Russia cld only be the exception to the rule – I shall never deny having said this ...'[57]

But a tsar's son was not about to be thwarted by a British queen. Within days, Grand Duke Sergei arranged to call on Ella in Germany. Queen Victoria heard of his visit and sent a flurry of letters. 'I am rather distressed that Serge is ... coming,' she told Victoria of Hesse on 4 September 1883. 'I can't tell you how I dread that marriage for her. Believe me it wld be misery for her as the climate, Society etc are pernicious there – And darling Mama ... never wld hear of one of her girls going there'.[58] Still anxious a few days later, she issued a much stronger warning. If Ella married Sergei, 'in fact it will be her ruin'.[59] Dreading the outcome of his visit, she could not resist writing for the third time in a week to Victoria of Hesse. Ella, she feared, would 'be taken in – for Heaven and Earth will [be] moved to get hold of her ... Believe me when I speak so strongly against it'.[60]

In the presence of her handsome grand duke, eighteen-year-old Ella felt confused. Sergei conveyed the authority of a man seven years older, his forceful presence not lightly dismissed, his grey-green eyes conveying his sensitivity and reserve. Had she treated him badly? She trusted him as a cousin; he shared her passion for music and literature; his character, Ella decided, was 'true and noble'.[61] Such a delightful partner seemed to offer immense security. She accepted him once again, despite the conflict she felt with her grandmother. Grandmama queen was old and a widow of many years: what did she know of romance? Entombed in her isolation, seeking out her constant reminders of grief: how could such a woman understand the irrepressible feelings of youth?

It was left to Victoria of Hesse to be the bearer of this unwelcome news. The response from across the English Channel was swift and strongly worded. A series of cautions were sent to Victoria of Hesse for 'our sweet but <u>undecided & inexperienced</u> Ella'. The queen warned once again of 'the <u>very bad state</u> of Society & its <u>total want of principle</u> ...' She judged the Russians to be '<u>so</u> unscrupulous' and '<u>totally</u> antagonistic to England'.[62] A month later she was still worrying that Ella 'will be <u>quite lost to me</u> ...' Ella must set conditions: to live out of Russia as much as possible and not to marry before the age of twenty. The queen was much vexed that Ella was being 'changeable and <u>unaccountable</u>'.[63]

Ella summoned up the courage to write on 13 October 1883. She was now convinced her happiness lay with Grand Duke Sergei. Despite the weeks of coaching at Balmoral, Ella wanted to go her own way. The queen could not bring herself to respond immediately. She had received Ella's letter, she told Victoria of Hesse, 'but I <u>really</u> do <u>not</u> feel <u>quite</u> able to answer her <u>yet</u> – as I <u>do</u> feel this prospect <u>so very deeply</u>'. Ella should have taken good 'Fritz of B [Baden] ... she wld not easily find so good a person'.[64] Possibly to shield her sister from their grandmother's forceful impact, Victoria of Hesse wrote to the queen that Christmas to reassure her that on the terms of the marriage 'nothing is settled decidedly'.[65]

The Russian groom was in no doubt about how to dazzle his German princess with a flamboyant extravagance that brought a whole new meaning to the word 'excess'. When Grand Duke Sergei returned to Germany in February 1884 for the public announcement of his engagement to Ella, he brought such a stunning collection of Fabergé jewels that they would have filled a shop window. There were rare and glittering gems to adorn his bride, some once worn by famous Romanov predecessors. In a romantic scene he asked her to try them all, and once her delicate throat and wrists were sparkling with gems he painstakingly decorated her dress, pinning each treasure in place until the very weight was almost a burden. As if this magnificent gift was not enough, millions of pounds were settled on Ella in the form of personal funds from the tsar himself, with an estimated value of some £700 million today. Ella was now richer than Queen Victoria herself. Her younger sister Irene reported to their grandmother, perhaps a little enviously, that Sergei had given Ella 'most beautiful jewels', exquisite Indian shawls, as well as the very bracelet that their great-aunt, the Empress Marie, had received from the late Tsar Alexander II on their engagement.[66] For young women brought up without extravagance, the Russian grand duke had opened a door through which a seductive world without boundaries was glimpsed, where life appeared to be lived in a more glorious way.

Queen Victoria understood the high price of all this. Almost as though she had a premonition, she could not stop herself lamenting Ella's choice. Her granddaughter was a gentle, trusting young woman with no experience of the dangerous world out there, walking unknowingly towards a cliff edge. In New Year 1884 the queen turned to Victoria of Hesse's future husband, Louis of Battenberg, the horrific assassination of Sergei's father still not far from her thoughts. The terrible state of Russia was 'shown by this most horrible last nihilistic murder', she told Louis. She had learned that Sergei's palace was very near the Anichkov Palace in St Petersburg, so 'it makes one shudder to think of her [Ella] going there'.[67] At the same time Queen Victoria endeavoured to accommodate her granddaughter's wishes. There were formalities to go through, photographs were exchanged, and plans made for her to meet Sergei. Ella tactfully agreed to sit for a portrait for her grandmother. 'It will be a pleasure to sit for you,' she wrote politely.[68]

But such efforts to appease her grandmother received a serious setback in late April 1884, when Queen Victoria arrived at Darmstadt for the wedding of Victoria of Hesse to Prince Louis. The older members of the Hesse family had an explosive secret that they could not bring themselves to reveal immediately. Ella and Irene met their grandmother at Darmstadt Station, and waiting at the door of the Neues Palais were Alix and her good-looking brother, Ernest, who had grown 'immensely tall'. All the handsome Battenberg brothers had gathered; the groom, Louis, was accompanied by Alexander of Bulgaria – who at the time was under consideration as a husband for Moretta – and their younger brother, Henry. Queen Victoria was also introduced to

Grand Duke Sergei, who she found 'very tall and gentleman-like' but 'pale and delicate looking'.[69] Everything was going well until a few days before the wedding, when it fell to the unfortunate bride to reveal the bombshell. There was to be a second Hessian wedding on the same day as her own: her father, Louis of Hesse, wanted to marry his mistress, Alexandrine de Kolemine. This woman had the drawback of being both divorced *and* Russian. Queen Victoria was stunned.

The queen's strategy when she was seriously put out was to avoid entering into any direct discussion with the offending party, but to set out her views in writing. Although they were all under the same palace roof, grandmama queen was not to be seen. Instead a strongly worded invective emerged from her rooms. This strategy had the merit that she could not be contradicted. She asserted her authority, while avoiding any risk of a challenge to it. The deeply offensive marriage 'would lower him [Louis of Hesse] so much that I cld. not have him near so much as before,' she warned Victoria of Hesse. 'To choose a Lady of another religion who has just been divorced ... wld I fear be a terrible mistake ...' It would 'shock' the wider family and 'do him immense harm in his own Country'.[70]

Her son-in-law would not listen. Ignoring the queen and somewhat insensitively overshadowing his oldest daughter's wedding, Louis of Hesse went ahead with his own marriage secretly on the same day. Shocked guests called their carriages and departed, first among them the mighty Hohenzollerns who saw it as a terrible disgrace. The queen was angry; she felt her own presence in Darmstadt had been exploited to provide respectability to the arrangement. It was time to reassert her authority. She ordered Bertie to instruct Louis that his second marriage would be annulled. The queen herself wrote to the British ambassador to ensure the German authorities speeded up the elimination of this highly unsuitable Russian woman from the family tree. During the high drama, the queen failed to notice that her youngest daughter, Beatrice, or 'Baby', her most faithful companion, had fallen in love with the third fine-looking Battenberg brother, Prince Henry. This additional shock was kept from the queen for a few weeks.

Ella paid one final visit to her grandmother some weeks before her own wedding in June 1884. The small family party at Windsor was under strain. Almost frightening, almost absurd, her beloved grandmother would not speak to Beatrice, but pushed notes across the table to communicate, such was her acute distress at the idea of her youngest daughter's proposed marriage. Ella's imminent departure to the other side of the continent heightened her sense of loss.

'I cannot say how sad we were leaving you,' Ella wrote politely to the queen. Her grandmother's farewell gift of a bracelet was a treasured memento 'which has made me love you more than ever'.[71] She left Windsor in its summer glory, the powerful image of her grandmother swathed in black, pushing notes across the table, a symbol of the controlling, restrictive, eccentric world she was leaving behind. Independent Ella was determined to go her own way. Exciting new horizons beckoned in Russia. 'I think I know what I am doing,' she told her grandmother, '& if I am unhappy, which I am sure will never be, it will be all my doing.'[72]

Twelve-year-old Princess Alix of Hesse felt excited and curious when she accompanied her family into the heart of the mysterious Russia for Ella's wedding. Their reception in Russia in June 1884 was like something from the pages of a fairy story. The interior of the train conveying them ever further north-east towards St Petersburg on the Baltic coast was decked in white flowers, scenting the train like a hothouse. When the Hesse family arrived at Peterhof Station there was the Russian tsar himself, Alexander III, a great bear of a man, with his diminutive wife, the Empress Marie Feodorovna. Queen Victoria had warned her Hessian granddaughters that she 'does not look upon [the Tsar] as a gentleman'.[73] But the alleged ungentlemanly qualities of the Tsar of all the Russias were not on display. Alexander III welcomed the bride and her family with considerable warmth and appeared the quintessential family man.

Outside the station a show of Romanov wealth awaited them: golden carriages drawn by horses perfectly matched with white plumes and golden reins, the liveried postilions glittering and showy as princes in the summer sunshine. The scene cast its inevitable spell and Alix, who was fascinated by the journey, was 'in a very cheerful mood' as they travelled to the Peterhof Palace by the sea on the Gulf of Finland.[74] The Peterhof was no modest, German ducal palace; everything proclaimed the imperial might of the family into which Ella was marrying. The palace had been modelled on Versailles by Peter the Great in the early eighteenth century and completed with Romanov excess. High water fountains formed a dramatic cascade between the upper and the lower gardens. Inside, the exquisite interiors housed treasures that spoke of Romanov glory: paintings illustrating great Russian victories, gilded French antiques, finely crafted Chinese cabinets and Fabergé ornaments. The Hesse and Romanov families became further acquainted in this setting of lavish beauty beneath skies of such northerly latitude that the sun never fully set. It was as though darkness itself was banished as Ella was feted by her new Romanov relations in the all-night glow of St Petersburg's luminous June skies.

After two weeks it was time for Ella to make her formal entrance into St Petersburg by the side of the popular new tsarina. Alix and other family members followed in a long procession of carriages that wound their way slowly through the streets to the magnificent Winter Palace. Victoria of Battenberg (formerly Hesse), by now somewhat dazed by the number of palaces, referred to it simply as 'the Big Palace'.[75] There was nothing to cloud their entry that summer's day; no reminder that this was the very place where Alexander II had died after the terrorist attack by People's Will. Victoria of Battenberg told her grandmother of the great enthusiasm of the peaceful crowds. She did not know that police had been drafted in from other cities to keep the Romanov clan safe.[76]

Wearing diamonds once owned by Catherine the Great, some so weighty that they hurt, the bride made her historic entrance into the chapel of the Winter Palace.[77] The powerful mysticism of ceremony was hypnotic. The air seemed heavy with music as many priests were singing and chanting, interweaving melodies that soared upwards, filling the vast space with a sense of the sublime. Almost intoxicating, incense drifted over the congregation, obscuring richly coloured icons, but finally revealing the bride processing steadily through the crowd, her silver dress encased in jewels, a pink diamond tiara framing her face. Ella appeared elevated to a star on some vast and gilded stage. She seemed not to be made of common clay. 'It was all like a beautiful dream,' her sister, Irene, told their grandmother. The costumes were like 'a scene out of the middle ages'. Ella seemed like the romantic 'Circassian princess whose trousseau consisted of a Bushel of pearls'.[78] Alix's cousin, Princess Marie of Edinburgh, was equally entranced. 'Her beauty and sweetness was a thing of dreams.'[79]

There was one person present who was not preoccupied with the bride: the sixteen-year-old tsarevich Nicholas, oldest son of Alexander III. The heir to the Russian throne found that his eyes were held by a young German princess standing near the altar in a white muslin dress. He could watch unobserved, catching glimpses of her even features framed by roses clipped to her blonde hair. It was Ella's youngest sister, Alix. In the coming days, as Nicholas saw more of Alix in the many celebrations in the imperial palaces of St Petersburg, he singled out this new member of his immediate family as special.

Nicholas did not take after his Romanov relatives but bore a much more striking resemblance to his British cousin, Prince George, Eddy's younger brother. Their mothers were sisters and the two cousins, George and Nicholas, although living far apart, could be mistaken for twins; the same short stature, dark hair and large, expressive eyes. Nicholas was just as bright and clever as George, Ella told the queen, 'only a little calmer'.[80] Polite, even-tempered, with an easy charm, there was a softness to Nicholas that Alix immediately warmed to. At formal events, Nicholas found that little Alix was often at his side. Although no longer a child, Nicholas was not too old to join in the younger children's games. He had 'a terrific romp' on one occasion with 'darling little Alix' and her brother, Ernest, he wrote in his diary. 'We jumped about together on the net ... went completely wild on the maypole ... fooled around a lot on the swing' and even 'told each other secrets'.[81]

Alix was accompanied by her governess, Miss Jackson, but there was far too much excitement to settle down to study. 'I have been much with little Xenia [Nicholas's younger sister] and her brothers and only come to our rooms at bedtime so Miss Jackson hopes that you will kindly excuse me not writing sooner,' Alix apologised to Queen Victoria on 18 June. 'It is very pretty here and I enjoy myself very much.'[82] Alix wanted to see everything; she had a sense of fun and her happy laughter was heard everywhere. Nicholas was completely absorbed by Alix, 'whom I really liked a lot' he confided to his diary. Less than a week later he was sure. 'We love each other,' he wrote, the day they drew their names together on a window in the Italian House. Nicholas was 'very very sad' when it was time for her to go.[83] He tried to give 'darling little Alix' a memento, a beautiful brooch. Confused by his token of affection, Alix later returned it.

For the tsarevich, the grand wedding of his Uncle Sergei in St Petersburg was a turning point in his life. His new 'Aunt Ella', now known as 'Her Imperial Highness Grand Duchess Elisabeth Feodorovna', was less than four years his senior. As their paths crossed at the Russian court over the following months they became close friends. Ella appreciated his gentle personality and gradually she came to think of the possibility of a union between her new nephew and her sister, Alix.

Queen Victoria was soon alarmed by reports that appeared to endorse her anxieties about Russian marital alliances. It was widely rumoured that Ella was not happy and that her supposedly devoted husband was having affairs with junior officers in his regiment. The queen was sufficiently troubled that she consulted the British ambassador in St Petersburg, who conducted enquiries but was unable to provide her with reassurance. The case remains unresolved today with Ella's most recent biographer, Christopher Warwick, concluding that 'the balance of probability still suggests that Serge was gay'.[84] Apart from concerns over his sexual orientation, Ella's relatives also worried about the powerful control he exerted over his young wife. Sergei ruled the household in a way that brokered no opposition and was known for his quick temper. There was 'something almost menacing about him', observed Ella's cousin, Marie of Edinburgh, as though 'there was a tyrant within him'.[85]

If Ella ever felt she had been taken in by her feelings of attraction to Sergei, she was not about to admit it. Innocent, trusting, but fiercely independent, she had wilfully ignored her grandmother's advice. Now she had her pride. Possibly, too, she was confused. She had strong feelings for Sergei and when he reprimanded her, even in public, it was very easy to believe that she was wanting in some way. She lost no opportunity in her letters to her family to slip in a word about her happiness. 'It makes me always so heartily glad when I hear how happy you both are,' she wrote to her oldest sister's husband, Louis of Battenberg, 'it is so pleasant that we four enjoy the same perfect contentment.'[86] She also enlisted her sympathetic brother, Ernest, to help scotch the rumours. Ernie, as he was known in the family, believed the hateful gossip originated with Ella's original admirer, Kaiser Wilhelm, who was exploiting jealousy of Sergei's elevated position within the Russian court.

Ella found it was not easy to reassure the queen. Her marriage remained childless and three years later her grandmother was still worried. 'I'm glad Ella says she is happy,' the queen wrote to Victoria of Battenberg on 15 February 1887, 'but it is the <u>whole</u> position in such a <u>corrupt</u> Country where you can trust <u>no one</u> & where politics are so antagonistic to one's own views & feelings wh. is so sad & distressing to <u>us</u> all.'[87] She returned to her suspicions in her next letter. 'Ella's constant speaking of her happiness I don't quite like,' wrote the queen. '<u>When</u> people are very happy they don't require to <u>tell</u> others of it.'[88] But Ella was a fortress, her feelings resistant to any probing. She wrote to reiterate 'the very deep love' she felt for her grandmama, 'as if you were my own Mother', but gave nothing away. 'All I can repeat is that I am perfectly happy.'[89]

Unexpected news during the spring of 1887 compounded the queen's feelings of loss of control over her Hessian granddaughters. Without any discussion, Irene, the third Hessian daughter, became engaged to Wilhelm's younger brother, Henry. 'It is impossible for me to tell you what a shock your letter gave me!' the queen wrote to Victoria of Battenberg in February 1887. 'Indeed I felt quite ill.' Queen Victoria was 'deeply hurt' at Irene's behaviour. 'How can I trust her again after such conduct?' she lamented. The two older daughters had at least kept her informed of developments prior to any announcement. But Irene's behaviour was ungrateful and out of order. After having been a mother 'to a gt extent' and been 'so vy intimate ... this want of openness has hurt me deeply,' she wrote. It reminded her of Ella and Sergei's engagement, 'wh I grieve over as much as ever'.[90]

These concerns compounded her fears about 'lovely Alicky' and she soon returned to her theme. 'You must prevent further Russians or other people coming to snap her [Alicky] up,' she insisted to Victoria of Battenberg on 2 March 1887. She wanted her granddaughter settled in Britain. 'I feel very deeply that my opinion & my advice are never listened to,' she complained. 'It was not before Ella's marriage was decided on wh dear Mama wld never have allowed to come abt ...'[91] She remained concerned at Ella's strong influence. Since their mother Alice's death the Hessian sisters had developed a close bond. What chance did Prince Eddy have with Alix? And how could Alix ever be safe? The very idea of her marriage to the Russian heir, Nicholas, was of a different order of danger to any match with a Russian grand duke. Her favourite granddaughter would thereby be in a prominent and dangerous position.

All this charged history lay behind Queen Victoria's invitation in the summer of 1888 to both Alix and Eddy to visit her at Balmoral. Ella too was invited, her grandmother perhaps hoping for a frank discussion, but Ella was unable to leave Russia. It is known that the queen wrote to Eddy 'on the subject', making her views plain.[92] Although this letter has not survived, the lethargic prince understood that he was to appear at Balmoral ready to show some interest in his pretty young cousin. Queen Victoria was determined to avoid another unwelcome Russian engagement behind her back and intended to steer proceedings towards a favourable conclusion for Alix, Eddy and the British throne.

Queen Victoria, Prince Albert and five of their nine children. Prince Albert saw the future marriages of their children as a way of spreading British liberal values and facilitating the peace of Europe.

Queen Victoria's large family and their guests at a garden party in Chiswick Park in 1875, painted by Louis-William Desanges. 'The royal mob', as the queen called her family, secured her position as Europe's great matriarch.

Victoria and Albert's oldest daughter, Victoria or 'Vicky', on her sixteenth birthday, when she was already engaged to the second heir to the Prussian throne.

The assassination of
Alexander II of Russia
in 1881 marked the birth
of a modern form of
political terrorism.

Queen Victoria's prestige
increased with Britain's
rising imperial and industrial
supremacy until she came
to occupy a unique position
apparently unequalled by
any other sovereign, and
was universally known
simply as 'the queen'.

As second in line to the throne, Queen Victoria's oldest British grandson, Prince Albert Victor or 'Eddy', was seen by many as 'first prize' in the marriage stakes. The truth was rather different.

rincess Alix of Hesse was courted by future heirs to the British and Russian thrones.

Princess Elisabeth of Hesse inspired strong feelings in the future Kaiser Wilhelm II.

Prince George, Duke of York, was in no hurry to marry.

Spirited Princess Marie of Edinburgh or 'Missy' had many admirers, including, allegedly, a young Winston Churchill.

4

Alix and Eddy

'You must prevent <u>further</u> Russians ... <u>coming</u> to snap her up.'

Queen Victoria to Victoria of
Battenberg, 2 March 1887

Sixteen-year-old Alix of Hesse arrived at Osborne on the Isle of Wight on 31 July 1888 with her nineteen-year-old brother, Ernie, and soon found herself singled out for special attention by the queen.[1] Before Prince Albert Victor, or Eddy, was invited to join the party, the queen wanted time with Alix alone. This would give her a chance to assess her granddaughter's suitability and also, without a word being said, to show Alix the magnificent prospect that could lie before her as a future British queen.

Day after day Alix was honoured as the queen's trusted companion, alongside Beatrice, her youngest daughter. There were intimate drives in the open carriage around the island and courtesy trips to see visiting dignitaries such as the Empress Eugenie, wife of Napoleon III, who was staying at Osborne Cottage. After months of painful silence, the queen had agreed to Beatrice's marriage to Henry of Battenberg on condition that they both live with her. Beatrice's life continued to revolve around her mother, and Alix was warmly welcomed into their close circle, enjoying informal days reminiscent of her childhood visits. Sometimes she walked with Beatrice beside the queen in her pony chair around the Italianate gardens and the estate, or took tea in the 'Swiss Cottage', the wooden chalet that Prince Albert had brought from

Switzerland years ago, or sat under the trees, joined by Beatrice's own children, one-year-old Alexander, and the new baby, known as 'Ena', or Victoria Eugenie. Summer days passed happily with Alix integrated into the queen's daily routine.

After three weeks Alix travelled with the queen and Beatrice to Balmoral. This draughty, forbidding mansion was the queen's favourite retreat, hallowed ground rich with memories where she could almost regain the life she had lost. In this haven she could pull up the drawbridge and keep the world at bay. Balmoral, as at Windsor, harboured a particular atmosphere in the corridors that led to the queen's apartments. 'The hush round Grand mamma's door was awe-inspiring, like approaching the mystery of some sanctuary,' recalled another granddaughter, Alix's cousin, Marie of Edinburgh. There were 'silent soft-carpeted corridors' that were somehow 'always approached from afar off', where people only spoke 'in hushed voices and trod softly'. A series of doors opened noiselessly 'like approaching the final mystery to which only the initiated had access'. The final door opened to reveal a little old lady in a flounced black silk gown whose voice was seldom raised and yet who projected a powerful presence. Although she was 'small and unimposing' she knew 'so extraordinarily well how to inspire reverential fear'. Such was the queen's cult of seclusion at Balmoral that Marie of Edinburgh could barely remember being invited to her apartments but only being permitted to see her outside. Despite this she still felt her grandmother 'was the central power directing things … the arbiter of our different fates'. Her '"yes" and her "no" counted tremendously', and she did not shrink from 'interfering in the most private questions'.[2]

But Alix found herself in a special position where she was not held at a distance like many of the queen's other granddaughters. When Ernie returned to Germany on 24 August, she remained at Balmoral, accompanying her grandmother to her most sacred haunts, places of desolate beauty such as Corrie Mulzie, Dantzig Shiel, Glen Gelder and Linn of Muich. They went out in all weathers, sometimes stopping for tea with faithful staff or taking presents to people living on the Balmoral estate. Queen Victoria took a great delight in the Scottish Highlands, observing each change such as 'the wild roses now in full bloom and the blue bells in quantities'. The ritual varied little regardless of the elements. In September the mists drew in and on one occasion the view was blotted out by an early fall of snow. The queen admitted it had 'turned raw', her one concession to travel in a closed carriage.[3]

Their tranquil circle was breached by family news of the outside world. Recently bereaved Vicky was the most prolific correspondent and her letters invariably brought news of 'the dreadful state of affairs at Berlin'. The queen was touched to receive a bracelet from her daughter 'with dear Fritz's hair' on the anniversary of 'poor dear Vicky's engagement day 33 years ago. All so bright then and now! It is too sad,' she wrote, feeling deeply that the calamity that had befallen her daughter was a misfortune for the whole of Europe.[4] Without her husband to help, Vicky worried about her daughter Sophie's forthcoming marriage to the heir to the Greek throne, Prince Constantine. She dreaded the great distance that would separate them, especially with 'the future of Greece and the Dynasty not being very secure' and the 'East being such a powder barrel'. Queen Victoria found Vicky's constant 'grief and trouble ... distresses me so'.[5]

The chaos of the outside world was kept at bay at Balmoral where the queen appreciated the simple and unvaried routine. Their company for dinner was not large, revolving each evening around Beatrice and her husband, the queen's private secretary, Sir Henry Ponsonby, her maid of honour, Harriet, with an occasional sprinkling of guests such as the Archbishop of Canterbury. Sometimes the gathering was enlivened by visitors from far away such as the tsarina, Empress Marie Feodorovna, who came to see her sister, Princess Alexandra. Queen Victoria noted with satisfaction that her granddaughter appeared to be able to hold her own well in the circle at Balmoral, overcoming her youthful reserve. Alicky was 'in good heart and not shy now', she told Victoria of Battenberg.[6]

Prince Eddy did not join the party until 10 September, bringing a friend, Major Miles, 'a very nice, gentleman-like & quite superior man', wrote the queen.[7] There were many opportunities for Eddy and Alix to see more of each other, sometimes joined by his mother and sisters. Any awkwardness about the situation could be deflected with talk of the season's inevitable highlight: the theatricals planned for 5 October. The queen took a special delight in the tableaux that was not entirely shared by her grandson, 'for they took up lots of time when I might have been stalking or doing things more amusing', Eddy confided to his brother George.[8] The queen obliged her guests to share her enthusiasm. On 25 September they visited the Ball Room and the queen 'tired my hand at painting some of the scenery'.[9] She returned with Alix later that day to see the lights tested. Over the coming days there was much to do; a stage was installed, scenery completed, costumes were devised and fitted, and early October was taken up with rehearsals.

The culmination of this effort came on 5 October 1888 when guests gathered in the evening in the ballroom at Balmoral. All the staff from the estate were invited as well as guests from outside. This year the theatricals were designed to celebrate the birthday of Beatrice's husband, Henry, with each tableau illustrating a different letter of his name: 'Henry Maurice'. For the very first letter 'H', Eddy was on stage with Alix as they enacted a vignette called 'Harvest'. The following evening they reached the 'U' in Maurice and it was Eddy's embarrassing misfortune to have to parade before the company as a bridegroom to enact the word 'Union' at a Hessian peasant wedding. Whatever his feelings he managed to act the part of being in the raptures of love, despite being dressed in an uncomfortable and unflattering peasant costume. He was spared the charade of marrying Alix onstage. She took another part, while his sister, Louise, gamely played the bride. Fortunately, he managed to avoid having to double up as a 'Romeo' that evening for the 'R' – the part gallantly volunteered by a guest, Sir F. Edwards.[10]

Queen Victoria was moved, finding the scenes and their senti-ments 'really beautiful', blissfully unaware of any potential awkwardness. It perhaps occurred to Eddy that his stage role as bridegroom was uncomfortably close to a bigger charade play-ing out in his grandmother's mind. The queen's interest in Alix above all her other grandchildren was so apparent that neither he

nor Alix could hardly miss her intention. But despite the openings created by the tableaux, he could not quite bring himself
to the crucial point of making an approach to Alix. She was so
young and he was unsure how to interpret her ambiguous signals.
'Alicky is still here and is much grown,' he wrote on 7 October
to her brother-in-law, Prince Louis of Battenberg. Eddy had not
corresponded with Louis for a long time, but now the theatricals
were over he wrote at length, passing on all the family news and
revealing a little of his admiration for Alix. 'She's looking prettier
than ever, and will I am sure be very handsome when she grows
up,' he observed.[11]

It was not until 10 October 'that dear sweet Alicky left'. The
queen found at once she 'missed her so much'.[12] Over the course
of Alix's visit of two and a half months rigorous assessments
as to her suitability for Eddy had been made by her probing grandmother. Queen Victoria declared herself delighted.
'Darling Alicky is dear & good & clever,' she wrote to Vicky
in Germany, perhaps a little insensitively since Vicky's own
daughters appeared to have been passed over. Alix stayed in
Buckingham Palace on her way back to Germany, affording her
another glimpse of the favoured prospect that could be on offer.
She wrote to her grandmama thanking her 'over and over again
for all the kindness and affection you showed me'. Although
there was no direct mention of Eddy in her letter, Alix referred
to the very happy time she had had.[13]

Queen Victoria's plan appeared to be taking shape. On cue,
indecisive Eddy seemed more sure of his feelings. He confided
in his younger brother, George. Alix had only just left Balmoral,
he wrote on 12 October 1888. 'She's a lovely girl now and everything that is nice, and I have got my eye on her; you know what
that means.'[14] Later he claimed to Alix's brother-in-law, Louis
of Battenberg, that it was at this point that he realised he was
in love. 'Inwardly I was longing to tell her so,' he wrote, 'but
thought I had better wait my time.'[15] Everything augured well for
the British throne.

Even at a great distance, almost a continent away, Ella understood exactly what was going on and felt under no illusion as to what this could signify. Her youngest sister's favoured position with the queen, the long drives in the country, the intimate luncheons, the careful attention: the message was all too plain. Grandmama intended Eddy and Alix to marry. Ella immediately poured out her feelings to her brother, Ernie. She found the very idea of Eddy 'marrying Alix quite dreadful'. First cousins 'is best to avoid', she explained, 'but the chief thing is that he [Eddy] does not look over strong & is too stupid – you would see that clever girl turn into a flirt as she is so pretty & England with a stupid husband not at all the place for her ...' Ella raised the subject of marriage to Eddy with Alix herself and was reassured that her sister 'said she never would'. But Ella feared that she might be persuaded because 'of the lovely country' and being so close to family. Ella was convinced her sister 'would not be happy'.[16]

Ella acknowledged that her strong stance on this issue reflected her own 'selfish wish' for her youngest sister to join her in Russia.[17] Her letters to those closest to her do hint at the pain of separation from her immediate family. She had shared a room with her oldest sister, Victoria, all her life until she left home and 'you can well imagine how I miss her', she confided to Louis of Battenberg. 'How I long to see you all.' When Victoria became pregnant, Ella calculated the months before it was safe for her sister to travel and longed for each scrap of family information since 'being far away news is so precious'.[18] When a visit was arranged, 'I hardly dare think of it for fear our pleasant plans being deranged.' Sometimes the pain of isolation from her family was almost visceral. She was not looking forward to returning to St Petersburg where she felt like a bird in cage, she admitted to Louis, but she liked the Peterhof since once 'we were all together there'.[19] The memory of her family filling these echoing marbled halls brought comfort. Her oldest sister was happily settled, but perhaps her youngest sister could fill the void. Early in 1889 Ella and Sergei invited Alix to join them for six weeks.

Alix returned to St Petersburg with her father Louis of Hesse and brother Ernie, and the visit could not have made more of a contrast to her recent trip to Balmoral cloistered with her elderly grandmother. The twenty-year-old tsarevich was at the Warsaw Station in St Petersburg to welcome the Hesse party, along with a number of grand dukes and Alexander III himself. Nicholas was struck at once with how Alix had changed; 'she has grown up a lot and become much prettier,' he wrote in his diary.[20] The party went first to the imperial palace, the Anichkov, to take tea with Empress Maria Feodorovna. As the two families talked, the empress composed and at ease in surroundings of exquisite beauty, Alix could not know that the tsarina sometimes cried when she left her sister, Alexandra, in England at the thought of returning to her 'Russian prison'. Indeed, as a guest of Grand Duke Sergei at the Sergeivsky Palace opposite the Anichkov, Alix did not detect the dangers in Russia that her grandmother described; she was cocooned in a world apart. The days that followed were carefree, filled with artless pleasures, larking around in the Jardin de la Tauride and the grounds of the Anichkov, playing in the snow, racing down the ice-bound hills in a sparkling winter world with no hint of threat. Nicky, as Alix now called the tsarevich, joined them every day and there are frequent references in his diary to the sheer joy of those afternoons skating together. He saw Alix at her best, at ease in the intimacy of family.

At night, palaces of unimaginable splendour formed the backdrop to balls and entertainments on a lavish scale. Alix had a chance to meet St Petersburg society at concert balls at the Winter Palace, the *bal noir* at the Anichkov Palace, and at the Russian ballet and opera. The tsarina came alive in company; she drew people to her and charmed any gathering. By comparison, through Russian eyes the handsome German princess appeared tense. Ella had personally supervised Alix's 'coming-out' in Germany the previous autumn. Her first ball had been held in the Neues Palais, Darmstadt, and Ella had travelled from St Petersburg to make sure it was a success. Alix in white muslin, with lily of the valley framing her face and her bodice, had made a striking impression.[21] St Petersburg society proved to be much more demanding. Alix's undisputed beauty was not enough; she needed poise and ease in company as well. She struggled, occasionally rigid with nerves on this vast marbled and gilded stage where the watchful audience sometimes appeared hostile to the provincial princess from Darmstadt.

But for Nicholas, Alix stood apart, her loveliness undiminished by her nervousness. He sought her out at dances; the cotillion, the mazurka, they danced sometimes till they were exhausted. He felt himself to be strangely animated; everything felt uplifting and wonderful. She provoked a certainty in him that was out of character. 'My dream is some day to marry Alix H,' he wrote later. 'I have loved her a long while and still deeper and stronger since 1889 when she spent six weeks in St Petersburg. For a long time I resisted my feeling that my dearest dream will come true ...'[22]

Ella noticed that Alix also was in buoyant mood, radiating happiness in the company of the tsarevich, becoming once again the 'Sunny' of her early years. The conflicts that Alix actually felt are perhaps indicated by a dream filled with anxiety that she faithfully recorded while she was in St Petersburg. She was in a hospital with her oldest sister, Victoria, and all of a sudden 'Grandmama comes in and a shot is fired at her ...'[23] It was as though part of her mind was echoing the queen's warnings, which did not tie up with her experience. The impressions Alix took back to Germany were all favourable; Russia was not as grandmama described. Ella appeared to be living the most wonderful life having made a very successful marriage to a Russian grand duke. The tsarevich himself seemed the very opposite of an autocrat in the making; he was gentle and fun. That spring she exchanged affectionate notes with Nicholas from Darmstadt.

Ella gave Nicholas a memento of her sister's visit: a photograph of Alix with Ernie and herself, painting around the frame images of all the happy times they had shared. Nicky found it 'charming' and described it to Alix: 'there is the ice, the big hall, the skates, a clown, *the* window with 3 lights, a cotillion-ribbon and a basket with flowers from Aunt Sacha Narychkine's ball ...' and many other remembrances. Another photo of 'you and her [Ella] together' in their ball dresses he kept 'constantly' before him. When he saw Ella their conversation 'always', he told Alix, went back to her stay in St Petersburg. Ella encouraged Nicky in his feelings for Alix and told him explicitly, 'I prayed so deeply for you both to bring you together in love for each other.'[24] Ella also confided to Alix how much Nicky thought of her.

Just how much the possibility of such a match was in the minds of the Hesse sisters is also hinted at by the papers of Victoria of Battenberg. It was around this time she made a serious study of the Romanov family tree and lists of all the Russian sovereigns in direct line and the key events of their reigns. To understand the Russian religion her notes show she went to the lengths of studying the schism in the Roman Catholic Church in the eleventh century in which the Eastern Church divided from the Western Church.[25] Meanwhile their brother, Ernie, under instruction from Ella, was valiantly trying to manage 'grandmama queen'. He had already written to her flatly denying any rumours. 'Darling Grandmama, I want to tell you so much that all what is written in the newspapers is simply nonsense.' He had watched Nicholas and Alexandra together closely, he told her, '& I can only say that not a single idea has come into his [Nicholas's] head about it'. To add to the obstacles, the emperor and empress 'think just as little about anything between A & N as we do'.[26]

Queen Victoria was not fooled for one minute. She had a way of knowing exactly what was going on. There was no doubt in her mind of the urgency of taking the matter in hand. She invited Alix to Balmoral once again in the summer of 1889 hoping that in the Scottish Highlands romance could flourish with Eddy. This time there would be no bashful holding back; no English reserve. She was quite resolved to raise the question of marriage with Eddy for herself. The queen was blunt about trying to establish beforehand what hope there was for Eddy. She knew that Alix had visited Ella in St Petersburg and therefore feared the worst. 'She [Alix] shld be made to reflect seriously on the folly of throwing away the chance of a very good Husband, kind, affectionate & steady,' she wrote to Victoria of Battenberg, '& of entering a united happy family & a very good position wh is second to none in the world! Dear Uncle and Aunt wish it so much & poor E. is so unhappy at the thought of losing her also!' Fearing some Russian interest, she enquired 'What fancy has she got in her head?'[27]

Eddy could not be certain what had transpired in St Petersburg. As Alix's visit approached, the prospective groom was in a state of some nervousness. Twenty-five-year-old Prince Eddy had to endure the pressure of courting his cousin under the searching gaze of his forceful grandmother. He was now certain that he loved Alix, that he had loved her the previous year, and wanted to declare his feelings. But he feared his grandmother's meddling might work against him. Before he met Alix he confided his worries to her brother-in-law, Prince Louis of Battenberg.

'For years' he had been fond of Alix, he told Prince Louis on 6 September 1889. He had 'told no one with the exception of my parents, and that only a short time ago. But last year Grandmama wrote to me on the subject, and was very nice about it; only I fear that she or someone else may have told Alicky, which was I think a great mistake, and as you say relations can only spoil my chance by mixing themselves up in the affair. I guessed that myself last year, and therefore was very careful how I approached Alicky and did not give her the slightest sign that I loved her.' He felt extremely anxious, he told Louis, 'but you may be sure I will do all I can to persuade Alicky that I love her for herself and for herself only and that my parents and relations have had nothing whatever to do with it as far as I myself am concerned ... I can't tell you what a happy creature I shall be if it only comes off right, for I do indeed know what a prize there is to be won ...'[28]

As Alix prepared to travel to England and Eddy nervously planned how to propose to her, a police investigation was under-way in London that would have devastating consequences for his reputation and, as a result, his prospects as a suitor. This unexpected turn of events was sparked by a seemingly inconsequential finding on 4 July 1889 at the London Post Office headquarters at St Martin's-le-Grand in the city. A fifteen-year-old telegraph delivery boy, Charlie Swinscow, was found with far more cash in his pockets than he could possibly earn in a week. Careful probing by the Post Office's internal police prompted Swinscow to reveal that he 'had got the money ... for going to bed with gentlemen'. Swinscow divulged the names of other messenger boys who were similarly engaged in supplementing their wages at a location in a rundown part of town north of Soho. The Post Office constable quickly established that 19 Cleveland Street was nothing less than a male brothel.[29]

The case escalated rapidly to the Postmaster General, who passed this hot potato on to Scotland Yard. It did not take detectives long to discover that members of the aristocracy had visited the brothel. The person named most frequently by the Post Office boys was a 'Mr Brown', who turned out to be none other than the head of the Prince of Wales's stables: Lord Arthur Somerset. As the younger son of the Duke of Beaufort, Lord Arthur was not heir to the family mansion at Badminton, Gloucestershire, but made his way in the world working as head of stables for Bertie, who affectionately called him 'Podge'. The Post Office boys' testimony was soon backed up by police surveillance of Cleveland Street. 'Podge' appeared to be deeply implicated.[30]

Such was the seriousness of the matter that within a couple of weeks the police investigation was referred to the Director of Public Prosecutions, the Home Secretary, and by 24 July to the prime minister himself, Lord Salisbury. At this point the investigation ran into unexpected delays. Salisbury, who sprang from a long line of statesmen whose service dated back to the time of Elizabeth 1, was allegedly a subscriber to the maxim 'whatever happens will be for the worse and therefore it is in our interests that as little should happen as possible'.[31] Here was a man who understood that for certain delicate matters there was real value in a little 'masterly inactivity'. He favoured downplaying the scandal and advised against the extradition of the proprietor of the male brothel, Charles Hammond, who had fled abroad. Letters between the Attorney General and the Director of Public Prosecutions during August reveal their strenuous efforts to avoid charging Lord Arthur Somerset.

Somerset meanwhile hired a young criminal law solicitor, Arthur Newton, who was earning a reputation defending those caught in awkward or shady circumstances. Newton was also acting for the Post Office boys, whose case was to be heard in court in early September. In the hands of Newton, the scandal took on an altogether astounding dimension. The Public Prosecutor, Sir Augustus Stephenson, was advised by his deputy, Hamilton Cuffe, on 15 September: 'I am told that Newton has boasted that if we go on a very distinguished person will be involved (PAV).'[32]

In other words – Prince Albert Victor.

Arthur Newton appeared to be threatening the authorities. If his client, Somerset, was charged, the scandal would implicate none other than Queen Victoria's grandson: the very prince whose estimable qualities and position she was trying to promote to Princess Alix of Hesse.

———

'Sweet Alicky, looking lovely arrived just before tea,' Queen Victoria noted on 13 August 1889 in her journal. A luxurious summer stretched ahead for the Hessian princess, first by the sea at Osborne and then in the Highlands at Balmoral, although her visit was not without pressure. The queen had sent her presents earlier in the year; a pretty shawl in April, a beautiful jewel for her birthday in June, which, Alix replied, made her think 'of the best and dearest of Grandmamas, who always knows how to make people happy'.[33] Their polite exchanges masked the queen's serious expectations. Talk of marriage was in the air: Bertie's oldest daughter, Princess Louise, had just married the Duke of Fife. Bertie's oldest son, Eddy, still unattached, was soon to join the party. Alix realised that these were weeks that could change her life forever.

On 22 August the queen, Beatrice and Alix made 'a cheerless crossing' from the Isle of Wight to Portsmouth and travelled by train to Wales. The queen was to give Alix a taste of a royal tour, her first in this region for many years. In spite of intermittent rain, the grey-slated mining towns and straggling villages were transformed by flags and draperies and the enthusiastic crowds filling the narrow streets. The queen watched sheep-dog trials on the misty Welsh hills, where she marvelled at the skill of the dogs and their masters. Alix and Beatrice visited a coalmine at Ruabon, where Alix didn't hesitate to go underground to see the shafts for herself. Choirs, sometimes forty strong, serenaded them through the Welsh valleys, and when the royal party finally departed the queen was gratified that 'the good people sang "God save the Queen" the whole time till the train left the station'.[34] Whether at any stage the growing rumours about Prince Eddy reached the queen is not clear; there were opportunities, for her diary shows she did have meetings with both Lord Salisbury and the Postmaster General, Mr Raikes, in late August.[35]

Alix and her grandmother did not reach Balmoral until the end of the month. If Alix was anxious about being pressured about her possible forthcoming marriage she had an ally at hand in the shape of her older brother, Ernie, who was there to greet them. The days soon fell into a familiar pattern with quiet mornings followed by carriage rides out in the afternoon to places of personal interest to the queen and full of wild beauty such as Loch Nagar or Aberarder. Occasionally, Alix found herself alone with her grandmama over tea, which gave the queen tantalising opportunities to try and gauge her granddaughter's feelings before Eddy arrived. Alix was not easy to read, except for Ernie, in whom she confided.

It was 'a fine fair morning' with 'a splendid sky' on 9 September 1889 as Prince Eddy made his way to Balmoral.[36] 'I little thought what I had to expect, and to learn, on my arrival,' Eddy confided later to Louis of Battenberg.[37] He had never broached the subject of marriage with Alix directly, but there were grounds for optimism. Relatives whose opinion he valued, such as Prince Louis, had given him encouragement, his grandmother had welcomed Alix into the heart of the British royal family, and he was ready to offer all that he could give. As his carriage wound its way across expansive Scottish landscapes, brilliantly lit under the late summer sun, there was every reason to feel both apprehensive and excited. This was the day when his life might be transformed. The occasion: a luncheon party at which both he and Alix would be present. If he could engineer a suitable moment alone with her, he intended to find out her feelings towards him.

Any air of confidence that Eddy could summon for this first meeting was soon dispelled. Ernie took him to one side 'soon after my arrival and had a long talk to him on the subject', Eddy recorded later. Ernie warned Eddy that his sister would not find a proposal of marriage welcome. He advised the prince not to raise the subject. Eddy was dismayed. 'Have I offended her in any way?' he asked. Ernie could offer little by way of explanation, 'which makes it all the harder for me to understand', Eddy recorded.[38] Not being a man overburdened with self-confidence or overwhelmed by strong feelings, he allowed himself to be persuaded by Ernie. Enough had been said for Eddy to lose his courage and endure the lunch, deflated.

Bertie came to Balmoral the following day without his son, perhaps hoping to clarify the position. On 11 September the queen's party, in turn, visited the Wales family, who were with their newly married daughter, the Duchess of Fife, at Mar Lodge, a sporting lodge some eighteen miles from Balmoral. Eddy struggled with the awkward situation with his first cousin, uncertain whether or how to advance his case. The queen, harassed by the heat and the journey, took tea outside in the shade of the veranda, and left others to explore the estate and see the ballroom.[39] The Fifes had guests that day, so any discussions about Alix and Eddy were limited, a hushed word here or there.

It was left to Eddy's grandmama to probe the delicate subject of Alix's romantic inclinations on his behalf at Balmoral. The indomitable queen was perhaps surprised to find an equal forcefulness of character in her young granddaughter. Alix appeared to know her own mind with an unfailing certainty that did not diminish with the searching concerns of her grandmother. Eddy was not her first choice. Indeed, over the course of an awkward conversation with her grandmother, Alix managed to convey the unwelcome message that she had no desire to marry Eddy at all.

Eddy's practical younger brother George had a clear measure of the situation by the end of the week. Along with all-important news of the stag shoot at Balmoral he told Louis on 15 September, 'it is all over between her and Eddy'. Alix had been bold enough to admit 'she does not care about him sufficiently to marry him but is very fond of him as a cousin'. George admired her 'very much for saying it out straight'. Much better, he thought, than any kind of vagueness. Eddy had taken the news 'very sensibly', he reported, but 'was very low'.[40]

Eddy was, in fact, deeply wounded. Alix's rejection was humiliatingly personal; no princess could dream of more glittering prospects than the future British throne. He himself was found wanting in some way that was yet unknown to him. As the glorious Indian summer swiftly faded in late September, the weather suddenly raw and cold, Eddy found the opportunity was fast slipping from his grasp. Beautiful Alix remained unobtainable. He left Scotland for a long tour of the empire on 1 October; Alix departed the next day. Once again she stopped at Buckingham Palace for a few days before returning home. Relaxed at last with her beloved brother Ernie, they roamed around London all day, taking in art galleries and visiting the theatre, Alix relieved to have stated her feelings and shaken off the pressure.[41]

There was no such relief for Eddy. He was convinced he was in love and several days elapsed before he could bring himself to confide in Alix's brother-in-law. 'I said nothing to Alicky,' he told Prince Louis on 7 October:

> but now begin to regret that I did not, for I might have explained things a little better if I had. For I can't really believe Alicky knows how much I really love her, or she would not I think have treated me quite so cruelly. For I can't help considering it so, as she apparently gives me no chance at all, and little or no hope; although I shall continue loving her, and in the hope that someday she may think better of what she has said, and give me the chance of being one of the happiest beings in the world. For I should indeed consider myself so, if I would only call her my own. I am almost certain, as certain as most people are who are in love with a girl, that I could make her happy, if she would only give me a chance of doing so ... I am sure you feel for me in my disappointment or you would not have taken the trouble to write me such a nice letter as you did. Grandmama was extremely nice about it all and said some very kind things

to me, for as you know, she was always in favour of a union
between me and Alix and spoke to me on the subject last year ...

Eddy asked Louis to find out the 'real reason why Alix does not
care for me, and if I have <u>ever</u> offended her in any way'. He could
not quite bring himself to give up hope and asked Louis to find
out 'what you think of my prospects and whether I shall <u>ever</u>
have a chance again with Alicky'.[42]

Queen Victoria, too, was stunned and 'most sad'. She turned to
Alix's oldest sister, Victoria. 'We have still a faint, lingering hope
that she <u>may</u> – if he remains unmarried, after all when she comes
to reflect & see <u>what</u> a sad & serious thing it is to throw away
such a marriage with such a position, & in such an amiable family
in her Mother's country – where she would be received with open
arms,' she wrote on 12 October. As if to spell out the attractions
clearly, she added, 'Moreover Eddie is not stupid, is very good,
affectionate & a good looking young man.'[43]

———————

This hardly ringing endorsement from Queen Victoria was soon
reduced still further by a rumour considered so shameful it was
enough to dent the confidence of any anxious suitor. Once Lord
Somerset's solicitor, Arthur Newton, claimed that a detailed
investigation of the Cleveland Street male brothel would implicate none other than Prince Eddy, the 'gross scandal' took on a
new dimension. Unwilling to pursue lines of inquiry that might
possibly expose a member of the royal family to criminal charges,
the authorities continued to downplay the case – while trusted
members of the Prince of Wales's staff discreetly endeavoured to
make sense of it.

Bertie's private secretary, Sir Francis Knollys, and his
Comptroller, Sir Dighton Probyn, went to interview Lord
Arthur Somerset on 16 October 1889. Bertie had complete faith
in his head of stables. Infamous for his heterosexual appetites,
the Prince of Wales could not believe Lord Somerset had visited
a male brothel 'anymore than I would if they had accused the

Archbishop of Canterbury'.[44] Somerset himself exuded all the self-confidence of his position as a young aristocrat of good family, asserting his innocence and urging Probyn and Knollys to interview his lawyer, Arthur Newton. It would appear the honourable gentlemen of the prince's household 'were very strongly impressed against' the possibly crooked solicitor.[45] They urged Somerset to hire a different solicitor, a step he was curiously reluctant to take. The indefatigable Probyn and Knollys pursued their inquiries all the way to the prime minister, who was abroad but was greeted with a telegram from them as he set foot in Dover on 18 October. It is perhaps a measure of the urgency that Lord Salisbury agreed to meet them as soon as he arrived at King's Cross, from where he was due to take a train north to his family home. Without exactly being explicit, the prime minister managed to convey to the horrified Probyn that there *were* grounds for the allegations against Somerset. His arrest could not be delayed for much longer. The rendezvous at the busy station, the platforms heavy with smoke from the steam trains, somehow escaped the attention of the press. But the news did not escape Lord Somerset, who evidently got word of his imminent arrest and fled the country that very evening.[46]

By now rumours were spreading 'on the street corners ... and all the clubs of the Metropolis' that leading members of the aristocracy, perhaps even Prince Albert Victor too, were implicated. The press started to make veiled references to the Tory government looking after its own. Finally by mid-November the *North London Press* broke ranks and published names: the Earl of Euston and Lord Arthur Somerset. Both men had been allowed to leave the country, claimed the editor, Ernie Parke, because their prosecution would incriminate 'a far more distinguished and more highly placed personage' in their 'disgusting crimes'. Euston sued for libel, the case soon attracting the interest of the foreign press, who had a field day. In France *La Lanterne* alleged '*une douzaine de Lords*' were involved in the Cleveland Street scandal, while in America, Eddy was openly referred to as a 'wild young prince' who was 'physically and mentally something of a wreck'.[47] He was condemned as possessing 'all his father's vices' without any of his compensating virtues and was 'not half the man in all the attributes of manly makeup' of his younger brother, George. the *New York Times* concluded on 10 November that there was 'a general conviction' the prince 'was mixed up in the scandal'.[48] Such was the outrage felt among the public that 'Marlborough House is daily assailed with anonymous letters of the most outrageous character', reported the *Cardiff Times* on 7 December. Both Bertie and his wife Alexandra were receiving communications 'of a monstrous character'.[49]

Beatrice's destruction of many of Eddy's records after her mother's death has served the prince badly over the years, creating a vacuum in which the wildest conspiracy theories have flourished. By the 1960s, Prince Albert Victor's name was demonised to such an extent that some claimed he was none other than Jack the Ripper, the serial murderer who mutilated his female victims in the streets of Whitechapel in 1888. This notion has been repeated by many authors despite the fact that Eddy's whereabouts on key nights in question can be proved from surviving records. Regarding the Cleveland Street case, at the time, Lord Arthur Somerset created the impression that he had fled abroad to avoid drawing Prince Eddy into the scandal. Having pointed at the prince, Somerset would say no more, beyond revealing that he had never taken Eddy to the male brothel himself. Whether the prince was supposed to be a regular visitor to the male brothel or the guileless victim of some ill-judged prank – Somerset's lips were sealed. There remains the possibility that Prince Eddy was innocent. Somerset's lawyer, Newton, could have encouraged his client to make false claims about a royal connection to the brothel, hoping this would stop any official investigation in its tracks. Years later Newton's career ended in two scandals that speak volumes for his unscrupulous character. He was suspended from law practice in 1911 for misconduct in selling a client's story to the press and later struck off entirely for falsifying data.[50]

While it is not possible to establish whether the prince had visited Cleveland Street, biographers are in agreement about Eddy's unspecified 'dissipations' from this time. The future heir to the throne was causing his parents anxiety because he was 'dissipated and unstable', according to Edward VII's biographer, Sir Philip Magnus, 'dissolute and essentially trivial' for Princess Alexandra's biographer, Georgina Battiscombe, and infatuated with 'every form of dissipation or amusement' for James Pope-Hennessy.[51] Even his mother, his most devoted ally, who had for years invariably referred to her adored oldest child as 'good' and 'dear', was beginning to see him as 'a naughty bad boy', according to Georgina Battiscombe.[52] Bertie was 'much annoyed at his son's name being coupled with this thing', and his staff, such as Sir Dighton Probyn, referred to 'cruel and unjust rumours' relating to his oldest son.[53] Any hope Bertie and Alexandra entertained that they might shield the queen from the news was no easy matter given the alarming comments in the foreign press. But whatever her private views, Queen Victoria behaved as though she had not heard the rumours, and if she had, they were beneath her contempt. In late 1889 she was still entertaining hopes of uniting Eddy with her favourite granddaughter, Alix, suggesting that she did not think badly of him. Her letters show her to be kindly disposed to her oldest British grandson, still seeing him as a 'dear good boy'.

As for the prince himself, in the autumn of 1889 he was safely abroad, part of a wedding party, very aware of his position and wondering whether all the gossip about him had reached the ears of the distinguished guests. The occasion was the marriage of his Aunt Vicky's daughter, Princess Sophie, to the Crown Prince Constantine of Greece. The royal clan descended on Athens, drawing representatives from several European dynasties. Vicky, her son, Emperor Wilhelm, and her daughters came from Germany. The British royal family was represented by Bertie and Alexandra. The tsar and tsarina sent their eldest son, Nicholas, Eddy's first cousin. The two cousins were almost certainly aware that they both had an interest in Alix.

For Eddy, the prolonged wedding ceremony could only serve to underline his own feelings of disappointment and humiliation, his prominent role in the proceedings supporting Sophie drawing attention to his unmarried state. Despite the setback at Balmoral he could not quite give up hope of Alix, and once again he took

Louis of Battenberg into his confidence.[54] He could not know that
Nicholas had written endearingly to 'darling Alix' as soon as she
returned to Darmstadt from Britain.[55] Nonetheless, as the disap-
proving headlines in the foreign press were whispered around the
court, it was hard to conceive of anything more crushing to his
fast-diminishing hopes.

From Greece, Prince Eddy travelled to India for an extensive
tour. He wrote to Queen Victoria from Bangalore in late November,
most anxious to please. The trip was proving most 'instructive'
and had already taken him on 'very hot and dusty' journeys from
Bombay to Poona, Hydrabad, Madras and Mysore. He told her
of big receptions, balls and speeches, acknowledging that he 'thoroughly understood' he was honoured 'merely because I am your
grandson'. Everywhere the enthusiasm was 'very touching' and
he enjoyed colourful highlights: seeing wild elephants herded into
a keddah, shooting Sambar deer and snipe, and trying for a lion
in the jungle.[56] His travels took him on to the northern frontier
and a camp not far from Lahore where there were a great many
troops. 'To give you an idea of the size of the force,' he wrote to
his grandmother, 'when drawn up in a line [the troops] extended
for over a mile and three quarters.' The infantry were equally
impressive at Rawal Pindi with many different races working side
by side: 'Highlanders, Irish, English, Sikhs, Gurkhas, Dogras and
Pathans.' He hoped he was not leaving an 'unfavourable impression behind me' in India, but nothing could quite redeem Eddy
from the hounding in the American press.[57] Sir Francis Knollys and
Sir Dighton Probyn were unflagging in their efforts to limit the
damage and were almost certainly behind a rebuttal printed in the
New York Herald on 22 December condemning the slander against
the prince: 'a more atrocious or a more dastardly outrage was never
perpetrated in the Press'. Christmas came and went with Prince
Eddy still overseas and Alix still holding her ground, displaying an
unwillingness to listen to the advice of her English relatives.

In the New Year the gossip of European courts was overtaken
by stunning news from Germany. After a prolonged wrestle for
power, on 20 March 1890 Kaiser Wilhelm II finally 'dropped the
pilot'. Bismarck, the very man who had been instrumental in the

unification of Germany and had consolidated the power of the German emperor, was now dismissed by this same power 'like a butler'. Vicky was quick to alert her mother to the dangers. Prince Bismarck's dismissal was 'a dangerous experiment', a first step towards her son's increasing absolutism. Without Bismarck there was no check on the grandiose aspirations of her son. 'William fancies that he can do everything himself,' she warned Queen Victoria, adding a few days later, 'I am afraid William is a most thorough despot.' She could only see an ominous future for the German Empire. 'The seeds of evil sown during the Bismarck era' were now to be nurtured by her own son, who 'has learned to play the despot from him'.[58] The queen knew that her grandson wanted good relations with Britain and she was obliged to play her part to welcome him, however sore her feelings about his treatment of Vicky.

In late April 1890 the queen made a short private trip to Darmstadt on her return from holiday in France. She was greeted at the station by her son-in-law, Louis of Hesse, and then 'dear Alicky' and two of her older sisters, Victoria and Irene, stepped into her carriage, the queen delighted to be reunited with these granddaughters with whom she always felt a special bond.[59] If she hoped for a word in private with Alix to find out whether her feelings about Eddy had changed, her opportunities were limited. A steady stream of visitors hurried across Germany to see Queen Victoria. She was overjoyed to see Vicky, who arrived with her daughters the next day. Then Wilhelm rushed to Darmstadt to speak to his grandmother. 'He came up to see me at once,' she wrote in her diary. He wanted the queen to understand that 'it would have been impossible' to go on with Bismarck, 'his violence in language and gesture had become such that he had to put a stop to it'.[60] His wife, Dona, now the proud mother of five sons, also came to pay her respects to the queen. Finally, on 28 April there was a chance for the queen to drive out privately with Alix and her father Prince Louis. It was pouring with rain but they made the best of it, driving to the beautiful Prinz Emil Garten, modelled on an English landscape garden, and then on to Secheim, a picturesque old house nearby.

Whatever passed between them, the queen finally settled her mind on the question of Eddy and Alix. On her return to Windsor Castle she confided to Vicky on 7 May 1890, 'I fear all hope of Alicky's marrying Eddy is at an end. She has written to tell him how it grieves her to pain him, but that she cannot marry him, much as she likes him as a Cousin, that she knows she wld not be happy with him & that he wld not be happy with her & that he must *not* think of her.' Alix's oldest sister, Victoria, had also written to Eddy, 'very kindly'. Evidently much pressure had been placed on Alix. 'It is a real sorrow to us and they have tried to persuade her,' the queen continued, 'but she says that if she is *forced* she will do it, but that she would be unhappy & he too.'[61]

Queen Victoria, not a woman to be opposed lightly, had a private admiration for her strong-willed granddaughter. 'She shows gt [great] strength of character as all her family & all of us wish it, & she refuses the greatest position there is'. But her seventeen-year-old granddaughter was not playing the game and she was convinced that Ella lay behind it. In July 1990 she asked Victoria of Battenberg 'to take care & <u>tell</u> Ella that no marriage for <u>Alicky in Russia</u> wld be <u>allowed</u>, then there will be <u>an end of it</u>...'[62]

5

Eddy and Hélène

'Such a marriage is utterly <u>impossible</u>.'
Queen Victoria to Prince Eddy, May 1890

Prince Eddy arrived at Folkestone in early May 1890 after a seven-month tour of the British Empire, his confidence at a low ebb following Alix's wounding refusal. He was soon back at Marlborough House in the protective embrace of his mother and his doting younger sisters. It was not long, however, before an envelope arrived from Windsor Castle bearing Queen Victoria's seal. A formal letter from the queen, imbued somehow with her indomitable spirit, could create foreboding in a young man who tended to drift on the wind. Sure enough, his grandmother began somewhat ominously with: 'I wish to say a few words about the subject of your future marriage ...'[1]

Queen Victoria pointed out to Prince Eddy that he must 'resist all the wiles and attempts of intriguers and bad women to catch you'. She had lost no time in alighting on another suitable candidate in the two weeks since reaching a final conclusion on Alix. Her second choice as a bride for Eddy was none other than Vicky's favourite youngest daughter: eighteen-year-old Princess Margaret or 'Mossy'. The queen knew Margaret as a well-balanced and highly respectful grandchild; tactful enough to seek her permission before writing to her and grateful enough to thank her grandmother for the slightest consideration.[2] Margaret had sensed that she was not top of the list of prospective brides, admitting on one occasion that she 'quite envied Alix ... being near you'.[3]

But now there were a number of reasons why the queen expected her grandson to look favourably on this most amiable German cousin. Firstly, there was a great shortage of princesses to choose from, 'for of course any Lady in Society <u>would never</u> do', the queen instructed Eddy on 19 May 1890. No one could doubt Margaret's Hohenzollern pedigree, which stretched back to Frederick the Great on her father's side and generations of British royalty on her mother's. Secondly, although the queen admitted that plain Margaret was 'not regularly pretty', nonetheless she 'has a very pretty figure'. In addition she frequently expressed a great love for 'dear England' and to cap it all, she was available and 'you will be able to see her shortly'.[4]

For Eddy the prospect of Kaiser Wilhelm's youngest sister descending on Sandringham with marriage in mind was not an attractive one. He had known his cousin Margaret for many years and did not feel drawn to her, still less to the prospect of closer ties to the Kaiser as a brother-in-law. Knowing that this match would please the forceful mother-daughter alliance between his grandmother and his Aunt Vicky, Eddy no doubt felt the pressure. But as the queen was perfectly well aware, the prospect of an alliance to a princess from the German ruling house had already sparked controversy between Eddy's parents. Although Bertie was not opposed to Margaret, the queen knew from her private secretary, Sir Henry Ponsonby, that Princess Alexandra 'would object most strongly and indeed has already done so'.[5] Ever since Prussia had invaded Denmark, the home country of Eddy's mother, Alexandra had nursed a grievance against Germany and this had found new focus in her loathing of Kaiser Wilhelm. In her view the '<u>emperor of All and Mighty Germany</u>' was 'mad' and 'a conceited ass' who was behaving 'worse and worse to his poor Mother', quite apart from being 'most frightfully rude and impertinent' to his Uncle Bertie as well as a perfect 'beast' who was unreasonably 'infuriated against <u>England</u>'.[6] She viewed the prospect of a closer unity with the mighty Hohenzollerns with alarm.

In anticipation of Queen Victoria's next move, Princess Alexandra and her daughters had also given thought to Eddy's future marriage while he was away and had arrived at a different conclusion to the queen. Most conveniently, they had discovered a *French* princess who convinced them that she had strong feelings for Eddy: eighteen-year-old Hélène of Orléans. Dark haired, blue-eyed Hélène did not have the classic beauty of Alix of Hesse, but she was pretty and had the tremendous advantage that she was not German. Her air was aristocratic, her figure tall and slim, her personality full of vitality. With her headstrong and impulsive nature, she formed a striking contrast to the detached and self-possessed Alix.

Eddy had known Hélène for some years since the French princess had spent large periods of her childhood in England. Her father, Philippe d'Orléans, Comte de Paris, although not currently in possession of a throne, had little doubt of his high social standing. But as Princess Alexandra was perfectly aware, there were immense problems with a Protestant future heir to the British throne becoming allied to a Catholic princess, one whose family history raised delicate diplomatic issues between monarchist Britain and republican France. For the fortunes of the Orléans dynasty had been intimately entwined with tempestuous French politics over the last hundred years.

—————

A century earlier, Hélène's great-great-grandfather, Louis-Philippe d'Orléans, was a man of great wealth, with the added cachet of being a cousin to the Bourbon French king, Louis XVI. His circumstances changed dramatically in 1789 during the violence of the French Revolution. France became a republic in 1792 to the rallying cry of a new revolutionary song, 'La Marseillaise', exhorting citizens to take up arms against foreign tyranny and treacherous kings. Louis-Philippe considered himself a liberal and a moderniser. He adapted to the times, changing his name to 'Citoyen Philippe Egalité' and voting for the death penalty for his cousin, the king. None of this helped him during 'the Terror' in which many thousands were deemed 'enemies of the revolution' and executed in mass killings. In November 1793, a month after Marie Antoinette was executed, Philippe Egalité in turn was carted off to the guillotine.

The Revolution was followed in nineteenth-century France by periods of stability interspersed with further insurrections in which Hélène's Orléanist forebears almost regained their former royal glory. After the Napoleonic Wars the original Bourbon royal line was restored to power in France until a second revolution in 1830 swept the Orléanist line of the family into power. Hélène's great-grandfather, Louis-Philippe, reigned for eighteen years as 'King of the French' until an economic crisis in 1848 sparked yet another revolution.

At Buckingham Palace in London, Albert came to Victoria on 25 February 1848 bearing the shocking news from France. 'The king has abdicated & left Paris,' he said. At first, it was not possible to know the fate of the French royal family. Victoria felt 'bewildered and petrified'. The centre of Paris was 'in possession of the mob who were destroying everything', she wrote in her diary. It was hard to think of anything but 'these dreadful French affairs'.[7] On 1 March came definitive news: 'Monarchy and Royalty [in France] have been abolished,' she recorded. 'The people are going on in a disgusting way.' Victoria offered sanctuary to the exiled French king, who was a distant relation by marriage: his daughter, Louise, had married the queen's Uncle Leopold of the Belgians in 1832. Now the 'King of the French' was reduced to fleeing his country as plain 'Mr Smith', 'wearing spectacles … a cap & his whiskers shaved off' and travelling as an ordinary passenger, Queen Victoria wrote on 4 March 1848. 'How indescribable does that sound?'[8]

For years there seemed no hope of an Orléanist restoration and Hélène's forebears adapted to life in exile at Claremont, near Esher in Surrey. As a grandson of the exiled Louis-Philippe, her father was styled 'Prince Royal', and became a pretender to the French throne when his own father had a fatal carriage accident. Meanwhile the Second French Republic, forged in the heady idealism of 1848, was undermined within three years by Napoleon's nephew, who consolidated power and declared himself Emperor Napoleon III. His downfall came twenty years later during the

German wars of unification, which culminated in war between France and Prussia. With Napoleon III's surrender in 1870, a Third French Republic was born. But after the ignominious French defeat, it was opposed by the radical 'Paris Commune', which briefly seized power in the French capital.

Once again, Queen Victoria followed the violent insurrection in troubled Paris, transfixed. Telegrams poured into Osborne House in the spring of 1871. The news from France was 'dreadful', she wrote on 8 April. 'The Commune has everything their own way & they go on quite as in the days of the old Revolution in the last century, though they have not yet proceeded to commit all the same horrors ... They have burnt the guillotine and shot people instead.'[9] For communists such as Karl Marx, the Paris Commune, led by socialists, anarchists and radicals, was blazing a trail for a radical new model of 'revolutionary government'. For the British queen, the Commune was appalling, 'nothing can exceed its state of Moral and Physical degradation'. The possibility that the radical ideas of the excitable French might spread to Britain was much discussed at Osborne.[10] The French government struggled to regain order during May. The magnificent imperial Tuileries Palace went up in flames and there were 'fires raging in every direction and great fears for the Louvre', the queen wrote on 25 May. Two days later she was stunned when the 'horrid Communists' shot the 'wretched Archbishop' and dozens of prisoners. The Third French Republic regained control by the end of May but faced a changed Europe. Newly unified Germany was now the greatest power on the continent.

The troubled Third French Republic wrestled not only with the rise of Germany and then the extreme left of the Paris Commune, but also with the political right who argued for a return of the monarchy. The government permitted the Orléans family to return from exile in June 1871, the very month that Hélène was born in Twickenham on the outskirts of London. The Comte took his family back to Paris and a significant part of the Orléans fortune was restored, but his own grandiose ambitions created problems. At the marriage of his eldest daughter, Princess Amélie, in 1886 to the heir to the Portuguese throne, Prince Carlos, the

Comte proved just a little too kingly and flamboyant, a rallying point for French royalists. The republican government expelled the pretender to the throne and fourteen-year-old Hélène returned with her family to exile in England, taking up residence at Sheen House in Richmond.

The Comte de Paris and his wife, the formidable, cigar-smoking Marie Isabelle d'Orléans, a crack shot who could hold her own with any honourables on the hunting grounds, became an accepted part of Bertie and Alexandra's circle. Queen Victoria, too, regularly invited 'The Paris' as she called him, to royal events. Nonetheless, she was astute enough to realise that the British must not offend their closest neighbour, republican France. Any match between the English throne and a daughter of the exiled pretender to the French throne could pose delicate complications.

But Princess Alexandra saw only that the Comte de Paris's second daughter, Princess Hélène, combined Parisian chic with a lively personality that made her a much more sympathetic companion for her son than Alix of Hesse. She and her daughters were enthralled over the winter of 1890 when the French princess hinted that she had feelings for Eddy. When Eddy returned from India his sisters could not contain the secret for long. 'The girls told me that dear Hélène had been fond of me for some time,' he confided to his brother George. He admitted this was a surprise for Hélène 'never showed it in any way', but his sisters were adamant: 'the girls constantly told me how she liked me'.[11] There was little Eddy could do that month to find out Hélène's feelings for himself since she was abroad on a European tour. But even before the prince had a chance to advance his interests, somehow his all-seeing grandmama appeared to know what was in his mind.

'I wish to say that I heard it rumoured that you had been thinking and talking to Princesse Hélène d'Orléans!' Queen Victoria wrote appalled on 19 May 1890. 'I can't believe this for you know that I told you ... that such a marriage is utterly impossible.'[12] For almost two centuries, since Parliament's Act of Settlement of 1701, no Catholic or person married to a Catholic could accede to the throne. If Eddy proceeded with the marriage it would provoke a constitutional crisis. The queen instructed him to steer well clear of the French princess. 'None of our family can marry a catholic without losing all their rights ... You should avoid meeting her as much as possible,' she ordered.[13]

Eddy did the exact opposite, encouraged by his mother. The queen had just conferred on the prince a new title, 'Duke of Clarence and Avondale', bringing him new responsibilities as a peer, but that very week he disobeyed her order, writing encouragingly to Hélène on 27 May. 'Dearest Hélène ... how pleased I am to hear you have returned again,' he began. Her 'nice little letter' had given him 'so much pleasure while I was in India'. He had been delighted 'to know that you had not quite forgotten me, although I was so far away'. He expressed a desire to see her 'before very long and be able to tell you something of my travels which may interest you'.[14] On cue, Eddy's sister Louise, the Duchess of Fife, invited Hélène to her home at Sheen Lodge. This soon proved to be a most convenient rendezvous where romance blossomed rapidly, nurtured by the women of the Wales family in secret opposition to 'grandmama queen'.

Eddy soon found that whereas Alix of Hesse had been hard to read, her inner feelings unassailable and with, he detected, a certain coldness towards him, the French princess was agreeably frank and direct, with a warmth that was hard to resist. He saw that she was 'everything that is nice in a girl ... and gradually perceived that she really liked me', he told George. 'Well this went on till one day she came to lunch and came up to the girls' room afterwards.'[15] Falteringly, charmingly, Hélène came to reveal that she had been deeply in love with him for several years but had felt unable to show her feelings. Knowing full well that Eddy was destined for Alix, she had admired from a distance, her devotion undimmed. For Eddy this was a revelation. Could it be possible, after the fruitless years of courting Alix, that this French princess had all along been nurturing a secret passion for him? Certainly Hélène had been very private about her feelings. Could she really be in love with him? Or was this what his grandmother referred to as the 'wiles and attempts of intriguers' out to snare him?[16] That very day the subject ran quickly to marriage, 'but then the unfortunate point of religion came in', Eddy confided to George, and Hélène 'feared it was quite impossible to think of marrying or anything of that sort'.[17]

Unknown to Eddy, within two weeks of his daughter's return, the aspiring Catholic Comte was looking for a loophole to find out whether there was a way around the religious problem. After generations of his family seeking to restore their fortunes in France, suddenly a glorious rise to the British throne had opened up before him. The Comte's first daughter had already become Queen of Portugal. If his second daughter succeeded in marrying a future heir to the British throne, the ascendancy of the House of Orléans, for so long adrift, would be secure. He saw the prospect in most honourable terms. This could be a watershed year between Catholic and Protestant faiths. Could the laws of the Catholic Church bend a little to accommodate the circumstances? For example, the Catholic Church required that the offspring of a mixed marriage must be brought up as Catholics, but any heirs to the British throne had to be brought up as Protestants. Could the Catholic Church contemplate granting permission for children of a mixed marriage to be brought up as Protestants? What were the prospects of a royal marriage between his Catholic daughter and Protestant second heir to the throne? He went to seek the advice of the most senior Catholic prelate in the country, Cardinal Manning, Archbishop of Westminster.

The archbishop 'weighed carefully and anxiously' the points raised by the French Comte. Regarding the Catholic law that children of Catholics should be raised as Catholics, this was a 'natural and divine law', he concluded on 22 June 1890, from which the pope had never permitted any deviation. The archbishop had applied this law all his life and having searched his conscience, would find it 'impossible to act otherwise'. The only alternative was to alter the laws of England by changing 'Laws of Succession' so that a Protestant king could raise Catholic children. The archbishop was convinced that this would be politically and morally unacceptable and that 'the slightest contact of the Catholic church with the public and political life of the country' would be met with the greatest hostility. He was conscious that this was an issue that affected not just the 'happiness of the two Families' but also 'the salvation of souls', and so for the archbishop there was no hope for the marriage.[18]

The Comte was nothing if not ambitious. He felt the need for a second opinion and began to contemplate approaching the highest Catholic authority in the world: the pope. Drafts survive in the Comte's hand showing that he considered this a most commendable cause. 'The heir to the throne of Henry VIII and William of Orange wants to be able to seek the hand of a Catholic princess of the highest lineage,' he wrote. The prince would have to forfeit his throne to marry the Catholic princess, but was it not possible for the Catholic Church to change the rules? 'There must be no stipulations on the religion of the children who will be born of this marriage,' he continued. The Comte saw a great destiny for Prince Eddy if he married a Catholic queen: 'will not all Europe see this as a great event?'[19] Although not generally thought of as Europe's most illustrious prince, Eddy was about to have his hour of greatness thrust upon him.

Almost 2,000 miles away in St Petersburg, the very princess who had just declared her love for Prince Eddy was also being short-listed by the Russian tsar and tsarina as a suitable consort for the tsarevich. Envoys from Alexander III considered the French princess, Hélène, a most promising candidate, who was said to possess great charm and self-confidence. But the tsar faced opposition from Nicholas, supported by Ella, who would not give up on Alix of Hesse.

Nicholas first raised the question of marrying Alix with his father in 1889 after her visit to St Petersburg, but Alexander III would not give his consent, convinced that Alix of Hesse was not suitable. The very qualities in Alix that appealed to Queen Victoria, such as her antipathy to the social whirl, were seen as failings in the Russian court. The princess from Darmstadt was too shy and gauche to be an empress, unable to measure up to what was required in the imposing Russian court. Queen Victoria soon discovered that she had an ally in the Russian emperor and warned Victoria of Battenberg, 'moreover Minnie [Empress Maria] does not <u>wish</u> it. In short <u>that</u> cld <u>not</u> be.'[20] The queen was not pleased to learn that within weeks of issuing instructions to Victoria of Battenberg that no marriage between Alix and Nicky 'wld be <u>allowed</u>', Alix was back in Russia again at Ella's invitation, with her father and oldest sister.

Ella was overjoyed. She had 'longed for them to come', she told the queen. They stayed at Sergei's country house, Ilinskoye, a private estate of over 2,000 acres some forty miles from Moscow. The late summer of 1890 passed and they relished the timeless tranquillity of the place, boating, fishing and bathing on the River Mosca, playing lawn tennis or chatting on the balcony that ran the length of the first floor. There were carriage tours to meet Ella's friends in the neighbourhood, among them Prince Felix Yusopov, one of the richest men in Russia. Yusopov had a 'palace-like country house', observed Victoria of Battenberg, reminiscent of Versailles with its fountains, statuary and an eighteenth-century theatre. Even the pigs in the piggery enjoyed the latest modern novelty, electric light.[21]

Nothing occurred in her visit to alert Alix to the dangers of the great injustices of Russian society as depicted by her grandmother. Ella presided with great charm over village fetes and fairs, which gave Alix a brief glimpse of the lives of the poor. The peasants appeared to Alix to be 'good natured' and deeply respectful to the royal party, welcoming '*their* Grand Duchess'.[22] Russia once again worked its magic on Alix, who was beguiled by the beauty of the scenery and the apparently simple, trusting relationship between the peasants and the nobility. She had been expecting to see Nicholas but a last-minute change in his schedule made this impossible.[23] It is likely that the emperor intervened to keep them apart.

Queen Victoria was exasperated to learn that Ella continued to conspire to bring Alix and Nicky together, and she expressed her disapproval in the strongest terms to Victoria of Battenberg on 29 December 1890: 'I had <u>your assurance</u> that <u>nothing was</u> to be <u>feared</u> in that quarter, but I <u>know</u> it <u>for certain</u>, that in spite of <u>all your</u> (Papa, Ernie's & your) <u>objections</u> & still more <u>contrary</u> to the <u>positive</u> wish of <u>his Parents</u> who do <u>not wish</u> him to <u>marry A</u> ... in spite of all this, behind <u>all</u> your backs, Ella & S [Serge] do <u>all</u> they <u>can</u> to bring it <u>about</u>, encouraging and even urging the Boy to do it!'[24] The queen's source was Princess Alexandra, who had been informed by her sister, the tsarina herself, 'who is very much annoyed abt it', she continued, adding that Victoria of Battenberg must '<u>never</u>' reveal her source. But now Queen Victoria had had enough. Beautiful Ella was beyond any kind advice. It was time to insist on firm rules. '<u>This</u> must <u>not</u> be <u>allowed to go on</u>. Papa <u>must</u> put his foot down & there <u>must</u> be no more visits of Alicky to Russia,' she ordered with her usual imperiousness. 'He <u>must</u> & <u>you</u> and Ernie must insist on a <u>stop</u> being put to the whole affair. The state of Russia is <u>so bad,</u> so rotten, that at any moment something dreadful might happen & tho' it may not signify to Ella, the wife of the Thronfolger [heir to the throne] is in a most difficult and precarious position.'[25]

The queen was well informed about the continuing worries over the security of the Russian royal family through the tsarina, 'Aunt Minnie'. For greater safety, Alexander III had settled his family in the Gatchina Palace, some thirty miles south of St Petersburg, which had the air of a fortress, with its defence wall, a moat, cannon and hexagonal towers. The imperial family settled in the Arsenal wing and the palace soon became known as 'the Citadel of Autocracy'. The revolutionaries responded to Alexander III's repressive regime by developing underground terrorist cells, but these were frequently infiltrated by his secret police, the dreaded Okhrana.

In February 1887 the Okhrana learned of a new plot to assassinate the tsar and fifteen suspects were arrested. Five of the terrorists were hanged, including a twenty-one-year-old science student at St Petersburg called Alexander Ulyanov, who admitted responsibility for making the bombs.[26] Like the members of the People's Will before him, Ulyanov made a heroic but doomed stand in the courtroom, pointing out the injustices of tsarist Russia and the rightness of his cause and insisting he would die for his country. News of frightening incidents continued to reach the British press. The tsar had another narrow escape from assassination seven months later at Kutais in Georgia. A Kouban Cossack was arrested for 'having upon him explosives in a handy form', claimed the *London Evening Standard*. He was a member of the South Russia Revolutionary Society 'and aimed to make an attempt on the Emperor's life'.[27] Queen Victoria did not want this kind of alarming future for Alix and was reassured by the fact that the emperor and empress also did not support the match.

Ironically, in their search for a suitable princess for Nicholas the tsar's advisors alighted on one of the very candidates Queen Victoria had favoured for Eddy: Princess Margaret. A Hohenzollern princess who was accustomed to the pressures of the court at Berlin would be a far more suitable consort than Alix. Margaret had a reputation for being outgoing and socially at ease and was well liked in the royal family.[28] Nicholas's protest that he would rather spend his life in a monastery than marry Margaret was ignored by his father. But as Nicholas's family weighed up the best bride for him, Princess Hélène had an advantage over her German rival. For Alexander III, a French princess brought the added advantage of helping to symbolise a new bond being forged between autocratic Russia and republican France.

Since Bismarck's Triple Alliance of 1882, in which the central European countries of Germany, Austria-Hungary and Italy had formed a military agreement, both Russia and France appeared exposed. A great swathe of central Europe was pro-German. To the east, Germany and her allies threatened Russia's border with Europe. To the west, France feared the growing strength of Germany on her northern border. For years Bismarck had built an intricate web of secret alliances to balance the Triple Alliance. He strengthened German ties with Russia firstly through the 'League of Three Emperors', a treaty of neutrality between Germany, Austria-Hungary and Russia that aimed to preserve European monarchies against republican France. When this failed owing to differences between Austria and Russia in eastern Europe, Bismarck negotiated a separate treaty between Germany and Russia known as the 'Reinsurance Treaty', which continued to isolate France and provide safeguards if Germany was attacked by France, or Russia by Austria.

During the crisis of Bismarck's dismissal in 1890, the Iron Chancellor's 'Reinsurance Treaty' with Russia was due for renewal, but Wilhelm and his new chancellor, Count Leo von Caprivi, declined to do so. This was a crucial choice. The future of Russo-German relations hung on this decision. Neither the Kaiser nor Caprivi fully appreciated the diplomatic safety net fashioned by Bismarck.[29] Alexander III had hoped to renew the secret treaty but was snubbed. Wilhelm's changeability and capricious statements on foreign policy soon heightened tensions with Russia.

Warily, the autocratic tsar began to look to republican France, which was investing heavily in Russian infrastructure. Industry was booming in Russia in the 1890s; iron and steel in the Ukraine, oil in Baku, and railways that began to criss-cross the country. French funds helped to oil the wheels and symbolise the unlikely new friendship. A pretty French bride and young Russian groom might serve as an iconic bond between their two countries. Nicholas hated finding himself in conflict with his mother, who began to drop hints about the suitability of the French princess as the perfect wife and empress. The tsarevich knew he could not disregard the wishes of his parents.

In July 1890 Prince Eddy returned to his regiment in York, but his mother and sisters hatched a plan that would help to advance his cause. Eddy's sister, the Duchess of Fife, invited him, Hélène and her parents to her husband's sporting estate at Mar Lodge in the Scottish Highlands five miles from Braemar. Queen Victoria was still at Osborne, unaware of these forbidden developments. The fact that a message reached the Comte de Paris from the queen, in which she charged him 'to avoid all meetings' between his daughter, Hélène, and Eddy, proved no impediment. By a rather convenient 'ill fortune' – as he later put it – the communication from the queen came the day *after* his arrival at Mar Lodge. 'Had I received it the day before, we would not have gone there,' he exonerated himself to the queen later.[30]

While Hélène's father had been doing his best to resolve the religious issue by tackling the saintly guardians of sin, Eddy's father was preoccupied with a rather more earthly matter, possibly arising from his son's 'dissipations'. With unfortunate timing, just as love and marriage appeared almost within his grasp, Prince Eddy was suffering from ill-health once more. Historians have speculated that this was a recurrence of his sexual infection.[31] He was taken ill in late July with a 'sharpish attack of fever' and the young locum who was visiting him daily, Dr Alfred Fripp, was invited to accompany him to the Highlands. Fripp was most discreet about his diagnosis in his letters home, although he did reveal that he had to give detailed directions about Eddy's diet and also limit his smoking since the prince 'smokes himself until he is stupid'. Fripp urged his own parents not to breathe a word of this, since the Prince of Wales 'is afraid the public will get the impression that his son is a chronic invalid'.[31]

Journalists, however, were not completely fooled. At Aberdeen Station the prince was spotted by one reporter who noticed that he 'looked jaded and ill, heavy-eyed and sallow complexioned', and with Dr Fripp in 'constant attendance'.[32] The press soon worked out that the prince was in the care of a doctor staying close at hand in the Fife Arms Hotel. Fripp worried that 'the cat is out of the bag', and indeed not all of the press was obliging enough to write – as claimed – that the prince had been involved in a riding accident.[33] The *Leeds Times* on 30 August considered the prince was 'really weak' and 'suffering from a marked general debility'.[34] For the *Yorkshire Post* there was 'not the slightest foundation' for claims made in a number of 'foolish journals' that the prince 'was suffering from Indian fever'.[35] As the mystery deepened, one reporter commented angrily in the *Sheffield Evening Telegraph* on 28 August that 'no one is told the nature of the illness which has now continued in a more or less degree for several weeks'. The *Huddersfield Chronicle* had a solution: the prince was 'sick with a malady common to youth: namely love'.[36]

The prince may have been pale and sallow but he was indeed blissfully happy as he spent enchanted days at Mar Lodge with

Princess Hélène. 'I naturally got to like, or rather, to love her, by the manner she showed her affection for me which I soon found out,' Eddy explained to his brother George.[37] The relationship between Eddy and Hélène blossomed, quickly running into open declarations of love. 'I had a long talk to Motherdear about the dear girl and she said if I really wished to win her, it was to show her how fond I was of her and then try and persuade her to change [her religion] for my sake.'[38]

Eddy soon understood that for a Catholic, changing religion 'is a terrible thing' like a crime, he told George. At first Hélène would not even contemplate such a step. 'I had a hard job of it as you may imagine and Motherdear also talked to her about it.' The poor girl, he continued, was pulled in all directions and did not know what to do, until finally she 'told me she would do anything for me. So at last with a great effort she said she would do this great thing for my sake.' Eddy saw this as a 'noble act' on Hélène's part, an act of immense sacrifice. Here was the confirmation that she loved him.[39] At last he dared to propose – and to his amazement she accepted. This was the moment to exchange rings, which would mark their engagement without complications. The prince was ecstatic. For him it was a 'blessed day' that he would never forget. He had solved the conundrum of royal love: here was a pretty princess who declared her love for him and who he, in turn, felt he could love. There was just one outstanding obstacle: 'Grandmama Queen'.

'Motherdear hit upon a capital solution,' Eddy related to George, although it 'rather took me aback at first'. Alexandra, like Eddy, was 'in such a state of excitement that I hardly know where to begin', she confided in her youngest son, George. 'What do you think. Dear <u>Eddy</u> and sweet <u>lovely</u> Hélène are <u>engaged</u> to each other! Altho' still a <u>dead secret</u> so you must hold yr <u>tongue!</u>'[40] The princess had concocted a little scheme that just might work on her mother-in-law. For all Queen Victoria's forbidding persona, Alexandra recognised that she had a strong romantic streak. The queen had just arrived at Balmoral, where she was likely to be at her most relaxed and off guard. Alexandra concluded that Eddy and Hélène must make a direct personal appeal – something impulsive and passionate. If they explained their deep love for one another the queen could only be moved.

Queen Victoria was greeted with the customary agreeable sense of order when she arrived at Balmoral on 26 August 1890. The grounds were pleasantly green and 'all my Highlanders with the pipes [were] drawn up on the lawn'.[41] The queen was accompanied by Beatrice and her family and the unvarying Balmoral routine was quickly restored. It was a cold, wet morning on 29 August when she took presents to people on the estate. After luncheon, Alexandra arrived with Eddy, Hélène and two of her daughters. Hélène's presence was innocently explained away on the grounds that she and her parents were visiting Mar Lodge. After a while the queen retired for some quiet to her rooms, her suspicions still not aroused. It was not long before there was a knock on the door. There was a messenger. Prince Albert Victor wished to speak with her. The queen granted her permission.

Eddy took Hélène's hand in his and led her down the interminable corridors towards the queen's apartments. He felt certain that his grandmother would find grounds to be angry both at the prospective liaison and the intriguing behind her back. 'You can imagine what a thing to go through,' he told his brother George. It was difficult to predict how the elderly queen might behave or whether she even understood the heated passions of youth. 'I did not at all relish the idea,' he continued.[42] The queen had an extraordinary ability to get her own way, however unreasonable her argument. This might be his last time with Hélène. With mounting anxiety they entered her room. Each declared their undying devotion to the other and awaited the queen's response.

But his grandmother softened on meeting the charming possible reformer of Eddy. The formidably astute and perceptive matron of Europe momentarily suspended disbelief. What was abundantly plain to Queen Victoria was that standing before her, in the pleasing shape of this dark-haired, wide-eyed princess with the headstrong temperament, was the very thing she was looking for. The French princess exuded inner strength and conviction; her good looks and stamina were exactly what was required to improve the breeding of the dynasty. Already she appeared to

have inspired Eddy into this uncharacteristically dynamic course
of action.

After some discussion to ascertain the strength of their feelings
for one another, Queen Victoria asked whether Hélène would be
prepared to give up her Catholic religion. The queen had met her
match. The French princess, eyes full of emotion, tears on her
cheeks, spoke with great passion: 'For him, only for him. Oh! Do
help pray do,' she cried. If the queen would only consent, Eddy
pleaded, 'I shall be grateful to you to the end of my life'.[43]

To his immense relief Queen Victoria succumbed to the
romance of it all. She was prepared to accept the marriage. The
queen 'promised to help us as much as possible', Eddy confided
to George, 'and I have been to see her several times since'. He
admitted that enlisting his grandmother's support had rested on a
little deception. She had been much swayed by the romantic idea
of a young couple so much in love that they had settled on this
impulsive appeal for themselves. Her lethargic grandson, at last,
appeared to be acting decisively on his own account. 'This as you
know was not quite true,' Eddy told George, 'but she believed it
all and was quite pleased.'[44] In the heat of the moment Eddy had
lied outright to his grandmother: 'I have not told Mama even,' he
had said.[45] Princess Alexandra now colluded with Eddy, writing
to the queen after the crucial interview as though she had only just
heard. 'What astounding but delightful news,' she exclaimed, all
innocence, on 30 August. The 'two loving hearts' were attached
'far more deeply than we had any idea of …'[46]

The queen was so taken with Hélène that she spoke that very
day with Arthur Balfour, the minister in attendance at Balmoral
who, most conveniently, was also a nephew to the prime minister,
Lord Salisbury. At stake was a constitutional issue: could Eddy
marry a former Roman Catholic or would he have to abandon
his future throne? The queen was at her persuasive best. She
was extremely keen to see 'the young man married', she said,
and there was 'a dearth of suitable Protestant princesses'. As
Balfour explained to his uncle, 'all the little German princesses
of a marriageable age are, according to her, totally ignorant of the
world and utterly unfit for the position'. By contrast the queen

regarded Hélène as 'clever' and 'healthy withal' – the very woman she was looking for who had the potential to 'be the making of her husband'. Balfour warned the prime minister that the 'sovereign has been touched through the grandmother', she was in 'melting mood', and was 'absolutely won over to the marriage'.[47]

This weighty matter, brought to the prime minister's attention at the weekend in a rush of female emotion – 'they are moved even to tears', Balfour warned him – prompted Lord Salisbury once again to seek various stalling tactics. The girl should meet with the Archbishop of Canterbury, of course, and what did her father say about the question of her religion? Evidently there was some amusement for both uncle and nephew over the shortage of royal brides, for Balfour wrote again on Saturday 30 August with further clarification on this issue. 'The Hesse girl won't have him,' Balfour explained, and that apparently left only 'a Mecklenburgh and two Anhalt princesses … According to Her Majesty they are all three ugly, unhealthy, and idiotic'; and to boot, 'penniless and narrow-minded … they might do perhaps … for a younger son but &c &c …' Balfour was unimpressed with the notion that the 'heroine' had been in love since the age of sixteen, still less with the 'ingenious theory which makes apostacy the conclusive mark of disinterested love'.[48]

Queen Victoria thought little of taking on the flattening combination of Salisbury and his nephew, not to mention the Lord Chancellor. She intended to do 'all in my power' to promote 'dear Eddy's and sweet Hélène's ardent wishes!' she told Bertie on 7 September. Two days later the queen wrote again with detailed points of strategy and by 20 September she felt she was making headway.[49] Meanwhile Bertie was secretly embroiled in diplomacy of an even more delicate kind. When the queen gave her blessing to the match, he had written at once to his comptroller, Sir Dighton Probyn, who was at Mar with Alexandra. Bertie advised that Dr Fripp must 'have an interview' with his wife, 'and tell her candidly what he has said to you, so that she may know how matters are, which are far more serious than she has any idea of …' Probyn duly passed Bertie's orders on to Dr Fripp. 'Hide nothing from the princess,' he advised. Alexandra, at last,

was to learn the truth about her son's ailments and their implications. Probyn also urged the doctor to do all he could to ensure a
'permanent restoration to health, no mere tinkering up for a few
years but a lasting cure. The gout and *every other ailment must be
completely eradicated* from the system.'[50]

According to some writers it was not just 'the gout' that had
to be eliminated. Patricia Cornwell has concluded that there was
another mopping-up operation discreetly underway around this
time concerning 'two ladies of low standing'. The more daring one,
a 'Miss Maude Richardson', was allegedly blackmailing the prince
and the money that had already changed hands had prompted
further demands. Under the vigilant eye of the barrister George
Lewis, who specialised in representing wealthy clients caught up
in such careless follies, the matter was being unobtrusively cleared
up.[51] However, the authenticity of the letters Eddy is supposed to
have drafted to George Lewis has been questioned.[52]

Meanwhile, the bride-to-be, blissfully unaware of any troubling secrets of the groom, left Balmoral to tackle one of her own.
Although her father, the Comte de Paris, had initially encouraged
the match, she knew that he assumed she would remain a Catholic.
For him this was an inviolable precept, his strength of feeling
recently affirmed by the Archbishop of Westminster. Yet somehow, carried away on impulse – first with Eddy, then the Princess
of Wales, and now before the queen of Great Britain – Hélène
had agreed to change her religion. Until the age of twenty-five she
needed her father's permission to take such a step. Eddy wrote
sympathetically on 31 August, 'I hope you won't worry yourself
too much, you darling, although I know you have a terribly hard
task before you. But the sooner it is done the better I think, and
get the worst over, for it must come. What would I not do to help
you in this …'[53]

When the Comte learned what had happened he was angry.
His daughter had 'blurted out words' to the queen 'whose significance she cannot measure', he told his wife, Isabella.[54] For Hélène
to abandon her faith would potentially be to expose him and his
family to serious criticism. Many might see her conversion as a
matter of selfish ambition to become the queen of Great Britain.

While the Comte saw his daughter's motives as pure and disinterested, it was a matter of honour, he explained. If she changed her religion for marriage she would lose the support of Catholics and Protestants alike for abandoning the faith in which she had been confirmed. Catholics would hate her for her unfaithfulness; Protestants would have no reason to trust her. Politically, too, he could now see the problems. The French Republic might take offence at the match and the Germans could feel threatened by a British-French marital alliance. The Comte's conversation with his daughter was 'serious and painful', Isabella told Alexandra on 31 August. Her husband 'will never give his consent to a marriage made under such conditions', she wrote. She believed Eddy and Hélène must wait for seven years until her father's consent was no longer needed. 'God will inspire us, I am sure. Console your son as I am trying to console Hélène.'[55]

Meanwhile Eddy was sublimely happy, intoxicated with love. The prince, portrayed for years as 'backward' and 'abnormally dormant', proved to be perfectly articulate in expressing his love. He wrote almost every day to 'my own sweet darling' or 'my own beloved one'. Her letters were treasured, he told her, as he read them 'over and over again':

> To think that a darling like you should really love so much this unworthy creature, which I know and feel I am, is too lovely for words. You will be all in all to me, which, however, you are now indeed, my darling, and ever in my thoughts, night and day ... It makes me half-wild to think I have no power to help you now in your distress you darling ... The more I think of it all the more dear you are to me, and that you should have gone through all this for my sake too, is indeed the truest devotion. You are indeed to me an angel upon the earth, and the sweetest one too that ever lived, or was ever dear to a man ...[56]

Prince Eddy's great romance gave him new confidence, creating an uncharacteristic courage when dealing with 'Grandmama queen'. He told his brother George that he would 'never give up this dear girl' and found that a little deception came easily.[57]

'Grandmama came over here to tea on Monday and was as nice as could be about it all,' he told Hélène on 2 September. 'But I won't tell her yet what your Papa has said, for I think it best to keep it from her for the present ...' He was also worried that Hélène's father might be angry if he found out that they were writing to each other and forbid the correspondence. 'Tell me ... if there is any fear of this for if so, I will send my letters through Louise,' he wrote to Hélène a week later.[58] Fired with the idea of love he felt he could take on his grandmama, the Comte and the British government. 'I feel you are more than half mine already, and it would take a very little to make you mine altogether and for good and all ... I feel as if I could do anything and stick at nothing, and very little persuasion would induce me to carry you off ... and then people might say what they liked and I would gladly bear the consequences ... I feel I could do anything for you my darling.'[59] When the Comte went away, he begged 'my own sweet darling' to wear the ring he had given her. 'Whenever I look at the one you gave me, it reminds me of the day we exchanged and the day you promised to be mine, and I yours, forever,' he told her on 21 September 1890, the hot red wax of his letters sealed by two entwined hearts. 'Nothing on Earth would turn my resolve to stick to you whatever happens,' he assured her. 'Even if I had to wait 50 years or more.'

The records do not reveal at what stage Dr Fripp had his 'little talk' with Princess Alexandra nor whether any word of this reached Hélène. But they show in mid-September that Queen Victoria herself expressed a desire to speak to Dr Fripp about her grandson. Her sudden arrival at Abergeldie put the household in a fluster. The doctor was relaxing in a hot bath when his valet rushed in with news that he was about to be presented to the queen by the Prince of Wales. Feeling hot and bothered, Fripp suddenly found himself ushered in before the queen, her sober presence summoning up the essence of respectability. Momentarily at a loss, he instinctively raised his voice, 'bellowing' as he did with Princess Alexandra. 'I am not deaf!' the queen corrected him. She, too, felt awkward. The prudish queen had such an abhorrence of medical examinations that her own highly uncomfortable prolapsed womb was only discovered after her death. Enquiries of a more intimate or sexual nature were not within her customary range. Dr Fripp formed the impression she was trying to put him at his ease. The conversation began with watercolours and moved on to painting in general followed by polite enquiries about Fripp's good father – before the queen finally broached the subject. What was the state of the Duke of Clarence's health? With Bertie standing there like an adjudicator, making absolutely sure the doctor imparted as little as possible of a sensitive nature to his mother, Fripp found himself responding in a reassuring manner, revealing little. The queen seemed satisfied and brought the audience to an end.[60]

While the prince was convinced that love would win through, Hélène's resolve began to falter during October. Although she may not have known of her fiancé's secret health problems, her father's claims that the proposed marriage was 'a crime' and 'vile cowardice' began to undermine her confidence. Hélène did not wait for others to tell her what to do. She decided to go to the Vatican to see Pope Leo XIII for herself and did not confide in her fiancé until her travel plans were finalised. 'I owe it to my conscience to remain Catholic,' she wrote to Eddy on 27 October from Stowe House. 'Only one person in the world can lower the barriers, the obstacles and that is the Pope.' She was ready to throw herself at his feet. There was no chance for Eddy to intervene. 'When you receive this letter I will have already left.' The next morning she added a few more words, hoping that she had not 'lost your feelings'. Knowing 'the nobility' of his heart, she wrote, 'you would never want to unite your fate to a woman who, even for love of you, committed a dishonourable act in her own eyes'.[61]

Hélène travelled incognito with friends of her parents, the Baron and Baroness de Charette. It took three days for the small and sombre party to travel south to Rome. Hélène drafted a message to explain her predicament to the pope and they were granted an interview a few days later. Dusk was gathering, shrouding the vast complex of the Vatican in a strange half-light, the Baron observed, yet Hélène recognised the magnificent St Peter's Basilica at once.

As they made their way across St Peter's Square the Baron realised that Hélène was 'trembling, her emotions reaching a peak': her future was out of her hands. A cardinal came to greet them, ushering them down narrow corridors that gave onto a large and unexpectedly bright room. There was an elderly man in a white cassock, sitting on his throne. The pope indicated to the princess to sit beside him and the Baron spoke for a while to allow Hélène the chance to regain her composure before they left her to speak privately.

After a while the Baron heard a bell summoning them to return. They found Hélène pleading her cause, 'in tears by the Holy Father's knee'. The Baron was much moved to see the Holy Father 'reaching out with both his hands to the princess who pressed them over her heart'. She was crying and he 'looked on with great compassion' at this 'Daughter of France' at his feet, 'imploring forgiveness and mercy for her first and only love!' But the pope saw his duty clearly. 'It is useless, you know that I cannot compromise on the principles I represent,' he said.[62]

Eddy was distraught when Hélène's letter arrived at Sandringham with the news. 'Your last has made me feel quite miserable,' he wrote on 7 November. 'But I will never give up hope as long as I have life in my wretched body ...' He could not help himself, he explained, he thought of her from morning till night. 'You are beloved by me more than any woman in the world. It is quite impossible I could ever love another woman again.' He seriously considered abdicating his throne. This was an unexpected deviation from her plan that Queen Victoria found 'extremely annoying'.[63] Bertie's private secretary, Sir Francis Knollys, wrote to Sir Henry Ponsonby with reassurance. 'I doubt from what you write to me whether the queen understands Prince Eddy's character,' he began. 'She certainly does not if she believes he could marry Princess Hélène "at all costs".' Eddy had been making all sorts of wild claims, 'but he would no more carry his threats into execution ... than he would attempt to jump over the moon'.[64] Bertie knew more about his son than his wife or his mother and evidently felt that the queen had allowed herself to be taken in. By December, Bertie had identified another suitable bride, the

pretty Princess of Saxe Altenburg, who 'would be snapped up
if they did not look sharp'. He was 'a little annoyed' with his
mother, Knollys revealed to Ponsonby, since 'the queen is trying
to persuade his son to wait for the other one'. This was 'running
after a shadow', he felt, 'but if the queen encourages Prince Eddy
to hope that there is still a chance of the French princess I am
afraid he will not think of anyone else'.[65]

Eddy was not to be deflected by the Altenburg princess. He
continued with long, devoted letters to Hélène, from Scotland in
the autumn, Sandringham over Christmas, Osborne in the New
Year, and his Cavalry Barracks in January 1891. In February he
confided to his brother that he would 'never give in' and 'shall feel
the happiest man in England if it only comes right some day'.[66] He
had absolute faith in his future with Hélène. He was convinced of
her love. Somehow they would make it happen; she could change
her religion at the age of twenty-five. They swapped treasured
mementos, photographs, lockets, hair, seals and other tokens of
affection with Eddy signing in desperation, 'your devoted lover
for life'.

But on 1 May 1891 Hélène finally wrote a letter that left no
room for hope. 'The political obstacles are insurmountable,' she
explained, and as for those raised by religion, 'I cannot dishonour
you and I will not cast them aside ... I must ask you to release me
from my word ... I beg you, do not try to fight against my decision, it is irrevocable, we must not see one another again. Do your
duty as an English prince without hesitation and forget me ...'[67]
The words were so final, with no vestige of hope, that she thought
it best for her mother to deliver the letter by hand.

It took the French countess, Isabella, three weeks before she
was able to see Princess Alexandra and her son. When they finally
met on 29 May 1891 the scene was 'terrible', Isabella reported to
her daughter. There was no easy way to break the news; she only
found 'the courage to bear such emotions' because she loved her
daughter deeply. Over the course of two and a half hours, first
with Alexandra, then with Eddy, she tried to explain that it was
finished. Eddy's confidence was demolished. He found it hard to
believe that Hélène, 'of her own free will', had decided 'that it all

should be over between us'. For him their future separation was unbearable; 'it almost breaks my heart to think our lives will be spent apart,' he wrote. His emotions, reported the countess, were 'at first violent, then in despair'.[68]

Eddy made one final appeal to his grandmother. He wanted the queen to use her influence to persuade Hélène to change her religion. She 'absolutely refused this' and although convinced that Eddy was heartbroken, Queen Victoria told him 'he must have the courage to renounce the idea for ever'. This was his princely duty no matter what it cost him.[69]

6

Eddy and May

'Any Lady in Society *would never* do.'
Queen Victoria to Prince Eddy, 19 May 1890

The years of thwarted ambition in pursuit of a bride for Eddy, and the unforeseen complexities that appeared to attend every effort, were soon to rebound on his younger brother, Prince George. In the spring of 1891 Queen Victoria turned with some urgency to the matrimonial prospects of the third in line to the throne. If twenty-five-year-old Prince George could be induced to marry this would, at least, provide continuity into the next generation, whatever impediments accompanied Eddy's endeavours to achieve wedlock.

But Prince George was growing into a young man of unusually narrow focus, who enjoyed singular pursuits in which romance did not play a leading part. When his older brother had been sent to Cambridge, George had continued his career in the Royal Navy, although he did not enjoy the 'beastly exams'.[1] Constant travel across the empire, anxious reminders from his parents to avoid any kind of 'dissipation', and his own father's bad example held out before him: this combination was not conducive to encouraging a reserved young prince in romantic adventures. 'Alas Society is very bad in these days,' the queen warned George. He should 'avoid the many evil temptations' and keep 'your dear grandpapa's name before you'.[2]

George's letters suggest that he felt his position to be on the periphery, frequently missing the family gatherings that he read about in the newspapers. 'I wish I could have been present at your wedding,' he confided to Prince Louis of Battenberg from Bermuda. 'I am all alone,' he wrote a few months later. His mother, father and Eddy were in Ireland. 'I wish I was there too.'³ Birthdays were hard. 'I missed being at home very much that day,' he wrote to his grandmother in June 1886 from Malta.⁴ Christmases too: 'I shall miss being home at dear Sandringham very much,' he wrote from Bermuda in December 1990, 'but unfortunately in this world one cannot have everything one wants.'⁵ He still missed his mother, father, Eddy and sisters 'dreadfully', but 'trust the time will go quickly so that I can come home again'.⁶

Nonetheless he applied himself and saw much of the world as he progressed steadily through the ranks of the navy. As a young lieutenant, in 1886 he accompanied his Uncle Alfred sailing into the heart of the Ottoman Empire. 'The finest sight of all is as you come up the Bosporus and first see Constantinople with the different palaces, mosques and minarets and the enormous number of ships going up and down,' he told his grandmother. They stayed in a Kiosk (pavilion) in the gardens of the fabled Yildiz Palace and were received by the sultan himself, Abdul Hamid II. The sultan of the empire that was the 'sick man of Europe' was himself unwell, and could not receive them for three days, wrote George. Abdul Hamid, the very sultan responsible for the Bulgarian massacres at the start of the Russo-Turkish War, was courtesy itself to Queen Victoria's grandson, presenting him with a fine Arab horse and a diamond cigarette case. When the sultan went to Friday prayers, George took note of the large numbers of Turkish troops who 'marched uncommonly well, all drilled by German officers'.⁷ Two years later he joined Uncle Alfred on a royal visit to Spain for the opening of the Universal Exposition in Barcelona. It was a surprise to see the infant king, Alphonso VIII, a two-year-old boy, who was carried in by his nurse and placed on his throne. The Spanish king was 'not very pretty' but he 'behaved quite wonderfully and never cried once'.⁸

As a naval officer George had to keep abreast of the fast-changing technology, such as the rapid improvement in torpedoes. 'Everything has become obsolete that I learned four years ago,' he told Louis of Battenberg, '& so I have to begin it all over again, first unlearning what I learnt before.'[9] George made steady progress through the ranks, appointed to his first independent command in 1889 on HM Torpedo Boat 79. By 1891 he was promoted to the post of commander, in charge of the gunboat HMS *Thrush*, stationed in Halifax, Canada.

Prince George made the best of his travels but he did not enjoy the navy. He suffered badly from seasickness and his intrinsic shyness combined with his elevated position as royalty contributed to his being one step removed from the camaraderie that other officers could enjoy. His tutor, the Reverend John Dalton, had described him as having a 'nervously excitable temperament', prone to 'fret at difficulties' and 'make mountains out of molehills'. Over the years the endless discipline to which he had been exposed, first in the classroom and then the navy, had shaped his character. Any nervous impulsivity or even childhood exuberance was now channelled into polite formality. His letters refer to 'cheery parties', 'capital games', 'jolly weeks in Scotland', and of course the huge number of stags or partridges shot. A strong sense of duty coloured his personality; he could be self-contained, rigid in his preferences, perhaps even emotionally repressed.

On leave, Prince George invariably returned to Sandringham where his most marked enthusiasms were for stamp collecting and shooting – neither pursuit enhanced by female company. Indeed, there appeared to be no princess currently available whose main interests quite matched those of George whose daily life was, in fact, agreeably free of the need to marry anyone. In his mid-twenties he remained devoted to his mother and she to 'my own sweet darling old Georgie boy'.[10] Her letters to him were written as though he was still a child, openly acknowledging that she hoped she would find him unchanged in every way: 'I hope my sweet Georgie does not alter himself'.[11] Even when Prince George was promoted to commander of his own gunboat, she signed off 'with a great big kiss for your lovely little face'.[12]

Princess Alexandra's own childhood, brought up in the gregarious and fun-loving Danish court, seemingly in a permanent holiday mood, left her with memories of irreplaceable happiness.

Her own marriage had been shaped by her husband's endless betrayals and her increasingly isolating deafness encouraged escape into the happy private world she created for her children. She clung onto her sons' childhood years, delaying their maturity into adults and taking comfort from keeping her children close. It has been suggested that her abnormally intimate affection for Prince George was 'compensation' for her frustration over Eddy's behaviour. Intriguingly, Alexandra's letters to Eddy have not survived and it is entirely possible that they were written in the same whimsical, even infantile manner.[13] Both Eddy and George adored their mother and neither discouraged her over-protective stance. For years George responded in the same childish style and only much later in his adult life did he talk of the 'selfish' nature of her demands. Both boys appeared sensitive to the hurt she suffered from their father's behaviour and both feared his bad temper. She served as their devoted protector, a buffer between them and their father and Queen Victoria, whose letters were full of unsolicited advice, usually of a frank nature.

Princess Alexandra's response to Queen Victoria's new-found interest in Prince George's love life was to make light of it. 'Well & now about your <u>Matrimonial</u> prospects!!! Ha ha ha!' she wrote teasingly to George in April 1891. 'You are <u>quite</u> [double under-lined] right to think Grandmama has gone mad on the subject – & <u>it is too ridiculous</u>.'[14] But despite the efforts of 'Motherdear' to reduce the pressure, George began to recognise that his brother's difficulties in finding a bride could rebound on him.

Prince George replied to his grandmother's unasked-for concern for his private life with a cautionary tale of his own. While he accepted her view that lovelorn Eddy 'will anyhow have to wait some time', he still felt that Eddy should be her priority, pointing out in February 1891, 'I don't call Eddy too young [for marriage], he is 27.' George believed that 'marrying too young is a bad thing' and cited the gruesome fate of the heir to the Austrian throne, 'poor Crown Prince Rudolf', to back up his case.[15]

Under pressure from his father, Emperor Franz Joseph, the twenty-two-year-old Austrian prince had chosen sixteen-year-old Princess Stephanie of Belgium. George believed that Rudolf, who was 'a very wild young man', had been further unbalanced by his unhappy marriage. This led to his shocking suicide pact in 1889 with his mistress, Baroness Mary Vetsera. Rudolf 'killed this poor girl & brought the most terrible sorrow & shame on his poor wife and parents'.[16] Rudolf's parents were broken by the violent death of their only son; indeed his mother, the legendary beauty Empress Elizabeth, never quite recovered from the shock. Rudolf's death also had wider implications in breaking the direct line of Hapsburg succession, which served to weaken the authority of the dual monarchy of Austria-Hungary, whereby the Hapsburg Emperor Franz Joseph served as monarch to both countries. The Austrian succession in time passed from the liberal Rudolf to his reactionary cousin, Archduke Franz Ferdinand.

With this tragic tale as a salutary reminder, George was anxious to dampen his grandmother's enthusiasm for matchmaking. 'The one thing I never could do is to marry a person who did not care for me,' he pointed out in February 1891. 'I should be miserable for the rest of my life.'[17]

Meanwhile the supposedly broken-hearted Eddy confounded the expectations of those close to him by the enthusiasm with which he embraced the 1891 London season. Far from withdrawing from society in his anguish over Hélène's painful decision, the prince graced all the glittering events of the day, balls, charity events and Ascot week. The reason for this unexpected light-heartedness was that the prince believed he had fallen in love again. This time it was with a woman who he knew would be absolutely forbidden to him, not just by his grandmother but by his parents as well: the daughter of the Earl of Rosslyn, Lady Sybil St Clair Erskine.

Nineteen-year-old Lady Sybil was a debutante of exceptional beauty which, unusually for the time, she embellished still further with make-up. Her lively, flirtatious personality, combined with her stunning looks proved to be a heady distraction. Since Lady Sybil was a commoner, Eddy realised his grandmother would never approve any romance between them. The queen had reluctantly given her consent for Eddy's younger sister, Louise, to marry into the aristocracy, but she would never grant permission for a non-royal match for a future heir to the throne. His new-found love would be equally unwelcome to his parents. Lady Sybil's half-sister, Daisy Warwick, was having a passionate affair with Bertie, and Eddy's long-suffering mother was hardly likely to welcome an alliance with the family of her husband's mistress. Nonetheless, Eddy could not help himself. He was convinced that he was in love and recklessly began to write heartfelt letters to Lady Sybil.

Although he had thought it 'impossible' until a short time ago, 'to ---- more than one person at the same time', Prince Eddy confided to Lady Sybil on 21 June 1891, he now realised that 'exceptions will happen'. He promised to explain how this could be next time they met and urged her 'to cut out the crest and signature' of his letter, 'which would prevent anyone understanding it', if it fell into the wrong hands. The following week he pressed his case. 'I wonder if you really love me a little?' he asked, hoping so much 'if you did just a little bit ...' Once again he urged Lady Sybil to show the letters to no one. 'You can't be too careful what you do in these days, when hardly anybody is to be trusted.'[18]

The very day of his first love letter to Lady Sybil, duplicitous Eddy also sat down to write to Queen Victoria, thanking her for her 'last kind and important letter' and expressing a rather more serious view of love. The prince was keen to make his grandmother believe that he was still grieving for Princess Hélène. 'I was indeed deeply touched by all you said in your letter,' he wrote on 21 June 1891, 'and feel certain that I have your sympathy in this truly heavy trial. It is hard to forget and will be impossible for a long while to come, for my love for the dear girl had become so deeply rooted.'[19] The prince was at pains to remind his grandmother not just of his heartache, but also his virtues. That very month his father appeared in court as a witness in 'the terrible business', as Eddy put it, of the Tranby-Croft affair, a gambling scandal that shamed the monarchy. Eddy promised his grandmother he understood 'the country's feeling with regard to gambling and betting ... but as I have never had the slightest inclination for that kind of thing I may easily promise you that no bad example will ever be set on my part'. His interest in cards extended only to whist, which he understood to be 'such an instructive game'.[20]

Meanwhile, the beguiling, teasing Lady Sybil thought nothing of carelessly leading on the hapless prince. Eddy appeared to be in love with love, swayed this way and that, without a central anchor, and unable to make any headway without falling under the vigilant gaze of some maiden aunt or private secretary. It seems likely that Bertie soon learned of his son's new love interest and was furious. By early August, Eddy's parents and grandmother were united in their concern for his future – although each alighted on a different solution.

Bertie was convinced that his erring son should be despatched for another very long tour of the colonies as soon as possible and was in no doubt that this should be seen as a 'punishment'.[21] The queen, who had seen much of Eddy during the Kaiser's recent visit in July, was still preoccupied by Eddy's lack of knowledge of European countries. 'To be "Insular" for a private individual is a disadvantage but for a Prince, it is in these days a real misfortune,' she told Bertie on 4 August 1891.[22] She was strongly opposed to dispatching Eddy to the colonies once again; he had already 'been dosed with them' (double underlined).[23] Eddy was in urgent need of learning about Europe. 'A Prince ought to be Cosmopolitan, ought to have seen with his own eyes, the difference in other countries to his own.' Italy, Spain, Austria, Hungary, Russia, Turkey and Holland were a blank to him. 'As I am getting old I feel more and more anxious about all this,' the queen told Bertie.[24] But Bertie would not agree to Europe, insisting his son must be 'out of harm's way' on a Colonial Expedition, where there was no danger his son's affairs might overlap with his own. Wherever his son went, Bertie wrote on 5 August to his mother, the real problem lay within Eddy himself and his own 'apathy and disinclination to work ... A good sensible Wife – with some considerable character is what he needs most – but where is she to be found?'[25]

Queen Victoria already had the matter in hand. Unknown to the artless Eddy his shrewd grandmother had her eye on the next candidate. After three fruitless years endeavouring to bring about a match for her grandson with first Alix of Hesse and then Hélène d'Orléans, the queen was prepared to broaden her search for prospective brides. During 1891 she alighted upon a most unlikely candidate, one known to the prince but long overlooked: Eddy's impoverished cousin, Princess Victoria Mary of Teck, widely known as 'May' after the month of her birth. The queen told Lord Salisbury on 4 August 1891 that she would not send Eddy off to the colonies again merely to please her son and daughter-in-law. He must go to Europe where at least he might see princesses, and 'even if he did not succeed in finding one, it might reconcile him to Princess May Teck'.[26]

Within two weeks, the queen had the agreement of both her son and daughter-in-law. An 'entirely confidential' letter between the Prince of Wales's private secretary, Sir Francis Knollys, to the queen's private secretary, Sir Henry Ponsonby, reveals how rapidly Eddy's future had been settled. Knollys told Ponsonby that of the three options that lay before the prince, both his parents were in agreement that their son must be reconciled to 'Number 3':

1 The Colonial Expedition
2 The European *cum* Colonial plan
3 To be married to Princess May in the spring

Regarding 'No 3', continued Sir Francis, 'I think the preliminaries are now pretty well settled, but do you suppose Princess May will make any resistance? I do not anticipate any real opposition on Prince Eddy's part if he is properly managed and told he <u>must</u> do it, that it is for the good of the country, &c &c.'[27]

This just left the outstanding question of whether proposal 'No 3' fitted with the prospective bride and groom's expectations of married bliss.

For many seasoned observers in this high-stakes game of royal courtship, the princess in question in Knolly's 'No 3' was a rank outsider, far down the list of potential brides for Eddy. This was for reasons beyond her control, which significantly blighted her chances: for Princess May was not a true blue-blooded royal princess. Her mother, Princess Mary Adelaide, Duchess of Teck, was of splendid royal lineage as granddaughter of George III and a first cousin of Queen Victoria. But May's father, Prince Francis of Teck, from the German kingdom of Wurttemberg, was deemed insufficiently royal as the son of a mere Hungarian countess. On account of her mixed or 'morganatic' blood, the Duke and Duchess of Teck's daughter, May, appeared doomed in love. She did not have the right pedigree for marriage into a royal line – unless perhaps to a younger son of some small and inconsequential kingdom – but was far too royal to consider anyone else, no matter how wealthy.

As a 'serene highness' rather than the more elevated 'royal highness', Princess May had endured social events that were little more than marriage markets, where her personal assets were discussed and linked to princes way down the pecking order, such as the Prince of Naples, who May deemed 'terribly short & not beautiful to behold'.[28] Over the years there were one or two other royal suitors who for good reasons were struggling to find a match, such as Kaiser Wilhelm's brother-in-law, Ernst Gunther, the Duke of Schleswig-Holstein, a prince dismissed by Queen Victoria as a 'worthless' and 'wretched creature' or simply 'odious Gunther'. The queen was 'much amused' to learn that May turned him down 'at once', especially since the Kaiser's wife, Dona, proudly insisted that her 'charming brother' would never stoop to making such a proposal.[29]

It was not just Princess May's pedigree that led to her being overlooked as a serious contender in the royal marriage market. An indefinable stigma attached to the Tecks, at least in part of their own making. Not only did May's father bring no fortune, estate or Grand Duchy in tow, but what assets the Tecks did have at their disposal had been carelessly squandered by his spendthrift wife, who was unable to resist creating an extravagant royal lifestyle. The Duke and Duchess of Teck enjoyed a London apartment in Kensington Palace and a country home at White Lodge in Richmond Park courtesy of the queen, as well as a parliamentary annuity of £5,000 a year, but by the early 1880s they had run up very large debts. Their repeated appeals to relatives for help eventually fell on deaf ears. In 1883 the Tecks faced serious financial difficulties and were obliged to auction prized possessions and leave the country to escape their creditors.

The night of their departure on 15 September 1883 had been a moment of disgrace not easily forgotten by sixteen-year-old Princess May. A small gathering of relatives came to see the Tecks' departure at Victoria Station, with at least one of them, Aunt Augusta, Grand Duchess of Mecklenburg Strelitz, weeping uncontrollably. There were no scenes, no speeches; the family and a scattering of servants waited quietly on the platform in their travelling cloaks, putting a brave face on their humiliation, their possessions for the foreseeable future now contained in trunks around them. The screeching of the engines, the steam and grime, the lack of dignity of their position could only underline any qualms about their new itinerant life. Low as they were on the list of potentially desirable visitors to the gilded palaces of Europe, an uncertain future lay ahead.

After a suitable absence of two years, Queen Victoria permitted the Tecks to return from abroad. Princess May's mother devoted herself to numerous charitable works but the Tecks failed to become part of the royal inner circle. May's parents continued to count against their daughter in the marriage market. The very idea of May's mother, Princess Mary Adelaide, 'haunting Marlborough House makes the Prince of Wales ill', Arthur Balfour told his uncle the prime minister on 30 August 1890.[30] Bertie had been heard to make unkind references to Mary Adelaide's more than ample proportions, on top of which 'Fat Mary', as she was known, could also be wearyingly loquacious. True, she was popular with the public, an affable and colourful participant in royal duties, but nonetheless Bertie had no desire to see her making herself too comfortable in his London home. As for May's father, Prince Francis, the Duke of Teck, Balfour's understanding was 'they hate

Teck'.[31] Whether this was on account of his inability to manage
the family's means or for some other reason is not clear.

The seasons came and went with Princess May unable to find a
suitable husband. Fast approaching the grand age of twenty-four,
she appeared to be passed over. Her hopes of a good marriage had
evaporated and May was resigned to a dutiful life, her hours filled
with needlework and assisting in her mother's charitable ventures.
The first hint that May had brighter prospects arrived in January
1891 with an invitation to spend a few days at Sandringham. In
spring a further boost to May's chances came with a request for
recent photographs from the queen herself. Finally, in October
that year the Tecks received a message that could raise their
fortunes to unimaginable heights. Queen Victoria required the
company of the two oldest Teck children, Princess May and her
brother, Prince Adolphus or 'Dolly', at Balmoral. Princess May
was to join that elite and rarefied circle of princesses summoned
to the queen's favourite retreat for the royal scrutiny.

Queen Victoria had studied May's photographs and saw a
young woman of pleasing appearance whose steady gaze and
even features had potential. May did not have the arresting beauty
of Ella or Alix of Hesse; her bone structure was not so delicately
chiselled, her deep-set eyes were slightly too close together, and
her hair was styled in the fashionable frizz of curls that Queen
Victoria did not care for. But she was not unattractive and besides,
far more important than her looks was her personality. Was she
the 'good sensible Wife – with some considerable character',
which even Bertie now agreed Eddy needed most?[32] The queen
was eager to decide this for herself and did not see the need to
invite Eddy, his parents or even May's parents to Balmoral – a
point that rankled with 'Fat Mary'. Mary Adelaide had not been
invited to her cousin's Scottish retreat for over twenty years.

As Princess May and her brother Dolly sped to Aberdeen to
meet their forbidding 'Aunt Queen' in early November 1891,
May could have little idea just how far the plans for her future
had advanced over the summer – and in what unromantic terms.
It had fallen to Bertie to inform his son of the delightful news of
the decision about his marriage in a delicate father-son exchange

skirting around the subject of yet another possible bride. If Eddy had any doubts about committing himself, his father cleared the matter up by informing Eddy that his duty lay in a proposal to Princess May. By 10 October, Knollys was in a position to inform Ponsonby that 'you might like to know that so far the question of the proposed marriage is going on well. The Prince of Wales has been in frequent communication of late with his son on the subject and Prince Eddy is willing & I don't suppose Princess May will make any real difficulty ...'[33]

But first the bride-to-be had to get through the queen's vetting. Princess May arrived at Balmoral in the late morning on 5 November 1891 and she and her brother Dolly found themselves prominently positioned either side of the queen at luncheon. It was the start of an exhaustive inspection that took ten days under grey Scottish skies. If May herself wondered at the surprising invitation and the unnerving examination coming from this short, grey-haired empress with the eagle eyes and the mind of a lawyer, she took care not to show it. That very afternoon, when the queen returned from her drive with Beatrice, the queen asked May to join her for tea.

The queen's journal indicates that she was not displeased with her first impressions, finding May and her brother 'both so good looking'.[34] The next day also met with her satisfaction: 'May looked so pretty and has charming manners.'[35] By the third day, May was elevated to that exclusive circle of princesses favoured with an invitation to accompany the queen for her afternoon drive, on this occasion to Dantzig. Beatrice invariably announced which of the queen's guests were selected for this rare honour. The carriage rides were a key part of the vetting, as the queen's ladies-in-waiting were well aware. 'One test was for her to be driven through the mountains in the Queen's four-horse carriage, getting out now and then to admire an icy waterfall,' observed Louisa, Countess of Antrim.[36] The mountains were indeed 'sprinkled with snow', the air bitingly cold, but May politely considered it 'a very pretty drive'.[37]

On thorough inspection Queen Victoria ascertained that May had put her enforced exile abroad to good use, studying German and art and gaining a much valued European perspective. May's strong sense of duty and respect for her parents was also apparent; there was much to discuss of her role supporting her mother with the household management and charitable responsibilities. May had the advantage of being older than previous princesses auditioned for the post. She appeared mature and steady; there was no waywardness, no impulsiveness or unwelcome revelations. The queen also saw in May a woman who held royalty in the highest esteem. Unlike her Hessian granddaughters, who had grown up welcomed into the inner fold and took for granted the long days at Balmoral waiting on the queen's wishes, for May all this was a novelty. While the Hesse girls expected to marry for love, May had a deep sense of duty and a desire to do her best for the monarchy. Queen Victoria appeared to be opening a door onto an exciting vista as part of the inner circle and May was fully sensible of the honour.

There is no indication in either Queen Victoria's journal or May's that the queen was tempted to reveal her exact purpose. If there was a transition from vetting to hinting at what might be expected of May and testing her reaction, neither made a record of it. The visit passed apparently uneventfully; there were the inevitable theatricals; hymn practice in the chapel; May played with Beatrice's children, and her husband, Henry, taught her the mazurka. The queen felt comfortable enough to take Princess May to the retreat that meant most to her, Glassalt Shiel, a private lodge on Loch Muich. This 'Widow's House', expanded after Albert's death, set in the deep shadows of the surrounding hills, was for the queen a sanctuary within the sanctuary of her treasured Scottish retreat. It was mostly shared with her daughter, Beatrice, and the seasonal midges, but on one 'fearfully cold' day she invited May and her brother to lunch there.[38] From this hideaway the queen confided her impressions of May to her daughter Vicky.

'We have seen a gt deal of May & Dolly Teck during these 10 days visit here & I cannot say enough good of them,' she wrote. May was 'very pretty' and 'so sensible' and 'so vy carefully brought up'.[39] No doubt a little put out to find even May elevated above her own youngest daughter, Margaret, who once again appeared to be passed over, Vicky enquired whether the queen found May a little 'shallow'?[40] The queen had plenty of opportunities to consider such potential defects; on 8 November – a day which even the queen found 'raw and dark' – she took May out alone; two days later May was required to walk beside her in the pony chair.[41] Perhaps a little insensitively, Queen Victoria replied to Vicky in glowing terms: May was 'well informed' and 'a superior girl'. The queen took leave of May 'with regret' on 14 November having reached her conclusions – their parting overshadowed by a worrying telegram from Bertie saying that Prince George was ill with suspected typhoid.[42]

Alongside reports of George's illness, the papers began to speculate about Eddy's match. 'The queen delights to honour her [Princess May] on all occasions', observed the *Edinburgh Evening News.* [43] The *Derby Daily Telegraph* concluded that Prince Albert Victor's engagement 'will shortly be formally announced'.[44] It was presumed by all involved that May would accept the role if it was offered. After all, what other chance would she have of a marriage, let alone marriage to the second heir to the throne. As for Eddy, he was not required to fall in love with this paragon of virtue. For Queen Victoria, there was just one outstanding question: when would he propose?

It was soon clear there was an unexpected hitch. The prospective groom had changed his mind. 'It seems, oh dear no, the Duke of Clarence will not hear of it!' the bemused Lady Geraldine Somerset wrote in her diary on 29 November, shortly after the queen had given her permission. '[He] Is immensely annoyed at its being universally talked of, declares he does not like her, & that he has no idea of being coerced & roundly declares it shall not be.'[45] But Eddy was not a young man in possession of a strong hand.

Just at this most delicate time, unfavourable reports reached the queen about her grandson. For so long his indulgent and powerful champion, she appears to have learned enough about Eddy in late November to change her attitude. Queen Victoria was sufficiently troubled to write to Princess Alexandra expressing great concern about her grandson's rakish behaviour and 'dissipations'. Whatever she learned caused such a furore that Knollys wrote despairingly in December 1891 to Ponsonby: 'I ask again <u>who</u> is it tells the queen these things?'[46]

So what were these unfortunate 'things' that caused such a rumpus behind the scenes in early December 1891? It is not possible to tell from the surviving records but press reports highlight at least two possibilities. First, there was the tragic case of a pretty chorus girl, Lydia Miller, who had been found dead on 4 October after taking carbolic acid. Some British papers, such as the *Manchester Courier* and *Lloyd's Weekly Newspaper*, insinuated that the unfortunate woman had been Eddy's lover: 'the deceased … was the *petite amie* of a certain young prince'.[47] The British press alleged that Lydia's mysterious royal lover had been with her recently and the foreign press was still less inhibited, naming the prince directly. 'Prince Albert Victor … is said to have had intimate relations with the dead girl', reported the *New Zealand Herald* on 11 November 1891, at the very time that the queen had been feting Princess May in Balmoral. The *Perth Daily News* was equally explicit that the chorus girl 'was the recipient of attentions of the Duke of Clarence and Avondale … although she was the nominal mistress of Lord Charles Montagu'.[48]

The sad case of Lydia Miller was not the only scandal linked to the prince that autumn. One report in the New Zealand press claimed that the blackmailer, Maude Richardson, also resurfaced at this untimely moment. 'The attachment he [Eddy] formed for Miss Richardson became so pronounced that it came to Her Majesty's ears and she threatened at one time to cancel his engagement to Princess May', claimed the *Auckland Star*. 'Confronted at last with the alternative of losing May, the Duke of Clarence ceased his visit to Miss Richardson … She wrote to him threatening to cause a scandal if he discontinued his visits.' The press reports of Eddy's links to Lydia Miller and Maude Richardson remain unverified.[49]

Whichever scandal reached the queen in the late autumn of 1891, Eddy woke up to the fact that he was in serious trouble. It fell to Bertie to have another painful conversation with his errant son, and he was in a position to inform his mother on 3 December 1891 that she could 'make your mind quite easy about Eddy'. The prince 'has made up his mind to propose to May'.[50] Bertie knew exactly how best to stage manage the happy occasion, even advising Eddy against a visit to Windsor next month, 'for the Tecks are there ... as it would look as though all arranged affair'. He informed the queen that Princess May was invited to Sandringham in the New Year where 'everything will I am sure be satisfactorily settled then'.[51]

Whatever was said to the prince, he felt the need for speedy compliance with his parents' and grandmother's wishes. Suddenly he no longer saw the point of a prolonged courtship of May. Nor did he wait, as planned, for the New Year. The very day that Bertie reassured the queen of his son's intention to propose in January, Eddy had a chance to meet May at the residence of the Danish ambassador to England, Christian de Falbe, at Luton Hoo in Bedfordshire.

———

Princess May's carriage approached down a curving driveway, neatly manicured lawns to either side. If the potential bride had any misgivings about the rumours she had read in the newspapers, she appears to have kept them to herself. The extraordinary prospect of one day becoming the Queen of Great Britain outweighed any niggling worries over the veracity of any tittle-tattle in the press. Through the window of her carriage the grand residence before her was a glimpse of the glamorous future that might lie ahead. The entrance way was a six-pillared portico, two stories high, and the long facade of the house ended in bow-shaped rooms, creating the impression of two towers as if this was a castle. Once inside the grand hallway, stately interiors stretched out before her, overlooking neat ornamental gardens to the rear. The guest book spoke of many distinguished visitors. If May was a little daunted, she kept her composure.[52]

The third of December 1891 was a wintry, overcast day; May described it as 'dull'.[53] There was nothing significant to mark her

day, nothing to alert her to Prince Eddy's intentions. The long
hours spent on the vast estate were without any hint of romance.
She passed her time walking with the ladies who accompanied
the shooters. In the late afternoon prospects brightened. The
Falbes were holding a county ball. Carriages began to arrive and
the spacious rooms filled with guests in all their finery. May's
mother, ever hopeful of her daughter's chances, had bought her
a striking mauve dress ornamented with beads, at sufficient cost
to provoke criticism from one friend, Lady Geraldine Somerset:
'Monstrous,' she said. 'Over forty pounds for *one* gown!'[54] As
time passed, May's hopes of some pleasant attention from Eddy
began to diminish.

The ball was underway before the prince came to see her and
invited her to follow him. He led her up the wide, curved stairway, the sound of the music receding as they reached the top floor.
May could only suspect the long-awaited moment – implied but
never formally confirmed – might be close. They walked down a
corridor into a room he had evidently selected in advance. May
described their conversation in unemotional terms in her diary.
'To my great surprise Eddy proposed to me during the evening in
Mme de Falbe's boudoir. Of course I said yes – we are both very
happy …'[55]

For May it was a moment to treasure, a confirmation of her
success. There was nothing to indicate she felt a strong attraction
to Eddy, but this was not expected or required. She held the royal
family in the highest respect and saw her duty as paramount. She
would become a future queen, her children heirs to an empire.
For a twenty-four-year-old woman, who at the beginning of the
year had felt her hopes of marriage were fast diminishing, it was
a heady victory. The engagement was meant to be secret but both
she and Eddy found it hard to conceal. Later that evening when
May confided in her friends, she could not contain her delight
and danced around the room. The world had suddenly become
dizzyingly exciting for a princess whose emotions were rarely on
display.

Eddy, too, appeared pleased. The strain of years of uncertainty
fell from his shoulders as the matter was settled in a way that

satisfied all concerned. He did not feel the need to spend a great deal of time with his fiancée. The next day he went shooting in the grounds, waiting until the evening to see Princess May. For both the prince and the princess, the ambiguity of their positions, the slight sense of inadequacy that they had somehow failed to meet expectations, were removed almost instantaneously. While there is no sense in the records of a strong mutual attraction or powerful meeting of minds, there was a shared relief that they could help each other. On 5 December, once formal engagement photographs were completed, the prince left to inform his grandmother at Windsor.

It was pouring with rain when he arrived, but the queen was still out in her carriage. On her return, 'I suspected something at once,' Queen Victoria later recorded when she was informed Eddy wished to see her. 'He came in and said, "I am engaged to May Teck". I was delighted. God bless them both. He seemed pleased and satisfied. I am so thankful as I had much wished this marriage thinking her so suitable.'[56] She sat with her grandson for some time, confident that the monarchy was in good hands for the future. The following day she was still so excited that she confided to her diary 'could think of little else but the great event'.[57] She passed on her delight to Vicky in Germany. 'Certainly she is a dear, good and clever girl, very carefully brought up, unselfish and unfrivolous in her tastes. She will be a great help to him. She is very fond of Germany too and is very <u>cosmopolitan</u>.' The queen could foresee no difficulties. 'I think it is far preferable than <u>eine kleine deutsche Prinzessin</u> [a little German princess] with no knowledge of anything beyond small German courts etc. It would never do for Eddy ...' Perhaps understanding Vicky's feelings about all this praise for May above her own girls, Queen Victoria added, 'I can understand that many things must make you very sore, but many are <u>really unavoidable</u> ...'[58]

Not all reactions were quite so favourable. On 5 December, Lady Geraldine Somerset had occasion to write in her diary that she had received a note from the 'darling Princess of Wales ... And!! Announcing to me that dear Eddy and sweet May are engaged to be married!!!! So!! For it is so! And God of Heaven

<u>what</u> [underlined five times] a weak wretched fool he must be! This day week "indignant at the idea of being talked into it and wld not hear of it" & within a week is made to propose! Yt is all those vile intriguantes at beastly Luton! ... What a world this is!'⁵⁹ The following day Lady Geraldine was still simmering. 'At Marlboro House now of course they pretend P Eddy has always wished it!!!! ... Not a week since both admitted he was indignant at the idea of being coerced into an arrangement he did not wish!!! Now however ... it is a love match on both sides!!!! (neither of them caring more for the other than I do!!) & that the only opposition to it was by the Q! who wld not hear of it! But now is all for it ... so like her ... dear guileless Ps of Wales who was "so afraid May might refuse him"!!!! She cld indeed have spared herself anxiety on that score.'⁶⁰

There was indeed a changed mood at Marlborough House. '<u>This time!</u>' Princess Alexandra wrote with relief to Queen Victoria, 'I do hope that dear Eddy has found the <u>right Bride</u> at last and that <u>nothing</u> will prevent him and dear May from spending a very happy future together.'⁶¹ At last Eddy's prospects, and with them the future of the British throne, appeared secure. Telegrams began to arrive from across Europe. At Darmstadt, Louis of Hesse was 'glad Eddy is engaged', though he found himself reflecting on Alix. 'We all wished once to see his desire fulfilled,' he telegrammed the queen.⁶² Alix wrote somewhat awkwardly to let the queen know that she had not sent congratulations to May 'as we never corresponded & it would have been rather difficult', but added 'I hope & trust that May will make him very happy.'⁶³ Ella telegrammed her 'delight' at the news.⁶⁴ Kaiser Wilhelm also sent congratulations, taking the opportunity to remind his grandmother of the threat to German peace in the growing cordiality between France and Russia.

Princess May herself found her quiet life transformed overnight. It was raining when she arrived from the country at London's St Pancras Station on 7 December. Wearing a beautifully cut blue velvet suit with lace trim, she stepped down from her saloon carriage to find a large and enthusiastic crowd waiting to cheer her. The princess 'appeared somewhat embarrassed at the demonstration but bowed her acknowledgement in a pleasing fashion', according to reporters, while her parents were 'much gratified' by their daughter's reception.[65]

Princess May's warm welcome at the station was in striking contrast to her experiences eight years previously when her family had slipped unseen from the country in disgrace. Then the small gathering had been fighting back tears; now there was applause for the future bride. For the first time in her life, she was the star attraction. The family travelled in an open carriage, to the evident delight of the crowds who gathered along the route, through Bloomsbury and Piccadilly to Marlborough House. The onlookers were in no doubt that this rather shy princess was to be their future queen. It was only when the rain became heavy that the Tecks were obliged to close the carriage en route and the bride could no longer be seen.[66]

———

While Queen Victoria had grounds for optimism that everything was falling into place for her British grandson, there was plenty to trouble her regarding her other grandchildren, especially her favourite, Alix of Hesse. She had all but forbidden a Russian marriage for Alix, but Ella continued to fight her sister's cause behind the scenes. Convinced that Alix was in love with Nicholas, she plotted to help the match along 'when the deciding moment arrives'. Ella sent her older brother, Ernie, detailed instructions about how to manage the queen. Firstly, he should be 'very careful' about what he let out in any casual conversation with 'Grandmama'. Secondly, if he was probed for information, he was to deny that there was anything between Alix and Nicholas. If asked for a view about Nicholas, Ernie was to say 'what a perfect creature he is & adored by all & [that Alix] deserves this loving being in every way'. She impressed on her brother that Nicholas himself 'was feeling very lovesick'. Finally, she pointed out that their grandmother was grossly prejudiced about Russia, 'through all the idiotic trash in the newspapers'. Youthful Ella considered that 'Grandmama

Queen' has 'impossible untrue views and founds all her arguments on facts which probably never existed ... God grant that
this marriage will come true.'[67]

Apart from the queen's forceful opposition, Ella knew there
was another crucial impediment to the match. If Alix wanted to
marry Nicholas, as a future tsarina she would be obliged to join
the Russian Orthodox Church. The Hesse children had been
brought up as Lutherans, a branch of the Protestant faith named
after the German priest, Martin Luther. Alix and her sisters had
taken their vows of confirmation and to go back on these oaths
would be a very serious matter, one that Ella knew could well
cause suffering for their father, Louis of Hesse.

Although Ella had not been obliged to change her faith
on marriage to a grand duke, in 1891 she decided to join the
Russian Orthodox Church. It would be sinful, she told her
father, to remain Protestant purely for the sake of appearances,
when in her heart she shared her husband's faith. This was a
matter of conscience about which she had passionately strong
feelings. At the family home in Darmstadt, Grand Duke Louis,
Ernie and Alix were stunned. For Louis, his daughter's rejection
of her confirmation vows shook him so deeply it disturbed his
own sense of inner peace, her actions all the more baffling since
this was not required of her. It was Queen Victoria who was
unexpectedly accepting of her granddaughter's decision, earning
Ella's undying gratitude. 'I shall never forget ... the comfort-
ing joy yr dear lines gave me,' Ella wrote to the queen from
Moscow. It was 'such a happiness' to have the same religion as
her husband.[68]

Dressed in white, beautiful Ella appeared radiant during her
conversion ceremony in April 1891, as though greatly moved.
The mysticism of the Russian Church, with its powerful holy
symbols, gilded icons and colourful saints, inspired her and she
always said that her conversion fulfilled her dearest wishes. But it
was not long before rumours about her began to circulate, which
Ella believed yet again came from the Kaiser. Ella had always
maintained that she had been under no pressure from her husband.
But the timing of her conversion did indeed coincide with Sergei's

promotion to become Governor General of Moscow, and some claimed that to enter the Kremlin he was required to have a wife of the same faith.[69]

It could not have been lost on either Ella or Queen Victoria that her wholehearted embrace of the Russian Orthodox Church might help pave the way for her sister to marry the heir to the Russian throne. Still fearing a Russian marriage for Alix, in the autumn of 1891 the queen alighted on another plan. She had searched through her trusty *Almanac de Gotha*, a 1,000-page tome published in Germany that listed all the vital statistics about every prince, grand duke and *Landgraf* that mattered: their title, rank, estate and so on. There among the many German princes was one who stood out above the rest: a second cousin to Kaiser Wilhelm known as Prince Maximilian of Baden.

The twenty-four-year-old German prince was not known for his good looks, his title and prospects carrying all the promise. His face was not quite handsome, the eyebrows and moustache heavy, his nose a prominent feature. But he had other attributes that made him excellent husband material in the eyes of Queen Victoria. His education in law and administration was first rate and he had a keen interest in liberal politics. As a descendant of the Grand Duchy of Baden in southern Germany, he had the security of a wealthy family behind him. Worried about whether to raise the matter with Alix directly or whether this might prove counter-productive, the queen turned to Victoria of Battenberg. 'I wish dear Alicky shld some day marry Max of Baden, whom I <u>formerly</u> wished for Maud,' the queen explained, her letter highlighting the endless gyrations of matchmaking. Her youngest Wales grandchild, Maud, who she had hoped would marry Max, she now thought was suitable for Ernie (although he was resisting the idea), freeing up Max for Alix. Fearing that Prince Maximilian of Baden was excellent husband material who was bound to be snapped up, the queen hoped that 'dear Papa will <u>lose no time</u> in inviting him'.[70] Louis of Hesse duly succumbed to the pressure and the hopeful Prince Maximilian descended on Darmstadt within a month, confident of his excellent prospects of securing the hand of Queen Victoria's granddaughter.

Given the encouragement he had received from the queen it must have been a surprise to find his prospective bride did not prove at all obliging. Alix felt mortified at being put on the spot, and 'threatened with the danger of marrying without love or even affection'. She thought she was being manoeuvred, a mere pawn in elaborate power games. Her feelings about the German stranger before her did not compare with the warm friendship she had appreciated with tsarevich Nicholas. Comments she made years later highlight the pressure she felt from her grandmother. 'I vividly remember the torments I suffered when ... [Max of Baden] arrived at Darmstadt and I was informed that he intended to marry me. I did not know him at all and I shall never forget what I suffered when I met him for the first time.'[71] Nineteen-year-old Alix trusted her own feelings more than any advice she received from relatives. There was too much advice. She made a firm stand. It was left to Victoria of Battenberg to break the unwelcome news to the queen.

On the very day that Ella was received into the Russian Orthodox Church, 2,000 miles south in Athens another of Queen Victoria's granddaughters changed her faith. Sophie, Crown Princess of Greece, joined the Greek Orthodox Church of her husband, Constantine. But Sophie's conversion caused uproar in the House of Hohenzollern in which her brother Kaiser Wilhelm's increasingly disturbed and tyrannical behaviour was on display before the wider family.

The trouble began when Sophie came to Berlin for the wedding of her younger sister, Moretta. Thwarted in her love for Alexander, Moretta had finally settled on a minor German prince, Adolf of Schaumburg-Lippe, but the happy family celebration was marred as news of Sophie's planned conversion spread. Vicky, like Queen Victoria, took a liberal view. She did not 'think it wrong' and hoped that Sophie would find happiness 'sharing her husband's faith'.[72] But the Kaiser's wife, Dona, opposed her. She summoned Sophie to a meeting and became overwrought, threatening her sister-in-law not only with Wilhelm's fury, but the wrath of God. 'You will end up in Hell,' she screamed.[73] When Dona went into premature labour a few hours later with her sixth son, the Kaiser blamed Sophie.

The rapid escalation of the argument bears all the troubling hallmarks of the German emperor's maniacal and deluded way of thinking. First, in Wilhelm's mind the issue was transformed into a personal attack on himself. It was inexplicable, he claimed, that Sophie 'entirely refused to acknowledge me as the Head of her Family and the Church'. Having personalised the issue, it was then supercharged with emotion. 'If my poor Baby dies it is solely Sophie's fault and she has murdered it,' he claimed.[74] Despite the fact that the baby was patently healthy, he still found reason to blame his English mother yet again, falsely insisting that she was responsible for his sister's conversion. Finally, he felt the need to defend himself against illusory attacks and banned Sophie from returning to Germany.

The wider family in Greece, Britain and Germany had a chance to witness the Kaiser's troubling behaviour. For Vicky, he was a 'conspicuous tyrant', Alexandra saw him as 'a great ass', Bertie was appalled, Sophie's sisters Moretta and Margaret were boiling 'with indignation' and despairing that 'things will never go on peacefully in Berlin', while Queen Victoria 'grieved'.[75] Sophie's appeals against the ban proved futile, prompting her to telegraph openly to her mother: 'Keeps to what he said in Berlin. Fixes it to three years. Mad.' Sophie made no attempt in her communication to conceal the word 'Mad'.[76] Queen Victoria wanted to help the troubled German house but recognised, as she told Vicky, that she could not intervene directly between Wilhelm II and Sophie. But she did have some leverage over the Kaiser and knew how to use it without saying a word.

The queen signalled her disapproval of the German emperor by greeting his long diatribe blaming his sister with an eloquent silence. Knowing he was keen to make a state visit to Britain she advised Vicky to invite Sophie to Germany in due course with her husband. Wilhelm 'will not dare to arrest the Crown Prince of Greece!', she reasoned, and he in turn 'would be very ill-received here' if he proceeded with banishing his sister.[77] Sure enough, the Kaiser did not take action when Sophie and Constantine went to see Vicky in July 1891. In turn, his state visit to Windsor that month passed without incident, apart from the occasional strained moment between Wilhelm and his Uncle Bertie, who he had seen fit to criticise over the gambling scandal, the Tranby-Croft affair. Wilhelm was pleased with his reception in Britain and wrote to the queen afterwards, expressing his desire to pursue 'the fulfilment of those great problems which were so ably begun by dear Grandpapa Albert'.[78]

But Wilhelm had neither the insight nor the diplomatic skill to fulfil his grandfather's vision of peace. With power increasingly concentrated in his hands in what Vicky called his 'personal government', the German emperor had unwittingly edged Europe one step closer to war. When he failed to renew Bismarck's Reinsurance Treaty with Russia, Wilhelm flattered himself that his relationship with Alexander III was an adequate guarantee, not realising that the tsar had no trust in an emperor 'who throws his weight about ... and fancies that others worship him'.[79] With no secret treaty with Germany, the tsar moved swiftly to consolidate Russia's relationship with republican France.

Too late, Wilhelm woke up to the new threat. A week after the Kaiser's visit to Britain in July 1891, Alexander III hosted the French fleet at Kronstadt near St Petersburg, home to the Russian admiralty. The German emperor was immediately alive to the danger. Was this friendly gesture the first step towards a future military alliance between France and Russia that would leave Germany between them exposed on both sides? That summer when the returning French fleet was invited to England by the British government, it appeared to the Kaiser that his grandmother was endorsing newfound ties between France and Russia.

The queen was, in fact, on the spot, since she happened to be hosting the Kaiser's younger brother, Henry, and her granddaughter, Irene. Almost farcically as the French fleet drew near, Bertie hurriedly took his German cousins on a cruise on his yacht, the *Aline*, out of the way of the approaching French. The queen watched their fleet slowly approach Osborne Bay from the

Upper Alcove, the lights of all the ships reflected across the bay as dusk fell. At a reception for French officers at Osborne the next day, the 'Marseillaise' was played. Like the tsar before her, the queen concealed her distaste for the republican melody, politely standing throughout, 'which gratified them greatly', she wrote.[80] Vicky was sympathetic. The 'Marseillaise' was 'horrid', she wrote to her mother, a 'symbol of violence' that was 'closely associated with the massacre of kings, aristocrats and priests'.[81]

The movement of the French fleet gave weight to an idea that was beginning to loom large in the Kaiser's mind that summer and was charged with emotions of dread and fear: encirclement. He saw any understanding between the French and the Russians as a menace to the peace of Europe. Wilhelm could not see the extent to which his own actions had fostered French and Russian fears, pushing the nations closer together, nor the skill with which Bismarck had taken care to cultivate the Russians. Now a sense of threat was in the air. Vicky wrote to her mother explaining that the Kaiser was not at all popular and that there was uneasiness 'that the Russians and French will take this opportunity of making war ...'[82]

For the Kaiser, there was another dimension to Europe's shifting Great Power alliances. Instead of royal alliances keeping the peace, as envisaged by his grandfather, in the Kaiser's disturbed mind the mirror opposite appeared to be true. There was a cabal of royal relatives with significant power, heads of state spread across Europe, who appeared to be talking about him, laughing about him, perhaps threatening him. Within this wicked circle he saw his suave and sophisticated Uncle Bertie as the ringmaster, who was inspiring the conspiracy against him.

In London, Princess May's warm reception at St Pancras Station proved to be just the start of an extraordinary few weeks. Her rags-to-riches royal romance captured the heart of the British public. Telegrams of congratulations poured into Marlborough House from 'nearly every crowned head in Europe' and heads of state from far-flung colonies.[83] Although in reality Eddy and May had only enjoyed a brief courtship and could scarcely be said to be in love, up and down the country the press saw things differently.

The engagement was 'purely a love affair throughout', according to the Devon press, which reported Princess May was 'very much in love with the Duke of Clarence'.[84] A 'pretty love story' it was, too, in the Manchester press. 'It has been an open secret years ago that Prince Eddy's heart was set on Princess May.' The prince had 'remained constant' and now Eddy and May 'seemed all in all to each other'.[85] In the *Dundee Evening Times* the Duke of Clarence was a different man: 'Tall and elegant in the smart uniform of his corps [he] looks as fit to be fallen in love with as the prince in the fairy tale', and the bride is 'bright and unaffected'.[86] While in Yorkshire the news was 'received with gusto and general satisfaction', according to the *Evening Post*, which claimed that Queen Victoria had opposed the match and sent the prince abroad to thwart his attachment to May. But the prince showed 'great strength of will' and his 'constancy and perseverance have overcome all difficulties'.[87] So lyrical was the press about the strength of their love 'triumphing over all obstacles!' that Lady Geraldine Somerset was prompted to comment in her diary on the 'columns of rot' from the 'twaddling and asinine' press.[88]

But Lady Geraldine's cynicism was out of step with the national mood. After years of Queen Victoria's mourning and Bertie's infidelity, the nation was ready for what the papers called 'a royal love match'.[89] Almost overnight, May and Eddy were *the* couple that high society wanted to meet. The bride and groom enchanted the crowds by appearing together in London. There were celebrations at Marlborough House, they visited the theatre, charity concerts, society events, and even posed romantically in a gondola at the Venice Exhibition at Olympia, which May found 'very pretty and well arranged'. She made plans with her mother for her trousseau and drove with Eddy in a hansom cab to St James's Palace 'to see our rooms and choose papers etc'.[90] Her future life was taking shape and for the princess who had long been overlooked it was thrilling to be swept from one glorious event to another, each one vying for the acknowledgement that it was at their party that the princess was the dazzling centre of attention. Even Bertie was won over, declaring that 'May is the most charming girl he has ever come across.'[91] He wanted a magnificent wedding for the young couple at St Paul's Cathedral, a royal pageant that would delight the nation. But on the prime minister's advice, St George's Chapel in Windsor was deemed more suitable and a date was set: 27 February 1892.

The queen was delighted but managed to strike a more sombre note when she welcomed May and her family to Windsor. The thirty-year anniversary of Albert's death was fast approaching and at the forefront of her mind. As though to underline the solemnity of their commitment, on 12 December 1891 she invited the newly engaged couple to the royal burial ground at Frogmore. They walked across the neat lawns, still wet from the heavy rain of the previous days, to the Royal Mausoleum. 'This day thirty years ago was the beginning of great anxiety,' she wrote in her journal later.[92] Once within the thick stone walls the air was colder, the room was dark. Standing before the granite sarcophagus, a sombre reminder of the transience of life, Eddy and May were to receive Prince Albert's blessing from the grave.[93] For Queen Victoria this was a defining moment. In the hands of this sensible, dutiful young woman, sanctified somehow by Albert's spirit, the future of the British monarchy seemed assured.

May's mother, Mary Adelaide, made an exuberant contrast. Against all the odds the Tecks had won the first prize and nothing could allay the buoyant mood. There were telegrams and invitations to send and all the thrill of the wedding plans. May and her mother commissioned the wedding dress material; the finest white silk broché made at a Lancashire silk mill with a wreath of roses and rosebuds in the centre. Christmas at White Lodge was a sublime moment that could never be spoiled for the Teck family. The wedding was just two months away. On Boxing Day the Tecks joined the Fifes and other guests for a dance in Sheen. The lighthearted mood, the optimism about her future, the Christmas atmosphere all combined to bring an exciting close to 'a most eventful year' for May.[94] The celebrations were due to continue after Christmas at Sandringham where May joined her fiancé in the New Year. Eddy had much news to tell her about the appointments for his first household staff, who had just been chosen.[95]

There was thick fog at Sandringham with many guests suffering from flu and when Eddy, too, caught a chill in the New Year at first he thought little of it. People wanted to congratulate the newly engaged prince and had brought gifts for his twenty-eighth birthday. He was well enough to write to Prince Louis, who had done so much to advise him over his hopes for Alix three years before. 'I suppose my engagement took you somewhat by surprise, as it did a good many people,' Eddy wrote on 5 January 1892, 'but I think I have done the right thing at last in getting married ... I feel certain she [May] will make the best of wives, and dearest companion.' His thoughts were of his wedding; he wanted Louis to come, which 'would please me more than anything'.[96]

The biting chill continued and there were skating parties on the lake in front of Sandringham, which had turned into a sheet of ice. While others in the family managed to shake off the infection, including George, who May noted was 'looking thin' after the typhoid, Eddy did not improve.[97] By his birthday on 8 January he stayed in his room with May, who was dutifully dealing with their voluminous correspondence. 'Eddy still in bed', Princess Alexandra telegrammed the queen at Osborne the next day.[98] Her oldest son seemed to have no resistance to this strain of influenza. Bertie warned the queen on 10 January that Eddy had 'now developed some pneumonia in the left lung'.[99] May was beginning to feel 'fearfully anxious'. Long hours waiting for any sign of improvement were punctuated with short walks with his youngest sister, Maud.[100] Word began to reach the wider family that things were not right. The influenza 'has developed into inflammation of the left and a little of the right lung', the queen alerted Vicky on 11 January. 'Is it not terrible?' The queen worried about the effects of this sudden illness on Bertie and Alix, who 'are very sorely tried'. At the very least, the wedding would have to be postponed.[101]

Less than a week after his birthday and in a matter of hours, Eddy's influenza turned into a fight for his life. By now the alarming developments were being announced across the empire. Regular news bulletins described his illness as 'grave' at first, but soon changed to 'critical'. With 'no abatement of the unfavourable symptoms', a large crowd gathered silently outside the Wales's London residence, 'many of them ladies', reported the *West Australian*. The awful possibility that Prince Eddy might lose his life just as he had become engaged added to the alarm. There was immense sympathy for Princess May whose popularity 'has doubled and trebled' since her engagement.[102]

Confined to the small anteroom by Eddy's bedroom at Sandringham, the Prince of Wales and his family along with Princess May waited with helpless anxiety. The queen, still at Osborne, alerted to each rally and each devastating setback in a flurry of telegrams, wanted to fly to Sandringham. 'There could not be a question of your coming here,' Bertie ordered his mother. There was nothing that she could do. 'Our darling Eddy is in God's hands.'[103] Princess Alexandra, her face 'wretched, imploring', would not leave Eddy's side, willing him to live.[104] During the night his temperature rose sharply. He slipped into feverish delirium, which was all the more painful for May since it was not her name he called, but 'Hélène'. The doctors were at a loss. The chaplain came, his prayers a comfort. May, dazed and wretched, her emotions unable to keep up with the shock, saw her fiancé transformed before her eyes, his face taking on a strange livid hue, his pulse weakening, his chin projecting forwards as he struggled for each breath. In the morning of 14 January 1892, barely six weeks before his wedding, the second in line to the throne died. 'Our darling Eddy has been taken from us,' Bertie telegrammed the queen. 'We are broken hearted.'[105]

At 9.55 a.m. an official at Marlborough House told the waiting crowd that 'it was all over'. The city seemed to come to a standstill. The signs and sounds of death appeared during the morning, creating a sombre backdrop to the capital. By 11 a.m. all the clubs in the West End had closed their blinds, shops were shuttered, offices locked. Black flags or drapes, like a malignant growth, hung from windows, omnibuses and trains. Reverberating through the London streets the tolling bells reminded the nation of its loss.[106] The news spread from city to city and crowds gathered in disbelief. 'It is impossible to give an idea of the shock with which the news came to the public,' reported the *Edinburgh Evening News*.[107] Although the second in line to the throne was not well known, people responded to the tragic circumstances of his death at a time that should have been full of happiness. Princess May now had to prepare not for a wedding, but a funeral.

The extravagant arrangements underway for a fine royal wedding at Windsor Castle were transformed into preparations for the prince's burial. 'There is something sadly dramatic,' observed Sir Henry Ponsonby's biographer, in the way the flow of letters to the queen's private secretary concerning Prince Eddy's marriage switched 'with hardly a break in the sequence' to arrangements for his funeral.[108] Black-edged letters and telegrams of condolence poured into Osborne, Sandringham and Marlborough House. The groom lay at Sandringham, surrounded by flowers such as May blossom that were to feature at his wedding. His mother and May were quite unable to bring themselves to leave him. Queen Victoria was stunned, 'too much stunned to take it in as yet! A tragedy too dreadful for words,' she told Ponsonby.[109] Forty-eight hours later it still felt 'like a horrible dream'.[110]

The press devoured the story and there was a huge outpouring of grief for the 'lost king'. 'Such sympathy was never known, not only from my vast empire but also from other foreign nations,' the queen wrote in her journal.[111] The following day Eddy's 'dear remains' were taken by train to Windsor for the burial. As though it were still his wedding day, 'not a vestige of black drapery has been employed', reported the *Manchester Courier*.[112] At Windsor Station the waiting room was transformed with white and purple flowers, lilac, lilies of the valley, white azaleas, fresh-cut orchids and other choice flowers. The coffin of the young prince was transferred to a gun carriage and taken through the packed streets to St George's Chapel. Eddy's father and brother, George, still dazed by what had happened, led the mourners walking behind the coffin. The queen had been advised not to attend the funeral and as a result had urged Bertie 'I wish no other princesses to go.'[113] Princess Alexandra refused to obey. 'My darling Eddie would have wished me to take him to his last resting place,' she telegrammed the queen. 'So I shall hide upon the staircase in a corner, unknown to the world.'[114]

There were magnificent floral tributes, including a wreath measuring fifteen feet of white flowers, from the Emperor and Empress of Russia to 'Our Beloved Nephew'.[115] But it was a simple symbolic gesture that brought the tragedy home to the nation. May's father gave away her wreath of bridal orange blossoms to Bertie, who then placed it gently on Eddy's coffin. May found it 'too sad for words' to see his coffin 'close to the altar at which we were to have been married'.[116] To the press she became 'the sole object of the nation's sympathy as a widowed maid'. Under an ancient statute for a princess betrothed to a future heir to the throne, there were reports that she could not marry for another five years, adding 'further gloom' to her 'dismal' circumstances.[117] Her rags-to-riches story had, apparently, ended in rags again, her future as an old maid apparently assured. May bore her grief with dignified restraint but she felt 'utterly crushed'.[118] All that remained of her 'bright dream of happiness' were two rings, her mother reminded the queen.[119]

After years of effort, Queen Victoria's matchmaking to secure the British throne had ended in a catastrophe. 'Poor darling Eddy was so good and gentle I shall miss him greatly,' she confided to Victoria of Battenberg.[120] As for 'poor May', her whole bright future had become 'merely a dream'.[121] The very idea that the 'poor young Bride', personally selected by her, had gone to Sandringham to celebrate her fiancé's birthday only 'to see him die', was unbearable. 'It is one of the most fearful tragedies one can imagine,' she continued. 'It wld sound unnatural & overdrawn if it was put into a Novel.'[122]

Accustomed as she was to dealing with grief and weaving the rituals of mourning into her daily life, Queen Victoria's powerful sense of loss that spring was compounded by another family tragedy when her son-in-law, Louis of Hesse, also died. Her Hessian grandchildren, at a young age, had now lost both parents. 'It adds to my quite overwhelming grief to think of your distress,' she wrote to Victoria of Battenberg, '& dear Ernie and

Alicky alone – <u>Orphans</u>!! It is <u>awful</u>. But I am <u>still there</u> & while I live Alicky, till she is married, will be <u>more</u> than <u>ever my own Child</u> – as you <u>all</u> are …'[123] She felt bound even more tightly as a mother to her two remaining unmarried Hessian grandchildren, especially Alix.

This second death, so hard after the first, proved too much. 'Everything goes wrong,' she confided in despair to Vicky. The queen's matchmaking was in disarray. It seemed impossible to bring Albert's dream to fruition and the harder she tried the more it was pushed out of reach. The sudden loss of Britain's future heir, the endless crisis created by her own German grandson and the trials that beset her favourite granddaughter, Alix, now parentless and irresistibly drawn to the temptations of dangerous Russia – the queen felt 'broken hearted, crushed, bewildered'.[124]

PART TWO

The High Summer of Royalty
1892–1901

7

George and Missy

'Grandmama has gone mad on the subject ...'
Princess Alexandra to Prince George, April 1891

It was a colder winter than usual and the icy chill outside seemed
to pervade the atmosphere at Sandringham as the royal family
struggled with their loss. Alexandra could not be comforted. Her
oldest son, who had always been so loving, was now beyond a
mother's reach. Prince George, still frail from his recent typhoid,
found the loss of his brother, and all the implications that
followed, difficult to bear. His grief mixed with fears about the
responsibilities ahead as a future king, for which he felt so unprepared. Telegrams poured in from concerned relatives. 'Feel for
you awfully,' wrote his cousin, Nicholas, from Russia.[1] Prince
Eddy had shouldered the great expectations of being the heir, a
burden that had shaped his life and protected George. Suddenly
the British throne looked vulnerable. As the prince on whom the
future of the British line would depend, it was George's turn to
experience the full force of Queen Victoria's consideration.

The Wales family arrived at Osborne in early February 1892,
the queen anxious to help her grandson in his new role. Although
Prince George did not suffer from any 'constitutional lethargy'
like his older brother, at twenty-six he had not yet demonstrated
his grandfather's breadth of intellectual interests or his father's
winning charm. Some described him as dull, a stickler for royal
protocol, deeply attached to his mother who leaned on her only
surviving son more than before. Alexandra was 'the very picture

of grief and misery', Queen Victoria observed, and 'so nervous about her other children'.[2] George worked hard to put the queen's mind at rest that he could meet his new obligations. 'I think dear Georgie (of Wales) so nice, sensible, and truly right-minded,' the queen reported to Vicky, 'and so anxious to improve himself.'[3] Marriage was high on her list of priorities as the most potentially improving accomplishment of all.

Prince George wrote to his grandmother after their short visit. 'I shall never fail to come to you for advice when I feel in need of it,' he promised on 13 February, anxious to keep her enquiries at bay.[4] The queen's reply the next day was full of sympathy. She felt 'so [underlined twice] very deeply' for him. There was, however, a gentle hint. The Tecks had now arrived at Osborne and the queen remained impressed with her protégé. 'Poor dear May' looked 'crushed but is so nice', she reminded her grandson.[5] A couple of weeks later the queen wrote more searchingly to 'Darling Georgie, I am longing to hear how you feel and how you spend your time? All is so changed for you since that dreadful 14th January that you must have many anxious and serious thoughts ...'[6] George knew that in his new position the queen would regard his marriage with some urgency. It was not long before her shortlist of possible brides for Eddy was transferred to his younger brother. Top of her list was 'poor dear May'.

The queen found May looking 'sad and thin' but maintaining commendable composure, her emotions under control. Her mother, Mary Adelaide, commandeered the conversation, unable to stop herself repeating every detail of Eddy's demise, while May sat silently, barely able to hide her unhappiness at her sudden change of circumstances. Memories of her triumphant return from Luton were still fresh in her mind, but the door that had been suddenly flung wide open had slammed shut again. Her prospects shrank to the familiar round of charities and parental obligations. On the dreaded 14th – the first-month anniversary 'since poor dear Eddy was taken' – the queen took May out after luncheon alone and found her 'very quiet and sensible but [she] says the contrast is terrible'.[7]

Princess May, like George, found the situation one that tested her to the limit, her parents' shameless pretensions greatly adding to her embarrassment. As the tragedy had unfolded, her father had paced around the rooms of Sandringham mumbling, 'it must be a tzarevich, it must be a tzarevich'.[8] His implication was all too plain to the royal family. Alexandra's younger sister, Dagmar, had once been engaged to Tsar Alexander II's oldest son, Nicholas. When her fiancé had died shortly before his wedding the Danish princess had married the tsarevich's younger brother, now Alexander III. The Duke of Teck could not have conveyed more explicitly his ambitions for his daughter: May should marry Eddy's younger brother, George.

To compound this excruciating humiliation for the princess whose feelings were never on show, her mother, too, devised a scheme to advance her chances with George. Bertie was planning to take his grieving family to the south of France in the spring for a complete change of scene. Mary Adelaide's insistence that 'poor May' in her unhappiness would also benefit from the restorative Mediterranean air was understandable to all. What was highly indecorous as far as Bertie was concerned, indeed quite inexplicable, was that of all the resorts on the French Riviera, May's mother found it necessary to select Menton, a mere two miles from the Wales's own holiday destination at Cap Martin. Bertie soon found all his original objections to Mary Adelaide reawakened, her over-familiar and ample presence grating on his mind.

Prince George and Princess May were unavoidably thrown together in late February 1892, when Bertie and Alexandra invited her to join them as the original wedding date between May and Eddy approached. The Duke of Devonshire had offered Bertie the use of his country house, Compton Place in East Sussex, and as Saturday 27 February dawned, it could not have made more of a contrast to the celebration that had been planned. The royal family walked along the cheerless esplanade, the dreary expedition in an uninviting setting perhaps an unconscious choice that fitted in with the family's desolation. It was 'dreadfully cold', May wrote in her diary, but despite the chill wind they braced themselves for another walk on the downs. She 'felt overcome' when Bertie and Alexandra gave her 'a lovely charming bag' that Eddy had ordered for her, and their own planned wedding gift: a brilliant rivière of diamonds. It was hard not to be caught off guard; the river of diamonds, a gift beyond price in her normal life, was now a forceful reminder of all that was lost.[9]

Her parents' thinly disguised ambitions invited comparisons between George and Eddy. May knew enough about George to be aware of his strengths compared to his older brother. There were no troubling rumours of 'dissipations' attached to his name that had been beginning to give May cause to wonder what she had been taking on with Eddy. George seemed dutiful, dependable, straight-forward, not drawn to the excesses of his overbearing father. His devotion to his mother hinted at a softer side to his nature hidden behind the layers of reserve. Above all he held out the prospect of the British throne, restoring the tantalising opportunity that had been fleetingly on offer. But his feelings were inscrutable. May was a strong woman. Duty she understood; her life had been shaped by it. Romantic love was elusive, perhaps unreliable. She had been prepared to accept her opportunity with Eddy and turn it into something good. What was duty if not a loving act?

Shortly after the Wales family had left for the French Riviera in early March the Tecks also set out. A family friend had inter-vened, discreetly steering Mary Adelaide away from Menton to a villa at Cannes, forty miles along the coast from the Wales's desti-nation: far enough apart never to meet, near enough for May's mother to hope.

———

Prince George did in fact have his own view on the subject of matrimony and had already singled out a special favourite of his own: Princess Marie of Edinburgh, known in the family as 'Missy'. Prince George had long felt an attraction to 'dearest Missy', but since she was ten years his junior he had held back. At the time of Eddy's death she had turned sixteen and under renewed pressure to marry, George could no longer keep his feelings to himself.

As the oldest daughter of the queen's second son, Alfred, the Duke of Edinburgh, Missy had a remarkable heritage, descended from both the British and Russian royal families. Through her father she was a granddaughter of Queen Victoria, and through her mother, a Russian grand duchess, she was also the granddaughter of Alexander II. The young princess had a vivid memory of the day of the tsar's assassination in 1881; it was the first time she had ever found her seemingly invulnerable mother weeping, 'an overwhelming, unheard of cataclysm', she wrote in her memoirs.[10] The grand duchess had hurried to St Petersburg while five-year-old Missy had stayed with her British grandmother at Windsor, who found her 'so innocent and dear with her fine golden hair, fair face & charming smile under her little black cap'.[11]

For George it was not her remarkable pedigree that was Missy's special attraction. Nor the fact that at sixteen she had grown into 'a remarkably pretty girl', according to her cousin, Victoria of Battenberg, with even features, thick blonde hair and blue eyes.[12] Her unique feature was harder to describe. There was something irrepressible about Missy, a joie de vivre, an impulsive spirit that had already inspired a number of followers, including a young Winston Churchill, who allegedly admired from afar. Missy could remember playing with Winston as a child. He was 'red-haired, freckled and impudent', she wrote, and even then displayed 'a fine disdain for authority'. She felt they had 'a sneaking liking for each other' and eventually the young Winston 'threw away all pretence' and openly declared his preference. 'Before witnesses [he said] that when he was grown up he would marry me!'[13] In early 1892, however, the seventeen-year-old Winston had not come forward to claim his supposed childhood sweetheart and Missy was still free.

The knight in shining armour of Missy's youthful games had always been Prince George, who she had known from her earliest years. Growing up at Eastwell in Kent, surrounded by its inviting parklands with great stretches of grass, she soon shared his love of outdoor pursuits. Along with her three younger sisters, Victoria-Melita, nicknamed 'Ducky', Alexandra and Beatrice, the 'Edinburgh girls' had been a tomboy presence in George's life. They were regularly invited to royal residences and in her memoirs Missy recalls the delight of afternoons playing in the gardens of Buckingham Palace. Their governess was obliged to bring spare smocks because she and her sisters would invariably get filthy, drawn as they were to the 'dirtiest, blackest' part of the gardens, the aviary. Surrounded by rare and beautiful birds, 'peacocks, silver and gold pheasants and every sort of duck and goose', the cousins played make-believe games of bandits, pirates and intrepid explorers.

Then there was the thrill of Cowes week, heightened by the excitement of the ferry. Once again the Edinburgh girls led by impulsive Missy were often shown up by the Wales sisters, Louise, Victoria and Maud, whose white starched dresses and sailor hats appeared to Missy impeccably neat. When it came to summer, Missy 'simply adored Scotland ... which touched some special chord in me'. The dramatic landscape, coloured in 'half tones; browns, buffs, purples, grey, every possible tint of these, and the hills in the distance blue, that special blue that distance alone can attain': all this stirred her as it did her British grandmother. There was something 'legendary' about the scenery, she wrote, 'which powerfully moved the soul'.

Princess Marie of Edinburgh was not as carefully educated as Princess May but she had a natural intelligence and eye for detail and has left vivid cameos of the close-knit circle of royal relations she shared with George. Her earliest impression of his mother, Alexandra, was at a shooting party at Eastwell. Aunt Alexandra had chosen to wear a striking red velvet gown with a flowing train. Five-year-old Missy found herself 'speechless with adoration'. Her own mother may have been a Russian grand duchess but she was not exactly a beauty and had settled into plump middle age with a somewhat disgruntled air. By contrast her Aunt Alexandra's loveliness appeared 'invincible ... exquisite and flowerlike'. When this 'velvet clad apparition' volunteered to see the children take their bath, 'I gazed at her over my sponge, spellbound,' recalled Missy. Curious details held her attention, such as Alexandra's beautiful hands and the gold snake bracelets that entwined around her arm with gems for eyes. 'So much did this bracelet seem a part of Aunt Alix that one had the feeling that it had grown on her arm.'

Missy was less sure of her Uncle Bertie. 'He was too patronizing, he lorded it too much over everyone ...' Even his famed geniality could be unnerving; his laugh was a sudden outburst, 'a sort of crackle'. As for her Aunt Vicky, Empress Frederick from Germany, 'who spoke English with a strong foreign accent', she appeared a learned woman 'with a tendency towards the "blue stocking"', rather eager to demonstrate her 'superiority over commoner mortals'. Missy was struck by Aunt Vicky's eyes that were 'extraordinarily blue' and her manner that 'was exceedingly sweet with us children'. Nonetheless she sensed that her Aunt Vicky could be 'forcible, incisive, penetrating'. Vicky's good-looking husband, Uncle Frederick, had also made a lasting impression. Years later Missy could still see him on his last summer visit at the time of the Golden Jubilee in 1887, frail but trying to make light of it. On one occasion he had walked down to Osborne beach. Already voiceless, he had tried to join in with the children and 'pretended to bombard us with sand and dry seaweed'.[4]

From her earliest years, Missy was aware that the most important person in this royal constellation, 'dwarfing all others', was 'Grandmama Queen, the all-powerful'. Her presence 'was felt in all things, even when she was not actually seen'. Without a word being said, her silent wish somehow appeared to be 'the arbiter of our different fates'. Missy could not help noticing that her aunts and uncles, the queen's children, 'were in great awe of "dearest mama"; they avoided discussing her will, and her veto made them tremble. They spoke to her with bated breath, and even when not present she was never mentioned except with a lowered voice.' The queen's inner sanctum at every residence was approached with such extraordinary hushed deference that this created the expectation in a child's eyes of a formidable presence inside. It was something of a surprise to find the doors led to 'a small, unimposing little woman ... not idol-like at all, not a bit frightening'.

Indeed, the source of her grandmother's remarkable authority was not easy to understand as a child. The queen seemed 'almost as shy as us children'. Missy found 'conversation was not very fluent on either side' and she imagined that the queen was as relieved as her visitor when an audience was over. Her rooms, too, were homely, smelling of orange flowers, even when none could be seen. There were pictures of Grandpapa Albert, in such quantities that they 'appeared the first and foremost spirit' of her rooms. All this domesticity was balanced by a heavy workload. Missy felt her grandmother's dispatch boxes commanded her attention for so long that they 'seemed almost a part of Grandmama herself'. In later years, looking back at this period, Missy found she 'cannot help marvelling at the prestige' the queen possessed. It was almost 'fetish-like'; her presence, her personality, the places she inhabited 'had something of shrines about them, which were approached with awe'.[5]

Of all her childhood experiences it was her years in Malta that stood out for Princess Marie. A special affection sprang up between her and her cousin George, and for years afterwards their carefree Malta days appeared as an oasis of delight as though permanently bathed in a summer glow. It all began in 1886 when her father, Alfred, who had a career in the navy, was posted to Malta to assume command of the Mediterranean fleet. Prince George was stationed nearby as a lieutenant on HMS *Alexandra.* Missy's parents kept a room for George at their official residence in the San Antonio Palace and he was a frequent visitor. Missy appreciated her cousin and soon felt George was her 'beloved' friend. 'What fun we had with George, what delightful harmless fun!' Missy wrote.

For Missy and her younger sister, Victoria-Melita, arriving in Malta from Britain in the mid-1880s was like waking up in an exotic land. Standing on the flat roof of their residence on her first morning, Missy felt a wild sense of joy at the scene before her: 'a walled-in oasis, Eastern and secret-looking, a maze of trees, mostly of kinds quite unknown to me ... a lovely mass of colour saturating the whole place with exquisite fragrance ... An enchanted world!' Beckoning enticingly beyond the walled gardens lay an unknown land of improbable beauty, which the girls could explore on their treasured white ponies. In the evening the setting sun created a 'stupendous illumination'; the sky, 'burning red, as if on fire', and the sea all around them 'caught up in its reflection as did the rocks on the harbour', created the impression of a world where 'Earth, heavens and sea were ablaze'.

Into this magical setting, Cousin George had entered their days like a breeze from England; practical, safe, sensible, brotherly. Although older than Missy he joined in their high-spirited games. 'He used to drive us in a high, two-wheeled dog cart,' she recalled. They shared exhilarating days out riding. George 'had a horse called Real Jam, a beautiful glossy bay'. He was companionable at family picnics at the weekends, adept at keeping order between the rowdy sisters and above all, without fail, always loyal to Missy, taking her side when she got into scrapes. On one occasion when she was banished from riding for a week, 'I can still feel what a delicious relief it was to lay my humiliated head upon his shoulder, and to weep my heart out ...' His handkerchief wiped away her tears and he consoled her with 'Poor dear little Missy ... poor dear little Miss ...'[16]

Louis of Battenberg was also stationed in Malta in the 1880s and his wife, Victoria, has left vivid impressions of family gatherings with her Wales and Edinburgh cousins. 'Life was more leisurely there,' wrote Victoria of Battenberg. There were few private carriages; people used 'carozzas' or pony carts, and goats 'were met with every street'. When she escorted the exuberant Missy and her sisters, they would 'gallop along the hard roads', while she would follow at a 'sober trot'. Victoria often sat with her Aunt Marie taking tea in the gardens of the San Antonio palace while her younger cousins played. The Edinburghs hosted many dinner parties and balls; a particular highlight was the fancy-dress ball during carnival week where, it seemed, the entire population turned out to dance traditional Maltese square dances in the sun-drenched streets.[17] In this vibrant carefree world, far away from the restrictive formalities of the British court and his grandmother's watchful concern, George was captivated by his pretty cousin, Missy.

Prince George referred to his Edinburgh cousins as the 'dear three', although Missy had the impression that she was his dearest. Uncertain of himself in this confusing world of transition from

childish games to real romance, George held back from expressing his feelings. Missy, too, with a childish crush on the captain
of her father's ship, gave no sign of encouragement. But Missy
was convinced she was George's 'decided favourite, there was no
doubt about that whatever'.[18] Secretly, George felt that they had
'an understanding'. He wrote to 'my darling Missy' whenever he
was away on his travels. 'You are always in my thoughts,' he told
her on her fourteenth birthday in 1889, sending her 'a great big
kiss [for her] sweet little face'.[19]

Their opportunities to meet easily came to an abrupt end in
1889 when Queen Victoria's plans intruded on their life in Malta.
It had always been Prince Albert's wish that his second son
should inherit the Dukedom of Saxe-Coburg after his brother,
the childless Duke Ernst. By the late 1880s Duke Ernst was
unrecognisable from the once charming older brother who had
accompanied Albert to England forty years earlier. A lifetime of
excess combined with venereal disease to make his future uncertain. The queen judged it best for her son, Alfred, to move his
family to Coburg in preparation for taking over the duchy. Alfred
built a substantial home on the main square, which became known
as 'Palais Edinburg', and settled his wife and children there. The
young Princess Marie was transfixed at the sight of Great Uncle
Ernst. It was hard to believe this 'terrible figure' was the brother
of the almost sacred Grandpapa Albert, whose noble spirit was
held up before them all. Ernst might 'have been an ogre', wrote
Missy, squeezed into 'a frock coat too tight for his bulk', his eyes
bloodshot, 'his sallow face marred by liver spots', and treating his
wife with 'abominable, insulting indifference'.[20]

Inevitably, George saw less of Missy after her move to
Germany, although there was one opportunity in 1890 when
he visited Coburg with his father. George was still enchanted
by the exuberant, irrepressible Missy. Her love of the outdoors
remained untempered by the efforts of her new German governess, the disagreeable 'Fräulein', to turn her into more of a lady.
Missy was an excellent horsewoman and critical of her German
riding lessons, which were 'not so amusing as riding out of doors,
to keep going round in the school gets rather a bore'. She thought

nothing of becoming caught in a thunderstorm in an open carriage despite the fact that 'we all got very wet' and loved to sit out late in the garden.[21] George wrote to her afterwards. 'What fun we had … when we danced'. He felt bold enough to address her as 'Darling Missy' when he wrote in the New Year of 1891. 'You are constantly in my thoughts,' he told her, signing himself 'yr most loving & devoted old Georgie'. He sent her a crystal clock for Christmas 1891 inscribed endearingly 'Darling Missy'.[22]

Prince George had initially sought his mother's advice about a formal approach to Missy in spring 1891 when Queen Victoria had first 'gone mad' about his marriage prospects in the wake of Eddy's failed alliance with Hélène. Princess Alexandra was discouraging. Missy was not yet sixteen and it was too soon 'in every way!!', she wrote back, 'particularly as the bride is not in long petticoats yet!!!'[23] Princess Alexandra was not an entirely disinterested party. She doted on her son and was in no hurry for him to marry, and she also found much to dislike about the new German influences on the 'Edinburgh girls'. Princess Alexandra could not know of the extent of Missy and her sisters' revolt against their German tutor's efforts to uproot their British past. 'We loved England deeply and clung with all our hearts to that love,' Missy wrote. The Edinburgh girls despised their German tutor, who they called 'Dr X', and pitted themselves against him 'with that magnificent courage of children whose gods are attacked'. As for 'Fräulein', who became his fiancée, Missy soon decided that her 'ingratiating' and 'honeyed' style disguised a pernicious character that was 'as destructive as a dangerous bacillus'.[24]

But Princess Alexandra saw only that the Edinburgh girls 'now have quite a foreign accent living so long abroad and surrounded by Germans,' she told George. She also objected to the way Missy's mother, the Duchess of Edinburgh, was rushing Missy's entry into German society, 'the girl being a perfect baby yet – altho Aunt Marie begging her pardon does all she can to make her old before her time which I think the greatest mistake which I know you think also and what do you say to Aunt Marie having hurried on the two girls confirmation & in Germany too, so that now they won't even know that they have ever been English'.[25]

Princess Alexandra's comments to George about Missy were insensitive enough to trouble any nervous suitor.

George was sufficiently concerned about Missy's sudden removal to Germany and early confirmation to raise the matter with his grandmother. Queen Victoria, always ready to suspect an ulterior motive in other people's behaviour, for some reason saw no harm in it. 'Coburg is a second country to us all, being your dear Grandpapa's country,' she replied on 31 July 1891. Uncle Alfred's prolonged absence in the navy 'is not popular nor any good for him in Germany naturally'. This made it 'quite essential' that the Duchess of Edinburgh should live at Coburg with the children. As for the older girls' confirmation, the queen told George this had arisen because Missy and her sister, Victoria-Melita, were 'so very fond' of their elderly religious instructor, Superintendent Muller, who had 'so deeply impressed the girls'. The Edinburghs were 'afraid he might not live to confirm them if he waited much longer'.[26] If George was unconvinced by this explanation he did not press it further. The queen had a remarkable facility for not seeing anything that reflected unfavourably on herself and failed to spot that the hurried confirmation was an act of rebellion by the Duchess of Edinburgh.

Missy's Russian mother – also called Marie – was, in fact, anxious to consolidate her exit from Queen Victoria's sphere of influence. The Duchess of Edinburgh had been delighted to move to Germany and her confirmation of the girls in the German Lutheran faith was a strong statement of her own independence and control after years of nursing long-held grievances at the British court. The speed with which she broke away from her British ties was just the latest in a long line of conflicts that had simmered throughout her marriage. Prince Alfred and Grand Duchess Marie had married in 1874 despite prolonged opposition from their parents, and within weeks problems had arisen that had prompted Alexander II to send complaints to Queen Victoria.

As a daughter of a tsar and an 'imperial highness' in her own right, Grand Duchess Marie could not understand her lowly ranking in the British court. By marrying the queen's second son, she came behind Queen Victoria's daughters and Princess Alexandra in order of precedence. 'I believe my mother felt this rather sorely,' her daughter, Missy, observed later. The grand duchess believed in the superiority of her home country with a passion and held to Russian customs. She felt demeaned by the modesty of the British court in comparison with the palatial glamour of the Romanov court 'and was always just a little in opposition to the times', observed her daughter. Her rooms exuded a Russian air, the furniture from St Petersburg with a distinctive scent of leather and cedar wood, icons and Russian imagery on the walls. Even her boots were ordered from St Petersburg, both feet identical since the Duchess of Edinburgh did not agree with the British custom of a distinct left and right shoe.[27]

Above all, the Duchess of Edinburgh resented Queen Victoria's meddling ways. She was fully aware of the queen's Russophobia and had seen her hostile letters during the Russo-Turkish War. The queen's interference in the marriage of the grand duchess's younger brother, Sergei, to Ella had antagonised her still further. The grand duchess could not fail to know of the queen's prolonged opposition to any Russian match for Alix. As she prepared for the time when she would become Duchess of Coburg at the helm of a court of her own, she seized her opportunity to distance herself and her girls from this unbiddable and fussing old woman.

After Eddy's death, Prince George knew he must do his duty and marry soon; but he did not want to marry out of duty alone. He had always avoided exposing his own feelings and it was hard for him to find out whether Missy still had a special affection for him. She wrote again shortly after Eddy's death. 'My dearest George', she began. 'Let me also tell you how deeply I feel for you in your deep sorrow. How often I have thought of you all now, Oh! What a terrible blow for you all! Tell all cousins & dear Aunt Alix how sincerely we sympathize with them. How terribly sudden it must have been ... But what is the good of making you unhappy by reminding you afresh. Only know that I feel sincerely for you all. Your loving Missy.'[28]

The warmth expressed in Missy's letter was ambiguous. It did not rule out the possibility that she nurtured feelings for him, but equally it did not stray beyond the bounds of decorum.

Separated by being in different countries, aware that his every move was magnified by an inquisitive array of aunts and uncles as well as the all-consuming interest of the press, it was not easy for George to see how to transform his relationship from that of Missy's beloved cousin to her suitor. But Queen Victoria lent her support to the idea. It was agreed that Bertie should make an initial approach to the Edinburghs. George, too, wrote directly to 'Darling Missy'. All he could do was await her response.[29]

During March of 1892 the days passed for Princess May waiting in the south of France, with no word from Prince George. The Tecks' destination at Cannes, Villa Clementine, was all that her mother had promised: warmth, light, terraces with sea views, gardens ablaze with colour. The roses were in abundance, smothering the walls, tumbling over the olive and orange trees, scenting the salt sea air. Compared to the memories of Sandringham, the cold, cluttered rooms, the shocking scenes of Eddy's deathbed, the strain of feeling an outsider who reminded the family of their loss, May was now in a place where wounds might heal in private. But nothing could quite erase the pain.

Princess May became aware of feeling her loneliness in a way that she had not before, she confided to her friend, Helene Bricka, her former governess. As she approached her twenty-fifth birthday she felt her chances of marriage were fast diminishing. Her confidence wavered and she worried that her intrinsic shyness was taking over, but felt powerless to prevent it. 'I fear I am getting more reserved than ever,' she admitted. There was no escape from a dull aching feeling as though something 'pleasant' had 'passed out of one's life forever'.[30] She shrank from any discussions of her future and her father noted her alarm at the prospect of returning home.

The awkwardness of her position is perhaps highlighted by the actions of Eddy's sisters and mother. Although May had been Eddy's official fiancée, they treated the French princess, Hélène, as his real love. They exchanged intimate letters with Hélène referring to their shared grief and sorrow. 'He is buried with your little coin around his neck,' Princess Maud revealed to Hélène. Maud and her mother had secretly placed it on his body 'and nobody knew it'. For them, 'you were the one he really loved and now he is yours still, and nobody can take him away from you'. The oldest sister, Louise, went so far as to imply that 'God had been merciful' in taking Eddy, 'and done all for the best instead of him belonging to another', and that he was being kept above in heaven for Hélène, 'yours in death'.[31] For the Wales sisters, Eddy's idle summer days shared with Hélène at Mar Lodge had been the happiest of his life.

Their letters served to underline the unromantic, inconvenient nature of Eddy's alliance with May, as though it stemmed from duty only. Their sentiments implied that May was merely a cypher, someone to occupy the required position of 'wife'. Eddy's sisters told Hélène that Princess May 'never knew and loved him as you did'. They were soon exchanging locks of hair, poems and other memorabilia with Hélène. Even Queen Victoria acknowledged Hélène's special position, writing to her on 17 March 1892 'knowing your heart is still full', enclosing 'precious souvenirs' of Eddy. She asked Hélène to refer to her as 'Grandmama', underlining the closeness of her grandson's ties to the French princess and enclosing photographs of his burial place and dried flowers neatly preserved from bouquets placed on his coffin.[32] Queen Victoria also believed that May had never been in love with Eddy, a view that conveniently made an alliance with his younger brother easier to accept.

The Tecks spent uneventful days with carriage rides into Antibes, Nice and Grasse. The scenery was spectacular but it was an unsettling time to be in France. The press was full of what they called an 'anarchist dynamite conspiracy', which had suddenly erupted on the streets of Paris. 'Propaganda of the deed' had not been seen on this scale before in France and there was talk of a new phase of 'French Terror'. The attacks appeared to be targeted at the judiciary, striking at the very heart of the Third French Republic under President Sadi Carnot.

It all began shortly after the Tecks' arrival in France when an explosion on 11 March 1892 in the Boulevard Saint-Germain ripped apart the home of a prominent judge, Edmund Benoit. The police soon established that this was revenge for Benoit's tough sentencing of anarchists whose unauthorised march the previous year had ended in violence.[33] A few days later there was a second explosion at a military barracks in Paris. A police search of the lodgings of thirty-five known anarchists led to a veritable weapons arsenal in the northern suburb of St Denis: cyanide, sulphate of potassium, acid, electrical batteries, six bombs and 'various explosive machines'.[34] None of this stopped a third massive explosion on 27 March that injured six people at the home of another lawyer involved in the earlier anarchist trials. After a tip-off from staff at a restaurant on 30 March, the police finally caught up with their key suspect for the bombings: the notorious French criminal and self-proclaimed 'anarchist', François Ravachol. The Tecks had been planning to visit Paris later that spring and followed this new development closely.

Forty miles further along the coast, settled into a hotel in Cap Martin, Prince George also felt the intrusion of the outside world. Just before he left England a letter had come for him from Coburg in Germany. He had waited several years before he could bring himself to the point of enquiring about Princess Missy's feelings. Now her reply did not allow for much hope.

Missy wrote that she held him in affection as a cousin but he 'must not think that there was anything definite in the friendship that had sprung up between them at Malta'.[35] Could this reflect her true feelings? The carefully chosen words did not sound like Missy, who had always been so spontaneous. George could not know that the letter had been dictated by her mother, only that the understanding he had been convinced they had shared might never have existed. Had he misunderstood her? All around him the beauty of the Mediterranean was a vivid reminder of their time together in Malta, colourful childhood memories that now seemed to recede. George was not a man of overpowering passion; all his life he had done what was correct and approved. He did not have enough self-assurance when it came to his feelings to make a definite move. Instead, he let himself be guided by his parents as he struggled to adjust his state of mind.

Bertie passed on the disappointing news to Queen Victoria and on 2 March 1892 a letter duly arrived from Windsor for George casting a probing spotlight on his feelings: 'I know how much you <u>did</u> wish to marry her Missy some day,' wrote the queen, '& they say that you declared that you wld never marry anyone else! But <u>then</u> you did <u>not know</u> that <u>she</u> did not care to <u>marry</u> you nor that you wld be placed in a totally different position – which may oblige you to marry earlier when she would be almost too young and above all very inexperienced. I should also be glad however, to know what your <u>own</u> feeling is about it, for dear Eddy told me <u>all</u> about himself and showed me great confidence & I am sure you wld do the same. It is moreover <u>necessary</u> that I shld <u>know</u> the exact state of the case, so that I can be able to help you ...'[36]

There at a stroke were so many of the queen's characteristics: the insensitivity of her blunt reference to Missy 'not caring' for him; the straight talking about his obligations, including his duty to marry quickly; and her desire to meddle which required that she knew his feelings. But George did not feel the need to take his grandmother into his confidence in his reply. Nor was he in any hurry to contact Princess May of Teck as the queen wished.

George waited several weeks until the end of March before he sent Princess May a note. He and his father were visiting Cannes, he explained. Could they come over for dinner one night? George's letter to May hinted at his somewhat gloomy frame of mind. 'What a bore it is pouring today. There is nothing to be done but look out of the window and see the rain fall,' he wrote, evidently feeling trapped indoors. The sudden death of Uncle Louis of Hesse had also prompted painful thoughts. 'I am so sorry for all the poor cousins who are now orphans,' he continued. No note of optimism could be detected by May in George's letter; little to suggest hope.[37]

The Wales's yacht, the *Nerine*, eased into Cannes harbour in early April, joining the many boats in this private sun-soaked world, but not quite dismissing the anxieties for May about what might happen. Prince George had hoped their visit would not attract attention, but there was no chance of that. One or two more sober newspapers confined themselves to the facts, discreetly noting that Prince George was among the guests joining the Tecks for dinner in Cannes, but most did not stop short of speculation even running to wedding presents. According to the *Yorkshire Evening Post*, a dinner service made for Prince Eddy's wedding was being held over for Prince George and since 'the present is to be the same, Princess May will be the bride'.[38]

Prince George's arrival in Cannes crossed with another letter from the queen, revealing her increasing impatience. 'Have you seen May and have you thought more about the <u>possibility</u> or <u>found out</u> what her feelings might be?' she wrote brusquely on 6 April.[39] Less than two months had passed since Eddy's death and already she was expecting George to consider his dead brother's fiancée. But the prince had not come to Cannes to talk about a wedding.

George was attentive to May, but self-contained, his behaviour readily understandable as polite interest rather than affection. There was plenty of opportunity for each to assess the other discreetly since they were rarely alone. Gatherings of relatives and friends met to dine on the *Nerine* or one of the other yachts, or to go for a drive or a picnic – which on one occasion turned into a 'frog hunt', hardly a situation that might help romance along.[40] Her cousin was guarded, apparently the perfect English gentleman, his feelings hard to read. George was equally detached in his reply to his grandmother, taking pains to ensure she knew he had done his duty, while giving nothing away of his emotions. He wrote of the great heat, the fine air and the beautiful flowers in Cannes. Then he added, 'We saw Aunt Mary & May every day & dined with them twice at Villa Clementine where they are staying. I thought all three of them looking wonderfully well, the change and quiet there has done them good ...'[41]

The French public saw no reason for such British restraint. Even in republican France, May's story of royal love and tragedy had fired people's imagination. On one occasion the Wales and the Tecks, both families in black mourning, visited a flower market in Cannes. May attracted attention: a pretty young woman in widow's weeds and not even married, proclaiming her sad state among all the sunshine and flowers. With charming spontaneity, a Frenchman asked the princess whether she could accept a gift. When she agreed, he returned with a magnificent bouquet. His touching gesture was noticed by others and soon there was a small crowd, each person with flowers for the widowed bride. There were so many that Prince George was obliged to come to her assistance, and then the Prince of Wales too. The sombre mood was transformed for a moment. It was hard to resist the warmth of the French people's gesture and the Prince of Wales, a committed Francophile, was enchanted.

Despite such romantic moments, George did nothing to raise May's expectations during his visit to Cannes. With Missy he had felt there had once been a genuine affinity; he could trust in her warmth and affection, even if not her love. The queen wrote to him in early April with more news about Missy, which still provided little by way of an explanation. The Duchess of Edinburgh 'is in no way to blame. She never wished for her Cousin, who tho he is good & steady she does not particularly care for. She is not angry with you or bears you any ill whatever. What did hurt her dreadfully was a letter that was written wh. ought not to have been.'[42] If George had suspicions that Missy's dictatorial mother had taken the decision, rather than Missy herself, the queen was unaware of it.

Both George and May left the Riviera on their separate travels that spring, their futures unresolved. Princess May continued to follow the details of the nihilist violence in Paris that formed a disturbing backdrop to her European tour. Could the anarchist movement represent a threat to any British royal marriage – however safe it appeared? There had not yet been anarchist attacks in London on the scale of the Paris attacks. In France, the authorities appeared unable to keep order, despite the arrest of the ringleader, Ravachol. On the eve of his trial in April there were more reprisals as a bomb ripped apart the very restaurant in Paris where he had been arrested. Many people were badly wounded, including the restaurant owner, Monsieur Véry, whose injuries were so severe that his traumatised wife 'has for the time, lost her senses and is in a raving condition', reported the *Manchester Times*. Monsieur Véry revealed that he had repeatedly warned the police of death threats he had received after Ravachol's arrest, yet they had been unable to prevent the explosion at his restaurant. The jury was so terrified that the court, too, would be bombed that they 'yielded to the sentiment of terror' and gave lenient sentences. Their decision was 'a triumph for the dynamite party', concluded the *Manchester Times*. 'The expression on the Boulevards is a feeling closely allied to panic.'[43]

Princess May and her family left the Riviera to see relatives in Germany but took the opportunity to pass through Paris and see what was going on for themselves. On 5 May the Tecks began their tour at the *Conciergerie* to explore France's revolutionary past. They peered into the small, dark cells occupied a century earlier by Marie Antoinette and Maximilien Robespierre. In a dark, airless corner, under constant surveillance of the guard, Marie Antoinette had spent her last few days in her struggle to survive France's first revolution. In the 100 years since, France had seen two further revolutions, in 1830 and 1848, as well as the Paris Commune of 1871. 'Ravachol the anarchist is now shut up here,' May commented in her diary.[44]

It was hard to make sense of the many different strands of anarchism that had emerged. France, that hotbed of revolutionary thinking, had produced Pierre Proudhon, dubbed 'the father of anarchy', whose writings in the first half of the nineteenth century had advocated peaceful change. Proudhon believed in 'order in anarchy', a phrase that later gave rise to the anarchist symbol, the 'A' in anarchy circled by an 'O'. Proudhon had inspired the Russian, Michael Bakunin, who believed revolution was the only way to destroy the existing structures of power and usher in a new social order. Another strand of anarchism arose in Germany through the philosopher Max Stirner, who argued for 'egoism', a form of 'self-mastery' in which individuals were truly autonomous. His ideas would inspire a generation of existentialists and anarchists.

By the 1890s anarchism was no longer the province of theorists and dreamers but encompassed a wide range of direct actions. Swelling the ranks of Europe's disparate anarchist movements were recruits drawn from the squalor and stench of Europe's fast-growing industrial cities. Many championed new workers' movements and trade unions and hoped to use widespread strike action to grind the system to a halt. Amongst Europe's peasant populations, too, there were sporadic anarchist attacks across the continent from Spain to the Ukraine. Although some anarchists believed in peaceful means to bring about change, anarchy was indelibly associated in the public mind with dynamite and the birth of international terrorism. While in Paris the Tecks took the opportunity to have lunch with Lord Dufferin, the former ambassador to Russia who had been in St Petersburg ten years earlier when the idea of a new age of anarchist terror had exploded into public consciousness with the gruesome assassination of Alexander II.[45] Now dynamite conspiracies were becoming almost commonplace and captured the public imagination in the literary mainstream.

The means by which anarchy might destroy the existing social order was explored in Edward Fawcett's science fiction novel, *The Doom of the Great City*, published in 1892. Fawcett's fictional character, 'Hartmann, the anarchist', attempted to blow up the German Crown Prince as he drove over Westminster Bridge. The failure of this attempt fired his mission. 'We want no more "systems" or "constitutions" – we shall have anarchy,' declared Hartmann, who despised the hidden price paid for Victorian consumerism: 'Men will ... abjure the foulness of the modern wage-slavery and city-mechanisms.' Hartmann set out to blow up London in a 'tempest of dynamite'. His aim was 'to pierce the ventricle of the heart of civilization, that heart which pumps the blood of capital everywhere, through the arteries of Russia, of Australia, of India ... the fur companies in North America, planting enterprises in Ecuador and trading steamers on African rivers'. The tower of Big Ben was the first to topple, 'bruising into jelly a legion of buried wretches'. Then the Houses of Parliament collapsed, its pinnacles and walls 'riven asunder'. Finally,

Hartmann's dynamite was unleashed on the bankers in the city in 'a constant roar of explosions'. Fawcett's story showed how the anarchists and dynamiters captured dissatisfaction with all systems of power – not just constitutional but also financial – that propped up the great social injustices of late nineteenth-century Europe.[46]

Before leaving Paris, the Tecks went to see Véry's restaurant for themselves.[47] This was the site of the most recent anarchist outrage and on turning into Boulevard Magenta, the place was immediately marked out by a large pile of charred furnishings on the pavement. As they drew closer, they saw that the ground floor had been blown out entirely, empty space where windows should be. The ruined, blackened interior still had the power to shock. Innocent people would have stood little chance. The bomb had been placed by the door, trapping diners inside. The leading perpetrator, Ravachol, was taken to the guillotine in July defiantly chanting an anarchists' song, according to the prison chaplain:

Danse, dynamite,
Danse, danse vite,
Dansons et chantons:
Dynamitons, dynamitons![48]

The desire of the 'dynamite party' to spread mass terror was not easy to understand. Would such a movement grow and where would it end? Would monarchy survive into the twentieth century? As the Tecks left Paris on the Orient Express for Stuttgart, the image of the burnt-out restaurant was a chilling reminder of the threatening undercurrents of instability in Europe: a warning.

8

Missy and Ferdinand

'Cruel is the only word which really describes it.'
Queen Marie of Romania, *Memoirs*

After turning down Prince George, sixteen-year-old 'Missy', Princess Marie of Edinburgh, was unknowingly facing a battle of her own. The path she was being steered towards would come to cause her so much distress that even years later she found 'my pen seems to tremble in my hand when I set about recounting it'.[1]

Her ordeal began imperceptibly when she and her younger sister, Victoria-Melita, accompanied her mother as guests of Kaiser Wilhelm and his wife, Dona, at Wilhelmshohe, a handsome château near Cassel, some 200 miles from Berlin. Ostensibly, the event was a celebration at the all-important annual *Kaisermanover* of military displays and cavalry assaults. Missy had not yet come out into society officially. All innocence, she was trying to appear grown up – a lamb to the slaughter. Dressed in her best mauve-coloured gown, complete with a matching coloured orchid she had chosen, she made her entrance through the tall pillared doorway of the eighteenth-century château with her fifteen-year-old sister, armed with her mother's advice 'not to be tongue-tied'. It was like entering a different realm; before her were the grandees of the German court, all appearing at ease in this lavishly gilded world.

Despite Wilhelm's colourful personality, he was 'not a favourite cousin', Missy observed. She felt he could be brusque and boisterous in his dealings with the family, almost intimidating. 'There was something about him that aroused antagonism' and made her feel 'all prickly with opposition'. Although his obedient wife, Dona, now the mother of six strapping sons, tried to be charming, Missy sensed there was a pretence about her cordiality, 'her smile seemed glued on'. Doubtless it was a relief that evening for Missy to find herself seated for dinner nowhere near the German emperor and empress, but next to an attractive man, ten years her senior, who had a youthful, unconfident air. This was so marked that Missy remembered vividly his awkward habit of laughing readily – even giggling – to mask an intrinsic shyness and lack of ease. He was introduced as the heir to the Romanian throne, Crown Prince Ferdinand.

Missy thought little of the apparently chance meeting until afterwards, when it was too late. 'Was it all a plot,' she wondered. Were her relatives 'all in it'? There were other 'coincidental' meetings through her German cousins with Crown Prince Ferdinand of Romania, who was from the senior branch of Germany's imperial line, the House of Hohenzollern-Sigmaringen. It was only long afterwards that she reflected on her youthful joy and trust that made her suspect nothing. 'But for all that it was cruel,' she wrote, 'yes, cruel is the only word which really describes it; it was a sort of trapping of innocence, a deliberate blinding against life as it truly is ...' At no stage did Missy blame her Russian mother, but the Duchess of Edinburgh was the key player in arranging her fate – all the while the duchess's face appearing 'happy and expectant', inspiring her daughter's confidence.[2]

For some months the Duchess of Edinburgh had been working on a marital alliance for her oldest daughter that would suit her relatives in Russia and win favour in her new home of Germany. The duchess's choices were intimately bound up with the outcome of the Russo-Turkish War. Her father, Alexander II, had been humiliated at the Congress of Berlin in 1878 when Russian control in the Balkans was curtailed. At the time Romania was recognised as an independent country, freed from Ottoman control. It was in the interests of the duchess's older brother, Alexander III, to gain influence there with his niece on the Romanian throne.

There was a second beneficiary of the Duchess of Edinburgh's planned alliance who was not unaware of the scheme: Kaiser

Wilhelm. While Missy innocently pictured Romania in vague terms as 'a land of Romance, a land of Promise' somewhere far off in the east, 'near the Rising Sun', the Kaiser knew exactly how the land lay.[3] This was a Balkan country of strategic importance to the east of Austria-Hungary where he wanted to strengthen German influence. In 1881 his distant cousin, Prince Karl of Hohenzollern-Sigmaringen, had been crowned King Carol of Romania. Two years later Carol joined the treaty between Germany and Austria-Hungary (and later Italy) – his agreement so secret that the only copy was kept under lock and key by the king himself.[4] Since Carol was childless his nephew, Prince Ferdinand, became the heir to the throne. The duchess's proposed alliance for her daughter could only serve to bind the ties between the two countries still more tightly together.

After turning down Prince George, events came to a head for Missy in Germany with astonishing speed. Her mother took the view that as girls grow older they 'begin to think too much and have too many ideas of their own which complicate matters'.[5] She was keen to preempt this with her spirited oldest daughter. Missy and her younger sister, Victoria-Melita, were invited to Berlin to stay at the house of the Kaiser's older sister, Charlotte. Missy implicitly trusted her worldly 'Cousin Charly' and it was only later that she felt taken in. Charlotte contrived that the timid Crown Prince Ferdinand of Romania was a frequent visitor, a tactic that misfired when it became clear that Missy and her sister did not shine in their cousin's sophisticated Berlin set. The Duchess of Edinburgh hurriedly adapted her plans, making arrangements for her daughter to meet the Romanian prince in Munich. All innocence, Missy wrote to her grandmother on 21 May 1892 about her forthcoming trip to see her brother, Alfred. 'We like going to Munich as there are many interesting things to see and lovely pictures,' she told Queen Victoria.[6] Under her mother's expert direction, Missy found that she and the Romanian prince were frequently thrown together.

Missy's next meeting with the Crown Prince in Berlin brought matters to a swift conclusion. The venue was the German emperor's magnificent Neues Palais at Potsdam. Kaiser Wilhelm had transformed the galleries and reception rooms of Frederick the Great's baroque masterpiece into a palatial statement of the power and glory of the German Empire. Berlin's elite assembled in their finery under the newly electrified chandeliers, themselves the craftsmanship of the finest glassmakers. In this opulent setting, spurred on by Charly and other German relatives, somehow the reticent prince managed to find the crucial words.

'How he ever had the courage to propose is today still a mystery to me,' Missy recalled. 'But he did and I accepted – I just said "Yes" as though it had been quite a natural and simple word to say. "Yes" and with that "Yes" I sealed my fate.' Missy remembers no particular feeling; she hardly knew her fiancé. She was merely aware of 'the approving eye of Kaiser William'; 'the benignly conventional smile' of his wife, Dona, and her own mother: 'radiant'. Later in life she looked back on her incredible trust and 'simple mindedness'. Still no more than a child, she was unaware of reality and lived 'in a glorious, happy, healthy Fool's Paradise'.[7]

Later that night, as though the outcome had been expected, Kaiser Wilhelm held a magnificent banquet for the young couple. The feast took place in the seemingly enchanted white castle at Pfaueninsel, 'Peacock Island', on a river within the Potsdam estate. In the luxurious setting of the island retreat, Missy was the centre of attention, heady with excitement and champagne, convinced she had found happiness. Emperor Wilhelm rose to make a speech and announce his cousin's engagement, sealing the deal with his authority. Toasts were proposed. Hands were shaken. The deed was done. It was only afterwards, prompted by her more cautious sister, Victoria-Melita, that impetuous Missy paused to reflect that she had accepted a man virtually unknown to her. Her British father had not been consulted. There was also the question of 'Grandmamma Queen'. 'My conscience was not quite easy,' she recalled.[8] With good reason; the British royal family were not well pleased.

Queen Victoria was 'quite dumbfounded'. She was at Balmoral on the evening of 2 June 1892 when a telegram arrived from Alfred out of the blue. Her son was devastated, she noted in her journal, but 'did not feel he could withhold his consent' after being presented with a fait accompli.[9] The queen felt powerless and turned to Vicky to confide her feelings. A match between Missy and George had been 'the dream of Affie's life' and he worried about what lay ahead for his pretty oldest daughter in Romania. Bertie too, she wrote, was 'very angry' about the match, which seemed like a further insult to George.[10]

Vicky's replies to her mother reveal her suspicions that her own children may have helped engineer the match. 'I ... only hope that William did nothing to hasten matters – he has done that very often – not always with happy results.' It also struck Vicky as curious that her daughter, Charlotte, was 'very enthusiastic for Romania'.[11] Two days later she wrote again to the queen commenting on how strange it seemed that both Missy and Ferdinand 'should feel so <u>sure</u>'. Had they been manipulated in some way? She expressed her concern for George, recognising his disappointment, 'wh. I feel sure is great'. At least the engagement 'so completely clears the situation', she pointed out. There was no longer room for George to entertain secret hopes.[12]

Queen Victoria was blind to the possibility that the Duchess of Edinburgh had deliberately engineered the match in her determination to steer her oldest daughter well away from the British court and her own forceful control. Instead, the queen chose to believe that the duchess had herself been taken by surprise. The duchess put it about that she had gone to Potsdam to please Dona, who '<u>wished</u> Missy for <u>odious Gunther!</u>' her unappealing brother, Ernst, who had already been rejected by Princess May. Vicky recognised that this could not be the whole story. She noted the troubling fact that Alfred was away 'when his child was engaged!' with all arranged behind his back. As for Ernst Gunther, she understood that he was 'very anxious' to marry Missy's younger sister, Victoria-Melita, but did 'not find any favour wh is quite natural'.[13] Part of the queen's strength appeared to lie in her inability to see or brood on her weaknesses. She continued to air her opinions liberally on the match, unable to see her own influence on the outcome owing to her poor relationship with her Russian daughter-in-law. The whole thing had been done with most indecent haste, she thought. Added to which 'the Country is vy insecure & the immorality of the Society at Bucharest <u>quite awful</u>,' she told Victoria of Battenberg.[14] As for 'poor Missy', she is 'a mere Child'.

As word spread, Missy's match continued to evoke strong feelings. 'Disgusted,' declared Lady Geraldine, wrongly concluding that the alliance had been engineered by the British royal family to suit their own purposes. 'It does seem too cruel a shame to cart that nice pretty girl off to semi barbaric Romania ... to clear the way for May!!! Too bad.'[15] Princess May had reached her German relatives at Ludwigsburg when a telegram arrived in early June bearing the startling news. She could hardly fail to know of George's interest in his Edinburgh cousin. Now pretty, vivacious Missy was spoken for – whisked off the list of potential brides. This could only signify greater hope for the Tecks. There was no discreet holding back for Mary Adelaide. She wasted no time in making arrangements for them all to meet with Missy's mother to hear all the news at first hand under the guise of happy congratulations.

Prince George was in Denmark when he heard of Missy's engagement. A sparkling array of royal relatives had descended on Copenhagen from across Europe to celebrate the golden wedding anniversary of Alexandra's Danish parents, King Christian and Queen Louise. As the news broke in this imposing company George had to work hard to keep his composure. Many who knew he had hoped to marry Missy were there. He had offered her the prospect of being a future Queen of Great Britain. But the princess of his choice had turned him down, apparently rushing to marry an unremarkable prince in line for an inconsequential throne in a backwater of Europe. This was the ultimate rejection.

Prince George may have been lacking a bride, but arrangements were proceeding like clockwork for his smooth transition to the married state. Plans were underway for the prince to take up the very apartments allocated to Eddy in St James's Palace before George embarked on his married life. Over the summer of 1892 correspondence flowed to and from Sir Henry Ponsonby's office about the costs of repairing the apartments and adapting the bachelor cottage at Sandringham. George's income to keep up a separate establishment was arranged and 'in case of Prince George's marriage', wrote Ponsonby, sufficient funds were made available for him 'to make a settlement on his wife'.[16] Like his brother before him, the queen honoured George with a new title. Eddy had been elevated to the peerage as the Duke of Clarence and Avondale. George would become the Duke of York and his place and precedence in the House of Lords was being arranged.

With an almost disturbing seamlessness, he seemed to be stepping into his brother's shoes. It was as though his very identity was being moulded to take over not just Prince Eddy's role but also his home, perhaps even his bride. After Missy's rejection, Queen Victoria was clear that there was one obvious solution for her grandson George. There was a royal bride, already vetted and perfect for him. George must inherit not just his brother's throne, but his bride as well. As for May, Queen Victoria understood that any sensible girl would know that respect and the doing of one's duty, whatever disappointments life might offer, were the unvoiced creed of royalty. Love would follow.

The queen raised the matter again in May 1892, prompting Bertie to advise her not to push the case. After George's serious illness 'and then the shock he received when Eddy was taken from us', the Prince of Wales felt his son had not quite recovered. 'It would be bad for him', Bertie wrote to the queen, if he and May were pressed into it.[17] The queen at last acquiesced. 'Georgie shall be forgotten as you wish,' she promised him. But she omitted to say for how long.[18]

Among the royal glitterati who arrived in Copenhagen in June 1892 for the Golden Wedding anniversary of the Danish king and queen was George's cousin, the tsarevich. Twenty-four-year-old Nicholas was three years younger than his British cousin and slightly taller, his eyes a deeper shade of blue. They remained as alike as twins, even with the same brown-coloured hair, just starting to recede across the forehead. As future rulers of Britain and

Russia, between them they were heirs to empires that covered almost half the world. In the informal atmosphere of their grand-parents' Danish court, they had the opportunity for a lengthy exchange. Still feeling the loss of Eddy, George warmed to Nicholas and they talked privately together for hours, as brothers would. Both faced the same pressures to find a bride, and despite living thousands of miles apart, both felt the ubiquitous influence of Queen Victoria over their choice.

Nicholas knew that Queen Victoria, like his own parents, opposed his first choice of the beautiful Alix of Hesse. Unlike his Romanov relatives, Nicholas tended to indecisiveness, except when it came to Alix. He did not even have to think about it; he was sure he loved her. Whenever speculating on his future he always imagined her in his life, but could not see how this would happen. She seemed remote, unobtainable. 'I have struggled a long time against my feelings,' Nicholas had confided to his diary at Christmas 1891, 'and tried to persuade myself it was an impos-sible thing, but since Eddy gave up the idea of marrying her, or was refused by her, it seems that the only obstacle between us is the religious question. There is no other, because I am convinced she shares my feelings.'[19]

Alix was less certain. The obstacles to marrying the Russian tsarevich loomed large in her mind, first among them her absolute commitment to the Lutheran faith that guided all her actions. If she were to become a future tsarina she would have to convert to the Russian Orthodox Church. Although both Ella and her cousin, Sophie, had each joined their husband's faith, Alix saw this as an impasse. Her confirmation vows were sacred. She had committed herself to a Lutheran God and all the demands of the Lutheran Church in struggling to be a good Christian. This could not be cast aside for something as selfish – frivolous even – as romantic love, however strong her feelings might be. Compromise was not possible. The searching instruction of her religious teacher, Dr Sell, during her confirmation had made a profound impression. It was as though she was engaged in a permanent struggle to achieve a spiritual ideal, observed her lady-in-waiting, Baroness Sophie Buxhoeveden. 'She was always mentally fighting things out,

always striving to solve deeper questions while jealously keeping all this inner life from prying eyes.'[20] Her inner conflict was
heightened because she had not raised the idea of conversion with
her beloved father before he died. She had seen his anguished
reaction to Ella's change of faith. Not knowing his wishes, how
could she risk going against his spirit?

A change had come over Alix since the death of her father,
Louis of Hesse, the year before. With terrible irrevocability a
door had been shut and she felt herself to be alone. She appeared
to withdraw into herself, shrinking from family gatherings
where she could feel overwhelmed. Just like her grandmother,
no anniversary or birthday could pass without a lament. 'One
does miss our Darling more than I can say,' she confided to the
queen. 'Perpetually there are things one longs to ask him' was
a refrain she repeated as though longing for guidance from a
trusted parent.[21] Her future was undefined, possibly frightening,
and Alix found refuge by immersing herself in the day-to-day
task of supporting Ernie in his new role as the Grand Duke of
Hesse. The more she absorbed herself in her brother's life, the
more she felt comforted and safe. 'We live so quietly,' Alix wrote
to her brother-in law, Louis. She would accompany Ernie to
town for his audiences, entertaining herself while she waited by
picking cherries or buying flowers. Ernie needed support running
the household and in spare moments, she continued, 'we have
got the craze' of taking the carriage to beauty spots and painting.
Sometimes they went fishing, 'the other evening got 40 crabs in
the pond'.[22] Wrapped up in his life, she could avoid the pressures
of her own.

But her anxieties surfaced all too readily. It was at this time
that Alix began to suffer from various physical symptoms for
which doctors could find no cause. She apologised to the queen
after one trip to Balmoral in 1892. 'It was only such a pity not
feeling well as it prevented me from going out with you more
...'[23] A few months later she asked forgiveness for not replying
to a letter from the queen, 'but I was not well enough'. Specialists
were consulted but could not find anything physically wrong.
The possibility that Alix was suffering from a nervous complaint

could not be dismissed. Queen Victoria urged her to seek further specialist advice. 'It is such a nuisance having perpetually something,' Alix confided to her.[24]

Her greatest worry was over her future. Although Alix had not seen Nicholas since 1889, she heard about him through Ella, whose letters occasionally gave glimpses of her grandmother's warnings about Russia. Sergei's promotion to Governor General of Moscow in 1891 coincided with the brutal repression of Moscow's Jews in which 20,000 were expelled from the city. With a resurgence of unrest, Sergei wanted the city 'cleared of Jews' according to Alexander III.[25] Moscow police raided Jewish quarters, evicting hundreds of people with some violence. Over the following months Jewish families hurried to settle their affairs and escape from the city. Many were transported west, others were imprisoned or deported to Siberia, and thousands fled abroad starting a wave of emigration. In the harsh conditions a great many died and as the transports continued during the perishing winter of 1892, the plummeting temperatures prompted even the Moscow police chief to call for a halt until the spring. Ella, whose unwavering loyalty to her husband could admit no weakness, finally let down her guard, confessing to Ernie that she saw 'nothing in it but shame'.[26]

With their families opposed to any union, Alix and Nicholas had had no further opportunity to see each other and explore their feelings. The tsarevich remained under mounting pressure from his parents to consider alternative brides such as the French princess, Hélène d'Orléans. His mother's hints were becoming increasingly painful. 'I myself want to go in one direction,' the tsarevich wrote in early 1892, 'and it is evident that Mama wants me to choose the other one.'[27] Hélène was the only princess apart from Alix who was courted by both British and Russian thrones. It came as a relief to Nicholas to learn that she could not change her Roman Catholic faith. Russian envoys were also sent to the German court to find out about Vicky's youngest daughter, Margaret, but were informed that she too could not change her religion. Margaret wanted to stay in Germany near her mother and preferred Maximilian of Baden (the very prince who Queen

Victoria had singled out for Alix). Meanwhile in Russia the affectionate memories Nicholas treasured of Alix had to compete with
another woman cynically singled out by his father as a diversion,
the beautiful ballerina Mathilde Kschessinska, or 'Little K'.

This liaison had started one evening at the Imperial Ballet in
1890 when Alexander III ordered the beautiful seventeen-year-
old ballerina to sit next to him and told the tsarevich to sit the
other side, moving another pupil aside. 'Careful now, not too
much flirting!' said the tsar, knowing full well the likely impact of
what he had just said and done on the young ballet dancer. Sure
enough Mathilde 'fell in love with the tsarevich on the spot', she
recalled years later. 'I had but one desire, to see him again, even
from afar.' She was 'almost fainting' with desire on seeing him a
few weeks later, when the Imperial Ballet danced for the royal
family at the camp for army manoeuvres.[28] Mathilde made her
interest clear in every possible way. Thwarted for so long in his
pursuit of Princess Alix, by the spring of 1892 Nicholas was no
longer finding Mathilde easy to resist.

Shortly before his trip to Copenhagen, Nicholas confided his
confusion to his diary. 'I have noticed something very strange
within myself,' he wrote in April 1892. 'I never thought that
two similar feelings, two loves could co-exist at one time within
one heart. Now it is over three years since I loved Alix H., and I
constantly cherish the thought that God might let me marry her
one day.' Yet he also felt 'madly (platonically) in love with little
K. An amazing thing, our heart. At the same time do not cease to
think of Alix, although it is true, one might conclude from this
that I am very amorous ...'[29] But the tsarevich held back, refusing
Mathilde's desire to consummate the relationship. To make sure
she understood the strength of his feelings for Alix, he showed
Mathilde the entries he had made about Alix in his diary. Mathilde
persuaded herself 'he had only a fairly vague feeling for Princess
Alice'. To her father's immense disappointment, she wanted to set
up a home of her own where she could more easily become his
mistress. Mathilde found a place to rent in the English Prospect
in St Petersburg and waited for Nicholas's return from Denmark
'with a beating heart'.[30]

In the early summer of 1892 as Nicholas relaxed with George in Copenhagen at the home of their maternal grandparents, they seemed bound by their common fate, talking each night until late into the evening. Uncertain whether he could marry Alix, Nicholas felt he had no choice but to hold out as long as possible until he was forced into a marriage of convenience. George felt his time was running out. Once a suitable period of mourning had elapsed he would be required to reach a decision and set a date for his marriage. Despite Queen Victoria's promise not to pressure George, within weeks Bertie told his son that she had returned to her theme and 'was in a terrible fuss about your marrying'.[31] Princess May remained understanding and discreet about the continued uncertainty. 'I have thought so much of you all in Denmark,' she wrote to George from Ludwigsburg in Germany. Perhaps hoping to establish more common ground between them she aligned herself with his mother's dislike of Germany. 'I do not yet know when we shall return home. I hope soon for ... I cannot stand Germany for too long ...'[32]

George did not rush to reply to May, waiting until he reached Balmoral. Her comment about Germany did indeed strike a chord. Ludwigsburg 'must be rather a deadly place', he observed '& I quite agree with you that a month in Germany is quite enough for the likes of us'. George had evidently taken May into his confidence about the attentions of another princess, the overly keen Helena Victoria of Schleswig-Holstein, unkindly nicknamed 'the Snipe' owing to her prominent nose. 'The Snipe' had sent George a framed picture of herself – a sure sign of her interest. 'It will be a pleasure to welcome that beauty as yr bride,' Alexandra had teased George.[33] 'The "Snipe" is also here & as charming as ever!' George wrote to May from Balmoral.[34] The idea that this signified wedding bells somehow found its way into the British press. The betrothal of the prince 'to his cousin, Princess Victoria of Schleswig-Holstein, will be officially announced within the next few weeks', announced *The World* on 26 July 1892.[35]

For a prince such as George who was not romantically inclined, his short trip to Balmoral in June 1892 was not without complications that interfered with his sporting interests. He was obliged to join the queen and her guests including the hopeful Princess Helena for dinner and other engagements. The queen's curiosity about his feelings for May had to be circumvented, while wounding reminders of Missy's new life punctuated his short visit. Perhaps seeking refuge from 'the Snipe', he opted for a quiet day's fishing on 10 June, learning on his return that the queen had received letters from Missy and her mother, both apparently 'very happy about engagement'.[36] On 12 June they heard that Missy and her family were at Sigmaringen, the ancient family seat of the Hohenzollern-Sigmaringens, where she met her future in-laws including the King of Romania. Queen Victoria had a long private talk with George over breakfast one morning and reached a favourable conclusion. 'He is a dear Boy with much character,' she wrote in her journal.[37]

George left the queen in mid-June to go to London to take his seat in the House of Lords. The chamber was filled with those who wanted a sight of their future king standing solemnly before them in a scarlet robe with an ermine trim. Inevitably comparisons were drawn to his brother. 'Probably the attendance was larger than on the memorable occasion in 1890 when the late Duke of Clarence was introduced', observed the *Daily Telegraph*, and the prince delivered his oath well, in 'a clear, audible tone'.[38] At Queen Victoria's request the newly invested duke was to spend the autumn in Germany at Heidelberg. The queen's concern that her future heir had insufficient knowledge of European languages also transferred from Eddy to George. Could he learn the rudiments of German in two months?[39]

George endeavoured to meet Queen Victoria's high expectations. Apart from his studies, she also asked him to represent her at important functions. 'It is so good for you,' she wrote, 'to make acquaintance with all these foreign royalties.'[40] George found his visit to Berlin in his new capacity as second in line to the throne was quite an experience. His mother feared it would be 'tiresome' for him to meet 'with the Great William from Berlin and Potsdam too!!!'[41] But the German emperor went out of his way to give George a fine welcome. The Kaiser was unusually 'kind and civil to me', George informed his grandmother. 'I have never known him so nice.' They went together to Wittenberg for another golden wedding anniversary, this time for the Grand Duke and Duchess of Weimar. A prince from each reigning Protestant house was represented and some 300 guests sat down to luncheon in the very hall where Martin Luther, founder of the Protestant Reformation in the sixteenth century, had once been a professor. All went well, George reassured his grandmother, with the Kaiser even sticking to his notes, written 'very carefully' in advance.[42] George also took the opportunity while in Germany to see his Aunt Vicky and Ernie and Alix, who was 'looking thin and sad but very pretty', he told the queen.[43]

As for his German, 'I am working away hard,' George reported to the queen. 'I find it rather difficult but still I mean to do my best to try to learn as much as I can.'[44] Victoria of Battenberg was probably nearer the truth when she wrote that 'George was a good deal bored by his life in Heidelberg and felt himself too old to start working with a tutor again.' The zealous corrections whenever the prince attempted spoken German could be exasperating and evenings at home with the professor and his wife were so dull that George found relief in his stamp collection.[45] Nonetheless, duty prevailed that autumn as he followed the schedule laid out for him. He could not, of course, go to see Missy in Coburg, but she remained in his thoughts. 'I see from the papers that Aunt Marie and Missy are soon coming to England,' he commented to his grandmother on 10 October. 'But I suppose that is not true?'[46]

In December 1892 Missy did have the opportunity to present her bridegroom to her British relatives including 'Grandmamma Queen'. The introduction would take place at Windsor Castle and as the day approached Missy began to feel a sense of dread. Her fiancé 'was a complete stranger ... a stranger to all the beloved Malta atmosphere, to all, in fact, from which I had sprung'.[47]

Missy tried to put a brave face on it all for her grandmother, writing twice beforehand to let the queen know 'we are rejoicing on seeing you again soon'. She was beginning to appreciate the enormity of the separation ahead. 'It will be the last visit to Windsor for some time I suppose for me, as most likely in the first year anyhow, I will hardly get away.'[48] She reassured her grandmother 'I am not at all frightened to go away so far, and to a land so different to what I have been accustomed to.' But even Missy could not hide the fact that she was dreading the moment of parting from her family and all that she had known.[49] Once surrounded by the relaxing familiarities of England, she felt distressed at what lay ahead. Her fiancé's hesitant attentions could not fill this space, 'so I hid my inner desolation as best I could'.[50]

Queen Victoria's approach was one she always remembered, the 'tap-tapping' of her stick well before she came into view, the faint sound of the rustle of silk. Missy was waiting nervously with her family and her prince on 10 December in a handsome Windsor gallery, filled with pictures and statues. The corridor curved and the 'tap, tap' of the queen's approach could be heard quite distinctly before 'Grandmamma' suddenly appeared, seeming very small, her shyness not quite concealed. She addressed Missy's prospective husband in his own language, speaking in fluent German to this young descendant of the senior branch of the Hohenzollern line. In those few moments the queen, 'the censor and critic of all our lives', missed little.[51]

Queen Victoria already knew what Missy did not. The king of Romania, the forbidding King Carol, had been anxious to find a suitable bride quickly for his nephew, Crown Prince Ferdinand. Ferdinand had caused a scandal, having fallen in love with a woman at court, the beautiful Helene Vacaresco. Vicky had pieced together the whole story and informed her mother of the affair. Mademoiselle Vacaresco was 'scheming and intriguing' and 'not very lady-like or refined', according to Vicky. Nonetheless, she had the queen of Romania 'quite in her pocket' and had seduced Prince Ferdinand, who told King Carol that he intended to marry her.[52] The king would not hear of it and Ferdinand was despatched abroad in disgrace, under instructions to find a more suitable bride.

Missy did not yet know of the circumstances surrounding her fiancé's proposal and was convinced that her prince was passionately in love with her. Queen Victoria was concerned, despite reassurances from Vicky that Ferdinand was, in fact, 'nice and good'.[53] She took her granddaughter out for a private drive. Missy's youthful naivety was plain. She 'is perfectly happy and contented and does not seem to mind going so far alone. She looks so fresh and pretty', the queen concluded.[54] Her brief visit passed quickly in an atmosphere of polite protocol surrounding the inevitable introductions, discussions of the marriage treaty, and formal receptions for ministers and officials. Nothing was said to disenchant Missy about the prospects that lay ahead.

After introducing her Romanian prince to Queen Victoria, Missy had to face an even greater ordeal, presenting him to Prince George. The meeting occurred two days later. George had returned from the continent and arrived at Windsor in the evening with his parents and his sister, Maud. Missy chose her best gown and braced herself to meet her Uncle Bertie and others in his entourage, although she wrote later, 'I only remember Cousin George.'

It was her first meeting with Prince George since she had sent her hurtful letter of rejection and been beguiled into her fateful, impromptu decision. 'My heart is beating,' she wrote. 'I have always that sick feeling at heart that I am in some ways betraying all the things that I had loved ...'

Cousin George was suddenly before her, his blue eyes resting on her face. She took in an impression of his kindness, of all that had drawn her to him before.

'Well Missy?' he began.

There was a lump in her throat. When she found her voice she could not bring herself to talk of the times that meant something to them both, 'of the dear Malta days, for I could not have stood it just then'. She felt 'a traitor somehow'. She had carelessly 'cast in my lot with a stranger ... setting out upon an unknown sea'. The old safe harbour no longer provided anchorage and she felt 'intolerable heart ache ... to the point of torture'.[55]

In Germany in the New Year of 1893, when the time for leaving home in Coburg was drawing close, there was a scene between Missy and her father, Alfred, when, at last, British stiff upper lip no longer prevailed. Alfred had avoided talking to his eldest daughter in private but shortly before her departure he asked to see her. Missy entered his room and was astonished to find her usually taciturn and distant father in a state of considerable emotion. He hugged her and 'burst into tears, confiding to me that he could not bear to see me, his eldest and dearly loved daughter, go to such a far and unknown country, that he had cherished another dream for me, one which would have very differently shaped my future …' He seemed distraught, and 'could not bear parting from me …'

It took him time to find his composure, and when he did, his emotions were channelled into English understatement. She must never forget that she was 'a British-born princess and a sailor's daughter', he said. Missy, perhaps overwhelmed by his unexpected display of genuine feeling, took refuge in her own room and cried.

The marriage between Missy and the Crown Prince of Romania, which had provoked such strong feeling in the royal family, took place at Sigmaringen in Germany on 10 January 1893, a few months after her seventeenth birthday. The young bride, who had been instructed to spurn the British throne and even denied a chance to enter society and find out her worth for herself, now found her future immovably fixed. Missy felt such 'unbearable grief' as her train steamed out of Coburg, her family finally disappearing from view, it took all her courage 'not to cry out in my pain'.[56] Bravely she wiped away her tears to make her entrance into Bucharest, but her brief honeymoon in Germany had heightened her sense of desolation.

Missy had been unprepared for her husband's strong passion. Years later, when her mother had occasion to defend her daughter before King Carol, the duchess wrote tellingly of 'Ferdinand's sensual passion for Missy [which] finished by … repulsing her.'[57] During her honeymoon, Missy tried to respond to her husband, but felt a great void. 'There was an empty feeling about it all; I still seemed to be waiting for something that did not come.'[58] Within days she was pregnant. It was left to her mother's lady-in-waiting, Lady Monson, who accompanied her on the journey to

Bucharest, to enlighten the shocked princess as to why on arrival at the Romanian court she felt such malaise and sickness. In her memoirs, written years later, Missy made no criticism of her mother's actions apart from one telling remark: 'Mamma more than any other being I have ever known would cut off her nose to spite her face!'[59]

Queen Victoria did not attend Missy's wedding but it was not far from her thoughts. She knew full well what lay in store for her granddaughter and confided her true feelings to Vicky, whose own daughter, Margaret, was shortly to get married. 'I ought not to tell you now, who have this so soon before you, what I feel about a daughter's marrying,' began the queen, 'but to me there is something so dreadful, so repulsive in that one has to give one's beloved and innocent child, whom one has watched over and guarded from the breath of anything indelicate [and that she] should be given over to a man, a stranger to a great extent, body and soul to do with what he likes. No experience in [life] will ever help me over that …'[60]

Despite her strenuous efforts, Queen Victoria's matchmaking for her grandchildren was not going smoothly. George had lost Missy by being too slow to act and was now failing to propose to May. Continuing worries about Alix's future created a distinct sense of unease. And innocent little Missy had been dispatched to an obscure country to be given over to a stranger 'body and soul'.

9

George and May

'This must not be allowed to go on.'
                    Queen Victoria to Victoria of
                    Battenberg, December 1890

Prince George's return from Germany in late autumn of 1892 sparked renewed speculation that he would shortly be proposing to Princess May. When she was invited to Sandringham in early December for the anniversary of her engagement to Eddy, her mother, Mary Adelaide, thought this could be the long-awaited moment. But the solemn occasion passed with nothing said. Sandringham was a house still suffused in grief and feeling the pain of each anniversary, Eddy's last Christmas, his birthday, his death. 'We missed our darling Eddy too terribly,' George told the queen. 'Mama was so brave all the time.'[1] The Wales family found consolation by going 'into His dear room', still laid out as though he was alive, the fire warming the room. George found remembrances flooded back as though 'they were grown into my memory then & nothing can obliterate them'.[2]

On Christmas Day George did write to May at White Lodge with 'a thousand thanks' for her gift of a little pin that 'I will often wear', he assured her.[3] May replied with careful formality. She felt 'so grateful' to him for his letter and was 'deeply touched' by his Christmas gift of a brooch. Grief over Eddy's loss was something she recognised they shared. 'Everything came back so vividly to my mind, that awful night, the sad, sad ending, and all the misery,' she told him.[4] 'I could almost hear his dear voice,' George responded.[5]

The pressures intensified on George in the New Year of 1893. May was now out of mourning and George carried on with his duties – opening the new Royal Eye Hospital in Southwark, making the keynote speech for the National Society for the Prevention of Cruelty to Children – harried by reporters. There was much '<u>beastly</u> newspaper bosh', as his mother put it, with many of the newspapers expecting the announcement before the opening of parliament.[6] The marriage would be popular on account of 'the great sorrow' that befell Princess May a year ago, declared the *Pall Mall Gazette*, earning for her 'the affections of the nation in an especial degree'.[7] At court, too, there was an air of expectation as though the outcome was inevitable.

Queen Victoria's patience was wearing thin. Forbearance was not her strong suit when it came to matchmaking. It was inappropriate to delay. She urged George to come to Osborne later in January for a few days. 'I long to see you. You must not think I wish to press you in anyway but as you have made your mind up about May – pray do <u>not delay after</u> [double underlined] the 20th, for <u>her sake</u>, as well as the <u>Country's</u>. <u>Her position</u> is most trying & I think that <u>she</u>, Aunt Mary & Uncle Teck behave <u>most</u> discreetly and kindly. But you must <u>not</u> let the <u>trial be too long</u>.' Given that his parents also wished it, 'you shd <u>after the 20</u>[th] go quietly down to White Lodge and speak to A[un]t Mary and then to May. This wld be the most correct & not tell anyone wh day you are going. One cannot settle a <u>day</u> for <u>such a thing</u>.' With her thoughts still on 'poor Missy's wedding' she added somewhat insensitively, 'Poor Alfred never ceases regretting she is not to be yours!'[8]

But the twenty-seven-year-old prince held back, harassed by the decision. His mother was sympathetic, convinced he was being hurried. 'I too am worried to death about it,' she confided to him. 'I can so well enter into all your poor feelings.'[9] Princess Alexandra wrote to the ever-expectant Queen Victoria with stalling tactics, explaining that George 'required a complete change and a rest'. She proposed to take him and his younger sisters,

Maud and Victoria, who was unwell, on one last holiday together
in the royal yacht to see their Greek relatives. Removed from
the pressure, touring the Mediterranean in the spring, she hoped
Prince George would recover his spirits. It would bring him back
'fresh and less worried', she promised Queen Victoria, ready to
settle his affairs.[10] The queen agreed and Alexandra wrote reas-
suringly to George, 'yr poor much worried mind can rest at peace
for a bit'.[11]

On the day of his departure George wrote an apology to
Princess May. 'I am so sorry that I have seen so little of you lately,
only a passing glimpse now and again.'[12] He knew she would be
back in her home routine, her life revolving around her mother's
needs and the endless guild and charity commitments. Ahead for
him open seas and wide horizons beckoned while he wallowed
in the reprieve afforded by the royal yacht. 'It is a very pleasant
feeling to know that one can go where one likes when one likes,'
George admitted to his grandmother from Genoa. He took the
opportunity to remind the queen that his mother was still grieving and his sister, Victoria, remained poorly. The holiday was
doing them 'a world of good'.[13]

Two weeks elapsed before George wrote to May from the
island of Elba, describing his tour with a care for detail that could
give her grounds for encouragement. They had been in Pisa and
then on to Florence where 'in the two days we saw everything
we possibly could in the time, both the picture galleries, Pitti and
Uffizi, nearly all the churches … Weren't you there for nearly
two years once, I forget,' he asked casually. He included one or
two anecdotes such as the nicknames they had adopted in their
efforts to remain incognito, which was all 'rather fun' except that
there were so many English, 'they of course soon found us out,
which was rather a bore'.[14] May thanked him 'very warmly' for
his letter. She had been following his travels in the papers 'with
great interest'. The nicknames amused her and she had evidently
shared the details with her inquisitive mother, who was 'much
flattered' at Maud adopting her pet name, Maria. 'What on earth
made you choose "Jane" for "Motherdear",' May enquired. 'She
does not at all give me the idea of Jane!'[15]

George's next letter was from Palermo in Sicily just before Easter. He was 'very much touched' by the speed of her response, he wrote, reassuring May that she and her mother 'have often been in my thoughts'. He continued to describe the many wonderful sights in Rome and Naples where he had seen Mount Vesuvius, Pompeii and the Blue Grotto at Capri. Perhaps aware that his letter did not contain expressions of feeling for which she might hope, he added bashfully 'you must be sick of reading this very stupid long epistle & I have a great mind to tear it up only that I think it might be useful to light your fire with'.[16] May responded in a similar vein with her news of London. Both registered their attentiveness to each other. Neither let down their guard, deflecting expressions of their feelings into neutral descriptions of daily events, and so the polite courtesy continued in an intermittent exchange of letters around the Mediterranean.

By early April the Wales family was in Greece and giving no sign of coming home. In Corfu they met Empress Elizabeth of Austria, who was still grieving the loss of her only son, Rudolf. Prince George had a chance to catch up with his aunt and uncle, the king and queen of Greece, and his twenty-two-year-old cousin Sophie, already the mother of a 'delightful' little boy, George told the queen, 'who talks away in the most funny English'. Sophie and Tino's house in Athens was decorated in an English style, 'with a lot of pretty things in it', he continued.[17] In this relaxed setting with hazy views of the Aegean, George unwound, mulling over his anxieties with his aunt, Queen Olga, who was sympathetic. She had first met May shortly after the Tecks had travelled abroad in disgrace and had formed a favourable view.

Olga was not the only concerned aunt keeping an eye on the proceedings. Vicky travelled from Germany in late January to see her mother at Osborne. It was a rough crossing but mother and daughter, so happy to be reunited, went straight to the drawing room together 'talking of many things'.[18] There was much to discuss concerning the queen's grandchildren. Vicky's youngest daughter, Margaret, had given up on the unforthcoming Maximilian of Baden and married his friend, Prince Friedrich Karl, a future head of the Hesse-Kassel dynasty.[19] Missy, the new

Crown Princess of Romania, had been 'enthusiastically received' in her adopted country. As for the future of the British throne, Vicky was still trying to discern what special qualities marked May out as a bride for George above her own girls. 'She seemed to me a little stiff & cold!' Vicky confided to Margaret, her frank views perhaps summing up reservations that George also privately felt. Although May was being 'praised on all sides', Vicky found her lacking in charm, perhaps even 'rather dull – & superficial!' Nonetheless, she felt certain that May was enviably destined to 'be Georgie's Bride – and – have the first position in Europe, one may say in the world!'[20]

There was much to concern the queen and her daughter about the German emperor. Vicky had reached the point where she felt her own relationship with her oldest son was beyond repair. There was nothing she could do or say to guide him. Wilhelm had been keen to build an alliance with Britain, a plan that had been part of Grandpapa Albert's original vision. But the Kaiser's efforts to first charm and then intimidate Britain into an agreement had had little impact on British ministers. William Gladstone replaced Lord Salisbury at 10 Downing Street in 1892 and Lord Rosebery in foreign affairs, but ministerial comings and goings made little difference. British interests appeared best served by its 'Splendid Isolation', keeping the country out of European alliances and focusing on her empire. Any alliance Britain entered into would oblige her to go to war on behalf of her ally even if she did not want to – although the precise terms might vary from treaty to treaty. It was unthinkable to the leaders of the British Empire to lose control over such a vital matter. By avoiding the tangled web of European alliances Britain was less likely to be drawn into any war.

Wilhelm's hope of Britain joining the Triple Alliance between Germany, Austro-Hungary and Italy was receding by 1893 and in turn, his fears for Germany increased. He tried to use his grandmother as a lever to achieve his ends, writing long, demonstrative epistles and requesting trips to Windsor or Osborne, which she found wearing. He seemed ever more autocratic to the point of instability. '*Suprema lex, regis voluntas*' – 'The will of the king is the highest law' – he wrote on a visit to Munich, much to the concern of the *Reichstag*.[21] Vicky recoiled from his absolutism, what she called his 'Caesarism', and his needlessly bellicose speeches proclaiming his desire to lead Germany to glory. It was as though his very identity had fused with heroic legends of old, stepping from some ancient Valhalla to defend his country against all slights and insults, whether actual, imaginary or provoked by himself. He could not desist from intervening directly in foreign affairs and his opinions often stoked anti-British feeling in the German press. Sometimes ingratiating, sometimes rude, he struggled with his own raw feelings of anger and resentment at the apparently seamless workings of British power. Vicky's frustration was intense. Her son's folly was undoing her life's work. For the queen, who understood completely what might have been, it was hard not to share her daughter's lament. She felt Vicky had 'a sad fate, so young looking, so gifted, so fit for the position she should have held and her career cut so sadly short …'[22]

Vicky's visit came and went, her farewell to her mother on 20 March still stressful after all these years. She was 'much upset and so was I', the queen entered in her journal. Vicky kept saying her mother 'was her great comfort and blessing' and 'it pained her to leave me!' The queen found it equally hard, 'for I am old now and partings are very sad'.[23] During her visit Vicky had had no opportunity to see George, the elusive groom, who remained abroad in spite of the growing rumours. He did not set foot in England until late April, only to find his prolonged absences abroad since Eddy's death had worked against him.

Up and down the country press speculation was at fever pitch over the lack of action. Why had Prince George, 'who is now 28 years of age, not got married or at least engaged to be married?', demanded the *Lincolnshire Echo*. No one 'knows precisely why the heir to the throne prefers a life of bachelorhood'.[24] Since the death of his brother, 'few men have been more talked about than the Duke of York', pointed out the *Sheffield Evening Telegraph*. 'At first it was rumoured that he would marry Princess May of Teck; then it was confidently predicted that he would do nothing of the kind. Prince George was supposed to have placed his affections in another quarter', and people in authority admitted 'the general accuracy of this impression'. Was the future heir to the throne hiding a secret or shirking his matrimonial duty?[25]

The Star had an answer with the stunning claim that Prince George was already secretly married. The prince's frequent trips abroad appeared to have a reason: he was visiting his first wife – the unnamed daughter of an English naval officer. It was alleged that George had married her in Malta in 1890 and they already had one child. The 'unexpected and sudden' departure of the prince on his most recent tour 'was not unconnected' with his 'matrimonial adventure', claimed *The Star* on 3 May. The alarming rumour 'is being eagerly asserted and discussed and its confirmation or refutation anxiously sought'.[26]

It was against this background of painful speculation that the prince was invited to dinner with the Tecks on 2 May at White Lodge. For a young man such as George, whose intrinsic shyness with women was overlain by the straitjacket of years of instruction over how to behave, the circumstances of his meeting with May and her family could hardly be more embarrassing. The long delay in his approach, combined with repeated press conjecture that his feelings lay elsewhere, created the impression that he did not care for her. Was he visiting out of duty or on orders from the queen?

The evening was strained. May had had a busy day in town supporting a fund-raising matinee in aid of Poplar Hospital. A year had elapsed since Cannes in which they had seen little of each other and both George and May remained guarded with their feelings. As if repeated public pronouncements as to what those feelings might be were not bad enough, the presence of the abundantly effusive Mary Adelaide could only add to George's discomfort. If he had hoped to talk privately, or even propose, his opportunities vanished as May's mother remained in hovering attendance. Ever the optimist, May's mother came to the conclusion that a proposal of marriage would soon be forthcoming. She and her husband tactfully left White Lodge the following day.

May was alone, but the prince failed to call. Perhaps sensing the difficulties for George, his sister, Louise, who had done so much to facilitate the match between Eddy and Hélène, took matters in hand. On 3 May she invited Princess May to Sheen Lodge. When May arrived she was shown into the drawing room to find George had also been invited to tea.[27]

Even in the sanctuary of his sister's home, George still seemed helpless, uncertain how to seize the initiative. It was left to Princess Louise to give her brother a gentle nudge. After tea she encouraged him to take May into the garden. 'Don't you think you ought to take May into the garden to look at the frogs in the pond'?[28]

This may not have sounded like a promising prelude to a romantic proposal, but this was George, a man whose greatest passion appeared to be reserved for his collection of stamps or the grouse moor, and who may well have understood that a background of croaking frogs did not detract from what he had to say. Somehow in the garden he found the words '& I accepted him', May wrote later. There was no sense of passion or rapture in her diary. She too was notably unemotional, making no mention of her feelings, or those of her fiancé, merely adding that Louise was 'delighted' at their news.[29] Possibly she felt relieved at the time that the scene was devoid of any emotional declarations or unrealistic expectations, but afterwards she may have reflected whether this was the normal prelude to a happy marriage.

George took refuge in formalities, turning at once to the dutiful matter of sending a telegram to Queen Victoria asking for her consent. 'I answered that I gladly did so,' the queen wrote in her journal on 3 May. 'I have so much wished for greatest satisfaction.' When she returned from her visit to the mausoleum the next day she found George was waiting at Windsor. 'He seemed quite pleased and contented,' she thought.[30] The agonising uncertainties of his position were now lifted. The queen explained to Vicky the business-like manner in which the romance 'was settled'.[31] Whatever the feelings of the bride and groom, May's mother expressed enough happiness for them all. Mary Adelaide felt such unbridled joy, the news had to be telegraphed immediately to all her friends. Word spread rapidly around the family, and among the thickening pile of congratulations was a telegram from the 'Snipe', who was generous minded in her disappointment. George and May 'deserve to be very happy', she wrote. 'Everybody here seems quite delighted.'[32]

The press, too, was favourable. The *Telegraph* referred to 'a most auspicious arrangement', explaining to their readers that the royal couple had been drawn together through their loss, which had 'ripened into an attachment and affection' in which 'all England will rejoice'. The *St James Gazette* welcomed the fact that Prince George was not marrying a foreign princess, which would be bound to 'introduce fresh complications into our relations', but a 'daughter of England'. *The Times* was more measured, arguing the betrothal 'accords with the fitness of things' and seemed the 'most appropriate and delicate medicament' for a wound that was 'never wholly effaceable'.[33]

But not all the papers hit the right note. The story in *The Star* took off in the press and assumed a life of its own. In the royal household the fast-growing pile of press reports about Prince George's secret marriage prompted one member of the royal household, perhaps Sir Henry Ponsonby, to register his frustration with a handwritten note: 'the power of invention among the newspapers is extraordinary'.[34] It was widely believed that Princess May would be his second wife. Across town, letters of 'distress and anxiety' began to pour into Lambeth Palace, the London residence of the Archbishop of Canterbury, Edward Benson. The very idea that the clean-living and upright prince was a bigamist fired people's imagination. 'As a rector of a Parish which contains the High Road of the World,' wrote Septimus Pennington from St Clement Danes in the Strand, he understood Prince George was not only already married but with a second child due imminently. 'The body of public men with whom I constantly come into contact openly denounce the Church for conniving at this matter,' he stormed.[35] If the heir to the throne was already married then any additional marriage would be 'a gross piece of wickedness', observed the clergyman's son, Mr T. Bartlett of Westbury, Wiltshire, 'which in the case of anyone below royalty would be styled bigamy. Is it right that the laws of God should in these enlightened times be overruled by the laws of Man?'[36] 'Was the other wife still alive?' enquired Stanley Pelly, vicar of Alfreton in Derbyshire.[37]

The archbishop was a little unsure how to proceed. With arrangements in full swing for a grand royal wedding there was no easy way of approaching Queen Victoria on the delicate topic of whether her British grandson, in the words of Rector Arthur Hayes of Holmbury St Mary, was about to commit 'a fraud and a sin in the Eyes of Man and God'.

Such alarming rumours did nothing to ease the way for George and May, for whom the transition from a business-like agreement to something more romantic was not easy. Their difficulty in behaving like lovers rather supported the idea of a first marriage and their short engagement proved surprisingly stressful. The outward show expected by the whole country of a great royal romance formed a marked contrast to their actual experience. Five weeks into the engagement even George recognised something crucial was missing. 'I am sure you must think me cold and with very little feeling, as I never show it,' he wrote to his fiancée on 12 June 1893.[38] The next day he repeated his concern, drawing her in for criticism too. He regretted that 'we are somewhat cold & distant to each other'. He put this down to their both being 'so shy & that we have known each other so well for so many years that we hardly yet realise that we are engaged'. He promised to 'try & be nicer and show more feeling and you must do the same'.[39] He returned to his theme the next day, promising 'I will endeavour next time to be nicer to you and not so shy.'[40]

Their intense preoccupations with the engagement preparations helped to avoid placing too searching a spotlight on their feelings. George had his future household to discuss with the queen, appointments to be made, royal guests to accommodate, seating plans to approve for the many planned receptions, and wedding presents began to arrive in their hundreds: in fact, there

was a surfeit of every conceivable extravagance – but for the
luxury of privacy to get to know each other better. When they
were together, at least one observer was dissatisfied with what she
saw. 'There is not even a pretense at love making,' commented
Lady Geraldine Somerset. Both the bride to be and her mother
were 'in plus belle humeur!', with May 'radiant at her position'
but 'placid and cold, as always'. The prospective groom appeared
'nonchalant and indifferent'.[41] Whatever efforts George did make
to try to live up to the expected ideal appear to have got the better
of him. The queen urged him 'to say everything affectionate to
dear May', but the strained situation proved too much.[42] On 18
June, George found himself shouting at May and her mother.

He wrote the next day 'to say how ashamed I am of myself
for behaving so stupidly yesterday & losing my temper ... Of
course I was not angry with you my darling, it was not yr fault
... You must think me an awful ass, as I appear so cold & shy
with you ...'[43] His outburst was directed at Mary Adelaide, he
explained. Blazing a trail of good intentions, May's overbearing
mother succeeded in greatly adding to the tension. She was '<u>so</u>
obstinate about those tiresome people and would not let me go,'
May replied. 'Oh! I was so angry with her. I felt like a little devil
& I have not forgiven her yet.'[44] May found a way to reassure her
fiancé. 'I am very sorry that I am still so shy with you,' she wrote.
'I tried not to be so the other day, but alas failed, I was angry
with myself! It is so stupid to be so stiff together & really there
is nothing I would not tell you, except that I <u>love</u> you more than
anybody in the world, & this I cannot tell you myself so I write it
to relieve my feelings ...'[45]

Such a communication confirming – at least on paper – that
there was indeed some sort of romance to their alliance was
obviously helpful. Was his bride sincere, or was she writing out
of duty? Prince George's own reply by return on the same day
expressed his great relief at her words. 'I do indeed find it difficult
to express in words the happiness I feel in your telling me that
you love me. Thank God we both understand each other.' He
explained that although 'I may appear shy and cold', his love for
her was 'deep' and he could 'feel it growing stronger & stronger

every time I see you'. He blamed their stressful circumstances as the cause of their problems, hoping she would not lose heart. 'As now we are so worried and annoyed by the smallest thing that we only lose our tempers, which generally are very sweet, at least I know yours is & I hope you will find mine the same.'[46]

The pressure proved too much for George. He began to suffer from what he thought was neuralgia, with sharp nerve pain spreading to his face. On 24 June he slipped away from London to the beloved sanctuary of Sandringham. 'I must get rest and quiet,' he explained to May. 'It is absolutely necessary and up till now I have had no rest.' He felt 'in despair' at not seeing her, 'but if I am not with you in the body I am in the spirit'. He found it easier at a distance to express his feelings.[47] 'I love you with all my heart my own darling,' he wrote. Still unable to find more to say about his love, he adopted the expression his mother had always used for him, adding 'with a great big kiss for your sweet lovely face'.[48]

Three days later he confirmed that it was not neuralgia but toothache and he was on the mend. May asked 'when and where can we meet', but George did not return until the week of their wedding, sending a card on 29 June to say he was coming back that afternoon. He had agreed to meet his cousin, Nicky, the next morning and then 'any number of deputations'.[49]

———

In June 1893 the tsarevich set out from St Petersburg to represent the Russian royal family at George and May's wedding. It was Nicholas's first visit to England since he was a child, his invitation to stay at Marlborough House being at the express wish of his cousin, George.[50] The tsarevich hoped there would be an opportunity to see Alix. Hundreds of guests from across Europe were invited including Alix's family. Four years had now elapsed since they had been together in St Petersburg and Nicholas's 'dearest dream' to marry her had remained elusive.

There had been one other opportunity to see her fleetingly six months earlier at the grand wedding in Berlin of Vicky's youngest daughter, Margaret. Before leaving St Petersburg in January 1893, the tsarevich had at last succeeded in winning his parents' permission for him to find out Alix's feelings. But just at this longed-for moment, Alix seemed more remote than ever, purposefully making herself unavailable.

Alix's letter to her grandmother a few weeks before Margaret's wedding shows just how much she had dreaded the great gathering of the clan in Berlin. Ernie had put her under some pressure to accept Margaret's invitation and she felt she must, 'as I have already been asked for other occasions the last years & did not go', she confided to her grandmother. 'I dread it terribly, as I have a great dislike of such large festivities & esp now, that I have lost my own sweet darling papa, but it must be and I pray god may give me the strength to do my duty.' Anxiously, she had sought the protection of an older married relative and had found it in Aunt Vicky, who had agreed to Ernie's request to take Alix under her wing. 'If I had had to live in the Schloss with all the guests ... [it would be] far more tiring – as one would perpetually have to be running up and down,' Alix told her grandmother, carefully avoiding any reference to Nicholas.[51]

In freezing weather on his first morning in Berlin, Nicholas had been up early, leaving his visiting card with many of the princes and calling on his Aunt Vicky. Alix was nowhere to be seen. He had found himself buttonholed by Kaiser Wilhelm, who was determined to present the distracted tsarevich with the Order of the Black Eagle and obliged him to wear 'a particularly uncomfortable red cloak'. Finally, he saw her in the procession to the church. Alix looked beautiful, but so distant, with barely an acknowledging glance. Scarcely able to curb his impatience, Nicholas endured the lengthy ceremony on 25 January 1893, after which each guest had had to bow before the newly married couple. 'This pleasure lasted two hours,' he wrote. Surrounded by the insufferable formality of the German court, constantly cornered by one important person after another, there was little chance to speak to her. Alix had told him she was suffering from earache. Somehow they were always seeing each other at a distance, frozen glances across a great gulf. For the tsarevich it could not be called 'a pleasant meeting'. He felt dejected. 'We generally used to be about half a mile off from each other,' he wrote to her later. It was hardly the occasion for a passionate proposal.[52]

Wrapped up in her anxieties, resisting any challenge to her religious beliefs, fearing she might weaken, Alix was so cold to Nicholas that when he returned to St Petersburg he 'flew to my MK'. That very night he finally consummated his relationship with the ballerina Mathilde Kschessinska. 'I am still under her spell,' he confided to his diary a few days later. 'The pen keeps trembling in my hand!'[53] But for Mathilde, the intensity of their first night together was fleeting. Within weeks his interest diminished. Their relationship became routine, the evening starting with the customary sound of his horse approaching. He would bring her presents and was invariably kind and affectionate, but she sensed she was losing him. Nicholas's experiences with Mathilde only served to intensify his longing for Alix. As time passed he called less frequently and all the while his cherished dream of loving and marrying the unobtainable Alix became more important. Mathilde felt her 'torments grew' every time he set out to see relatives in Europe, convinced that he would meet Princess Alix.[54]

That was six months ago. It was a hot summer day in late June 1893 when the tsarevich arrived at Charing Cross Station in London for George's wedding. He was met by his Aunt Alexandra, Uncle Bertie and the groom, who welcomed him to Marlborough House. Nicholas was in a room next to George and the cousins, once again, found themselves talking into the small hours. Eddy's room was further down the passage, still unchanged, Nicholas told his mother. Uncle Bertie proved to be 'very friendly, almost too much', summoning his tailor, bootmaker and hatter to prepare his Russian nephew for the London season. The July heat, too, was overpowering and on occasion he felt dizzy.[55] He did not want to miss any chance to meet members of Alix's family: most importantly, 'Grandmama queen', who invited him to Windsor on 1 July. Knowing the special place she had occupied in Alix's life since the death of her parents, it was a meeting that the tsarevich wished to go well.

The date of their meeting coincided with the thirtieth anniversary of the marriage of Alix's parents, Alice and Louis, and Queen Victoria was feeling their absence. 'Both beloved ones gone from this world. Incredible!' she entered in her journal. She, too, was finding the weather oppressive; a close thundery heat. But this was the Russian prince who held such significance for her favourite granddaughter and the queen's interest went beyond the ceremonial. She stood at a vantage point at the top of the Windsor staircase to greet him, her small frame dwarfed by the uniformed officials around her, who were under instruction to show 'every possible civility'.[56] As they approached each other she saw at once that the tsarevich was 'wonderfully like Georgie'. He spoke in excellent English and she soon yielded to his charm, perhaps surprised to find a member of the mighty Romanov clan who was 'very simple and unaffected'. Nicholas, in turn, found her 'very friendly'. The queen 'talked a lot', he wrote to his mother, and awarded him an Order of the Garter in the Audience Chamber after the formal luncheon. He himself saw her as 'a round ball on unsteady legs' although he felt she was 'remarkably kind to me'.[57]

At the various functions in the build-up to the wedding day, the tsarevich met Alix's older sisters, Victoria and Irene, and her brother Ernie, but there was no sign of Alix herself. This time Queen Victoria had personally invited her. 'It is too kind of you asking me to come to the Wedding,' Alix had replied from Darmstadt on 2 June, 'but I fear it is impossible, as we have been about so much this year already and as Ernie cannot stop v long in England, the journey would be scarcely worth the while for me & there it is so expensive also ... Excuse my writing so openly but I thought it was only right you should know the reason of my not accepting your awfully kind invitation & hope you will not mind ...'[58]

This frank note provided a convenient excuse, but a shortage of funds seems unlikely to have been the main reason for her absence. By staying away, Alix avoided any possibility of her nervous complaints becoming obvious to the family. More significantly, she prevented any chance of matters coming to a head with the tsarevich. Torn between her attraction to Nicholas and her trust in her grandmother's views, she shrank from any decision. By staying away there was no chance of their romantic attachment coming under Queen Victoria's sharp scrutiny.

Nicholas made the best of his visit to London. Despite a tight schedule, he found time to visit Westminster Abbey, St Paul's Cathedral and the Tower. He rode in Rotten Row 'where the whole of Society goes' and marvelled at the freedom of London life where palaces were not prisons.[59] On the eve of the wedding, thousands of guests gathered for a garden party at Marlborough House. The tsarevich saw many familiar faces including Hélène d'Orléans, who was drawing admirers. The queen considered the French princess was 'in great beauty' while even the acerbic Lady Geraldine Somerset was prompted to observe 'how lovely she was in pink'.[60] She may have been considered a highly desirable young princess, but for Nicholas she was not the right princess.[*] There was no sign of the one he longed to see, his frustration scarcely eased by the repeated confusion over his similarity to the groom. Victoria of Battenberg saw people congratulating Nicky on his marriage, while one elderly gentleman gave George instructions that were intended for the tsarevich.[61] The garden party was followed by a dinner at Buckingham Palace where Nicholas found himself seated next to the queen, who was still intrigued by him.[62] Finally, there was a ball, but he 'didn't see many beautiful ladies', he told his mother pointedly. The tsarevich had to content himself with news of Alix from her brother Ernie, who the queen ensured was prominently positioned throughout the celebrations.

Whatever his own disappointments, Nicholas entered into the spirit of the occasion and reported everything back to his mother. Princess May was 'delightful, much better looking than her photographs, so quiet and simple ...' He enjoyed meeting her brothers and seeing the wedding presents, on display at first in the palace but transferred to the Imperial Institute. 'They were given everything conceivable,' he wrote home. 'Somebody even managed to present them with a cow.' His cousin George, he

---

*On 25 June 1895, Hélène eventually married Prince Emanuele, Second Duke of Aosta, a match that did not quite live up to her parents' original expectations.

thought, appeared 'very tired' in the run-up to the wedding. The groom appeared highly strung, pressed on all sides with all the 'frightful bother', Nicholas observed.[63]

Vociferous claims that Prince George was already married further added to the strain. At Lambeth Palace, Archbishop Benson faced a deluge of complaints from concerned parishioners. The news had spread as far as the Cape of Good Hope, where 'it causes great indignation', wrote Mabel and Edith Bourne from Richmond. 'You, we are told, at first refused to perform the marriage ceremony on July 6th but allowed yourself to be persuaded by Her Majesty the Queen on the grounds that the former marriage was morganatic.' The whole wicked business would 'do much to hasten the downfall of the English Throne'.[64] The archbishop was harassed by many similar worries. 'Has the queen pronounced his first marriage as invalid?' asked the Vicar of Alfreton.[65] If Prince George's marriage to Princess May was bigamous, he would be unable to receive communion. Might this render any future coronation invalid? To save the reputation of the Church the archbishop must publicly refute the allegations, stormed the Rector of Holmbury St Mary. He faced 'parishioners of all classes' who 'confidently and persistently assert' that the prince is already married. The rector sought the archbishop's permission to 'announce your corroboration of my denial to my parishioners ... publicly from the pulpit'.[66]

Under this onslaught, the archbishop felt obliged to defend his actions. He issued a statement denying that the royal bridegroom was already married. But the archbishop's denial only served to give the rumour credence. The press responded as though something was certainly being kept back.[67] Neither the queen, the groom nor his parents had been informed in advance of Benson's statement. All felt furious at the injustice that a prince like George, who had 'steered so straight' in life, as Alexandra put it, should be tarred with 'such base things'. The bashful groom felt traduced as he prepared for the big day. 'The whole story is a damnable lie,' he said.[68]

Privately, away from watchful eyes, George was beginning to unwind a little with his fiancée. 'You were so nice to me,' he wrote to May on 3 July, '& actually kissed me twice, I was so touched.'[69] It was three days before their wedding. Although he still could not express his feelings to her face, alone in his study he was beginning to find his own words. 'I adore you,' he told her on the two-month anniversary of their engagement. 'I feel so happy that I don't know how to thank you enough for having made me so.'[70] May sent her future husband a short note just before her wedding. 'I love you with all my heart. Yrs for ever & ever – May.'[71]

George and May's wedding on 6 July 1893 was one of those pageants through London at which the British royal family excelled, the press fast running out of superlatives to capture the excitement. 'Never has the English sun … poured its rays upon a more imposing spectacle, never have scarlet uniforms, cuirasses of steel, sabres and bayonets and gold lace reflected a more fiery light … never the plaudits of the people been more spontaneous and tumultuous', eulogised *The Times*.[72] For the *New York Times* it was quite simply 'one of the most magnificent Pageants ever seen in the streets of London'.[73] By 11.30 a.m. two million people had gathered in the streets, almost as many as for the queen's Golden Jubilee, before the many varied processions began to emerge from Buckingham Palace.

First to appear were thirteen open landaus conveying members of the royal family and their guests. The Duchess of Edinburgh shared a state landau with three of her daughters, but not Missy who was pregnant and remained in Romania. The tsarevich rode with his Aunt Alexandra and his grandparents, the king and queen of Denmark. This convoy was followed by the groom's shorter procession, which included Prince George, Bertie and Uncle Alfred, all looking striking in their naval uniform. Then came the bride and her entourage, May dressed 'simply and prettily', the queen noted, wearing her mother's lace veil. Finally, the queen's procession left amid a flourish of trumpets at 11.45 a.m. with a colourful escort of guards including Indian Cavalry. The

queen rode in the new State Glass Coach, wearing, in a concession to the jubilant mood, what she called her 'light black stuff'
softened by her own white wedding lace and small diamond
coronet from which hung her own wedding veil.[74] A diminutive
figure suffering from the 'overpowering heat', she was dwarfed
still further by May's mother, Mary Adelaide, sitting next to her,
acting as though she was the queen with royal gestures in abundance, beaming irrepressible joy, her delight uncontainable at the
applauding crowd.

Around them, the dowdy London streets were transformed.
Bunting and tapestries were flung over balconies, flags and banners
floated over rooftops and there were flowers in abundance. On
approach to the Chapel Royal, St James Street was festooned with
garlands of evergreens and baskets of flowers hung from Venetian
masts to make one long floral archway. Even the cynical Lady
Geraldine was prompted to comment 'it was 'Really lovely! ...
like a bower from end to end ... too pretty'.[75] Deafening cheers
announced the arrival of the bride who was followed by no fewer
than ten bridesmaids, chosen with some diplomacy. Among them
were George's unmarried sisters, Victoria and Maud, Missy's
younger sister, Victoria-Melita, the spurned Schleswig-Holstein
princess, 'the Snipe', and Beatrice's pretty daughter, five-year-old
Ena: all dressed in white satin with silver trim and roses in their
hair.[76] Throughout the proceedings Queen Victoria's face plainly
showed her 'pleasure' at the way the crowd 'expressed its approval
of the marriage, which it is believed to a certain extent her majesty
brought about', continued the *New York Times*.[77] For her it was
a day crowned in glory. Five years after her search began for a
suitable consort for the future heir to the British throne, Queen
Victoria had no doubt that the right bride for England, empire
and Prince George was walking down the aisle.

But even on such a red-letter day, further matchmaking could
not be neglected. There was yet another alliance on the queen's
mind that she 'ardently desired', according to Missy.[78] She had
not forgotten her two unmarried Hesse grandchildren, Alix and
Ernie. When their father died the queen had advised Ernie on his
new role as the Grand Duke of Hesse as though he were her son

and for some months her thoughts had turned to his dynastic obligations, her plans inevitably having a bearing on Alix's future.

The twenty-four-year-old Grand Duke of Hesse found himself singled out to ride with his grandmother in the procession and escort her into the wedding breakfast. As intended, the handsome grand duke stood out from the crowd, prominently placed at the queen's side. Carefully positioned on his other side, Ernie found his intended spouse, a tall, dark, sixteen-year-old girl, somewhat intense and with an unusual self-assurance: Missy's younger sister, Victoria-Melita or 'Ducky'. At first sight they appeared well suited, both artistic and sensitive, and in worldly terms, Missy observed later, with his status and her wealth, 'this was a match which promised every hope of happiness'.[79]

The queen had the satisfaction of seeing her plans take shape that day. Ernie and Ducky did seem to enjoy each other's company and George and May were a tremendous success. In public, the newly married couple received 'one unbroken ovation' as they processed through London to Liverpool Street Station.[80] Privately, the queen was 'much pleased' with 'dear May', and George also seemed to gain in self-assurance. 'I can't tell you, dearest Grandmama, how happy I am,' he wrote to thank the queen while on honeymoon at York Cottage at Sandringham. He and May had much in common, he told her, '& understand each other thoroughly, in fact I did not think I could be happy with any Lady as I am with her now'.[81] Prince George's letter is perhaps a tribute to the very qualities that the queen had long seen in May: her discretion, tact and keen sense of duty. While George imagined that his wife was as delighted as he was with York Cottage, she was disappointed that he had chosen the furnishings in advance from the dull Maples range, her own ideas on interior decoration ignored. It was not long before she found the closeness of his interfering family over-whelming, especially his doting mother. Nonetheless, she raised no objections. Her honeymoon proved to be the start of a prolonged repressive period in her life where she felt subordinate to her husband's will and narrowed by his limitations. George did not suspect this. 'I love her with all my heart,' he told his grandmother in November. 'She is quite charming to me and we get on so well.'[82]

Confident of her sound judgement as matchmaker, the queen increased the pressure on Ernie that autumn. 'I have written <u>twice</u> to Ernie about the <u>necessity</u> of showing some attention and interest,' she told Victoria of Battenberg. 'Pray tell it him and say he <u>must answer</u> me.'[83] But Ernie was neither sure of the choice of bride nor even how easily he could fulfil his role as husband. He was drawn to masculine company and his cooperation with his grandmother may have stemmed from his eagerness to allay suspicions in the wider world. The queen was in blissful ignorance of these complications. She soon found she had an ally in her second son, Alfred, who was keen to advance the match for his second daughter, Victoria-Melita, while his wife was away in Romania attending the birth of Missy's first child.

Alfred had finally inherited the dukedom of Saxe-Coburg Gotha in the summer of 1893 following the death of Grand Duke Ernst, and his wife gloried in her new position as the Duchess of Coburg. At last she was free to create a court of her own well away from Queen Victoria and the British court. For the duchess, Ernie's closeness to his grandmother counted against him as a prospective son-in-law. But after the fiasco of Missy's sudden engagement, Queen Victoria was not to be outdone. Almost as though in reprisal, perhaps also because she sensed Ernie's own hesitancies about the opposite sex, she would not let the matter rest. She enlisted Alfred and Bertie to support her cause, and under pressure, Ernie obligingly set out for Coburg in November to see his prospective bride.[84]

At Darmstadt, Alix of Hesse was appalled at the prospect of her brother's marriage. Despite being four years her junior, the prospective bride displayed a pushy self-confidence that eluded Alix. She disliked the idea of Victoria-Melita, with her regal airs, invading her sanctuary by Ernie's side. Alix had found the courage to stand up to the queen when pressured to marry Eddy, but her brother and cousin appeared to be caving in to her wishes. She felt the fate of her brother was inextricably linked to her own future and was convinced he was not in love.

The pressures intensified on Alix that month as she was forced into a decision about her feelings for Nicholas. When the tsarevich returned to St Petersburg after George's wedding he found it hard to live with the continued uncertainty. He wrote to Alix on the pretext of asking for a recent photograph: 'I would be so happy to have one near me,' he told her. 'Whenever I look into our garden ... I always think of that lovely time on ice, which seems now to be a dream.'[85]

Alix could not bring herself to reply in the same affectionate tone. She wrote a letter to Nicholas in November 1893 that would end his hopes. The tsarevich had advance warning of her intentions from Ella. When Alix's letter arrived he could not find the courage to read it. He had such a dread of seeing what she had written that her package stayed in his room on the table all night, unopened. It was not until the next morning that he could bring himself to read it.

'Dearest Nicky ... It must have been a stronger will than ours that ordained that we should not meet ... for like this it gives me the chance to write to you all my innermost feelings,' she began. Alix explained that she had thought over everything for a long time and concluded she could not change her religion. They could never marry. 'It grieves me terribly and makes me very unhappy. I have tried to look at it in every light that is possible, but I always return to one thing. I cannot do it against my conscience. You, dear Nicky, who have also such a strong belief, will understand me.' It was 'a sin' to change her faith. 'We are only torturing ourselves about something impossible and it would not be a kindness to let you go on having vain hopes, which will never be realised ... Goodbye my darling Nicky.'[86]

Nicholas wandered around the grand interiors of Gatchina Palace 'in a daze'. He felt as though there was no longer 'any possibility of happiness in the whole world', he wrote in his diary.[87] 'All my hopes are shattered by this implacable obstacle.' He struggled to appear calm at dinner with the family. Inside he felt 'his whole future life is suddenly decided'. His immediate impulse was to go at once and see her in Darmstadt. Then he vacillated. Alix had written with equal finality to his sister, Xenia, acknowledging that she loved him and that 'to hurt one whom one loves is fearful and yet I don't want him to go on hoping, as I can <u>never</u> change my Religion'. He turned to Ella for help but she had already been briefed by Alix not to provide encouragement. Ella felt compromised, prompting Sergei to write to Nicholas: 'Everything is over and my wife asks you not to mention this again.' Days passed and Nicholas could not bring himself to write to Alix accepting her decision. 'It is hard sometimes to submit to the will of God,' he wrote in his diary.[88]

It was late December before Nicholas felt calm enough to reply to Alix. He had been in such a 'sad state of mind', he told her. He felt so close to his cherished dream being realised, 'then suddenly the curtain is drawn and – you see only an empty space and feel oh! So lonely and beaten down!!' He pleaded with her. 'Oh do not say "no" directly, my dearest Alix, do not ruin my life already! Do you think there can exist any happiness in the whole world without you! After having *involuntarily*! kept me waiting and hoping, can this end in such a way?'[89]

Whether Queen Victoria's warnings influenced Alix's letter of rejection to the tsarevich is not clear. Alix seemed determined to come to her own decisions without the aid of interested parties. She was most unwilling to meet with her beloved grandmother. After declining to join the queen for George's wedding, she turned down a second invitation to visit that autumn. 'Your 2 [Ernie and herself] are terribly sorry not to come this year,' Alix wrote on 14 October. 'I hope you will forgive us for not coming ...'[90] She may well have felt angry about the strong influence the queen held over Ernie, but her feelings for her grandmother were inescapably bound up in the conflict she felt about her judgement.

It is perhaps no accident that the week before Alix sat down to write her letter of rejection to Nicholas, Europe was set alight by a renewal of anarchist violence – a persuasive echo of the queen's warnings. On 8 November 1893 at the Liceu Opera House in Barcelona, two bombs were hurled from the gallery into the stalls killing thirty people in the deadliest attack yet seen.[91] The perpetrator, an anarchist, Santiago Salvador French, claimed he sought revenge on 'bourgeois elites' who perpetuated injustice by supporting the state.[92] It was as though a sudden fissure had opened up in the smooth facade of European civilisation, giving a glimpse of a great tide of anger and resentment welling up beneath in the oppressed lives of the masses. Like volcanic springs, flashpoints of terror ignited across the continent. Hundreds were arrested in Sicily, and in Paris the dynamite conspiracy that had opened with attacks on the judiciary now reached the heart of government as a nail bomb was thrown by an anarchist in the French National Assembly. Royalty stood out as the most powerful symbol of privilege of all and the rising levels of extremist violence may well have contributed to Alix's caution.

In the muffled interior of the Kremlin palaces, that unbreachable fortress of autocracy, the noise and alarm of Europe's troubles were easy to forget. Ella did not see – or perhaps did not want to see – the growing dangers. Having acted as go-between and knowing Alix's feelings, she wrote a letter to Queen Victoria that could be interpreted as disingenuous. Ella urged the queen not to raise the subject of Nicholas with her sister and omitted to mention that the question of a proposal had come to a head. She may have been trying to allay the queen's fears or perhaps was seeking to prevent Alix gaining confidence in her decision by mulling it over with her grandmother.

'Now about Alix. I touched the subject – all is as before,' Ella wrote evasively, '& if ever any decision is taken which entirely settles this affair I shall of course, write directly. The best is to leave her alone as of course it is a very very sore heart one touches – well all is in God's hands & dearest Grandmama, if ever she accepts – your motherly love will be what she longs for most – alas the world is so spiteful & not knowing how long & how deep this affection on both sides has been – the spiteful tongues will call it ambition – what fools as if to mount this throne was enviable. Only love pure and intense can find strength to [take such a] a serious step. Will it ever be I wonder?'[93]

Ella underlined once again why she favoured this match. Nicholas came from a model family, she wrote, 'all heart and religion which ... brings them nearer to God'. She believed the dangers were overestimated. 'It will be a tough school but one

that prepares for a future life & thank God, much is exaggerated.'
Above all she wished it, 'because I like the boy'. It is perhaps
telling that Ella referred to twenty-five-year-old Nicholas as 'the
boy' as though her initial impressions had left an indelible mark.
Ten years had elapsed since she had arrived in Russia and Ella
still saw only his strengths, his charm, gentleness and unswerving
affection for Alix. His weaknesses were not yet apparent to her:
his inability to assert himself, his lack of authority and his unfit-
ness to rule. Nor did she seem aware of the degree to which he
followed the reactionary thinking of his father, although she did
know of the cruelties to which this could lead in the treatment of
the Jews of Moscow. Nicholas's ability to lead could have a direct
bearing on her sister's safety as a future tsarina, yet such thoughts
had not occurred to her. Queen Victoria had evidently raised the
possibility of Alix being the target of a terrorist attack, prompting Ella to blur the line between practical issues of safety and
spirituality. 'Are not our lives always in His hands?' she replied.
'And may we not all die suddenly. *"L'homme propose et Dieu
dispose"*.' [94]

Despite Ella's omissions, by Christmas the queen had the satisfaction of learning that her choices for Alix and Ernie were falling
into place. In fact, Ernie was so eager to oblige that his letter on
18 December 1893 almost reads like a proposal to his grandmother. As instructed, he had courted Victoria-Melita, who had
been 'so dear and kind', he told the queen, that he was 'certain
that if I wanted to ask her now she would say yes'. But the actual
proposal – which had not yet happened – appeared to be second-
ary to fitting the wedding arrangements around the queen. 'You
see I simply could not bear the idea that my wedding would be
without you,' he told Queen Victoria. 'It would make me too
unhappy.' Ernie had everything planned. He wanted the queen
to agree to come to the wedding on her return from Florence in
the spring, and when the timing was arranged he aimed to 'engage
myself as soon as possible'. As though his grandmother were the
bride herself, Ernie pressed her to agree. '<u>Do please</u> say <u>yes</u> …
it would make me the <u>happiest</u> being on earth … Please, please
darling Grandmama, say yes.' He asked her to telegraph using

just the word 'yess' to show she agreed with his plan. 'Ever your most devoted Grandchild ... Please say Yess!!!!'[95]

Queen Victoria did say 'Yes'.

On 9 January Ernie duly proposed and Ducky dutifully accepted.

Everything was falling into place for the perfect spring wedding. It would be in Coburg – the birthplace of Grandpapa Albert, the place Queen Victoria felt to be the family's second home. She had not been back there since her husband's death, but now her devoted grandson hoped to make everything feel right for her.

As for Alix, over the winter the queen learned the truth about her rejection of Nicholas through her daughter-in-law, Alexandra. 'I wonder if poor dear Alicky has talked to you abt the end of Niki's hopes,' Queen Victoria enquired of Victoria of Battenberg in February 1894. The queen was put out that 'our dear Ella always encouraged him instead of doing the reverse'. Over ten years Ella had done all in her power to oppose her grandmother and pave the way for her younger sister to join her in Russia. Now Ella had lost. Queen Victoria knew that Nicholas was 'miserable' about Alix's decision.[96] But her granddaughter had made the right choice. Whatever Nicky's great charm, the country was too dangerous. The matter was at an end.

icholas, the Tsarevich of Russia (sitting), with his first cousin, Prince George in 1893.
ey looked so similar that they were sometimes mistaken for twins, but were to have very
fferent lives.

Princess Victoria Mary or 'May' of Teck, photographed c. 1886, was a rank outsider in the royal marriage stakes.

Princess May and her family went to see the charred remains of Restaurant Véry in Boulevard Magenta, Paris, shortly after an anarchist attack in April 1892.

An anarchist attack at the Liceu Opera House in Barcelona in November 1893.

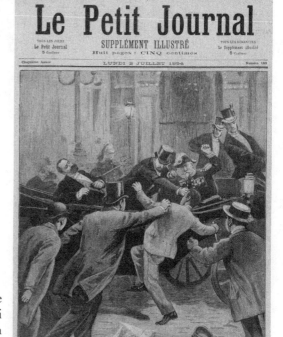

The assassination of the French President, Sadi Carnot, by an Italian anarchist in June 1894.

In a fictional account by Edward Douglas Fawcett in 1892, Hartmann the Anarchist and his crew destroy London in a 'tempest of dynamite'.

The high summer of royalty: Queen Victoria arrives at St Paul's Cathedral for her magnificent Diamond Jubilee celebrations in June 1897.

rowds watched in silence as their great queen made her final journey through packed ondon streets to her funeral on 2 February 1901.

Bloody Sunday in St Petersburg, 22 January 1905, led to the first Russian Revolution.

The remains of Grand Duke Sergei's carriage after his assassination in 1905.

Anarchist terror caught up with Queen Victoria's youngest grandchild, Princess Ena, on her wedding day in Madrid in 1906, when a bomb was thrown at the bridal carriage.

During the First World War, ten million people died and twenty million more were injured. Four empires – the Russian, German, Austrian and Ottoman – were swept away, and three of Queen Victoria's grandchildren lost their thrones.

10

Nicholas and Alix

'My blood runs cold ...'
> Queen Victoria on Alix's engagement,
> October 1894

In April 1894, Nicholas telegraphed ahead that he was on his way to Coburg. Ostensibly, he was to represent the tsar at Ernie's wedding, but for the tsarevich there was a far more crucial reason for his sudden trip. He wanted to speak to Alix.

Since the New Year there had been a different atmosphere in the palace at Gatchina. Alexander III had fallen ill with an ailment that was not easy to diagnose. Until this time, the evident vitality of the forty-nine-year-old tsar had created a blanket of security for those around him. Now Nicholas found his peace of mind revolved around his father's health. 'Thank God, we were able to breathe again today,' he wrote in his diary in January 1894 when his father improved. The tsarevich had been excluded from state matters by his father and was wholly unprepared for his future role. Nicholas did not even have the support of a consort at his side. Four months after Alix's first letter of rejection, his sister, Xenia, tentatively sounded her out once again.

Alix was unbending. 'Darling, why did you speak about <u>that</u> subject, which we never wanted to mention again?' she replied to Xenia on 11 April. 'It is cruel as you know it <u>never</u> can be – all along I have said so. It cannot be – he knows it – and so do not I pray of you, speak of it again. I know Ella will begin again, but what is the good of it, and it is cruel always to say I am ruining his life.' To make Nicholas happy she would have to commit a sin.[1] Nicholas heard about this repeat of her refusal just as he was about to leave for Coburg and was 'very upset', according to his cousin, Konstantin. He begged his mother not to force him to attend Ernie's wedding but the tsarina persuaded him to go. His mother wrote later that they parted with such 'a bad and *desperate* feeling ... that my heart bled as I saw you go'.[2]

Nicholas set out from St Petersburg accompanied by Ella, Sergei and other members of the Romanov family. It was a 1,200-mile trip, the imperial train driving at full steam through the endless countryside of Russian Poland and north-east Europe. Inside the luxuriously appointed carriage it was stiflingly hot and the tsarevich felt confined in the close atmosphere, unable to take his daily walk and clear his head. Alix had written that the subject must never be raised again, but he had to have the conversation with her, 'which I have so longed for and yet so feared'.[3] He dreaded to hear what she might say. After two days' travel they were in southern Germany and approaching Coburg. He went to change into his uniform.

There she was on the platform, all but lost amongst the large family reception party: the bride and groom, the bride's parents and sister, Missy, a guard of honour and a battalion of soldiers. At twenty-one Alix was the accepted beauty in the family, although not everyone agreed with this view. May's brother, Dolly, perhaps unkindly, observed to his mother that although she was 'very handsome', she 'looks very much like an actress'.[4] But Alix was no actress. Her intensity, her shyness, her inability to disguise her feelings: these traits had not left her. Suddenly, she and Nicholas were together on the platform going through the formality of a family greeting, enveloped in the noise and steam and crowds as they faced up to the awkwardness of seeing each other after her last painful rejection.

Queen Victoria had not yet arrived to assert any influence. The queen was travelling north to Coburg from Florence, much rested after a spring holiday. Her days in Italy had passed uneventfully. She could almost have been an elderly tourist out with her daughter, except for the retinue of ladies and servants in discreet attendance. She and Beatrice had taken breakfast on sunlit terraces overlooking vineyards and cypresses below and explored the grounds of their house, the queen taking turns in the donkey chair. They had driven through quaint old streets to see Michelangelo's sculpture of *David* and the Villa Medici and to gaze through the arches of the Ponte Vecchio at the sun setting over the Arno. The queen had found it 'too lovely', so peaceful, so quiet, the lilac-scented air 'too delicious', the setting 'quite heavenly'.[5] She did not leave Florence until 16 April, a few days before the wedding, unaware of the unwelcome proceedings already unfolding.

On his very first morning Nicholas seized his moment. Ella arranged for them to meet in her rooms. Alix struck him at once as having grown 'noticeably prettier, but looking extremely sad', he told his mother later. After a few minutes, Ella left them alone. The moment had come and Nicholas endeavoured to convey the strength of his feelings. 'I tried to explain that there was no other way than for her to give her consent and that she simply could not withhold it,' he wrote later. 'She cried the whole time and only whispered now and then, "No I cannot."'[6]

Nicholas could not bring himself to accept her 'no'. Her fervent conviction that to deviate from her spiritual path would be a sin was beyond any kind of rational argument, but for two hours 'I went on repeating and insisting ...' Alix wept but could not bring herself to accept his proposal. His appeal was irrelevant, from another sphere of thought. This was a question of faith and conscience, she said. Her Christian beliefs were immutable. To him it was as though she was struggling with unworldly forces bound up with her religious conviction that pushed her almost beyond endurance. He waited until she was 'calmer' before leaving her, profoundly saddened. All his hopes had come 'to nothing'.[7]

The opportunity was slipping away from the tsarevich. Queen Victoria arrived later that day in an unsettled frame of mind. On her approach to Coburg for the final leg of her journey from Munich, she found 'many conflicting feelings filled my heart'. Memories from long ago were as fresh as if from yesterday. Her first time in Coburg with Albert returned with great vividness. Remembering his joy as he had 'painted out everything' for her, the warmth and beauty of Italy receded and her habitual feeling of loss returned.[8] The Kaiser, of course, had laid on a smart reception. A squadron of her Prussian Dragoon Guards welcomed her at the station and escorted her to Schloss Ehrenburg, the seat of the House of Saxe-Coburg and where Prince Albert had been brought up. A large party was waiting for her: the tsarevich, Sergei and Paul from Russia, Ernie of Hesse, Ferdinand of Romania among the princes, and Victoria of Battenberg, Ella, Irene and Missy, Crown Princess of Romania among the princesses. To Missy it was as though her grandmother, encased in black, spread her 'sober glory' over the wedding party.[9]

Dismayed at the outcome of the morning, the tsarevich felt 'weary to his bones'. The next day he talked again with Alix, but this time 'touched as little as possible on yesterday's question'. He felt grateful that she was still prepared to meet.[10] But word of what had transpired between Nicholas and Alix began to make its way around the royal gathering. Alix had turned down not just the future heir to the British throne but also the Russian heir – twice. By the time Ernest and Victoria-Melita exchanged their own wedding vows on 19 April, for many the day was eclipsed by the tense exchange between Nicholas and Alix. Nicholas wrote to his mother later that he felt 'in a state of painful anxiety' and Alix seemed sorrowful, tormented by some 'final struggle'. While Ernie was convinced that there was still hope, the tsarevich seemed gripped by some kind of anxious fatalism. He told his mother the very solicitude of relatives 'made me even more afraid of something evil happening'.[11]

For the German emperor, this was no time for Alix's conscience or Nicholas's defeatism. Tantalisingly within his grasp was a rich prize: his German first cousin on the Russian throne. Wilhelm believed in blood relations to enhance politics. He was distantly related to the tsarevich, but the closeness of his blood ties to Alix might help to ease the strained relations that had developed between the two countries since he had dismissed Bismarck, and point the way to a new course.[12] More import-ant still, if he succeeded as matchmaker he would also acquire a new psychological weapon: Nicky's gratitude and indebtedness, a powerful card to call in later. The Kaiser visited Alix's rooms determined to change her mind.

According to Victoria of Battenberg he had a long conversation with Alix in which he challenged her religious scruples. The irony of this was not lost on Victoria. The Kaiser had been so enraged by his sister Sophie's conversion to the Orthodox Church that he had banned her from Germany and called her *'fahnenfluechtig'* – a deserter. Without appearing to see the contradiction, the German emperor now 'proved to Alix that it was her bounden duty for the sake of the peace of Europe' to sacrifice her conscience. Europe's future was at stake, he reasoned. Supercharged by his political ambition, he persuaded her that the difference between the two faiths was 'only superficial'.[13] Ella added to the pressure, highlighting similarities between the Russian Orthodox Church and their Lutheran faith. She was convinced her sister was in love and this would be her last chance to accept Nicholas. The forceful arguments of her relatives, the knowledge that her own life at Darmstadt was about to change, the tsarevich's absolute certainty: Alix's resolve began to weaken.

The following morning the Kaiser took the tsarevich in hand. Nicholas must ask again more forcefully, Wilhelm insisted. He felt a sword was called for and an impressive uniform of course, one that would make a statement and dazzle the most reluctant princess. Above all, Nicholas must appear masculine, confident and in charge. There must be no more introspection, only the glorious charisma of the winner. And some flowers perhaps: the romantic gesture to sweep her off her feet. Finally, the German emperor brought Alix to the house where Nicholas was staying. The tsarevich was ready to repeat his proposal. With the Kaiser, Ella, Sergei and other Romanov uncles waiting expectantly in the very next room, Alix and Nicholas were left alone again.

To his astonishment, 'with her first words she consented!' Nicholas told his mother. At last 'my darling, adorable Alix' relented. He found that he was crying, 'like a child', and she was too. Alix seemed different, 'her face lit by a quiet content', he wrote. Nicholas felt so happy it was as though 'the whole world is changed for me: nature, mankind, everything, and all seem to be good and lovable … I could not even write, my hands trembled so …' Alix too, seemed changed, becoming 'gay and amusing and talkative and <u>tender</u>'. He felt overwhelming relief and gratitude. 'I can't thank God enough for His mercy,' he wrote to his mother.[14]

Nicholas and Alix went immediately to Queen Victoria. She had just finished a leisurely breakfast with Beatrice when Ella arrived, 'much agitated' and 'begging' the queen to see Alix and Nicholas. 'I was quite thunderstruck,' the queen wrote in her diary when she heard the news. 'As though I knew Nicky much wished it, I thought Alicky was not sure of her mind. Saw them both. Alicky had tears in her eyes but looked very bright & I kissed them both.'[15]

Alix had already shown early signs of the traits that would make her spectacularly ill-fitted for her future role: her acute suffering in large public gatherings that made her shun society; the mysterious pains that made it hard to function – only a few days before Ernie's wedding she told the queen 'I have to keep as quiet as possible on account of my legs'; her ability to cling to ideas once her mind was made up.[16] All these characteristics would in time become magnified by her frightening experiences in Russia and lead her to play a crucial part in her and Nicholas's downfall. Queen Victoria was better placed than Nicholas to understand Alix's weaknesses, but even she had interpreted her granddaughter's wilfulness as a strength, and half-believed, half-hoped she would grow out of her nervous complaints. Ironically, the tsar's long-held desire to block the match meant that Nicholas had not had a chance to see her develop. The Alix he knew was the sixteen-year-old girl he had met in St Petersburg in 1889, who had responded to his attentions with an enchanting vivacity, becoming the adored, outgoing 'Sunny' of her youth. With characteristic self-deprecation Nicholas told Queen Victoria, 'she is much too good for me'.

Over coffee that morning, surrounded by the timeless peace of the Ehrenburg Palace, the queen confronted the instinctive fear she felt for her granddaughter as her ten-year campaign came to an end. Her reservations remained deep-rooted, but she responded to Nicholas and Alix's excitement. Of all the royal marriages of her grandchildren, this most undesirable match was unmistakably a love match. The queen was still thinking partly of herself when she wrote in her diary that night that 'Russia is so far', and also of Alix, 'the position is such a difficult one', but she was now resigned to the match: since they 'are really attached to one another perhaps it is better so'.[17] Each morning the couple joined her in the palace for coffee. The queen was full of practical guidance, urging Nicholas to ease the way regarding religious differences and accepting the bizarre quirk of fate that the heir to a country she had long regarded as Britain's enemy could now call her 'Granny'.

For the rest of their stay in Coburg, Alix and Nicky were inseparable. Those who saw them together were in no doubt of their feelings. For Nicholas it felt like 'walking in a dream, without fully realising what has been happening to me'. He drove with his fiancée out in the carriage in the warmth of the spring sunshine, he took her in the charabanc to The Rosenau, the birthplace of Grandpapa Albert, they watched the lawn tennis, drank tea and sat side by side at the banquets. He felt 'utterly enchanted' with her, 'brimming with pleasure' just to sit beside her on a bench for hours by the pond. Nothing was too much trouble. He summoned a choir across Europe from the Imperial Guard to sing for her. The tsarina was much moved by his letters home and 'shed tears of joy'. She and the tsar wrote affectionate messages to Alix to welcome her 'as their own dear child'.[18] Magnificent Romanov gifts soon followed: a bracelet studded with exquisite emeralds and a bejewelled Fabergé egg.

To the wider world, the remarkable union bringing closer ties between the royal houses of Russia, Germany and Britain appeared to embody some shining new hope. The alliance 'cannot fail to strengthen in the highest degree the guarantees of European peace', enthused the Morning Post.[19] The newly engaged couple 'may exercise a commanding influence on the destinies of more than one continent', forecast The Standard. As early as 1885 'Prince Bismarck tried to prevent the union for fear that England should reap some advantage from it', continued The Standard,

but the bride's sister, Grand Duchess Sergei, had used 'all her
influence to bring it about'. The betrothal indicated 'a complete
change' in the views of the tsar and was of 'high political significance' in linking the Russian heir to a cousin of a German emperor
and a granddaughter of the queen, 'who is also Empress of India'.
Such a happy event will even 'touch the heart of Asia and impress
the Orient!' On top of all this, after the recent 'estrangement'
between the 'courts of Berlin and St Petersburg', credit must be
claimed by the Kaiser for 'the "new course" in Germany', continued *The Standard*, noting his 'delight and elation'. [20] Reuters
observed that Emperor William 'received an ovation' from the
huge crowds that gathered in Coburg. The people 'vociferously
cheered him waving hats and handkerchiefs'.[21]

In London, telegrams poured into the queen's office in the same
vein, among them one from Archbishop Benson, expressing the
views of many that the match gave confidence 'as to future peace
and relations between such great nations'.[22] The new Liberal
Prime minister, Lord Rosebery, telegrammed 'that much public
advantage' would arise from the 'auspicious union', a view that he
repeated to the queen when they discussed the matter in person a
couple of weeks later.[23] The engagement, he felt sure, 'must tend
to Peace'.[24]

But the high hopes of the wedding masked a harsh new
European reality. The old world where a marital alliance could
influence foreign relations between countries was slipping away
fast. Just a few months before the engagement, the Franco-Russian
treaty had been ratified and formally announced. The Kaiser's
worst fears were realised as tsarist Russia and the Republic of
France sealed their military alliance challenging Germany's Triple
Alliance with Austria and Italy. From the beginning the purpose
of Bismarck's intricate alliance system had been to isolate France
and prevent a rapprochement with Russia. Just four years after
his dismissal by Wilhelm II, a new kind of Europe was beginning
to form, shaped by two opposing power blocs.

From her position as an outsider in the German court, Vicky
saw the dangers clearly. As early as June 1894, just a few weeks
after Alix's engagement, she warned her mother 'Wilhelm's one

idea is to have a navy which shall be larger and stronger than the British navy.' Vicky saw this as a danger that would destabilise the balance of power in Europe. She saw flash points too, arising over the race for colonies. Her son's desire for colonial expansion was making Germany 'quarrelsome and pretentious'. African colonies 'are of no use to Germany, only an expense and a trouble', she continued, prompting the Germans to suspect the English of 'falseness and treachery'. Although Bismarck had once opposed colonialism, he was speaking from his retirement in favour of it, Vicky explained, as a ploy for 'stirring up German indignation against England'.[25] For Vicky there was also the long-running fear over the 'Eastern Question', which 'crops up again and again', she despaired, papered over only with 'palliatives' by the Great Powers. After a visit to see her daughter, Sophie, in Greece, she foretold of the 'dangerous' threat to peace in the Balkans in South-East Europe. It would not take much, she wrote to her mother, 'to have the east in a blaze'.[26]

Queen Victoria felt protective of Alix and invited her for a long stay in England after the momentous events at Coburg. She hoped to delay the marriage as long as possible and have time to prepare her granddaughter for her role. Not long after their return to Windsor Castle she took Alix out for a drive. Once they were alone, the queen could no longer contain her curiosity. She had a tiresome cough and was finding the clear spring day 'rather raw', but this did not inhibit her. 'She began by asking me so many questions,' Alix wrote to Nicholas on 4 May 1894. 'When, how, and where, and what had made me change my decision and so on, till I no longer knew what to say ...'[27] Queen Victoria's efforts to understand her granddaughter's worrying choice appeared to exhaust her. The queen eventually fell asleep in the carriage and Alix was free to gaze at the beauty of Windsor Great Park in the late afternoon sun, the glimpses of the castle through the dark trees 'like a beautiful vision', she told Nicholas. Beside her was her beloved granny, the woman who had come closest to a mother figure in her life and who could never be replaced. The English scene before her was redolent of the very essence of her childhood security that was fast slipping away.

Once again, Alix was unwell, suffering from mysterious pains in her legs that made it difficult for her to walk easily. She left Windsor on 20 May to go to a spa in Harrogate for specialist treatment. On 9 June she wrote to the queen to say the pains were 'no better', but she still had high hopes 'the good effects of the baths will show itself' and was able to go out in her bathchair. The stress of leaving her grandmother was on her mind. 'I am sure his parents will often allow us to come over to you. Why I could not bear the idea of not seeing you again … I cling to you more than ever now that I am quite an orphan … Please do not think that my marrying will make a difference in my love to you – <u>certainly it will not</u>.'[28] Victoria of Battenberg, who went to visit Alix in Harrogate, thought her sister was suffering from 'attacks of sciatica'.[29] But the queen understood the anxiety that lay behind her granddaughter's complaint and wrote full of concern to her future grandson explaining that Alix 'requires great quiet and rest'. Alix's heartbreak over her father's death, concern for her brother, and the worry over her future, she told Nicholas, 'have all tried her <u>nerves very much</u>'.[30]

It was almost too much for the queen. She poured out her distress on 25 May to Alix's oldest sister:

> Oh! Darling Victoria, the more I think of sweet Alicky's marriage the more unhappy I am! <u>Not</u> as to the personality, for I like him <u>very much</u> but on acct of the Country, the policy & differences with us & the awful insecurity to wh that sweet Child will be exposed. To think she is learning Russian & will have probably to talk to a Priest – my whole nature rises up agst it – in spite of my efforts to be satisfied. – But I will <u>try</u> & bear it & make the best of it. Still, the feeling that I had laboured so hard to <u>prevent it</u> & that I felt at last there was <u>no longer</u> any danger & all in one night – <u>everything</u> was changed. Ella shld never have encouraged it originally as she did – at one time …[31]

The queen was reunited with Alix and Nicholas on 23 June at Windsor. It proved to be an eventful week. Hard on the heels of the family's delight in the birth of George and May's first son,

Prince Edward, came shocking news from Paris. The French president, Sadi Carnot, had been brutally assassinated. The queen heard the gruesome details through the French ambassador. The president had been returning from a banquet in Lyon when the assassin had managed to leap onto the step of his carriage, his dagger concealed by a newspaper. Carnot had lingered a few hours before dying of his wounds. The assassin was an Italian anarchist named Sante Caserio, who, the queen was told, 'glories in the deed'.[32] This latest outrage was particularly unnerving because it had proved impossible to protect the president in his own carriage. Behind the thick walls of Windsor Castle the grand gathering that assembled a few days later on 29 June seemed almost invulnerable. They assembled in the Red Drawing Room: the future Austrian heir, Archduke Franz Ferdinand, the Russian heir, the British heir, the queen; princes resplendent in their uniforms, princesses decked in their finery. 'Nicky led me in and I sat between him and the Archduke,' the queen recorded in her journal. 'Alicky looked lovely as always.'[33] But how safe were they beyond the walls of palace, castle or *schloss*?

The violence of 'propaganda of the deed' that had exploded into public awareness with the deaths of Alexander II and now the French president stirred the queen's anxieties for Alix's future in 'horrid Russia'. The tsarevich left on 23 July and there was one more week together at Osborne before the day came at last when Alix, too, had to leave. Victoria and Louis of Battenberg arrived after luncheon on 31 July, 'alas! to take Alicky away', the queen wrote. She felt she had 'watched over [Alix] since May' but was no longer able to protect the granddaughter she loved most.[34] The carriage disappeared from view, taking Alix to Trinity Pier where she boarded the *Victoria and Albert* to sail onwards to Flushing in the Netherlands. For weeks afterwards the queen felt a sense of foreboding about 'her dear life'. The queen begged Victoria of Battenberg that nothing further should be settled about Alix without her being consulted and pressed for Alix to return once more to see her before her marriage. 'I have a claim on her! She is like my own child,' the queen wrote. 'All my fears abt her future marriage now show themselves so strongly & my blood runs cold when I think of her <u>so</u> young most likely placed on that very unsafe throne ...'[35]

Relaxing with his family in his palace at Livadia in the Crimea, surrounded by stunning vistas of the Black Sea, Alexander III rallied in the late summer of 1894. For Nicholas it began to seem possible to believe in his father's recovery. He received frequent letters from 'my own darling Sunny' that had him 'in a mad state of excitement'. There was none of the English reserve that had characterised George and May's engagement. He wanted her 'madly' he told her and would cover her 'with greedy, burning loving kisses'. She replied to her beloved 'Boysy' that she would 'kiss you gently always more and more, till there is no escaping for you any more'. He replied by return. 'The state I'm in – a sort of gelatine!'[36] But their elation, unchecked by responsibilities, was not to last. By late September it became clear that Alexander III was suffering from an acute form of nephritis, inflammation of the kidneys. He was confined to his bed, and priests joined doctors in attendance. Thoroughly alarmed, Nicholas urged Alix to leave Darmstadt and join him with his parents in the Crimea.

Alix hurried from Germany, accompanied by Victoria of Battenberg to Warsaw, where Ella took over as her escort. The Hesse sisters were oblivious to the lack of ceremony with which Alix was met in Russia. The life of the little palace at Livadia revolved around the dying tsar, who was anxious to greet his prospective daughter-in-law with affection and respect. Alexander III would not receive her in his sickbed but found the strength to dress in uniform and wait for her in a chair, no matter what pain it cost him.

Queen Victoria followed events anxiously from Balmoral, her drives out in clear, frosty weather punctuated with the news from Livadia. On 22 October she learned that Alix had arrived safely and that the emperor was 'so pleased' to see her.[37] Reports in the British press sounded ominous. 'Along the muddy roads leading to Livadia, wagons accompanied by soldiers passed, loaded with india rubber cushions', reported the *Daily Telegraph*. 'These were filled with oxygen gas for the imperial patient.'[38] The telegrams that Nicholas and Alix faithfully sent each day showed that the tsar was weakening fast. Even so, she was 'much startled' on 30 October when Bertie and Alexandra announced that the tsarina had entreated them to set out at once. It was already too late. When the queen returned from her afternoon drive the next day, Beatrice was waiting with a telegram. Alexander III was dead. Although the news was expected, it still seemed 'almost incredible', the queen wrote in her journal. 'How my heart bleeds for … poor dear Nicky and Darling Alicky. May God help them.'[39]

At Livadia the sound of the guns announcing the tsar's death echoed across Yalta harbour, sounding doom-laden and incongruous in such a beautiful setting. Outside in the palace grounds, workmen prepared for the ceremony for the oath of allegiance. Inside, Alix witnessed the overpowering grief of her twenty-six-year-old fiancé, who 'cried himself out on the day of his father's death'. As they prepared for the Prayers for the Dead, she found the familiar pains in her legs had returned. Everyone in the palace understood that Nicholas was not equipped to be a tsar. For the new emperor, Nicholas II, it was as though his very soul was invaded by 'a terrible feeling of oppression'. His brother-in-law, Sandro, felt there was nothing now to stop the country from 'falling down a precipice'.[40]

Queen Victoria gleaned the bare facts in a succession of telegrams. Her granddaughter was received into the Russian Orthodox Church the very day after the death of the tsar. 'I long to hear more about it,' the queen wrote in her diary. Then came news that Alix, now Alexandra Feodorovna, would be travelling to Moscow and St Petersburg with her new family with the funeral train bearing the emperor's remains. 'Alicky must remain with her future husband & mother in law,' Ella explained. Under pressure from Nicholas's powerful uncles, the wedding was to take place after the funeral in St Petersburg. This news gave Queen Victoria 'rather a shock'.[41] There would be no last chance to see Alix before her marriage. '<u>Where</u> shall I <u>ever</u> see her again?' she wrote despairingly to Vicky.[42]

Ella did her best to create for her sister the same idyllic reception as a Romanov bride that she herself had experienced ten years earlier. Her letters to her grandmother convey her enthusiasm as she described Alix's sumptuous bridal costume. 'The dress is in embroidered silver cloth ... & very pretty,' she wrote on 17 November. Alix's hair would be piled high, apart from two long curls that would make 'a pretty frame for her face'. Her cloak would be of dark ruby velvet and ermine. 'I must say the latter is heavy and would be much prettier without,' Ella commented. Nonetheless, with the myrtle blossom pinned on her dress and the 'splendour of diamonds' crowning her head, 'Alix being tall will look perfectly lovely'. Her detailed sketches of her sister as a Romanov bride looked like something from the pages of the fashionable new American society magazine, *Vogue.* But even independent Ella could not quite conceal the exposure and insecurity they all felt without the protection of Alexander III. Nicky, she conceded, looked 'thin and pale', and she signed herself 'your loving "Own Child"', as though she, too, suddenly felt the need of a parent.[43]

However hard Ella tried to recreate the fairy tale for her sister, the circumstances were beyond her. At Windsor, Beatrice read out loud to her mother the reports of the funeral procession across Russia. The funeral train bearing Alexander III's coffin made slow progress from the Crimea to Moscow, the route lined with crowds waiting for a glimpse as it passed. They stood silently: this was the closest they would ever be to the remote, legendary figure, half-man, half-god, who had ruled their lives. With frequent stops for services in the open air, Bertie found it all 'very fatiguing'. There was no respite in Moscow where the streets were packed for the imperial procession to the Kremlin. Finally, on 13 November the funeral train arrived at St Petersburg, where it took four hours for the cortege to cross town in heavy fog and a bitter wind to the Cathedral of the Fortress of Peter and Paul.[44] Bertie's equerry, Sir Arthur Ellis, was struck by the chaotic security arrangements. Police were 'using and threatening a fire hose on the multitude near the cathedral' and 'not a single window was permitted to be open' as the cortege went by. The measures seemed to Sir Arthur a curious mixture of 'cruel interference and infinite laxity and the result is clearly the same, that the dastard who will give up his life in an attempt cannot fail to succeed'.[45] Inside the cathedral, the rapidly decomposing body of the tsar lay in state, his familiar countenance a fearsome black, his rotting flesh emanating a pungent odour of death. Royal mourners were obliged to lean over the coffin and kiss the icon in his hand during the many services. 'It gave me a shock when I saw his dear face so close to mine,' Prince George wrote to May.[46]

The queen lived through her granddaughter's experiences vicariously. She held a Memorial Service in Windsor Chapel on 19 November to coincide with the final funeral service for Alexander III in St Petersburg. 'A fine Russian hymn always sung at funerals ... was sung without accompaniment & was very impressive,' she wrote.[47] Her mind was filled with worrying thoughts. The one thing that she had understood to be of immeasurable danger for Alix had happened. There was no escape. She turned to her beloved Albert, looking for the comfort that she always found from being near him at the mausoleum. 'Tomorrow poor dear Alicky's fate will be sealed,' she confided to Vicky on 25 November. 'The dangers and responsibilities fill me with anxiety and I shall be constantly thinking of them with anxiety,' she continued. 'I daily pray for them.'[48]

Alix did not tell her grandmother what she admitted to her sister: her wedding on 26 November 1894 felt like an extension of the funeral, as though 'a mere continuation of masses for the dead' except she wore 'a white dress instead of a black'.[49] She seemed so frail and vulnerable to Nicholas's cousin, Grand Duke Konstantin, she could have been 'a victim destined for sacrifice'. Thousands of miles away at Windsor, the queen felt the same way. She held a large banquet in honour of the new tsarina and proposed a toast 'to the health of their Majesties the Emperor and Empress of Russia, *my grandchildren*'. The assembly stood as stirring strains of the Russian national anthem were played in the Windsor dining hall. It seemed almost impossible to believe that 'gentle little simple Alicky should be the great Empress of Russia'.[50]

Ella wrote to the queen putting the inevitable gloss on events. The Russian people were 'mad with joy' to see their new sovereigns, she observed. Alix had entered the Russian Church and was praying alongside the family, she and Nicholas had nursed the dying tsar, comforted his widow, and now were ready to do their duty: 'all this is understood with loving hearts by the people & they bless their young sovereigns and love them,' she wrote. 'I wish you could see and feel all this, it would be a true comfort to you as I see you are worrying about them.' Alix 'hardly feels her leg', she added.[51] For months afterwards she continued to reassure the queen. Alix 'is already adored for her tact and sweet winning manners' and 'that dreadfully sad look which papa's death printed on her has disappeared'.[52]

Prince George, who had struggled to feel any passion for his own wife May, did not miss the unmistakable signs of his cousins' evident happiness. Despite the pressure they were under he told Queen Victoria that he had 'never seen two people more in love'.[53] Alix herself told the queen of her 'utter happiness. I never can thank God enough for having given me such a husband.'[54] A famous exchange in Nicholas's diary conveys their strength of feeling. 'My bliss is without bounds,' Nicholas wrote. Alix discovered his journal and added an entry of her own: 'Never did I believe there could be such utter happiness in this world, such a feeling of unity between two mortal beings. I love you – those three words have my life in them.'[55]

Nicholas's reign opened with high expectations. Ever the idealist, Vicky saw his golden opportunity to reform Russia. 'What a benefactor to his country, what a saviour to his poor oppressed nation, what a godsend to Europe he might be!' she wrote to her mother on 3 November. She believed his gentle and sensitive character could be an asset. Nicholas formed such a contrast to his Romanov forebears, he might embrace the reforms started by his grandfather. 'No one ever had a finer mission. May the truth reach his ears and wise disinterested counsel. He might make himself adored.'[56]

But Nicholas let himself be guided by his forceful uncles, among them his Uncle Sergei, who encouraged him to follow the path set out by his father. Their grandfather's liberalism had led directly to his death, he reasoned. No one in the family could ever forget the deathbed scene of Alexander II. What could be a plainer demonstration that Russia was not yet ready for democracy? The land of all the Russias was ungovernable without the firm hand of autocracy. Those hoping for a revival of the reforms started by Alexander II were soon disappointed. Gentle Nicky, the quintessential quiet family man, aimed to continue his father's hardline policies. In January 1895 Emperor Nicholas II took to the stage before a delegation from Tver who sought greater liberalism. Such reforms were mere 'senseless dreams', he declared. 'I will maintain the principle of autocracy as firmly and unflinchingly as it was preserved by my unforgettable late father.'[57]

In clinging 'unflinchingly' to autocracy Nicholas did not just ally himself to the oppressive autocracy of his Romanov forebears. It was not long before the new tsar and tsarina became personally associated with their bloodshed too. The catastrophe occurred in May 1896 during the celebrations held for their magnificent coronation in Moscow. Governor General Sergei had overall charge of the arrangements and, according to Ella, laboured hard over the preparations beforehand. Twenty-year-old Missy, Crown Princess of Romania, now the mother of two children, travelled to Moscow with her husband, Ferdinand, and has left a vivid account of the unfolding drama. She was struck at once by how ill-fitted Nicholas and Alexandra appeared for their public roles.

A mass of people lined the streets to cheer the new imperial couple for their symbolic entry into Moscow. The funereal atmosphere was at last dispelled. The sun shone and bells rang out as the tsar entered at the head of the procession on a white horse. He had the ease of a good rider, Missy noted, but in his physical appearance he was 'less well cut out' for the part than his forebears. Missy's impressive Romanov uncles dominated the scene, tall, good-looking and 'so sure of themselves, so wealthy and powerful, real autocrats'. Nicholas was unable to project the same air of certainty. He seemed 'small, almost frail-looking' and unlike his uncles, his 'eyes were kind, had a caressing expression, there was something gentle about him and his voice was soft and low pitched ...' Nonetheless, he was the tsar and Missy felt he was loved and seemed 'imbued with mystic power'.[58]

Two golden coaches followed the tsar, 'such as children picture to themselves in fairy-stories, white horses, glittering trappings, pages, followers'. The tsar's mother, now Dowager Empress, was in the first carriage, in a gown 'of shining gold', her neck 'one mass of glittering jewels'. She judged her part perfectly, bowing with ease to the left and right to great applause. But Missy was concerned for Alix in the second coach. Although she was 'much more handsome than her mother-in-law ever was' and looked every inch the beautiful empress, she was quite unable to play the part. There was an awkwardness about her that could not be disguised. She 'does not smile and her expression is one of almost painful earnestness. There is a tightness about the lips which is disconcerting in one so young. There is no happiness in the large steady eyes ... It is as though she were holding Fate off at arm's length, as though darkly guessing that life might be a foe, she must set out to meet it sword in hand'.[59]

The five-hour coronation ceremony in the Cathedral of the Assumption in the Kremlin confirmed Missy's first impressions of the new emperor and empress. The setting could hardly have been more stunning. 'The very atmosphere seemed golden, a golden light enveloped the glittering assembly,' she wrote. The chants 'were almost unearthly. They rose and swelled, filling the church with such mighty waves of harmony that one's heart felt like bursting ... it was more like a dream than reality.' All eyes were on the tsar and tsarina, seen through a haze of incense, figures of such symbolic potency they were like 'two shining apparitions'. Standing side by side they could have been 'deities almost ... two diamond crowned figures at the zenith of their glory'. As sunlight suddenly flooded the scene it was almost possible to believe that they had indeed been chosen by God. But Nicholas appeared overwhelmed, 'the prodigious crown of his ancestors appeared to be too heavy for his head'. As for the tsarina, despite being 'imbued with a glamour that few ever achieve', she was 'all dignity but ... no warmth ... Her face was flushed, her lips compressed; even at this supreme hour no joy seemed to uplift her.' As the festivities continued, Alix struck her cousin as 'more and more pathetic'.[60]

The spectacular coronation in the ancient city of the tsars was overshadowed a few days later by a tragedy that came to be seen as 'a great sin', even an omen. The calamity also marked the start of a split between the Hesse sisters in Russia.[61] A feast was to be held at Khodynka Field, a former military training ground on the outskirts of town. Word spread fast of free food, beer and souvenirs – mugs and handkerchiefs with sweets and gingerbread. Some 700,000 people, many of them peasants who had travelled from the country, made their way to the site, almost double the numbers expected. A rumour that supplies would run out led to a stampede as the vast crowd surged forward. 'Nobody fully realised the danger,' observed Victoria of Battenberg. 'Those who stumbled were trampled down, others falling on top of them.' All morning 'we saw the dead and wounded carted past the Governor-General's house'.[62] Sergei insisted that the 'joyous occasion' should continue as planned that afternoon with thousands still waiting for the arrival of the tsar. Reluctantly, Nicholas and Alix submitted. They arrived at Khodynka to the triumphant fanfare of the national anthem played several times over, even as bodies were still being removed from the field.[63]

Missy witnessed at first hand the toll this exacted on Nicholas and Alexandra. They were scheduled to attend a glamorous ball at the French Embassy that night. Alix had had enough. She was 'cruelly impressed' by the disaster and resolved to take no further part in celebrations that day. She was opposed by Nicholas's uncles, notably Ella's husband Sergei, who insisted that the French must be honoured. Tearfully, Alix begged to be excused. 'God alone knows how much rather she would have stayed at home to pray for the dead!' recalled Missy. Ella agreed with her sister and as Sergei became more vehement, 'beautiful Aunt Ella's despair was pitiful to see'.[64] Both women intuitively understood that in their adopted land of mystic icons and superstitions the tragedy would be read as a portent. Both women wanted to pray for the souls of the departed. This was not a show of piety but central to their beliefs, essential to help expiate such a destructive and wanton act.

Overriding Alix's feelings, Nicholas was persuaded that they must attend the ball. The event was excruciating – the young tsarina even more rigid and nervous than usual, Sergei with a forced 'broad smile'. The family seemed suddenly split in two, the younger generation, notably the tsar's sister, Xenia, and her husband, Sandro, blaming Sergei bitterly for the tragedy and its mishandled aftermath. Why had he not made better arrangements with police for safety at Khodynka Field? At the very least, he should acknowledge the tragedy, rather than ignore it. And why did he appear to block a special inquiry into its cause? Alix and Nicky were tarred with serious failings that many laid at Sergei's door. Horrified at events and torn between her loyalty to her husband and her sister, Ella would not admit any blame. 'Thank God Sergei had nothing to do with all this,' she insisted.[65] Alix did not voice any criticism of Sergei, but for the first time both sisters had a chance to appreciate their grandmother's warnings in a new light.

On the other side of the continent, Queen Victoria soon had the measure of the situation. Three thousand dead, she recorded in her journal on 4 June 1896, '& there are grave accusations against the Police and others'. She was greatly distressed by the accounts of the funerals in the papers. 'The people of Moscow are showing signs of anger and exasperation at the frightful mismanagement of the authorities. It makes me anxious.'[66]

Victoria of Battenberg was also troubled. She knew that Nicholas could not shake off 'a feeling of profound depression' and the stress continued unabated for Alix. Even the tsarina's hand was 'swollen and red' as if 'she had been stung by a wasp', because so many people were presented to her during the celebrations.[67] Victoria's notes on her reading at that time show she studied *The Statesman's Handbook for Russia* – lent to her by Alix – which set out the far-reaching powers and rights of the tsar. But she also studied *Paris under the Commune* by John Leighton, showing how discontent had turned to open revolt in

1871, leading to what Marx termed 'the dictatorship of the proletariat'. In Paris the veneer of civilisation had proved wafer thin under the onslaught of revolution. What would it take for the same to occur in Russia?[68]

In the late summer of 1896 Balmoral's unvarying routine was upturned in preparation for the visit of the tsar and tsarina. Almost two years had elapsed since Queen Victoria had seen her granddaughter and in the weeks beforehand she was 'much occupied with preparations'. Arrangements were made for lodging Nicholas's huge entourage, ensuring their safety and providing a travelling escort. The Balmoral ballroom was adapted to become a dining room and a temporary passage constructed to make it easier for the company to reach it. On 21 September the queen drove to Ballater Station to inspect the welcoming decorations of Venetian masts and festoons. The place was 'prettily decorated', she noted, complete with a new portico over the platform. But in the event there was drenching rain on 22 September, 'the worst we have yet had', Queen Victoria observed as the Russian imperial yacht approached the Scottish coast.[69] She sent her two sons, Bertie and Arthur, to welcome the tsar and tsarina. It was evening before their imminent arrival was heralded by the sound of church bells and pipes. The queen was waiting in eager anticipation on the doorstep as an escort of Scots Greys came into view, followed by the pipers, a procession of torchbearers, and finally the carriage with Alix and Nicholas.

Nicholas stepped down first and the queen was struck that he appeared 'thin ... and careworn'.[70] She embraced him and then saw 'darling Alicky, all in white, looking so well, whom I likewise embraced most tenderly'. It was a great relief to see her at last, 'in great beauty' and positively blooming. They hurried out of the rain to the drawing room where to the queen's delight she was presented with her first Russian great grandchild, ten-month-old Olga. Olga had been born in November 1895 and her great-grandmother thought her 'a most beautiful child'.

After the many months of anxiety, it was 'quite like a dream' to see them at last and she spent hours happily talking with Alix.[71] Nicholas found the experience rather less gratifying as he was commandeered by his British uncles, who were keen to take him out shooting despite atrocious weather. Nicholas adored his wife and resented moments apart even after two years of marriage. The only consolation was that George came too and the rapport felt by the cousins immediately struck up again. 'We can at least talk over the good times,' Nicholas told his mother.[72]

The queen still believed in the value of family relations to enhance foreign diplomacy. The Russian visit was presented to the press as a private affair and many days did pass in the privacy of family, driving out to the Highlands, visiting relatives, and walking on the estate. This was poignantly captured in an early cinematograph – the first private family film – the jerky, grainy images revealing what looked like an ordinary family in their garden, the elderly lady in her bathchair, her dog on her lap, far removed from the image of a great queen and empress of a quarter of the globe.[73] But this was also the longest visit of any reigning monarch to see the queen and she took the opportunity to sound out the tsar on Russian foreign policy.

By the time of the tsar and tsarina's visit, the relationship between Germany and Britain had sunk to a new low, with hostility often surfacing between Bertie and his German nephew. Emperor Wilhelm had arrived at the Cowes Regatta in 1895 accompanied by German warships and exasperated his francophile Uncle Bertie by making triumphant speeches on the anniversary of the German victory in 1870 against the French. But such provocations faded into insignificance compared to the uproar that followed in the New Year of 1896 when Wilhelm sent a letter of congratulation to Paul Kruger, President of the Transvaal, a state in southern Africa, who had successfully suppressed a British coup. The coup, led by Dr Leander Jameson, had aimed to provoke an insurrection against the Boer government in the Transvaal and advance British mining interests in the area. The Kaiser's 'Kruger telegram' implied that Germany supported the Boers against the British.[74]

Wilhelm's congratulatory telegram to the Boers sparked a furore and came to be seen as a watershed in Anglo-German relations. Although a British raid had provoked the crisis in the first place, Londoners took to the streets to vent their fury at the Kaiser's response. German businesses and shops were attacked and there were anti-German demonstrations. Queen Victoria found the 'violent feeling against Germany' expressed in the British news-papers 'most distressing'.[75] She had hoped for a quiet time at Osborne and felt anxious and angry about the Kaiser's 'dreadful telegram'. Bertie was keen to punish the German emperor with 'a good snub', but the queen responded to her German grandson on 5 January with some tact.[76]

Their correspondence shows that the British queen could still exert a personal influence over the German emperor. 'As your Grandmother to whom you have always shown so much affec-tion and of whose example you have always spoken with so much respect, I feel I cannot refrain from expressing my deep regret at the telegram you sent President Kruger,' she began. She explained the trouble Wilhelm's telegram had caused while taking care not to allocate blame or intention. 'It is considered very unfriendly towards this country, which I am sure it is not intended to be, & has, I grieve to say, made a very painful impression here.' The British raid 'was of course wrong', she conceded, but nonethe-less it would have been much wiser for the emperor 'to have said nothing'. Finally, she asked for his help in trying to contain those who harm Anglo-German relations. 'Let me hope that you will try to check this ...'[77]

Her letter produced the desired effect and Wilhelm sent a confused but contrite answer to the 'Sovereign whom I revere and adore'. He implied that he had been endeavouring to uphold the queen's wishes but had been misunderstood by the press.[78] The queen, who considered his reply 'lame & illogical', passed it to Lord Salisbury, who had become prime minister in 1895 for a third time. Salisbury agreed it was best to accept the emper-or's explanations without examining too closely 'the truth of them'.[79] As for Bertie, the queen tried to teach him to take the same moderate approach when dealing with his nephew. She sent

Bertie a copy of Wilhelm's reply, pointing out 'it would not do to have given him "a good snub". Those sharp, cutting answers and remarks only irritate and do harm and in Sovereigns and Princes should be most carefully guarded against.'[80]

Vicky had reached a point of such anguish about her son that, it has been argued, she possibly came close to treason in her revelations to Queen Victoria on 24 October 1896. She revealed that Kaiser Wilhelm was pursuing a systematically hostile policy towards Britain and that the true purpose of his plan for a large battlefleet was to 'wrest fr[om] her the supremacy she has in the world'. Vicky perceived 'a systematic *enmity* in Germany to the '*Welt Stellung*' [world status] of the British empire', which had '*an aim* & a *purpose*', she told her mother. For years Germany would deny that its new naval programme was aimed against Britain, insisting it was to protect German trade and colonies. Yet here Vicky explained its real purpose to the British queen, well before Germany began building its fleet. Vicky even revealed specific details. Wilhelm had befriended men like Friedrich Krupp whose weapons manufactory in Essen had become the largest company in Europe. She pointed out to her mother that Krupp, 'the *greatest* manufacturer we have, who has a colossal fortune – has been ordered to buy some Docks near Wilhelmshafen, "Germania Docks", in order … to be able to have English ship builders & employ engineers etc to design and build ships for the German Navy that shall beat the English'. In her frustration she railed at her helplessness at her son's 'deluded & mistaken' actions: 'I can do *nothing, nothing* …' The cherished dream of Vicky's generation and her father's generation of the 'closest friendship' between the two countries was vanishing before her eyes.[81]

With Anglo-German relations at such a worrying point, Queen Victoria hoped it might be possible to create a closer understanding between Russia and Britain in the congenial setting of a family reunion at Balmoral. She was not the first in the family to try to sound out the tsar given the new closeness of family ties. Prince Louis of Battenberg, now brother-in-law to the tsarina, had met with Nicholas and his foreign minister, Prince Lobanoff, earlier in the summer of 1896. In the serene setting of Sergei's country estate, with its tall trees and wide river, they had talked through Russian interests as though they were brokering the world. Louis recorded Nicholas as saying 'we are best of friends with England' and he saw the 'outlook in Europe as generally hopeful'. The importance of ensuring that Russia's Black Sea Fleet could pass through the Straits into the Mediterranean and the Suez Canal, the tsar's anxious interest in the Far East, why Russia wanted to curb Japan's influence and see an independent Korea, Russia's need for an ice-free port, its lack of interest in Africa – all these topics were aired with some candour.[82]

Queen Victoria found Tsar Nicholas less forthcoming. She felt confounded that her conviction that Russia and Britain 'should go well together' as the world's most powerful empires to guarantee peace elicited little response. Both she and the prime minister, Lord Salisbury, found that the new tsar proved rather hard to pin down. For all his easygoing charm, there was a measured vagueness to Nicholas's replies that was a little frustrating from the British point of view. He was out of his depth and under instructions from his ministers not to fall for British blandishments. The Russian emperor would not be drawn into any comments on British affairs in Africa. He revealed little of his attitude to shifting Great Power alliances. He appeared to 'regret' German hostility to Britain and was sparse with information about his attitude to the French. When the queen queried the Franco-Russian alliance she did manage to ascertain that this was primarily defensive. Both France and Russia felt threatened by Germany.[83]

The queen felt dissatisfied after the Russian visit that she had made no progress with the tsar. She had asked whether he could try to ease Franco-British relations while he and Alix were on a state visit to France. But Nicholas failed to do so. He wrote briefly from Darmstadt excusing himself. His schedule for his short stay in France was packed and he 'never had the occasion' to raise her concerns. At a distance, however, he was a little more forthcoming about areas of difficulty between the Russians and the British. The British occupation of Egypt threatened Russian interests and could 'endanger peace' because it gave the British control of the Suez Canal. 'Politics alas! Are not the same as private or domestic affairs,' he told the queen, 'and they are not guided by personal relationships or feelings.'[84]

Ella also found family relationships were unravelling in a way that defied expectations. For years she had looked forward to her youngest sister joining her in Russia and fought for what she believed was the perfect match between Alix and Nicholas. As sisters in Darmstadt they had been close, but in their new roles in Russia, one as the empress, the other the wife of a grand duke, their relationship was sullied by malicious gossip and differences between their husbands. The aftermath of the tragedy at Khodynka lingered in the Romanov family as a 'burning question', observed Nicholas's cousin, Konstantin, which nobody liked to raise but which stood 'between us for so long like some terrible phantom of dissension'.[85] The sisters' pleasure at having each other in Russia was tainted. Ella was at pains to make sure her grandmother understood there was no rift between her and Alix or their husbands. 'May God grant we husbands and wives may always love each other as we do,' she wrote. The crisis that had sprung up overnight between Sergei and Nicholas at the time of the coronation had led to 'abominable lies' that Ella found 'simply disgusting'.[86]

Ella tried to set out the truth for her grandmother. She denied rumours that she resented her younger sister's higher rank or had refused to kiss the tsarina's hand. She had had no part in cancelling her sister's arrangements, as claimed. Her husband was wrongly blamed and she felt that this was taking a toll. 'Poor Sergei looks very thin,' she wrote. They both felt 'calumniated' by the rumours that 'we were not liked' in Moscow. They had very few enemies but were much more wary, 'our eyes are open'. Poignantly, Ella now saw it as a blessing that she and her sister would be living apart. 'In every way I find it lucky we live in another town than Alix, for her sake chiefly, it makes her quite independent.' Ella's long-cherished desire for her sister to join her in Russia had somehow been blighted from the very beginning.[87]

11

Ena and Alfonso

'Here at last will I rest with thee ...'
Queen Victoria's inscription for Prince Albert, 1862

For several days before her Diamond Jubilee of June 1897 to celebrate her sixty-year reign, Queen Victoria was 'a good deal agitated' for 'fear anything might be forgotten or go wrong'.[1] Feeling the increasing frailties of her seventy-eight years, the queen could no longer take for granted her ability to endure prolonged public performances. The tragedy at Alix's coronation was also not far from her mind. At least one paper did not dismiss the possibility of 'holocausts and wholesale massacres'.[2] Ella and Sergei arrived at Windsor shortly before the jubilee and after hearing their account of the Russian disaster the queen was convinced that Sergei had been wronged. The grand duke 'has had to suffer a great deal from wicked calumnies', she wrote in her diary, 'people having tried to lay on him the whole blame of the terrible disaster at Moscow'.[3]

Her concerns proved to be unfounded. As her carriage emerged from Paddington Station 'it was like a triumphal entry', Queen Victoria wrote in her diary. 'One mass of beaming faces' lined the streets all the way to Buckingham Palace. Feeling buoyed up by the momentum of the occasion, she was greeted at the palace by family members and then wheeled into the Bow Room to receive foreign princes and ambassadors. That evening she abandoned her black for a dress 'which had been specially worked in India', she wrote. 'The whole front was embroidered in gold.' In this uncharacteristically vibrant attire, adorned with diamonds in her cap and her necklace, the queen joined the glamorous assembly and was led into dinner by the Austrian heir, thirty-three-year-old Archduke Franz Ferdinand.[4]

All this was just the prelude. The day of the Thanksgiving Service for her sixty-year reign surpassed every conceivable expectation. It was 'bounteous Queen's weather', according to the papers; 'A never to be forgotten day', wrote the queen. Drab London streets were transformed early as hundreds of thousands massed on the pavements or piled into tiers along the procession route to St Paul's Cathedral. The capital looked like 'a fairy city', according to the *St James Gazette,* 'a glorious vista of living colour'. The crowd was held back by two lines of soldiers in vivid scarlet uniforms, colourful drapes hung from balconies, and red, white and blue flags waved from walls and roofs. As the queen passed, the streets became 'a great theatre ... quivering with life and emotion ... hats waved, handkerchiefs fluttered, every hand and arm at work, throats strained to shout, shriek or roar'.[5] Dressed in black brocade, a white feather in her jet bonnet, the queen was overwhelmed, sometimes smiling, sometimes with eyes filled with tears. 'No one ever I believe has met with such an ovation as was given to me passing through those six miles of streets,' she wrote. 'Every face seemed to be filled with real joy. I was much moved.'[6] It was, concluded the *St James Gazette, 'the* social function of the century ... the like of which has not been seen on earth ... It was a reception which has never been, and probably never will be paralleled.'[7]

This was indeed the high watermark of imperial and royal supremacy, those halcyon June days apparently the very zenith of British power and glory. At the pinnacle of it all, almost worshipped like a deity, was the diminutive queen, who remained in her carriage for the Thanksgiving Service on the steps of St Paul's, looking both 'very grave' and 'under the stress of emotion'. She 'suffered terribly' in the heat, observed Victoria of Battenberg, being 'lame and helpless', her hands 'like hot bricks'.[8] Nonetheless, as a figurehead for 450 million people, the 'Grandmother of Europe' was the very embodiment of British stability and prosperity, the representative of the collective achievement of a generation and the recipient of the gratitude of millions. Celebrations in her honour straddled the globe, from British-ruled India, Burma, colonies in Africa and the dominions of Australia, Canada and New Zealand. Now 'men of all races and colours marched under the flag', continued the St James Gazette. Londoners marvelled that people from far-flung countries spoke English as well as themselves. Foreigners were astonished at the orderliness of the London crowds. To all 'the greatness of the empire was brought home with force'.[9]

In the ten years since her Golden Jubilee at the height of the belle époque, Queen Victoria had helped to fulfil Albert's vision as her role as Europe's grandmother had blossomed. Her first-born grandson, now the thirty-eight-year-old Emperor Wilhelm, had ruled for nine years and secured the German branch of the dynasty with no fewer than six sons. Dona 'is getting quite grey', Prince George observed when he saw her in Coburg in 1896.[10] The queen learned of a new addition to the Russian branch of the royal family just two weeks before her Diamond Jubilee. Alix's baby daughter, Olga, was joined by a beautiful sister, Tatiana, on 10 June 1897. Closer to home, George and May had already secured the British line with two great-grandsons, Edward (the future Edward VIII) and Albert (the future George VI) – this latter prince named, of course, after 'his dear Great Grandpapa', and bestowed with a bust of the late Prince Consort as a christening gift. 'I know that when he grows up he will greatly value this beautiful bust,' George had written tactfully.[11] Queen Victoria's granddaughters, Crown Princess Sophie of Greece and Crown Princess Marie of Romania, had also presented her with great-grandsons, assuring the continuity of the Greek and Romanian branches of the royal family. With a number of her grandchildren still growing up – her youngest granddaughter, Ena, was only nine years old – there was no end to the possibilities for royal matches. Most recently, Bertie and Alexandra's third daughter, Maud, had married her Danish cousin, Prince Charles, although on this occasion the queen had excused herself from the wedding breakfast and slipped upstairs quietly to her room.[12]

But the image of dynastic impregnability that day was not quite what it seemed. The high summer of royalty was drawing to a close. Unlike at the Golden Jubilee, reigning monarchs in the family were absent from the great pageant through London. When the colonial secretary, Joseph Chamberlain, had proposed that the queen's jubilee should be a 'Festival of the British Empire' and that colonial representatives, rather than reigning monarchs, should be invited, the queen had gladly agreed.[13] Quite apart from the cost of entertaining foreign royalty, she was most anxious not to parade any family differences or allow personal squabbles to ease their way into the press and cloud the big day. For a destructive element was gnawing away at the roots of this apparently flourishing royal family tree, and it resided in the very feature in which the queen had placed her trust: family relationships. Above all, the German emperor had the power to threaten the entire great edifice. Vicky saw it clearly; the queen could not bring herself to believe it was true. If she worked hard enough at family diplomacy, if Wilhelm could be induced to behave, she hoped to safeguard Europe's stability.

In the late nineteenth century, Kaiser Wilhelm continued to consolidate his personal power in Germany. The cabal of ministers around him found their authority fast diminishing. Rewards went to the most sycophantic rather than the most able, such as the diplomat Bernhard von Bulow, who claimed the Kaiser was nothing less than a 'genius' and saw him alongside his grandfather, Wilhelm I, and Frederick the Great as 'the most impressive Hohenzollern who has ever lived'.[14] Bulow duly found himself elevated to secretary of state for foreign affairs in the summer of 1897, a prelude to his becoming chancellor in 1900. Gradually the post of German chancellor was being diminished to a mere satellite or courtier in obeisance to an increasingly powerful emperor.[15] Bulow supported Wilhelm's grand dreams of building a colonial empire, and to achieve it Wilhelm wanted to expand the navy. He promoted Admiral Alfred Tirpitz to run the German fleet, and Tirpitz soon redefined Britain officially as Germany's natural enemy. Fuelled by a belief in the power of the Hohenzollern dynasty, an increasingly autonomous and megalomaniacal

Wilhelm aimed to steer Germany to greatness and challenge
Britain's supremacy. He spoke of German *Weltpolitik* or 'World
Policy', and urged the case for German expansion, colonies and 'a
place in the sun'.[16] His sabre-rattling rhetoric aimed to win support
for large increases in funding for the German navy. The queen
confided to Vicky her 'great distress and anguish' over 'the bad
feeling' between Britain and Germany engendered by Wilhelm's
'speeches and colonial follies'.[17] Vicky shared her despair. 'Alas
these speeches at Kiel. How unfortunate and I must say absurd!'[18]
The era of the Kaiser's 'personal rule' was taking ominous shape
far beyond the reach of his grandmother.

But not quite. Wilhelm endeavoured to enhance German
power by devious manipulation of family relationships – and
here Europe's grandmother kept an astute eye on the proceedings. Wilhelm pressured Nicholas to sign a German alliance by
threatening him with claims that Britain was on the verge of
striking a deal with Germany. The German emperor was equally
underhand in dealings with the British, claiming that the Russians
were agreeing to deals against British interests in the east. The
queen suspected that her German grandson was inflaming rivalry
between the Great Powers – and despite her years of hostility to
Russia, turned to the tsar. Her famous exchange would expose the
Kaiser's duplicity.

'I feel I must tell you <u>something</u> which you <u>ought</u> to know and
perhaps do <u>not</u>,' the queen wrote to Tsar Nicholas in March 1899:

> It is, I am sorry to say, that William takes every opportunity of
> impressing upon Sir F. Lascelles [British ambassador in Berlin]
> that Russia is doing all in her power to work <u>against us;</u> that
> she offers alliances to other powers, and has made one with
> the Ameer of Afghanistan against us. I need not say that I do
> <u>not</u> believe a word of this, neither do Lord Salisbury and Sir
> F. Lascelles. But I am afraid William may go and tell things
> against us to you, just as he does about you to us. If so, pray
> tell me openly and confidentially. It is so important that we
> should understand each other, and that such mischievous and
> unstraightforward proceedings should be put a stop to.[19]

The tsar's reply was equally frank. 'It is a dangerous game he is playing at,' Nicholas concluded.[20] Their correspondence highlights the climate of fear and suspicion created by the Kaiser and also marked a softening in the queen's inimical stance towards Russia.

As the decade progressed long-held hopes for an Anglo-German understanding fell apart. The various initiatives that surfaced periodically came to nothing. Even Joseph Chamberlain, the man who could make the weather, according to Winston Churchill, could not bring about an Anglo-German alliance despite his strong desire to achieve it. Vicky heard the rumours and in her excitement urged her son on 31 May 1898 to grasp this 'world saving idea', which might never come again. It was the '*most blessed*' opportunity for peace 'that could happen *not only* for the 2 Countries but for the *world* and civilization!! ... My father's dream & your father's dream, and what they worked & slaved for, would come true.'[21] But all efforts foundered in the climate of mistrust between the two countries. For the British, an alliance with Germany would now have been tantamount to a hostile act against France and Russia and an endorsement of the Kaiser's hegemonic goals. The German emperor approved the Second Naval Law on 20 June 1900 to double the size of the German fleet; in the next few years three more bills would follow to strengthen the German navy, part of a predetermined plan to build up a naval force of some sixty warships by 1920. Vicky's warnings to her mother became ever more urgent. 'I think with fright and horror of the future,' Vicky wrote. 'It makes one mad to think of all the misery that may yet come.'[22]

Britain's much-vaunted imperialism was cast in a new light in October 1899 with the outbreak of the Second Boer War. In the opening months of the conflict the Boers of the Transvaal and the Orange Free State secured victories over the British. By December, on the thirty-eighth anniversary of her husband's death, the queen felt 'very low and anxious about the war'. As British losses mounted in January 1900, her distress appeared to affect her physically. She fretted with each new report, 'horrified at the terrible list of casualties'. The belief in British invulnerability was severely shaken. Long-held pride in the British Empire as an alleged moral or 'civilising force' was also dealt a bitter blow when the story broke of Britain's 'concentration' camps to contain Boer families in which some 20,000 Boer women and children died, many in epidemics. Shocking accounts of gruesome conditions in the camps added to the list of Britain's colonial failings, such as the failure to get to grips with famine in British India. British imperialism, for so long the glory of the nation, was taking on a different hue. There was outrage against the British treatment of the Boers in the European press, prompting the queen to write to the German emperor hoping that 'the German Press may cease abusing and reviling us and telling lies about our army'.[23]

Britain's 'imperialist war' also provided further ammunition for anarchists and terrorists. Bertie was targeted in April 1900 as he travelled to Denmark. He had reached Brussel-Nord Station in Belgium when a fifteen-year-old, Jean Baptiste Sipido, appeared at the carriage window and shot at him at point-blank range. Sipido was an anarchist who blamed British royalty for the Boer War. The queen was 'greatly shocked and upset', although it was soon clear that the bullet had missed. She continued to worry that Bertie's 'precious life' would be jeopardised and urged him to avoid events abroad.[24]

Towards the close of the century anarchists set a new benchmark by singling out soft royal targets. Queen Victoria was 'dumb with horror' when she wrote to Vicky on 11 September 1898 after the murder of the beautiful Empress Elizabeth, wife of the Austrian emperor.[25] The empress had been about to board a steamship on Lake Geneva in Switzerland when a young man appeared to knock into her accidentally. Her corset was so tight and the long industrial needle file he had used so fine that at first it was not clear there was anything wrong. But the empress fainted after walking on board and never regained consciousness. It was soon found that the four-inch industrial needle – sharpened to a fine point – had punctured her heart and a lung. The assassin, an Italian anarchist, Luigi Lucheni, was caught later that day. 'It was not a woman I struck, but an empress,' he said to police. 'It was a crown I had in view.'[26] Vicky, who had only recently met with the empress, wrote in some distress to her mother. She felt 'ill with horror' at the thought of Elizabeth's terrible death and had learned that anarchists were 'turning their attention to <u>Princesses</u>, who were more easy to get at'!'[27] But the next royal victim, in July 1900, was King Umberto I of Italy, followed just over a year later by the American president, William McKinley: both were murdered by anarchists. The great social divides that fuelled the rise of anarchism appeared increasingly impossible to resolve.

However powerful a weapon assassination proved to be, for an increasing number of radicals and revolutionaries it was not enough. Anarchists had been grabbing the headlines for years with sporadic incidents since the death of Tsar Alexander II in 1881, but the injustices of the social order appeared unchanged. One young Russian, Vladimir Ulyanov, whose brother had been hanged in 1887 by Alexander III for his part in an anarchist plot, had read Marx's *Das Capital* and translated the *Communist Manifesto* into Russian, and dedicated himself to spreading communist ideas. This led to his imprisonment and in 1897 he was banished to Siberia for three years. To the despair of his mother, who had already lost one son to the anarchist cause and did not want to lose another to Marxism, when he was freed in 1900, Ulyanov travelled back to Europe. He was absolutely sure of his mission. Only all-out revolution would make a difference: an 'international proletariat revolution'. This time he was writing under a new name: 'Vladimir Lenin'.

With the arrival of the twentieth century the queen was feeling old and tired, no longer certain of the future. Vicky saw more clearly than her mother that the troubles between Europe's Great Powers were shifting beyond the calamitous interventions of the Kaiser. Unlike her pragmatic prime minister and foreign secretary, Lord Salisbury, Queen Victoria still placed great faith in the power of personal relationships between royal heads of state; her matchmaking to extend European royal ties rested on this view. 'I only think, if it is <u>possible</u>, that in families all should be made up again, for life is so very uncertain,' she told Vicky.[28] The glorious past, in all its brilliance, must live on. Her grandson George understood the significance of continuity in her mind and was quick to reassure the queen after the birth of his third son, Henry, in April 1900, 'of course we will add Albert as his fourth name'.[29] The baby's godparents included Queen Victoria, the German Kaiser and Prince George of Greece.

The queen's health began to fail, with cataracts, rheumatism, lameness and exhaustion all depleting her strength. Her 'great anxiety' over the Boer War preyed on her mind, observed Victoria of Battenberg, along with the shock of her oldest daughter's illness.[30] Vicky was diagnosed with breast cancer in 1899, which spread to the spine. Mother and daughter continued their correspondence, now spanning over forty years. The queen tried to make light of her health troubles to Vicky but was obliged to enlist Beatrice's help to write over Christmas 1900. 'I have not been very well myself, but nothing to cause you alarm,' she dictated. Beatrice tried to shield Queen Victoria from the full horror of Vicky's illness, but the queen was not fooled. She was well enough to write herself a week later and sharp enough to see her daughter's deterioration. 'I am so grieved to see by your dear letters that your hands trouble you so …'[31]

At Osborne, Queen Victoria looked upon the New Year 'sadly', feeling 'so weak and unwell'.[32] Despite her tiredness and confusion, she rallied occasionally to sign papers or take a short drive, perhaps unable to relinquish her role of decades until a stroke robbed her of this last comfort. She lay in her room, which was crammed with precious mementos she could no longer see, her remarkable willpower no longer able to summon the strength for her to sit unaided. For two days she fought on, struggling to deal with the business of state through Beatrice until the last vestiges of strength ebbed from her.

In Germany, Vicky was utterly distraught at the news. Too weak to make the journey, she knew she would never see her mother again. Alix, who was four months pregnant and unable to travel, was also bereft. 'She did so love her grandmother!' observed her sister-in-law, Xenia.[33] Ironically, it was the queen's least favourite grandchild who held her on 22 January 1901 as she lay dying. The

German emperor had set out 'on personal impulse', according to Victoria of Battenberg, and would not be kept away. In those final hours the grandson who had caused her and her daughter such immense distress appeared to have 'a real affection and respect for Grandmama', continued Victoria.[34] Her family did not disclose that he was in the room and it was left to her doctor, James Reid, to arrange for the Kaiser to have a few moments alone with the queen. When Reid returned something stirred from the depths of her mind, from the great distance of all those years of tangled frustrations and hopes. 'The emperor is very kind,' she said.[35] She died with his good arm wrapped around her at 6.30 p.m. on 22 January 1901, surrounded by her family. 'Oh my beloved Mama. Is she <u>really</u> gone?' cried Vicky when she was told the next day. 'I wish I were dead too.' The former German empress had only seven more months to live.[36]

On 2 February, Queen Victoria's coffin was conveyed from Osborne to London, people kneeling in the fields as the funeral train passed in reverence for the woman whose loss was hard to imagine. There was an atmosphere of shock in the capital as her coffin, conveyed by eight cream-coloured horses, crossed London to Paddington, large crowds silently witnessing the passing of the mother of the country. She was the longest-reigning monarch in British history to that point and her death marked the end of an era.

Queen Victoria had envisaged a definite purpose to her final journey and this was fulfilled on 4 February, when her coffin was conveyed to the Royal Mausoleum near Windsor to be laid to rest beside Prince Albert. She had left instructions that on her death she was to abandon her widow's weeds. There must be no more black. This was the day her soul would be united with her beloved Albert, the man she had waited for grieving half a lifetime. All must be perfect; she had left explicit directions to make sure this was so. Her aged body, carrying the marks of time and decay, was in bridal white, her wedding veil beside her, and hidden forever amongst her clothes many mementos of her life, including a photograph of John Brown as well as Prince Albert's treasured dressing gown and a cast of his guiding hand.[37]

A gentle rain was falling outside in the grounds of Frogmore where she had sat so often, taking tea under the shade of a parasol, seeking comfort from his proximity. Marked indelibly above the door of the mausoleum were the words that had sustained her as a young widow almost forty years before: 'Farewell most Beloved! Here at last, will I rest with thee; with thee in Christ I will rise again.'[38] Now one by one the family came to kneel at her coffin. When Albert had died, Queen Victoria had commissioned a stone effigy of herself as a young woman that was to be placed beside him, fulfilling in death the moments she had envisaged so often when they were both young together. Their love immortalised in the two white youthful figures on their tombstone, they left behind a dynasty at the height of its power, their legacy apparently invulnerable. The fruits of their sacred union held positions on the world's mightiest thrones, the closeness of family relationships in her eyes promising Europe's peace.

The nineteenth-century vision at the heart of Victoria and Albert's matchmaking did not end with her death, but collided increasingly with an overwhelming and urgent impetus for change. Their wonderful dream of constitutional monarchies spreading across the continent, bringing order, peace and a stable form of political governance, was irresistible, an idyll somehow tinged with all the innocence of village England, the sound of leather on willow, the puritan work ethic and British stiff upper lip. But as the curtain rose on the twentieth century this vision clashed with something altogether more brutal and immediate in which moderation was swept away by an overpowering impulse for change. Nowhere was this manifest more forcefully than in Russia where the injustices and oppression of the masses that had fired anarchist and revolutionary thinking in the nineteenth century could no longer be contained by its crumbling autocracy. Queen Victoria's worst fears for her Russian granddaughters turned into a terrifying reality soon after her death.

By Christmas 1904, Ella and Sergei knew what it was to be hunted. Like Sergei's father, Alexander II, twenty-five years earlier, they lived with a heightened sense of danger. Sergei was convinced he had been a target for some weeks; and he was right. The revolutionaries who kept a close watch on his movements knew that Sergei had worked out that he was in their sights. 'He was running scared, changing palaces, trying to avoid a death that was already inescapable, already creeping up on him,' recorded Boris Savinkov, a member of the Socialist Revolutionary Party, which had superseded the People's Will.[39]

Tsar Nicholas had no solution for the countless hungry peasants roaming the land unable to survive on their meagre plots or the thousands of industrial workers in the cities striking against appalling factory conditions. As losses mounted during 1904 from his disastrous war with Japan, radicals and reformers turned on the tsar demanding an end to his authoritarian rule. Nicholas wavered, torn between those, such as his Uncle Sergei, who argued for strengthening autocracy, and those who argued for reform and the creation of a 'duma', or assembly with limited power. The mood in turbulent Russia was 'far too like that' of the years before the murder of Alexander II, observed Nicholas's cousin, Grand Duke Konstantin. 'One senses something unknown, but inescapable and terrible. It is as if the dam has been broken.'[40]

Ella knew the toll this exacted on Alix, who lived with her family imprisoned behind ever higher barriers of barbed wire at the Alexander Palace at Tsarskoe Selo, about fifteen miles from St Petersburg. The young grand duchesses, Olga and Tatiana, had been joined by two more sisters, Maria in 1899 and Anastasia in 1901. The arrival of a son and heir in August 1904 fulfilled everything Nicholas and Alexandra had worked for; the longed-for little boy, Alexei, contained their whole purpose. But for two days afterwards, the fresh bloodstains on his swaddling clothes soon brought the dreaded confirmation that her perfect baby boy suffered from 'the family curse', haemophilia. Enough was now known about it for Alix to understand that his disease had come through her line from Queen Victoria; haemophilia had already claimed the lives of Alix's infant brother, Friedrich, her favourite uncle, Leopold, and just six months previously, her nephew, Irene's young son, Heinrich. Alexei, too, could bleed to death from the slightest injury. Alix felt crucified daily whenever the bleeding started, unable to get away from the horror of what was happening to her beautiful, innocent son.[41] Her own health suffered and she withdrew still more from society. Exhausted from the nervous strain, hours passed on her daybed, a table with her daily occupations beside her, every surface around her crammed with portraits and memorabilia. Behind the looped-back fabric adorning her bedstead was a wall covered with brightly coloured icons.

In Alix's devotion to the Russian Orthodox Church, it seemed to Ella and her friends that she 'dipped into mysticism and was led astray'.[42] Her son's episodes of bleeding and the helplessness of the doctors appeared to throw Alix off balance and bias her judgement, making her susceptible to the claims of faith-healers. Eventually, she became totally dependent on one man, a Russian peasant and mystic, Grigori Rasputin, whose uncanny ability to relieve her son's suffering convinced her he had supernatural, God-given powers of healing. Olga, Tatiana, Maria and Anastasia supported their mother, adapting to her strained and idiosyncratic world. In their photographs from the early twentieth century, Queen Victoria's Russian great-granddaughters appear radiant, four young women on the brink of maturity. With their good looks and impressive pedigree they could expect happy and fulfilling lives; there is no doubt to be read on their faces that this is the story that will unfold.

But on Sunday 22 January 1905 a watershed was reached in St Petersburg. Thousands of workers processed peacefully to the Winter Palace to present a petition to Nicholas II, many bearing icons and images of the tsar. As the masses drew nearer to the town centre, the imperial guard opened fire. Over 1,000 died and many more were wounded, the dark shapes of the dying on the white snow an incendiary symbol of the misdirected power of the tsar. Nicholas II was not at the palace, but he was blamed nevertheless. Overnight he was no longer the peasants' 'Little Father' but 'Nicholas the murderer' and 'Nicholas the Bloody'. The cry went out for vengeance. Strikes and riots swept the country, which now shuddered to the violent convulsions of the first Russian revolution.[43]

Sergei had recently resigned his post as Governor General of Moscow, objecting profoundly to his nephew's instinct to listen to reformers. 'The people were not yet ripe,' he explained to his sister-in-law, Victoria of Battenberg, for 'a more liberal government in Russia'.[44] Sergei remained a hardliner and for many in Moscow he inspired loathing. Like his older brother, Alexander III, he was convinced that any attempt to liberalise Russia was an invitation to revolutionaries and terrorists to incite further revolt. Ella knew her husband's fears. He changed his routes and slept in different rooms; they rarely went out. Eventually, they moved inside the Kremlin, secure behind its thick fortified walls, soldiers keeping guard.

But one evening, not long after the massacre in St Petersburg, Grand Duke Sergei and Ella were leaving the Bolshoi Theatre where they had attended a performance for one of her charities. Glitteringly attired for the event, they sank back into the soft, white silk interiors of the carriage. Outside it was snowing. Unknown to them, Sergei's place of execution had already been selected: Voskresensky Square. The bomb throwers were waiting for the signal. The grand duke's closed carriage could be readily identified at a distance by its bright white lamps. Keeping watch near the theatre was Ivan Kalayev, a former student of St Petersburg University and a member of the 'Terrorist Brigade', a combat arm of the Socialist Revolutionary Party of Russia. His hands grasping one of the bombs were numb with cold. He saw Sergei's carriage and raised an arm. But as it drew alongside, he glimpsed Ella and two children inside and aborted the plan.[45]

Two days later, on 17 February, Ella was inside the Kremlin. The sounds of the city outside were muted by the heavy snowfall. She was accustomed to the familiar sound of snow ice falling from the Kremlin roofs in the thaw. Suddenly there was a different noise, so close at hand, a tower in the Kremlin might have collapsed. Then silence, 'so crushing that for some seconds we did not stir', recalled Ella's niece, Maria. The 'vague unease' that Ella had felt all day turned into sudden dread. Sergei had only just left. She ran out of the building. At the Nikolsky Gate there was a small crowd. People tried to stop her going near, but Ella would not be held back. Before her was a scene beyond comprehension.[46]

There on the white snow beside the remains of a destroyed carriage was a disembodied hand, a foot, part of a torso ... Irrationally, she fell on the snow and began to pick up the body parts as if she could somehow repair the damage. There was no sign of her husband's head or shoulders or his left arm. The crowd that gathered witnessed the grand duchess, apparently 'calm-faced', as though removed from the scene in a private world. The shock was too immense; her emotions could not keep up with the sight before her. A slight figure in a blue dress stained with blood, she 'rummaged around in the snow, which for a long while afterwards continued to give up small bones and bits of carti-lage, pieces of body and splinters from the carriage', Nicholas's cousin, Konstantin, wrote later. Sergei's rings were on his severed hand and now she carefully removed them. All that ran through her mind, she told her sister, Victoria, was that she must 'hurry, hurry' since Sergei 'hates blood and mess'.[47]

A stretcher was fetched and what could be found of his body was gathered up. A coat was placed over the remains. They were taken to the Chudov monastery where Ella began to pray. She was joined by her niece, Maria, who described Ella as 'white, her features terrible in their stricken rigidity', the expression in her eyes creating 'an impression on me I will never forget'. She was too shocked to cry. Maria was struck by the misshapen lines of the coat over the remains. There could not be very much left of her uncle, she realised, it seemed such 'a very small pile'. Beneath the stretcher, blood oozed and dripped to the floor.[48]

Family members greeted the news as though struck by light-ning. Alix was unable to comfort her sister. The tsar gave the order that it was too dangerous for close family in Moscow. 'Alix of course wants to go,' recalled her sister-in-law, Xenia. 'Mama too, but ... its too risky ... Poor Ella ... and she is *all alone* there.'[49] However, Ella's oldest sister, Victoria, left for Moscow as soon as she heard the news. The German emperor met her en route in Berlin. He was 'very kind and thoughtful', observed Victoria, 'and much worried about Ella for whom, since student days, he had a strong devotion'. Victoria found her sister 'very brave and collected' but unable to sleep or eat. Ella's only comfort was the chapel, as though her prayers removed her to another world.[50]

The badly injured terrorist, Ivan Kalayev, had been arrested at the scene. A few days after the murder, Ella went to see him in prison. She was escorted through the damp, dark passages, but she entered the cell alone in order to speak with him.

'Who are you?' he asked.

'I am the wife of the man you have killed,' she replied.[51]

In those moments of meeting the assassin, Ella came face to face with the full implications of 'propaganda of the deed' and the enormity of change that it called for. She told her sister, Victoria, that she was trying to save the murderer's soul. Sergei had always felt 'great distress for people dying unconfessed', and she hoped to 'awaken a feeling of repentance in him for the murder'.[52] Kalayev took her icon, but would not repent. He believed his own death would serve a wider purpose. 'Learn to look the advancing revolution in the face,' he told the judge later.[53]

Shut in the foetid cell, noting the intransigence of the doomed youth who embraced death as the only way to give his life meaning, royalty came face to face with anarchy. Ella could no longer escape what she had scrupulously avoided in her formative years: the great juggernaut hurtling towards them as Russia's oppressed and impoverished masses demanded change and would not be contained by the old social order with its privileged elites.

———

Even as the Russian revolution unfolded in 1905, Bertie, now Edward VII, was extending dynastic ties to the thrones of Europe with the assurance of a nineteenth-century monarch, spurred on occasionally in competition with the Kaiser. Queen Victoria's matriarchal mantle had fallen gently around Bertie's shoulders as the 'Uncle of Europe' on account of the number of his nieces and nephews who occupied positions of power. Appearing resplendent and secure in his dynastic power, he gloried in visiting his many continental relatives. In the summer of 1905 in the peaceful surroundings of Buckingham Palace he confided his thoughts to his long-standing friend, Louis of Battenberg, almost as though discounting the forces of revolution in Russia. 'I pass over any allusion to the events in the Far East and Russia,' he wrote on 15 July. 'They are a matter of History' and a subject 'too sad' to discuss.[54] He preferred to dwell on the bright prospects for the dynasty as Queen Victoria's many granddaughters continued to forge new royal connections in Europe.

'The King of Spain's visit was a great success,' Bertie continued knowingly to Louis.[55] When the king of Spain, Alfonso XIII, had revealed that he was looking for a bride, the British king and the German emperor had vied with each other to find a suitable consort. Wilhelm II had rushed to Spain to draw attention to the many eligible German princesses, under the guise of reviewing the Spanish fleet. The German emperor was reeling from the expansion of British interests in the Mediterranean and the brilliant success of his Uncle Bertie's recent trips in France, Spain and Italy. But it was Bertie who had the satisfaction of seeing Alfonso apparently charmed by a British princess: Queen Victoria's granddaughter, Ena, who was now eighteen.

As the Spanish royal romance blossomed, Bertie was enchanted by another glorious prospect that suddenly opened up in Scandinavia. As he explained to Louis, 'the great political event is the separation of Norway from Sweden and the former are determined to have my son-in-law, Charles of Denmark, as their king'.[56] Sweden and Norway had been united as one country under a Swedish king for almost a century, but by 1905 the Norwegians had had enough. They declared their independence and were looking for a monarchy of their own. Once again, the familiar fault lines in the family between Bertie and Wilhelm deepened over the issue. Bertie wanted his youngest daughter, Maud, and his Danish son-in-law, Charles, to occupy the Norwegian throne. This was opposed by the Kaiser, who considered one of his six sons eminently qualified for the role. But Prince Charles became the favourite and Bertie urged him to hurry to Norway in August 1905 'to prevent someone else taking your place'.[57]

To Bertie's frustration, Charles and Maud were not keen. Apart from Maud's desire to spend more time in her home country, they interpreted the events in Russia with rather more caution. There had been socialist demonstrations in Vienna, Berlin and other European capitals in support of the Russian revolution. Any new monarchy in Europe must reflect the wishes of the people, Prince Charles reasoned. The Norwegian people had not been consulted and might prefer a republic. To the alarm of traditionalists in the family, he threw the matter open to a vote.

The result of the Norwegian plebiscite in November 1905 was overwhelmingly in his favour. Charles and Maud set out for their new country as King Haakon VII and Queen Maud of Norway. No one had anticipated that the retiring Princess Maud would become the third of Queen Victoria's grandchildren to become a head of state, after Kaiser Wilhelm and Empress Alexandra. But for some who had served in Queen Victoria's court, the very idea of an elected monarch was unnervingly modern. It was just 'too horrible', observed the Duchess of Mecklenburg, 'for an English princess to sit upon a Revolutionary Throne'.[58]

Meanwhile Alfonso XIII's courtship was progressing and in January 1906 he asked Bertie's permission to marry Ena. Beatrice accompanied her daughter to France as she prepared for her conversion to the Catholic faith and everything augured well for the young couple. Princess Ena would be the fourth of Queen Victoria's grandchildren to be crowned, but the traumatic events of her wedding day would underline the tremblingly delicate balance of European stability and the position of monarchy within it. It would provide one of the most haunting images of collision between the nineteenth-century vision of royal match-making and the powerful modern forces for change.

Queen Victoria's 'royal mob' gathered in Madrid for the wedding on 31 May. The streets were festooned in vibrant Spanish colours, reds and yellows, while flags and tapestries hung from balconies and windows. Despite the searing heat, huge crowds jostled for a sight of the wedding procession from the Palacio Real: the plumed white horses, improbable gold carriages, the many royal celebrities including the Archduke Franz Ferdinand,

Prince George and Princess May, the Duchess of Coburg and of course the bride herself. Princess Ena in the bridal coach was wearing a white satin dress and long-flowing silver mantle exquisitely embroidered by forty Spanish women. Her pretty face, framed by orange blossom, could be glimpsed through her delicate veil of Alençon lace.[59]

The royal party filled the Gothic church of San Jeronimo. Stepping in from glaring sunlight outside, the small space seemed confined and close although lit for the first time with electric light. It was 'fearfully hot', Princess May noted in her diary, although it was only 10.30 a.m. when they took their places. The service was long and three hours elapsed before the bride and groom emerged to return to the palace in the bridal coach.[60] Bells rang out, cannon fired, and the cheering crowds craned forwards eagerly to catch a glimpse of their newly married queen and the king.

No one quite caught the moment when everything changed. A bouquet was thrown directly at the bridal carriage. It was unclear at first whether it fell from a balcony above, a window, or was thrown from the crowd. But in an instant the bomb concealed in the flowers transformed the holiday gaiety of moments before into a war zone.

'We saw the horses bolt and the crowd shrieking and surging and realised the truth,' observed Mrs George Young, the wife of the Second Secretary, watching from the window of the British Embassy. The ambassador was lunching with military attachés and officers, who 'gave some deep curses & in a twinkling were all out of the house'. The British soldiers surrounded the royal carriage and kept the king and queen from the frantic crowd. The new queen of Spain, dazed but unhurt, faced a scene of carnage. Fifteen people died that day and many more were injured. 'The police appear to have lost their heads,' continued Mrs Young, and the panic-stricken crowds 'nearly lynched a harmless countryman whom they thought was the assassin'.[61] The terrorist, Mateo Morral, killed himself and his guard when he was arrested two days later.

The royal party learned that the bomber had tried to gain entry to San Jeronimo. Had he succeeded probably none of them would have survived. Princess May took note of the royal family's close brush with death. 'We can only thank God that the anarchist did not get into the church,' she wrote to her aunt, 'in which case we must all have been blown up!'[62] The young bride was distraught. 'I saw a man without any legs,' Ena cried.

It was not the entwined flags of Spain and Britain that prompted press comment but the bride's bloodstained wedding dress, which like an ominous new flag symbolised the collision as the impetus to continue the old ways came up against a harsh modern reality.

As her cousins continued to marry into Europe's royal houses, Ella went further than any of Queen Victoria's other grandchildren in turning her back on the whole idea of matchmaking. The dreams that had dazzled her in her youth no longer seemed a worthy way to spend a life. As she adapted to the fast-changing times, the grand duchess who once inhabited Russia's finest palaces and commanded the admiration of all around her in her stunning gowns and Fabergé jewels could no longer be found. 'Aunt Ella, beautiful, beautiful woman', whose enchantment was like 'a fairy-tale apparition', according to Missy, Princess Marie of Romania, no longer wanted her birthright and everything that stemmed from it.[63] Grand Duchess Elisabeth Feodorovna wanted to take Holy Orders and become a nun.

Ella's spiritual convictions became all-consuming. Over the next few years she sold her possessions, even – perhaps tellingly – her wedding ring.[64] Her efforts became focused on creating her own Order, a perfect world in miniature dedicated to looking after others, which she named the Martha and Mary Convent of Mercy. She gathered around her like-minded women who were prepared to join her in dedicating their lives to Moscow's most deprived communities.

Ella's faith followed the true path of 'humility and love', according to her friend, Prince Yusupov, in contrast, he thought, to Alix's superstitious trust in faith-healers and mystics such as Rasputin. The sisters' differences in their interpretation of their adopted religion drew them apart. Alix felt let down by Ella, believing that she had 'lowered the dignity of the throne'.[65] By leaving her palace and giving away much of her fortune, Ella's actions revealed an implicit criticism of the excessive Romanov lifestyle in which Alix herself was trapped. Ella, the very person who had guided Alix to come to Russia in the first place, appeared to be distancing herself from the implications. The two sisters found themselves on opposing sides in a growing divide.

As empress, Alix chose the path of upholding autocracy and did all she could to strengthen Nicholas's resolve. Her son's future depended on it. Her faith in its importance was strengthened by Rasputin, whose apparent skill in relieving Alexei's pain lent weight to Alix's belief in the God-given mystical power of the Russian emperor. Rasputin's very existence was proof that God had sent her the help she needed to safeguard autocracy for her husband and her ailing son. In her terror, Alix's thinking became fixed around this one central idea to which she clung as if her life depended on it. By contrast, Ella found the obligation to help her fellow man had become her life's mission. Even when under instruction not to leave the Kremlin as violence spread in the autumn of 1905, she found a way to slip out to attend to the poor and the wounded.[66]

It was almost as though Ella was seeking atonement or redemption. She could not entirely escape the knowledge that Alix's life was infinitely harder because of her strong influence against their grandmother's advice. There was also the terrible burden of the sins of previous generations of Romanovs, emperors and empresses whose fabled lives had come at great cost to ordinary people. Nor could Ella dismiss the possibility that her pride and vanity had helped draw her to Russia in the first place, charmed as she was, not just by Sergei, but by the glamour, the wealth, the life of unimaginable excess that had been paraded before her. Possibly, too, she saw her choice as a way out of danger; if she dedicated her life to the people she might be spared extremist violence. Whatever the truth, Ella appeared to those around her as an inspirational figure, whose faith gave her life meaning. She defended her new path to the tsar, 'not as a cross but as a road full of light', and explained her 'longing to help those that suffer'.[67]

When Victoria of Battenberg visited Ilinskoye, Sergei's country estate near Moscow, in 1906 she was struck by the changed atmosphere in Russia. Before her eyes, disintegrating forces were at work in Russia and the certainties of the old world were disappearing. She saw houses on fire, read of a wave of assassinations of high officials, and had an escort of mounted guards at the station. At Ilinskoye, electric lights 'burned all night around the house' as protection against incendiary attacks. Ella appeared to her one step removed from the horror, 'distracted' by her dedication to help others. Even the glamorous villas on her country estate, which once housed aristocratic guests, were now home to those wounded in the Russo-Japanese War.[68] Victoria was at Ella's side in 1908 when the foundation stone was laid for the church at her convent and visited again the following year when the site had blossomed to include a hospital, a dispensary, a home for orphan girls and a separate house for disabled veterans.[69] Although Ella always claimed her devotion stemmed from her religious conviction rather than any ideological stance on the monarchy, her actions were the most far-reaching of any of her family and carried the implicit acknowledgement of a need for change. She saw herself as doing God's work as she attended to the sick and poor of Moscow. Knowing she could make a difference was sufficient reward.

The royal mob descended en masse on London in May 1910 for the funeral of the 'Uncle of Europe', but it was a last hurrah of a fading world, 'the old world in its sunset' in the words of Winston Churchill. After Bertie's death, George became the fifth of Queen Victoria's grandchildren to be crowned, with May (Mary) at his side as his grandmother had wished. Missy, Crown Princess Marie of Romania, was watching on 22 June 1911, as the forty-six-year-old George V and forty-four-year-old Queen Mary processed majestically down the long aisle of Westminster Abbey. They had emerged in middle age as the perfect example of what Queen Victoria required; sedate, upright, dutiful, upholding successful family values. From the Gothic choir stalls, Marie of Romania was struck by the serenity and dignity of the ceremony, 'a feeling of undisputed might' in which 'no tragedy lay beneath, no sense of fear or sacrifice'. British institutions seemed strong, resilient, trustworthy, including the centuries-old monarchy itself. 'The thrones they were mounting were, if I can so express it, seats of peace,' she observed.[70]

It was hard to avoid the feeling of a gathering storm. Royal marriages were proving to be irrelevant in the shaping of Europe's Great Power allegiances. Germany, the country with the most marriage ties to the British throne, never formed an alliance with Britain. Bertie had been widely perceived as paving the way for the 'Entente Cordiale' in 1904 between Britain and France. This agreement over colonial conflicts marked an important shift in European relations, bringing a new understanding between Britain and France and drawing to a close centuries of recurring antagonism.[71] This was followed in 1907 by the Anglo-Russian Convention, which addressed long-running disputes in central and south Asia, and which for Britain at least, provided some reassurance about the increasingly fraught state of European politics. Emperor Wilhelm never grasped that this new spirit of cooperation between Britain, France and Russia had been driven by a mutual fear of Germany. Instead, he held his uncle person-ally responsible for the perceived threat to Germany. Bertie, 'the Encircler', was the devil himself: 'He is a Satan; it is quite unbe-lievable what a Satan he is,' Wilhelm told his entourage.[72]

The speed of change may have been confusing, the signals hard to read, but there was no escaping the fact that Europe's Great Powers, still professing peace, increasingly squared up into two opposing camps. The 'Triple Entente powers' of Britain, Russia and France stood opposed to the Central Powers of Germany, Austria-Hungary and Italy. Europe was dividing into two massive armed power blocs, each side bristling with the new mass-produced weapons of the industrial age, stockpiling machine guns, high-explosive shells, dreadnoughts, submarines and aeroplanes. The Kaiser's efforts to weaken the Triple Entente and provoke discord between Britain and France in Morocco backfired, at Tangier in 1905 and Agadir in 1911 (the First and Second Moroccan Crisis), only serving to increase their unity. Unlike Queen Victoria, who found a way to manage Wilhelm, Bertie found it hard to contain his dislike. Within a few years of his mother's death, he had reached an impasse with his nephew. 'Trust him – never,' he told Louis. 'He is utterly false & the bitterest foe that England possesses.'[73]

Barely ten years after her death it was as though Queen Victoria's grandchildren in eastern Europe, tied to their thrones, were trapped in a crucible from which there was no escape. Marie of Romania was engulfed in the turmoil of south-east Europe as the troubled 'Eastern Question' erupted yet again. With the weakening Ottoman Empire and inflamed passions of nationalism in the Balkans, the very air was 'tense and electrical', she wrote.[74] The First Balkan War broke out in October 1912 when Montenegro, Greece, Serbia and Bulgaria fought for territory occupied for centuries under Ottoman rule. The following year yet another assassination would usher in the reign of Queen Victoria's sixth grandchild, Sophie of Greece. Her father-in-law, King George of Greece, was walking through the newly won Greek town of Salonika in March 1913 when he was shot in the back by a Greek vagrant, Alexandros Schinas, who claimed to be an anarchist. No sooner were Sophie and her husband, Constantine, crowned, than Bulgaria fell upon her former allies of Greece and Serbia, demanding a greater share of land won in the first war and triggering the Second Balkan War. Romania joined the fight against the Bulgarians in July 1913 and Princess Marie dedicated herself to relieving a cholera epidemic among the troops. 'It was my first initiation into suffering on a large scale,' she wrote.[75]

Victoria of Battenberg continued to visit her sisters in Russia and was with them during the fateful hot summer of 1914. Few anticipated that yet another assassination in an obscure part of Europe would, this time, set off the chain of events that would catapult Europe towards global war. The Austrian heir to the throne, Archduke Franz Ferdinand, was murdered with his wife

Sophie in Sarajevo in Bosnia on 28 June, but Victoria continued with her travels with Ella. They steamed up the Volga, struck by the great breadth of the river, the shores seemingly so far off. They stopped periodically for Ella to attend church services or visit convents, while Victoria went sightseeing. Victoria took the time to extend her journey into the Urals, exploring many new places, including Ekaterinburg where, even then, she sensed hostility. 'The population did not seem particularly pleased at the official visit,' she recorded. She drove past Ipatiev House on the main square several times, little knowing the significance it would later have in the family. 'It was pointed out to me as belonging to a rich merchant,' she wrote.[76]

By late July 1914 the atmosphere in Europe 'was so threatening' that Alix urged her sisters to cut short their tour. On 28 July Austria-Hungary declared war on Serbia. Russia mobilised in support of the Serbs and as Ella and Victoria made the last leg of their return to St Petersburg they were diverted several times to make way for troop trains. Germany declared war on Russia on 1 August. Russia declared war on Germany the next day and German troops invaded Luxembourg. On 3 August, Germany declared war on France and prepared to invade Belgium. The sisters reached St Petersburg on 4 August, the very day that Britain declared war on Germany.[77]

The German emperor would not recognise any part he had played as each unbelievable step unfolded, even though he knew that his unconditional support or 'blank cheque' to Austria-Hungary on 5 July had emboldened it to declare war on Serbia. Instead he blamed his relatives. 'Edward VII is stronger after his death than I who am still alive,' he said, as though Bertie had something to do with it from beyond the grave. As for his cousins, 'to think that George and Nicky have played me false!' Wilhelm permitted himself a glimpse of righteous indignation coming from the silver-haired, black-clad empress, his grandmama. She would surely be on his side. 'If my grandmother had been alive, she would never have allowed it,' he declared.[78] But she was dead, her influence gone. Soon the irresistible tide, the German Army, would change the map of Europe. 'Paris for lunch, dinner in

Petrograd,' the Kaiser had once declared, apparently unable to see the contradictions in his beliefs in his own innocence and his warmongering exhortations.[79]

Victoria of Battenberg's last image of her sisters was on 7 August, the day she set sail for Britain. Alix came for one last goodbye, bringing thick coats for her sea journey, the sisters stoically refraining from voicing their fears. 'I little dreamt it was the last time I should ever see my sisters again,' wrote Victoria.[80] She made her way from the Russian frontier to Stockholm and then Norway, visiting King Haakon and Queen Maud before catching the last steamer from Bergen back to Britain.

Victoria kept her sisters' letters and mementos. Among her papers was a poem Ella had sent her that expressed her feeling about her husband and her growing religious conviction. Ella's belief that God had spared Sergei from further pain sustained her. This was the marriage that Queen Victoria had never wanted to occur, but it seems that even after Sergei's death Ella was still defiantly proclaiming her love for him; a mere Victorian formality perhaps, or an expression of her true feelings? Carefully written out on thick, black-edged paper, the poem is untitled but bears only the telling date of her husband's death.

17 February 1905

Oh gallant upright spirit
Whose faithful work is o'er
Whom earthly joy and anguish
Will trouble never more
Who like a faithful soldier
Didst face a hostile host
Until a greater Master
Released thee from thy post!

Oh husband true and tender
Oh gracious gen'rous friend
To conscience and to duty
Found constant to the end!
God, in His Wisdom, took thee

From earthly love and life
God, in his Pity, spared thee
From further pain and strife!

On earth the souls that loved thee
Look upwards without fear
And in their hearts remaineth
The love they bore thee here.
Oh may a ray descending
From the great source of Love
Strengthen the heart that waiteth
To join thy peace above.[81]

12

The Fall

'She drove me away like a dog!'
Grand Duchess Elisabeth (Ella), December 1916

Queen Victoria's seventh and last grandchild to be crowned became Queen Marie of Romania on 10 October 1914, 'at a moment when the whole of Europe was on fire and flames were licking our every frontier', she wrote in her memoirs.[1] The new queen felt 'the future lay before us like a fiery portal we should have to pass; all the unknown lay beyond.' Swept along on a tide of national self-interest, the royal cousins stood on the very brink of a precipitous descent. 'Tomorrow was as separated from yesterday as with the stroke of a sword,' Marie wrote. 'There would never be any going back, no shelter could be found, we were out in the glaring light.'[2]

It is not possible in a few short pages to convey the scale of the tragedy that was about to engulf these royal cousins or to describe all the events that would sweep away the Europe of their youth. This brief summary aims to highlight turning points in their downfall in which Queen Victoria's crowned descendants found themselves pitched not just cousin against cousin, but husband against wife and sister against sister. Several of these key points in their lives have assumed almost legendary status, the stories told and retold across the twentieth century, with the reputations of the protagonists ebbing and flowing with new evidence or even transfigured from demons to saints.

Within a few months of Queen Marie's coronation in 1914, Europe was fastened into 'frightful bondage', wrote the First

Lord of the Admiralty, Winston Churchill, its great glory reduced into 'an immense battlefield'. Trench lines cut through Europe like a gaping wound, tearing up the meadows of Flanders and northern France as the armies of the British and French tried to halt the rapid German advance. The cannon and machine guns of the industrial age had already 'hurled death across battlelines' at Mons, Marne and Arras on the western front and at Tannenberg and along the Vistula on the eastern front. 'Havoc on such a scale had never even been dreamed of,' Churchill later observed, 'and had never proceeded at such a speed in all human history.'[3]

Kaiser Wilhelm was fighting against his cousins, George V and Nicholas and Alexandra. His sister, Sophie of Greece, and his crowned cousins in Norway, Spain and Romania had declared their neutrality. At her coronation Queen Marie of Romania felt 'a new and fearful page was opening before me'. During the ceremony suddenly she became aware that the people were calling out her name: 'Regina Maria'. There was something in the way they spoke 'that had within it a sound of hope'. Solemnly, she turned to face the congregation and lifted the veil that covered her face. The response was overwhelming. There was a united cry of 'Regina Maria', the voices rising into the vaults, 'as though I were their supremest hope'. In that moment Marie felt she had won; the stranger from overseas 'was theirs with every drop of my blood!'[4]

Despite her strong identity as Romania's queen, Queen Victoria's last granddaughter to be crowned also had an unquestioning faith in Britain that pitched her in opposition to her husband. She was convinced that Romania's neutrality was unsustainable, but King Ferdinand, a descendant of the House of Hohenzollern, believed their country's very survival lay with Germany. Romania shared borders with Germany's allies, he pointed out, and the German Army was 'invincible'. It was unthinkable to Ferdinand to fight for Britain against Germany and the Central Powers. Marie could not agree. 'I should die of grief if Romania were to go to war against England,' she replied. She turned to her cousins, George V and Tsar Nicholas, pleading Romania's interests. It was widely believed she 'swayed King Ferdinand's will'.[5]

When Romania did enter the war on the side of the British and their allies on 27 August 1916, Marie still believed in cousinly solidarity. 'I am happy we are together in these great and terrible times,' she wrote 'cousin to cousin' to George V on 12 September. 'We are a small country and we are risking our existence – we know it.' Although separated from Britain by 'the whole of Europe, yet we feel ... it is England that we trust'.[6] It was a critical moment. There was deadlock. The thundering battlefields of the eastern and the western front were devouring the young manhood of Europe. The Germans feared the small country of Romania with its large army and oil reserves could tip the balance against the Central Powers.

At German headquarters the Kaiser panicked. The all-powerful German Warlord who had projected German glory and military prowess for decades had rapidly turned into a shadow king. His grandiosity and self-belief were often overtaken by paralysing states of anxiety and on occasion he took to his bed.[7] But when news was brought to him of Romanian advances he summoned his two great generals from the eastern front to plan a counter-attack: Paul von Hindenburg and Erich Ludendorff. On hearing of the German counter-offensive, Queen Marie turned at once to Tsar Nicholas. It is 'as a woman and as a queen that I make my appeal to you, to the man and the Emperor!' she wrote less than six weeks after joining the war. 'We have come to the realisation that we are facing tremendous and immediate danger and that unless we are helped at once it may be too late.' Russia was the only Entente country that could realistically come to Romania's rescue.[8]

Queen Marie was working as a nurse in Bucharest in late September when she saw the blue sky blotted out by the exploding shells. 'Death streamed down upon us from the heavens,' she wrote. The Romanians were beaten back into their own territory, caught between Bulgarian and other troops invading from the south and German and Austro-Hungarian troops closing in from the north. On 6 December she learned of the fall of Bucharest as she fled on a crowded train. She felt she was 'struggling against invading floods of disaster'. The rapid German victory in Romania was bound to cause trouble in Russia, 'now we are so weak with our half-destroyed army and three-quarters of the country torn from us, all our riches gone! ... Everything is sad, sad, sad ...' Russia might do a deal with Germany. 'What then? What would be our fate? Wherever I turn nothing but terror, danger and pain ...'[9]

Family relations that had seemed strong and inviolable were proving irrelevant. George V had not been able to help. Her last hopes rested with the tsar. With immediate Russian support, there might yet be a chance for Romania. Marie wanted to go in person to Nicholas and plead Romania's interests. She wrote to her sister, Victoria-Melita, who was now living in Russia, having divorced Ernie in 1901 and married Grand Duke Kirill of Russia, a grandson of Alexander II, in 1905. But Victoria-Melita's reply was chilling. She advised Marie not to come under any circumstances. There was a crisis at the Russian court. Their cousin Alix was 'extraordinarily hated'. Marie was uneasy as she waited for news. 'Something uncanny and dreadful is going on there,' she wrote.[10]

Towards the end of 1916 the perilous fall for Queen Victoria's crowned grandchildren was gathering pace most quickly of all for Nicholas and Alexandra. Trapped in an unalterable mindset, the tsarina was greatly accelerating the unfolding tragedy.

During 1915 the Russians had been beaten back beyond Russian Poland on a wide front. Spectacular Russian advances against the Austrians proved hard to sustain. It was as though even the vast lands of Russia itself were against them, conspiring with the poor state of the railways to turn the transport of fresh soldiers and supplies into a home battleground. When unskilled Russians finally reached the front they were often without weapons, and were forced to wait to get a gun until the men ahead of them fell.[11] Line upon line of infantry was slaughtered by the German heavy artillery, which arrived at the eastern front with Teutonic efficiency.

Alix desperately wanted to share her husband's burden. Nicholas looked so ill; she felt sure she could help. Inspired by a mystical belief in his God-given autocratic powers, she impressed upon Nicholas that as Russia's 'chosen one' he should take personal control of the army. In his absence at the front, she would act as head of government for him. The tsarina turned to the one man who she knew understood God's will: the corrupt faith-healer, Rasputin. Soon she was running the government, leaning heavily on 'our Friend'.

Rasputin's every suggestion was pursued by the tsarina as though she had been personally directed by God. Key ministerial appointments were made on his whim. 'He likes our Friend' or he is 'Our Friend's enemy' was sufficient grounds for her to choose or reject a minister and her letters to Nicholas implored him to agree. 'God sent Him to us,' she reasoned.[12] This appalling state of affairs was sustained by Alix's blind faith. Such was her absolute conviction that she was saving Russia that her instinctive reserve vanished. 'I am no longer the slightest bit shy,' she wrote to Nicholas in September 1916. Indeed, she found the words came freely and forcefully, 'like a waterfall in Russian'.[13] Inevitably, the tsarina had access to military secrets, many of which she shared with Rasputin against her husband's wishes.

St Petersburg, now renamed 'Petrograd', was soon alive to the rumours. Rasputin was no man of God. His drunkenness, debauchery and thieving were common knowledge.[14] The tsarina was either a fool or a spy. His recommendations for top jobs were not guided by God, but by bribes and favours, perhaps even the enemy. Rasputin was indiscreet with his cabal of supporters. There was talk of treason.

Ella witnessed the hostility provoked by her sister's actions at first hand. In the summer of 1915 a vengeful crowd gathered outside the Martha and Mary Convent in Moscow. They demanded to see Ella, 'the German traitor', insisting that she, like her sister, must be a German spy. It was claimed she was conspiring with the tsarina to hide German agents, perhaps even her brother, Ernie, in the convent. Someone began throwing stones. Ella saw the swirling mass of people hungry for vengeance, their minds filled with the need to kill with no thought of justice. She walked out to meet the crowd, a solitary figure, appealing for calm. Her brother was not in the convent, she told them. They could search it for themselves. The mood remained ugly and it was only as soldiers arrived that the mob disbanded.

With her sister directing the government, in under a year and a half Russia's misfortunes at war accelerated as no fewer than four prime ministers and three ministers of war came and went with dizzying speed, not to mention top ministerial changes to other crucial departments such as agriculture. By the time the rout in Romania in 1916 was adding to Russia's military problems, men of no ability were in charge of crucial matters: how to supply enough grain to feed the army and how to transport supplies to the front. Russia itself was crumbling under the tsarina's interference. The marital alliance that had started in Coburg twenty-two years earlier with such extravagant hopes for peace not only now threatened the survival of the dynasty but had potential implications for all of civilised Europe.

The tsar himself was uncharacteristically irritable, his face assuming a gaunt, hollowed-out expression. When he tried to oppose one of his wife's judgements, she came to the army headquarters and pressured him in person. The tsar had all but surrendered his control of Russia's mighty autocracy to an illiterate peasant. Senior members of the Romanov family, including his own mother, pleaded with him to stop his wife's interference. The Dowager Empress believed Alexandra had lost her sanity.[15] The merry-go-round of inadequate ministers was destroying the tsar's authority. If Nicholas did not take control there would be no kingdom to manage. The tsar did not listen. He appeared pushed beyond endurance, utterly unable to resist his wife's endless entreaties. There was a defeated air about him as though his interior life was now dead.

The Romanovs also warned Alix, but their concerns were meaningless to her. The only voice she could hear was Rasputin's. Nothing could shake her faith in him. He alone understood the mysteries of God's plan. Her delusional world had its own internal logic, resistant to all outside threats. Anything said against him was 'slander'. Saints, she believed, 'have always been slandered'.[16] The criticism was just part of God's test. When shown photographs of Rasputin at the centre of an orgy, she insisted he had been impersonated. Those who spoke badly of him were coldly dismissed.

It fell to Ella to make one last personal appeal. She set out from Moscow bearing the hopes of the Romanov family. By this point the sisters 'did not get on at all well', according to her friend, Prince Yusupov, due to 'the tsarina's blind confidence in Rasputin'. Alix and Rasputin were aware of Ella's views. Ella was a friend of Yusupov's mother. 'Both of them plot against me and spread slander about me too,' Rasputin once claimed. 'The tsarina has often told me they are my worst enemies.'[17]

In December 1916 the two sisters who had once turned the heads of Europe's most eligible princes were briefly reunited. Ella was shown into the tsarina's rooms in the Alexander Palace. She had prayed to God to 'give her the powers of persuasion which had hitherto failed her'. Now she tried to find the words to explain the disastrous course her younger sister was taking. But once it became clear that Ella wished to talk about Rasputin, the sisterly warmth that she had hoped for evaporated.

The tsarina had long dismissed Ella's views by believing that she was part of a 'very bigoted' Moscow clique. The passion and sincerity of her pleading eluded her. Alix expressed her disappointment that her sister could believe in falsehoods. 'Rasputin was a man of great prayer,' she insisted.[18] She had no wish to touch on the matter any further.

Ella found it hard to accept her younger sister had become so unwilling to hear any view that conflicted with her own, so dangerously bound up was she with an imaginary saint. She tried again, but Alix had heard enough. Her trust in her sister had broken down.

As the two women faced each other in the Alexander Palace, they stood apart, separated irretrievably: Alix now, in all but name, the unreachable ruler of that ungovernable mass of land, tsarina of all the Russias; Ella in her grey nun's robes, retired from the world but with a much keener understanding of it.

A servant was summoned. The meeting was over. Sisterly ties, once so intimate, appeared to no longer exist. Ella went straight to her friend, Felix Yusupov, and members of the Romanov family. 'We all waited eagerly for her arrival,' recorded Yusupov, 'anxious to hear the result of the interview.' Ella came into the room 'trembling and in tears: "She drove me away like a dog!" she cried. "Poor Nicky, poor Russia!"'[19]

Ella herself endorsed what happened next – knowing full well the traumatic impact it would have on her sister.[20]

———

The steps taken by members of the Russian nobility in December 1916 to break the destructive hold of Rasputin have taken on the character of myth or legend. The chief architect of the plan was Ella's devoted friend, Prince Yusupov, whose own famous account casts his exploits as a heroic clash between good and evil, apparently touched by the supernatural as though he were struggling with the devil himself. But his actions would cost the Romanovs their last vestiges of moral authority.

On 29 December, Prince Yusupov invited Rasputin to his palace on the pretext that he could meet his beautiful wife, Irena, a niece of the tsar. Rasputin enjoyed being feted by the prince, little knowing that the cakes and wine he was served were laced with cyanide. Yusupov had reached a point where he and his friends saw murder as the only way to shore up Russia's ailing autocracy.

According to Yusupov's account, Rasputin consumed enough cyanide to fell a man, but still he did not die. Dressed in silks and velvet, at ease in the richly appointed room, he called for more of the poisoned cakes and wine. Time passed with Rasputin in exuberant mood, impatient to meet the beautiful Irene. Finally, in desperation, Yusupov pulled a gun and aimed for his heart at close range. Rasputin fell on a white bearskin, apparently dead. Yusupov's friends left to make arrangements for disposing of the body, leaving the prince on guard. Curious, he leaned over the dead man and watched, unbelieving, and in a state of shock, as first one eye opened, then the other, 'the green eyes of a viper'. With an expression of malevolent hatred, Rasputin rose to attack his murderer, clutching at Yusupov's jacket, grappling him down.

Yusupov broke free and fetched his friends, but they returned to an empty room. The 'dead' man was making his way across the snow-covered yard towards the gate. It took several more bullets to stop Rasputin, now heavily bleeding and lying in the snow.[21]

The claims made by Yusupov highlight the feeling widespread at the time, that Russia had somehow fallen under a supernatural influence. Analysis of the body, which was found below the ice of the Little Neva, has shed a rather more prosaic light on Yusupov's colourful account. The actual point of death was in the courtyard: a final shot in the forehead executed with the skill of a professional killer. This lends weight to the unproven claim that British agents may also have been involved in the murder, anxious to remove the one man who was having such a destructive impact on Russia's war effort – a view naturally denied by the British ambassador, George Buchanan, when questioned by the tsar.[22]

Whatever the case, the plot backfired. Once her initial trauma had subsided, Alix rallied as though fortified from beyond the grave by Rasputin's spirit. 'Our dear Friend … is yet nearer to us,' she told Nicholas.[23] The chaos in government resumed once again with the tsarina selecting and dispatching ministers. It was the tsar who, far from being released from the irrational hold of his wife, seemed destroyed from within, consumed by the fearful implications of the murder. He became silent, his face expressionless. From the sanctuary of his study, he shrank from further conflict, a ghost in the vast glittering palace.

Over the winter of 1916 Nicholas was in a state of helplessness, as though he had suffered a devastating nervous breakdown. Everything about him was world-weary, exhausted. One loyal advisor considered him 'unrecognisable', his face haggard, his large eyes 'quite faded' as though his spirit had vanished.[24] He behaved like a man doomed, trapped between the demands of his ministers to introduce reforms and stop his wife running the country, and her desire to enforce Russia's autocracy. Resigned to her control, he approved the construction of a secret passageway so she could overhear his conversations and advise him. He did not respond to the repeated warnings. The tsar's brother-in-law, Sandro, found a way to have one last meeting with the tsarina in

February in which he dared to say the unsayable. The tsarina had 'no right', in her blind stubbornness, to drag everyone 'down a precipice'. Alix spoke 'excitedly, hurriedly', but, Sandro felt, she had reached 'a state of complete and incurable delusion'. Nothing would shake her certainty that she knew best, guided as she was by the spirit of God through 'Our Friend'.[25]

By early 1917 the scandal of government corruption and the dysfunctional relationship at the helm sparked rebellion. There were momentous events on the streets of Petrograd in late February as the years of hardship and repression came to a head. The tsar was warned of the bread riots; he was warned that 60,000 men and women were on strike; he was warned on 7 March that the revolt was out of control. That evening he told his ministers he would introduce reforms. A few hours later he changed his mind. With characteristic indecisiveness, he avoided a decision and slipped away to the front. Unknowingly, he had squandered his last chance. On 11 March some of the troops sent to bring order refused to fire on the rioters. The mutiny lit the fuse of the second Russian revolution. The following day members of the imperial cabinet were arrested. Power lay with the duma and a new assembly, the Soviet, representing workers and soldiers. The tsar attempted to return – but it was too late. The railways were falling into the hands of armed revolutionaries. By 15 March, diverted to a railway siding at Pskov, 200 miles south-west of Petrograd, Nicholas was forced to abdicate.

Meanwhile, unaware of developments as she waited for her husband at Tsarskoe Selo, the empress tried to maintain her dignity, her memory taking her back momentarily to the security of childhood experiences. 'You Russian ladies don't know how to be useful,' she said as her retinue was moved into the royal family's wing. 'When I was a girl, my grandmother, Queen Victoria, showed me how to make a bed. I'll teach you …'[26] With Petrograd in revolt just a few miles away, it was a relief to see her loyal guards at the palace gates.

But on the morning of 15 March she woke early, perhaps disturbed by the unnatural silence outside. Looking out of the window at first light she was filled with a sense of shock. The scene outside was whitewashed with snow. There were no foot-prints. The grounds were empty; the soldiers gone. She and her children were utterly alone and unprotected. In the magnificent complex of palaces and pleasure gardens there was no one to help them in a world suddenly full of fear.

The following day servants brought posters from the city announcing the abdication of the tsar. Alix had lost her throne, the first of Queen Victoria's grandchildren to do so.

For all her horrific forecasts for the Russian monarchy, even Queen Victoria had not anticipated a crisis in which the best hope of survival for her beloved granddaughter Alix would lie with her cousins: Kaiser Wilhelm and King George. Still less, that they would ruthlessly abandon her in order not to jeopardise their own fate. Queen Victoria herself had provided sanctuary for fallen sovereigns, notably Louis-Philippe, King of the French, after the 1848 French revolution and his successor, Emperor Napoleon III, who went into exile in Britain in 1871. But an inglorious point was reached in the descent of the royal dynasty where betrayal became intensely personal.

George V was well informed of the catastrophe unfolding in Russia, fearing that Alicky was the 'cause of it all'. His immediate instinct was to protect his cousins. He telegrammed Nicholas promising 'I shall always remain your true and devoted friend', words of comfort that never reached the tsar.[27] The British prime minister, David Lloyd George, agreed to a request from Russia's Provisional Government for asylum for the imperial family in Britain. But within days George V became worried and level-headed calculation set in.

King George and Queen Mary had worked hard to live up to the high expectations invested in them by Queen Victoria. He had inspected troops and pinned on medals, she had visited hospitals and toured wards, invariably assured and in charge of her feelings. She was deeply moved but 'trained herself to talk calmly to frightfully mutilated and disfigured men … Her habit of self-discipline gave her complete physical control,' observed her lady-in-waiting, Lady Airlie.[28] Her rather more excitable husband, George V, relied increasingly on his wife and their dignified and dutiful efforts went a long way to converting the British monarchy into a symbol of the people during the war. Should he now ally himself with his autocratic cousin?

The newspapers were full of the dramatic scenes in Russia, images of the tsar beneath headlines announcing 'the Russian Revolution'. George's close kinship to Nicholas was underlined by their striking similarity. It could almost have been a photograph of George looking out from the newspapers, next to column inches on the riots and chaos in Russia. The tsar and his family were under arrest by Russia's Provisional Government 'for their own protection', reported the *Daily Mirror*. Mass rallies in Britain were held in support of Russia's long-suffering people, not their fallen tsar.[29] The birth of a 'Russian Republic' after centuries of autocracy ran alongside articles on the strength of republican sentiment in Britain. The tsarina was widely seen as a German spy. All this weighed heavily. George's dear cousin Nicky, formerly absolute Ruler of all the Russias, for many clothed still with that once awesome mantle of wealth and power, might attract unimaginable trouble in a democratic country. Would it be wise to offer asylum? Could it even jeopardise his own throne? Guided by his faithful private secretary, Lord Stamfordham, the king had a change of heart.

'His Majesty cannot help doubting ... on general grounds of expediency, whether it is advisable that the Imperial Family should take up residence in this country,' Stamfordham wrote on 30 March 1917 to the foreign secretary, Arthur Balfour.[30] However, Balfour did not withdraw the British government's offer of sanctuary, so Stamfordham wrote to him again on 6 April. 'I feel sure that you appreciate how awkward it will be for our Royal Family,' he wrote, urging that alternative arrangements were found.[31] Concerned that this letter was still ambiguous, he sent a stronger message that day which left no room for doubt. 'We must be allowed to withdraw from the consent previously given to the Russian government.'[32] But this, too, failed to produce any change of policy, so Stamfordham went in person on 10 April to lobby the prime minister. He explained it was 'the king's strong opinion' that his cousins 'should not come to this country'.[33] At last this produced the desired result. The British offer was discreetly dropped.

George V could be in little doubt about the precariousness of his cousins' position from the moment the imperial flag was lowered over the Winter Palace and the Red Flag was hoisted in its place.[34] By mid-April the British press revealed that the tsar was confined to three rooms at Tsarskoe Selo and the 'tsar and tsarina are forbidden to talk to each other' while Alix was under investigation for treason. Six weeks later Russia's Congress of Delegates discussed 'the captivity of Nicholas Romanov' and the transfer of the ex-tsar to the Fortress of St Peter and St Paul.[35] The Soviet argued he should be imprisoned for his crimes, pending trial, possibly execution. 'Ex-Tsar to be Tried', pronounced the headlines.[36] But George V did not change his decision; he merely obscured it, leaving Lloyd George to take the brunt of responsibility for the British government's decision.[37]

It was left to Kaiser Wilhelm to approve a critical resolution that would wield the killer blow. Grandpapa Albert's original vision had aimed to reduce the risk of revolution by gradual reform of Europe's constitutional monarchies. Now the Kaiser's government did the exact opposite and played an active role in 'revolutionising' Russia – a move that would backfire spectacularly and echo resoundingly across the decades to come.[38]

When America was drawn into the war on 6 April 1917, German generals faced a race against time. They needed to settle the war with Russia in the east before American soldiers could arrive in large numbers to break the deadlock in the west. The Kaiser's ministers alighted on a possible solution: they could destabilise the new Russian republic with help from Vladimir Lenin and his unruly gang of Bolsheviks. Russia's Provisional Government was committed to the war effort, but Lenin promised to end the war with Germany whatever the cost.

From his exile in Switzerland, Lenin lobbied the German government to permit him to travel through Germany to Russia. He won support at the highest level of the German government.[39] As Churchill later famously observed, Germany's war leaders 'turned upon Russia the most grisly of all weapons'. They transported Lenin and his thirty-two supporters through Germany with diplomatic immunity in a 'sealed' train 'like a plague bacillus'.[40] When Lenin arrived in Petrograd on 16 April he spoke to his supporters of an end to Europe's despised imperialism, an end to the 'imperialist war' and the beginning of the international peoples' revolution. He was bankrolled by the Germans, who also provided funds for the Communist magazine, *Pravda*, which soon changed its editorial stance, promising an end to the war.

Studies have shown that the Kaiser was fully aware of the plan to return Lenin to Russia and even joked about it.[41] To win the war, his generals needed Russia to fall to the Bolshevik revolutionaries, and the Kaiser did not think too closely about the price that might be paid – not just by his Russian cousins but by future generations.

In that turbulent summer of 1917 a second of Queen Victoria's granddaughters would lose her throne: Queen Sophie of Greece and her husband, Constantine of Greece.

Like her cousins, Queen Maud of Norway and Queen Ena of Spain, Sophie had supported her husband's neutrality during the war – but neutrality proved to be no easy option. Spain and Norway suffered from trade wars, leading to such hardships that there were food riots in Spain. Nowhere were the dangers of neutrality greater than in Greece, where Queen Sophie was a sister of the Kaiser, and like her cousin, Alix, was suspected of being a spy. From the very outset the German emperor did indeed threaten Sophie and Constantine that Greece would be treated 'as the enemy' unless they joined the Central Powers.[42] But the

Greek prime minister, Eleftherios Venizelos, backed Britain and her allies. When the Greek king and queen refused to support the Gallipoli campaign in the eastern Mediterranean in 1915, the Entente launched a vicious campaign against them.

The hatred inspired by French and British propaganda was so intense it almost cost Sophie and Constantine their lives. There was an oppressive heat on 14 July 1916 when a column of smoke was spotted rising over their summer palace at Tatoi near Athens. They took the car to investigate but in moments it was trapped. They had driven into a forest blaze, the sparks jumping twenty feet and creating a fiery wall in seconds. There was no time to turn the car around; Sophie grabbed her youngest daughter and fled back to the palace while Constantine tried unsuccessfully to reach others in their party. Seventeen members of the royal household lost their lives that day. Police soon found a pile of used petrol containers near the palace. Arsonists had tried to kill the royal family.[43]

To pressure the Greeks to turn against their neutral king and queen, the Entente bombed Athens and blockaded the country. By Christmas 1916 Sophie was driven to despair and finally turned to her brother for help. The Allies were 'trying to rouse the people against us', she explained on 26 December. 'A decisive and prompt attack [on your] part ... would mean for us the deliverance from the horrible situation in which we are.'[44] She encouraged the German emperor to launch an attack in Macedonia. All will be 'lost', she telegrammed again on 2 January 1917, 'if the attack does not take place immediately'. Her message to her brother one week later expressed her feelings against the French and British. 'May the infamous pigs receive the punishment they deserve! I embrace you affectionately. Your isolated and afflicted sister, who hopes for better times. Sophie.'[45]

A crisis was reached in June 1917 when the Entente presented the Greek prime minister with an ultimatum. The Greek king and queen must go into exile. If they failed to obey, Greece would be occupied and Athens bombarded again. Constantine and Sophie bowed to the pressures. Hurried enquiries were made as to which country would have them. Once again the British press was hostile and George V objected to a request for them to settle on the Isle of Wight. In this once honorary 'club of monarchs' for a second time the British king found good reason not to help a cousin.

On 11 June Constantine and Sophie drove to the coast where their yacht was moored. An anxious crowd had gathered and as the king and queen set out, people waded into the sea after them, calling for them to return. Sophie and Constantine made their way into ignominious exile in Switzerland, the cries of the people fading into the night as the Greek coast gradually slipped from view.

———

'Flaming Russia' appeared to Queen Marie of Romania 'a close and terrifying reality' during the summer of 1917, where 'anything could happen' as Bolshevik ideas spread across the country. Romania relied on its Russian ally, but discipline collapsed among the Russian soldiers. Their regiments in Romania turned against their officers and there was an air of menace among the men. 'Our hour of disaster seems to be coming nearer and nearer,' Marie wrote, feeling 'waves of anxiety which almost amount to panic'. The prospect of fleeing Romania was unthinkable: 'My grief over the situation is so great that I am like one great wound.'[46] Marie was even more stunned by a long letter from her sister, Victoria-Melita, in Russia, a 'soul torturing letter ... full of the blackest despair, and deepest most hopeless agony'. It was as though everything familiar and good in their lives was being swallowed up. Victoria-Melita felt there was nothing left, 'neither pride, nor hope, nor money, nor future and the dear past blotted out by the frightful present'.[47]

Although George V had declined to help his cousins Nicholas and Alexandra in Russia or Sophie in Greece, he did offer asylum to Marie. Romania had been a loyal ally. Possibly he still remembered those carefree Malta days and the princess he had once hoped to marry. Marie declined his help. Even though the Romania she knew was disappearing before her eyes, nothing would induce her to leave. The advance of the Central Powers was rapid. The German emperor was 'triumphantly promenading about the invaded part of our country', she wrote. For Marie, her Cousin Wilhelm now represented 'a brutal, a merciless tyranny'.[48]

In Britain, too, a virulent hatred of anything German was sweeping the country. As German 'Gotha' planes bombed British cities in the spring of 1917, the German roots of the royal family were called into question. The many German royal marriages in Queen Victoria's era now prompted awkward questions. During a stormy debate in the House of Commons the chancellor was asked whether he could 'state the names of all Royal or titled persons of German birth receiving pensions from the British taxpayer – some of whom were even living in Germany!' Was any 'redistribution of this money contemplated in view of the hardships endured by families of soldiers killed at the front?'[49] Such anti-German sentiment towards the royal family was growing. Even Lloyd George referred to the king as 'my little German friend'.[50]

George V had already distanced himself from his Russian and Greek cousins. Now he was urged to obscure his German origins. The British royal family name was 'Saxe-Coburg and Gotha', passed down the line from his German grandfather, Prince Albert. For Queen Victoria the ties to Coburg were sacrosanct and the many illustrious connections to Germany resounded through family names such as Battenberg, Hanover, Teck and Saxony. But such German ties 'have become utterly offensive to all true Britons', observed one press report.[51] The connections had to go. It was not just, as Victoria-Melita had written, 'the dear past blotted out'. Aspects of King George's very identity had to be effaced. His private secretary, Lord Stamfordham, alighted on the perfect solution: 'Windsor', a name resonant with all things British, conjuring up the solid security of the ancient castle that towered over the Home Counties and reached back through centuries of British history to medieval times. A royal proclamation on 17 July 1917 confirmed that all German names and honours would go. Battenberg became Mountbatten and the 'House of Windsor' was born.[52]

Over the summer of 1917 the former tsar and tsarina began to feel the consequences of George V's decision not to grant them asylum. Russia's Provisional Government lost its authority following heavy military losses, while Lenin's Bolsheviks held out the promise of 'Peace! Bread! Land!' The mood in Petrograd was ugly with half a million demonstrators on 16 July roaming the streets and mingling with the thousands of deserters. The royal family were secretly moved during August from Petrograd to Siberia and imprisoned in the remote town of Tobolsk, lost in a subarctic wilderness. 'We live as in a ship at sea,' Nicholas wrote to his sister, Xenia, confined in a small space, the days 'all very much alike'.[53]

Assisted by German funds, Lenin and his Bolshevik Party gained supporters in the large industrial cities, and on 7 November he and his party overthrew the Provisional Government. To strengthen his hold on power Lenin advocated violence 'in the interests of the people' to establish his Communist Party. 'Terror reigns everywhere,' wrote Marie of Romania on hearing of the collapse of law and order in Russia. 'It is the old story, the French revolution over again, probably worse. It fills me with horror.'[54] Lenin wanted to secure peace with Germany, but the Kaiser's armies progressed deep into Russian heartlands, almost to Petrograd, before a settlement was agreed. In March 1918 at Brest-Litovsk peace was signed between the Bolsheviks and the Kaiser and his generals. Lenin had surrendered some 400,000 square miles to the Germans, including Poland, Finland, the Ukraine and the Crimea.

Nicholas was devastated. For him, the 'Bolshevik scoundrels' had committed Russia to 'suicide'.[55] Lenin was no more than a German-funded 'traitor'. The part played by the German emperor added to Nicholas's grief. For Alix the idea of her own cousin triumphing over their abject defeat, celebrating his 'victor's peace', and gloating over a map of Russia as regions were dismembered between German allies, was too much to bear. The appalling terms of the peace deal made her family's suffering meaningless. 'All things for us are in the past,' she wrote despairingly to a friend.[56] When she heard that the Kaiser was asking for the Russian royal family to be sent to Germany, she was resolute: 'I would rather die.'[57]

The Kaiser also tried repeatedly to reach Ella through the Swedish Embassy. He had loved her once and now he did not forget her 'on the eve of terrible happenings', observed Yusupov in his memoirs. Ella, too, declined. She would not abandon her sister, or her new sisters who shared her life in the Order of Saints Martha and Mary. She sent word that 'she would never leave her convent, or Russia, of her own free will'.[58]

In late April 1918 a commissar travelled from Moscow to Tobolsk, his very arrival ushering in a renewed air of threat for Alix and Nicholas. Civil war had erupted across Russia between the Red Army that supported Lenin and the White Army that represented, amongst others, monarchists and foreign armies. Lenin had hoped to bring the former tsar to trial in Moscow, but recognising the complications he liaised instead with the Ural Soviet, one of the most virulently Bolshevik of all the Soviets. The train carrying the prisoners was intercepted by troops who moved them to their final destination: the mining town of Ekaterinburg in the Urals. They were confined within Ipatiev House, now redesignated 'House of Special Purpose'.

Yakov Yurovsky, who headed the Bolshevik guard watching over the Romanov family, received his final orders on 13 July 1918. There would be no trial. The Ural Soviet had decided the fate of 'Nicholas the Bloody' and his family. The weight of evidence indicates that Lenin approved the orders but took steps to ensure there were no official documents revealing his involvement.

At 1.30 a.m. on 17 July the imperial family was woken and told there was unrest in the town. They had to be moved to a different location. While supposedly awaiting transport, they were taken across the dark courtyard to the cellar – an empty room, the window barred with a grille like a prison. Alexandra asked for chairs. Two were brought in, one for Alexandra, while Nicholas placed Alexei beside her in the other. The young grand duchesses duly lined up behind them as though they were about to have their photograph taken; beside them stood their loyal doctor, valet, cook and maid.

There was silence. No reassuring sound of their escort arriving. No familiar faces.

Yurovsky returned, followed by his band of executioners. They piled into the room after him through the small doorway. As their numbers kept increasing, twelve in all, it was apparent these were not their guards for a journey. The men lined up opposite the frightened family like a firing squad.

'In view of the fact that your relatives are continuing their attack on Soviet Russia,' said Yurovsky, 'the Ural Executive committee has given orders to shoot you.'

For a split second, Nicholas moved instinctively forward to protect his wife and son.

'What? What ...' he began.

Yurovsky and his men fired at him at point-blank range.[59]

The former tsar fell to the floor.

Nicholas was spared the horror of seeing the fate of his daughters and son, an execution so grim that it has gone down in the annals of history as a symbol of the brutality of the new Soviet regime. The soldiers fired a volley of shots, enough to mow them down. There was utter confusion. Unaccountably, the girls refused to die. The bullets ricocheted off them. Even those that fell did not appear to be dead, clinging to their youthful lives amongst the growing wreckage of their family.

The killing became frenzied, the young princesses trapped in the small room fighting for their lives. It was incomprehensible, as though they were not made of mortal flesh. The maid also was strangely invulnerable, running against the back wall, trying to avoid the bullets by holding out a cushion. Plaster began to fall off the wall behind the prisoners, obscuring the soldiers' view with clouds of dust. The floor became slippery, covered in blood. The slaughter continued in the reduced visibility created by firing so many bullets.

'We set about finishing them off,' recorded Yurovsky later. The maid was stabbed, her hands sliced to shreds as she tried to protect herself from the bayonets. The girls' final cries were haunting even for the most committed of revolutionaries. Still, the carnage was not over. Groans were heard from Alexei, who had been protected by his father's body. The squad turned on him with kicks and blows until Yurovsky shot him in the head. Anastasia was the last to die, bludgeoned and finally shot in the head. At last silence presided over the mutilated bodies of individuals, who, only a short time before, had been enveloped in the certainty that they were the resplendent, the only true rulers created by God of the mightiest empire in the world.

For the efficient Yurovsky this was just one more order, successfully carried out. Now it was time to clear up the mess. The bodies were loaded onto the waiting vehicle and taken to a site in the Koptyaki Forest a few miles away. As the bodies were stripped, precious stones fell from the duchesses' clothing. Their bodices were almost entirely lined with prized gems that had protected them from the bullets, prolonging their agonising death. The bodies were doused with sulphuric acid and thrown in a disused pit. But daylight was approaching and the killers were desperate to conceal the evidence. Over the following two nights Yurovsky struggled to conceal their bodies despite ordering gallons of sulphuric acid and gasoline. The mighty Romanovs ended in a shallow grave by a roadside, their faces disfigured with blows to the head and acid burns. Alexei and Maria were dismembered, burnt and buried in a separate pit nearby.

As evidence of these murders was being hidden in the woods near Ekaterinburg on 17 July, the Ural Soviet determined the fate of Alix's older sister, Ella. She had been taken from the Martha and Mary Convent in late April and was now imprisoned in a disused school in Alapayevsk in the Urals along with several younger members of the Romanov family.

Ella and her relatives were woken in the night. Blindfolded, hands bound, they were driven into the surrounding forest. The carts stopped in a clearing and Ella was led first to the edge of a mine shaft some sixty feet deep. She was stunned with a blow from a rifle butt before being flung, still alive, into the shaft.

But there was water below and one of the executioners, Vassili Ryabov, later claimed that they listened to her struggles 'for some time'. They threw in her companion, Sister Varvara, only to hear more splashing 'and then the two women's voices'. One by one the men followed. According to Ryabov's account – no doubt much embellished in the retelling – voices could still be heard and so he threw down a grenade. When sounds continued to rise from below, 'I threw another grenade and what do you think? From beneath the ground I heard singing. I was seized with horror. They were singing the prayer, *Lord Save your People.*' The executioners gathered wood and lit a fire in the mine shaft. Even this did not silence the hymns, which 'rose up through the thick smoke for some time yet'. Eventually the singing stopped. No sound came from the shaft.[60]

Eighteen members of the Romanov family were murdered by the Bolsheviks and the rest fled, bringing a horrific end to one of the world's most legendary dynasties. The Romanovs had forged the rise of the Russian Empire over 300 years and unintentionally had taken a leading role in its demise.

———————

'The blood of the unhappy tsar is not at <u>my door</u>; not on <u>my hands</u>,' the German emperor declared when he heard the news.[61] Profoundly shaken, he seemed unable to grasp, or perhaps refused to grasp, any part he had played in the downfall of the last tsar and his family. But within a couple of weeks the Kaiser, too, had to face the reckoning.

It had taken over a year for the Americans to train and transport an army across the Atlantic, but at last, in the summer of 1918, the Americans were ready. To the overwhelming gratitude of the exhausted British and French troops on the western front, young men from America began to arrive in France at a rate of 10,000 a day. Shaking, nervous, Kaiser Wilhelm was stunned on 8 August 1918 when he learned of a new Allied offensive led by the British at Amiens, Germany's 'black day'.[62] The German war machine appeared to be at breaking point.

German troops continued to be beaten back and many surrendered. Ahead was humiliation, past glories stripped away. In early September the Kaiser retreated to his bed in a state of nervous collapse.[63] When he surfaced he found it hard to grasp the fast-changing situation. His surroundings on the imperial train bore potent reminders of his proud heritage: a photograph of him taking tea with Queen Victoria in the grounds of Osborne; a world apart, so safe and secure, from the closing years of the previous century. He could not accept that all this had gone.

Rallying on 10 September 1918 the Kaiser told Krupp workers in Essen that they must labour with renewed vigour, 'to you with your hammer … to me upon my throne'. With fanatical zeal he announced to the crews at Kiel that traitors would be shot.[64] But soon he learned that Bulgaria and Turkey could no longer fight. The Austro-Hungarian Empire was close to collapse. Germany could not continue alone. Confusion reigned in the German high command.

By a supreme irony it fell to the man once singled out as the ideal consort for Alix by Queen Victoria to agree peace terms: Prince Maximilian von Baden. Appointed chancellor on 3 October, Max von Baden tried to negotiate an armistice. The Kaiser's rule was disintegrating. It was only now, after the crucible of war that had cost the lives of millions, that the German emperor finally conceded what his English mother had advocated all those years ago. He wished 'to see the German people more closely involved … in the running of the affairs of the fatherland'.[65] Hurried efforts to democratise Germany's despised autocracy did not go far enough for the American president, Woodrow Wilson. The Kaiser's final days were haunted by the humiliating prospect of losing everything. 'I will not abdicate,' he told his interior minister on 1 November. 'It would be incompatible with my duties, as successor to Frederick the Great.'

But the German navy, the Kaiser's proudest achievement, erupted in revolt on 3 November to the sailors' rallying cry of 'Bread and Peace'. The spark of rebellion in Kiel spread like wildfire to other cities. The many royal dynasties of Germany began to crumble. Suddenly the possibility of a Bolshevik revolution in

Germany seemed real. The terrible sacrifice of war demanded a scapegoat, which increasingly took the shape of the Hohenzollern figurehead: the emperor. Even in the face of a German revolution, Wilhelm hesitated. Surely he could keep his Prussian throne?

On 9 November the Kaiser was told he could delay no longer. Revolutionaries on the streets of the capital were winning the support of workers and troops. The army was not prepared to fight German 'Bolsheviks'. Yet still he vacillated until the decision was taken out of his hands. Max von Baden released a statement for him: 'The Kaiser and King has decided to give up the throne.'[66] Germany was to become a republic. 'Treachery, treachery, shameless, outrageous treachery,' was Wilhelm's response.[67]

At 2 a.m. on 10 November, Wilhelm was woken and told his car was waiting. It looked just like any other car now, the insignia of emperor removed. He had been advised his life was at risk if he did not flee the country, but he appeared vacant, almost childlike as he did what he was told. At the Dutch frontier, the guards had not expected to see the former German emperor. They took his sword and his application for asylum. The former Kaiser waited for officials to process his request like any other traveller – the third of Queen Victoria's grandchildren to lose their throne. The ceasefire had been announced by the time he reached the sanctuary of Amerongen Castle, safe behind a guard of Dutch soldiers. Almost as though the whole thing had been a game and he had never really been an enemy of the British, he declared 'now for a cup of real good English tea'.[68]

At the stroke of the eleventh hour, of the eleventh day, of the eleventh month of 1918, the chimes of Big Ben rang out across London announcing the end of the First World War. Ten million people had died and twenty million more were injured. Four empires had been swept away, the Russian, German, Austrian and Ottoman empires – claiming their monarchies. Of Queen Victoria's seven crowned grandchildren, only George V, Marie of Romania, Maud of Norway and Ena of Spain still retained their thrones – and in Spain the monarchy was not to last. In 1931 Ena and Alfonso hurried into exile and, a few years later, the Spanish Civil War would pave the way for General Francisco Franco's military dictatorship and 'totalitarian state'.

From his Dutch exile, the former Kaiser Wilhelm, the prince who had always craved adoration, found himself loathed and reviled. Even his own cousin, George V, blamed him as 'the greatest criminal known for having plunged the world into this ghastly war'.[69] Many clamoured for his trial for war crimes and for his death. Prime Minister Lloyd George considered the prospect of putting the former emperor on trial in Westminster Hall. But Wilhelm escaped such scrutiny because the Dutch government declined extradition requests.

The former emperor took refuge in a world of his own. 'The historian stands bewildered and ashamed before the mountain of evidence documenting the crazed and racist opinions espoused by the exiled monarch,' observed the Kaiser's leading biographer, John Röhl, after a thirty-year study of the Kaiser's life.[70] Presaging Hitler's regime, the former emperor became consumed with the idea that 'the Jewish rabble' were responsible for his downfall. 'Let no German … rest until these parasites have been destroyed and exterminated,' he wrote in 1919 to one former German general, August von Mackensen.[71] The following year he told his former adjutant, Max von Mutius, the world would have no peace 'until all Jews had been clubbed to death'.[72] A few years later he wrote 'the best would be gas?'[73] No contradiction would be tolerated; no alternative view could be aired in his presence. His paranoid world shrank to one driven by hatred and loathing.

In Russia the Bolshevik revolution was soon consumed with the mass killings of the Cheka, or secret police. During Lenin's 'Red Terror', repression in a myriad of violent forms became widespread: ordinary civilians could face the firing squad, the notorious gulag system became established, and torture became almost commonplace. People could face execution simply for belonging to 'the possessing classes'. There were reports of barbaric torture reminiscent of the Spanish Inquisition for captured White officers or members of the clergy, and mass drownings of civilians. Tsarist autocracy was replaced with a 'revolutionary autocracy' that even Lenin's former friends saw as evidence of Russia's 'growing bestiality' as the Bolshevik 'murder machine' set to work 'as butchers'.[74]

Unable to leave the Crimea without her son, the former dowager empress, Maria Feodorovna, would not accept accounts of Nicholas's death. She waited and waited until the advancing Red Army in spring 1919 forced her to flee.[75] She learned of the continuing turmoil as Russia became the 'Union of Soviet Socialist Republics', or 'Soviet Union', in 1922. Lenin's death in 1924 did not bring an end to the misery as Joseph Stalin, General Secretary of the Central Committee of the Communist Party, seized power. Russia's new dictator cultivated the authority of a tsar and would become responsible for the deaths of many millions on a scale that dwarfed that of the Romanov tsars. Recent estimates suggest in excess of twenty million died under Stalin.

Europe's Great War exorcised the leading autocracies of Victorian times; the thrones proving to be tottering tokens of power, their figureheads mere miniatures caught up in the swift-flowing current of change. The royal family's fall mirrors the collapse in Europe's supremacy. The measureless sacrifice in the killing fields of the First World War cost the lives of a generation but would pave the way for Stalin's Russia, Hitler's Germany and the Second World War, during which some sixty million more were killed. The glory of Europe's belle époque years was forever eclipsed as Russia and America would emerge as the world's great superpowers.

Could all this have been avoided? Could Europe have marched without bloodshed through the process of democratisation and the transformation of its many monarchies to a continent of peaceful democracies, whether republics or constitutional monarchies? Prince Albert and Queen Victoria's vision of extending royal ties and developing a flourishing continental cousinhood was intended to enhance diplomacy and bring about peace and had its roots in the traumas inflicted on the continent in Napoleonic times. But the European cousinhood proved to be powerless – even harmful – in the face of the tectonic shifts in political power during the early twentieth century. The titanic clash, not just between nations, but of poverty against wealth, the disenfranchised against ruling elites, was on an undreamed-of scale, its resolution well beyond the scope of any one individual or any one family.

Queen Victoria has been condemned for her matchmaking by some historians as a control freak, whose manipulation of her relations went well beyond motherly feeling or her duty as queen. It is undeniable that the marriages of her descendants were an all-consuming interest and she rarely shrank from expressing her views. It proved impossible for her to implement Prince Albert's grand vision for the dynasty, her frustrations over the decades finding expression in her intimate correspondence with her daughter, Vicky. Nevertheless, she adapted to the changing times, exercising her strong need for control while still keeping the cherished dream in view. She had a powerful instinct for the survival not just of her family, but of the monarchy, an instinct whose immediacy and shrewdness shaped her character – and was rarely wide of the mark.

The dutiful Princess May might not have had the glamour and lively spirit that drew Prince George to Princess Marie, but even after Queen Victoria's death, May lived as though trying to meet her expectations, playing her part to the full in adapting the British monarchy to the times. The marriage against which Queen Victoria fought longest – that of Alexandra and Nicholas – may indeed have been a love match, but it proved to be highly destructive. The queen's instincts had warned her with the power of a premonition that Alix would be unsafe in Russia as tsarina but they failed to foretell the role her strong-willed granddaughter would play in her own downfall as well as the collapse of the Russian Empire. Alix's unswerving advocacy of autocracy and her belief in the divine power of the tsar sealed the fate of her in-laws and paved the way for the total rejection of the governing elite in Russia. How different might things have been had the weak tsar married plain Margaret, who shared her mother's enlightened beliefs and might have encouraged Nicholas to follow the reforming influences of his grandfather? Or if Ella had obeyed her grandmother's instructions to break her engagement with Sergei, thereby making a union between Nicholas and Alexandra less likely. Intriguingly, the man Queen Victoria judged most suitable for Alix, Maximilian von Baden, was the very prince who came to be seen by the Kaiser as an 'arch traitor' for his role in speeding up his abdication. Kaiser Wilhelm fulfilled the queen's early assessment as 'the enemy', becoming the worst possible caricature of royal power.

There remains one haunting 'what if?' in the tale of Queen Victoria's matchmaking. If Vicky's husband, Emperor Frederick, had not died of cancer, but lived to a ripe old age like his father, historians have speculated for years what might have been Europe's fate. The rapprochement between Germany and Britain to which Vicky's marriage had been dedicated? An Anglo-German understanding? Detractors from this view point out that Frederick may not have proved to be the liberalising force that was anticipated. Apart from his personality weaknesses that were not conducive to driving change, when Frederick ascended the throne after twenty-six years of Bismarck's domination, the liberals had long since lost their majority in the Reichstag and the tide had turned against the Albertine programme. But even Frederick's detractors agree that he would have been unlikely to steer the country on a warlike path. It is hard to imagine an early twentieth century with no naval arms race between Britain and Germany, no goading and inflammatory hostility in the German and British press, no clashes over colonies, and no grounds for the fears that provoked Anglo-French and Anglo-Russian treaties.[76] Victoria and Albert's idealistic vision did not encompass the possibility that their own grandson at the helm of the vigorous new country of Germany, his thoughts constantly directed towards his dreams of German power, would help to sow the seeds of destruction.

Events in Europe conspired to create the impetus for war, but Kaiser Wilhelm II and his generals were the first to draw their shining swords. Albert's hopes for a thriving and stable Europe ended in a way far from his original dreams – his fellow

countrymen as well as Englishmen lying in death together in
peace at last:

> In Flanders fields the poppies blow
> Between the crosses, row on row,
> That mark our place; and in the sky
> The larks, still bravely singing, fly
> Scarce heard amid the guns below.[77]

Grandmama's Little Poem

> Then come what will and come what may!
> As long as thou dost live, 'tis day

> And if the world through which we must roam
> Wherever thou art, there is my home

> I see thy face so dear to me
> Shades of the future I do not see.[78]

Acknowledgements

I would like to express my thanks to Her Majesty the Queen for her gracious permission to read the papers and correspondence of her great-great-grandmother, Queen Victoria, and to publish extracts. Unrestricted access to the many letters in the Royal Archives at Windsor Castle between Queen Victoria and her children and grandchildren provided a window into their innermost lives and made it possible to examine their hopes and dreams as well as the tumultuous conflicts behind the royal marriages that shaped Europe. My aim was to present an intimate portrayal and I am most indebted to the team at the Royal Archives for their support with my research over many months as well as their skill in deciphering Queen Victoria's handwriting in her later years when her eyesight was failing.

This book could not have been completed without the expertise of several scholars and historians who helped me along the way. I would particularly like to express my thanks to Jane Ridley, Professor of Modern History, University of Buckingham, for reading and commenting on the manuscript and for her compelling insights into the characters and the times. It was an honour to meet John Röhl, Emeritus Professor at the University of Sussex, who provided invaluable guidance on sections of my draft, helped me through the complexities of the German court in the late nineteenth century and opened up the world of Kaiser Wilhelm II. Discussions with Andrew Wilson at the Royal Archives and the British Library were always an inspiration and I am indebted to Andrew for many steers including Prince Albert's idealistic vision for Europe. Thank you, too, to Christopher Warwick for giving up valuable time to discuss Elisabeth of Hesse and her sisters and advising on extracts in my text. I would also like to thank Dr Richard Williams for his patience and generosity in commenting on the draft, and many others who assisted with the project.

In researching this story I owe a debt of gratitude to staff in several public archives including the Lambeth Palace Library, the National Archives, the British Library and the Parliamentary Archives. Karen Robson, John Rooney and the team at the Mountbatten Archives in the Hartley Library at the University of Southampton drew my attention to unpublished papers, poems and memorabilia collected over a lifetime by Victoria of Hesse about her sisters, and I am grateful for permission to publish extracts. Thank you to Prince Michael of Greece and Ted Rosvall for generously granting permission to publish extracts from the recently found correspondence between Eddy and Hélène in *Eddy & Hélène ... An Impossible Match*, published in 2013 by Rosvall Royal Books in Falköping, Sweden. Thank you also to John Röhl for permission to cite key correspondence from his outstanding three-volume biography of Kaiser Wilhelm published by Cambridge University Press between 1993 and 2014: *Young Wilhelm: The Kaiser's Early Life, 1859–1888*; *Wilhelm II: The Kaiser's Personal Monarchy, 1888–1900*; and finally *Wilhelm II: Into the Abyss of War and Exile, 1900–1941*. In addition, many thanks to Christopher Warwick for permission to quote from *Ella: Princess, Saint and Martyr*, Chichester, John Wiley, 2006.

In London it has been a great pleasure to work with my editor at Bloomsbury, Michael Fishwick, who nurtured this project from the outset and saw its potential. I would like to thank Bloomsbury's managing editor, Sarah Ruddick, for her excellent oversight, assistant editors Marigold Atkey and Jasmine Horsey, and also Richard Mason for his thoughtful copy-editing. In New York I have greatly enjoyed working once more with Clive Priddle, the publisher at Public Affairs, Hachette Book Group. Thank you to Jane Robbins Mize at Public Affairs for guiding the book through each phase of its American production. This project would never have happened without Gordon Wise at Curtis

Brown, who spotted the potential in the story from the beginning. I am indebted to Gordon for his skilful editorial insights and encouraging advice during each phase of the book's development.

Lastly, heartfelt thanks to friends and family who made it possible for me to complete this book. Thank you to Pete and Jo and most of all to Julia Lilley, whose imaginative ideas and wisdom sustained me through the years of writing.

Bibliography

Airlie, Mabell, Countess of, *Thatched with Gold*, Jennifer Ellis (ed.), London, Hutchinson, 1962.

Almedingen, E. M., *An Unbroken Unity: A Memoir of Grand-Duchess Serge of Russia*, London, Bodley Head, 1964.

Aronson, Theo, *Grandmama of Europe: The Crowned Descendants of Queen Victoria*, London, Cassell & Co, 1973, rev. edn 1994.

—*Prince Eddy and the Homosexual Underworld*, London, John Murray, 1994.

Azar, Helen (ed.), *The Diary of Olga Romanov, Royal Witness to the Russian Revolution*, Yardley, PA, Westholme, 2014.

Balfour, Michael, *The Kaiser and His Times*, New York, Norton & Co, 1972.

Battiscombe, Georgina, *Queen Alexandra*, London, Constable, 1969.

Benson, E. F., *The Kaiser and English Relations*, London, Longmans, Green & Co, 1936.

Bing, Edward J. (ed.), *The Letters of Tsar Nicholas and Empress Marie*, London, Ivor Nicholson & Watson, 1937.

Blumenfeld, R. D., *In the Days of Bicycles and Bustles*, New York, Brewer and Warren, 1930.

Bolitho, Hector (ed.), *Further Letters of Queen Victoria, from the House of Brandenburg-Prussia*, London, Thornton Butterworth, 1938.

Buckle, George Earle (ed.), *The Letters of Queen Victoria: A Selection from her Majesty's Correspondence, 1862–1878*, 2 vols, London, John Murray, 1926.

Butterworth, Alex, *The World that Never Was: A True Story of Dreamers, Schemers, Anarchists and Secret Agents*, London, Vintage, 2011.

Buxhoeveden, Baroness Sophie, *The Life and Tragedy of Alexandra Feodorovna, Empress of Russia*, London, Longmans, Green & Co, 1928.

Calder, W. M. (trans.), *The Memoirs of Prince Max of Baden*, New York, Charles Scribner's & Sons, 1928.

Carter, Miranda, *The Three Emperors*, London, Penguin, 2009.

Chester, Lewis, Leitch, David and Simpson, Colin, *The Cleveland Street Affair*, London, Weidenfeld and Nicolson, 1976.

Churchill, Winston, *The World Crisis, 1915*, London, Thornton Butterworth, 1927.

— *The World Crisis, 1916–1918*, Parts 1 and 2, London, Thornton Butterworth, 1927.

Clay, Catrine, *King, Kaiser, Tsar: Three Royal Cousins who Led the World to War*, London, John Murray, 2006.

Cook, Andrew, *Prince Eddy: The King Britain Never Had*, Stroud, The History Press, 2008.

Cornwell, Patricia, *Portrait of a Killer: Jack the Ripper – Case Closed*, London, Time Warner, 2002.

Corti, Egon Caesar, Count, *The English Empress: A Study in the Relations between Queen Victoria and her Eldest Daughter, Empress Frederick of Germany*, London, Cassell & Co, 1957.

Davies, Norman, *Europe: A History*, London, Pimlico, 1996.

Edwards, Anne, *Matriarch: Queen Mary and the House of Windsor*, London, Rowman & Littlefield, 1984.

Egremont, Max, *Balfour: A Life of Arthur James Balfour*, London, Phoenix, 1998.

Erickson, Carolly, *Alexandra: The Last Tsarina*, London, Constable, 2002.

Esher, Viscount Oliver (ed.), *Journals and Letters of Reginald Viscount Esher*, London, Ivor Nicholson & Watson, 1938.

Fawcett, Edward Douglas, *Hartmann, the Anarchist: The Doom of the Great City*, London, E. Arnold, 1892.

Fischer, Louis, *The Life of Lenin*, London, Weidenfeld and Nicolson, 1964.

Florinsky, Michael T., *The End of the Russian Empire*, New York, Collier Books, 1961.

Fulford, Roger (ed.), *Dearest Mama: Private Correspondence of Queen Victoria and the Crown Princess of Prussia, 1861–1864*, London, Evans Brothers, 1968.

— *Your Dear Letter: Private Correspondence of Queen Victoria and the Crown Princess of Prussia, 1865–1871*, London, Evans Brothers, 1971.

— *Darling Child: Private Correspondence of Queen Victoria and the Crown Princess of Prussia, 1871–1878*, London, Evans Brothers, 1976.

— *Beloved Mama: Private Correspondence of Queen Victoria and the German Crown Princess, 1879–1885*, London, Evans Brothers, 1981.

Gelardi, Julia, *Born to Rule: Granddaughters of Queen Victoria, Queens of Europe*, London, Headline, 2004.

Gilliard, Peter, *Thirteen Years at the Russian Court (A personal record of the last years and death of the Czar Nicholas II)*, London, Hutchinson & Co, 1921.

Gore, John, *King George V: A Personal Memoir*, London, John Murray, 1941.

Hanbury-Williams, Major-General, Sir John, *The Emperor Nicholas II, As I Knew Him*, London, Arthur L. Humphreys, 1922.

Harrison, Michael, *Clarence: The Life of HRH the Duke of Clarence and Avondale*, London, W. H. Allen, 1972.

Hibbert, Christopher, *Queen Victoria: A Personal History*, London, HarperCollins, 2001.

— (ed.), *Queen Victoria in Her Letters and Journals*, New York, Viking, 1984.

Hough, Richard (ed.), *Advice to a Granddaughter: Letters from Queen Victoria to Princess Victoria of Hesse*, Newton Abbot, Readers Union Ltd, 1976.

Ion, Theodore, and Brown, Carroll (trans.), *The Greek Supplementary Diplomatic Documents, 1913–1917*, New York, American Hellenic Society, n.d.

King, Greg, *The Last Empress: The Life and Times of Alexandra Feodorovna*, London, Aurum Press, 1995.

Kinross, Lord, *The Ottoman Centuries: The Rise and Fall of the Turkish Empire*, London, HarperCollins, 1997.

Kschessinska, Mathilde, *Dancing in Petersburg: The Memoirs of Mathilde Kschessinska*, Arnold Haskell (trans.), Alton, Dance Books, 2005.

Leighton, John, *Paris Under the Commune: The Seventy-Three Days of the Second Siege*, London, Filiquarian Publishing, 1871.

Longford, Elizabeth, *Victoria R.I.*, Stroud, The History Press, 1964, rev. edn 1999.

Magnus, Sir Philip, *King Edward the Seventh*, London, John Murray, 1964.

Marie, Queen of Romania, *The Story of my Life*, vol. 1 (1934), vol. II (1934), vol. III (1935), London, Cassell & Co.

Massie, Robert K., — *Nicholas & Alexandra*, London, Victor Gollancz, 1968.

The Romanovs: The Final Chapter, London, Random House, 1995.

Maylunas, Andrei, and Mironenko, Sergei (eds), *A Lifelong Passion: Nicholas & Alexandra, Their Own Story*, London, Phoenix, 1997.

McCrae, Lieutenant-Colonel John, *In Flanders Fields and Other Poems*, London, Putnam's Sons, 1919.

Michael of Greece, Prince, *Eddy and Hélène: An Impossible Match*, Falköping, Sweden, Rosvall Royal Books, 2013.

Montefiore, Simon Sebag, *The Romanovs, 1613–1918*, London, Weidenfeld and Nicolson, 2016.

Muller, Frank Lorenz, *Our Fritz: Emperor Frederick III and the Political Culture of Imperial Germany*, Cambridge, MA, Harvard University Press, 2011.

Newsome, David, *On the Edge of Paradise: A. C. Benson – The Diarist*, London, John Murray, 1980.

Nicolson, Sir Harold, *King George V: His Life and Reign*, London, Constable, 1952.

Noel, Gerard, *Ena: Spain's English Queen*, London, Constable, 1984.

Pakula, Hannah, *The Last Romantic: The Life of the Legendary Marie, Queen of Romania*, New York, Simon & Schuster, 1984.

— *An Uncommon Woman: The Empress Frederick*, London, Phoenix Press, 1996.

Ponsonby, Arthur, *Henry Ponsonby, Queen Victoria's Private Secretary: His Life from his Letters*, London, Macmillan & Co, 1942.

Pope-Hennessy, James, *Queen Mary, 1867–1953*, London, George Allen & Unwin, 1959.

Radzinsky, Edvard, *The Last Tsar: The Life and Death of Nicholas II*, London, Arrow, 1993.

— *Alexander II: The Last Great Tsar*, New York, Free Press, 2005.

Radziwill, Catherine, Princess, *The Royal Marriage Market of Europe*, New York, Funk & Wagnells, 1915.

Ramm, Agatha (ed.), *Beloved and Darling Child: Last Letters between Queen Victoria and her Eldest Daughter, 1886–1901*, Stroud, Sutton Publishing, 1990.

Ridley, Jane, *Bertie: A Life of Edward VII*, London, Vintage, 2012.

Roberts, Andrew, *Salisbury: Victorian Titan*, London, Phoenix, 2000.

Roberts, Cecil, *Alfred Fripp*, London, Hutchinson, 1932.

Röhl, John C. G., *Young Wilhelm: The Kaiser's Early Life, 1859–1888*, Cambridge, Cambridge University Press, 1993.

— *Wilhelm II: The Kaiser's Personal Monarchy, 1888–1900*, Cambridge, Cambridge University Press, 2001.

— *King Wilhelm II, 1859–1941: A Concise Life*, Cambridge, Cambridge University Press, 2014.

— *Wilhelm II: Into the Abyss of War and Exile, 1900–1941*, Cambridge, Cambridge University Press, 2014.

Rose, Kenneth, *King George V*, London, Weidenfeld & Nicolson, 1983.

Stockmar, Ernst Alfred von, *Memoirs of Baron Stockmar*, 2 vols, London, Longmans Green & Co (1873), pp. xv and xcviii.

Strachey, Lytton, *Queen Victoria*, London, Penguin, 1971.

Sullivan, Michael John, *A Fatal Passion: The Story of the Uncrowned Last Empress of Russia*, New York, Random House, 1997.

Van der Kiste, John, *Kaiser Wilhelm II: Germany's Last Emperor*, Stroud, Sutton Publishing, 1999, rev. edn 2014.

— *The Prussian Princesses*, London, Fonthill, 2014.

Vizetelly, Ernest Alfred, *The Anarchists: Their Faith and their Record, including Sidelights on the Royal and Other Personages who have been Assassinated*, Cambridge, Cambridge University Press, 1937.

Warwick, Christopher, *Ella: Princess, Saint and Martyr*, Chichester, John Wiley, 2006.

Weintraub, Stanley, *Uncrowned King: The Life of Prince Albert*, New York, The Free Press, 1997.

Wilhelm, Crown Prince, *The Memoirs of the Crown Prince of Germany*, London, Thornton Butterworth, 1922.

Williams, Robin Harcourt (ed.), *Salisbury-Balfour Correspondence*, Rickmansworth, Hertfordshire Record Society, 1988.

Wilson, A. N., *The Victorians*, London, Hutchinson, 2002.

— *Victoria: A Life*, London, Atlantic Books, 2014.

Ybarra, Thomas (trans.), *The Kaiser's Memoirs, 1888–1918*, London, Harper & Bros, 1922.

Yusupov, Prince Felix, *Lost Splendour*, Ann Green and Nicolas Katkoff (trans.), London, Jonathan Cape, 1953.

Abbreviations

Alix	Princess Alexandra of Hesse (Alicky), later Empress of Russia
Bertie	Albert Edward, Prince of Wales, later Edward VII
Ella	Princess Elisabeth of Hesse, later Grand Duchess Elisabeth
George/GV	Prince George, later George V
L of Battenberg	Louis of Battenberg
LPL	Lambeth Palace Library
MB	Mountbatten Archives
Missy (Marie)	Princess Marie of Edinburgh, later Crown Princess of Romania
PAV	Prince Albert Victor (Eddy)
PM	Prime Minister
Princess A	Alexandra, Princess of Wales, later Queen Alexandra
QV	Queen Victoria
RA	Royal Archives
Vicky	Victoria, Crown Princess of Germany
V of Hesse/ V of Battenberg	Princess Victoria of Hesse, later Victoria of Battenberg

Notes and Sources

PROLOGUE

1 RA VIC/MAIN/H/43/19, The Earl of Dufferin, 14 March 1881.
2 Ibid.
3 Edvard Radzinsky, *Alexander II: The Last Great Tsar*, New York, Free Press (2005), p. 414.
4 RA VIC/MAIN/H/43/39, The Earl of Dufferin, 16 March 1881.
5 RA VIC/MAIN/H/43/2, Telegrams 1–10.
6 RA VIC/MAIN/QVJ/1881: 13 March.
7 RA VIC/MAIN/H/43/39, The Earl of Dufferin, 16 March 1881.
8 *Standard*, 15 March 1881.
9 RA VIC/MAIN/QVJ/1881: 13 March.
10 RA VIC/MAIN/QVJ/1839: 27 and 29 May.
11 RA VIC/MAIN/QVJ/1839: 27 May.
12 RA VIC/MAIN/QVJ/1839: 28 and 29 May.
13 Radzinsky (2005), pp. 67–8.
14 RA VIC/MAIN/QVJ/1839: 29 May.
15 RA VIC/MAIN/H/43/11, Vicky to QV, 14 March 1881.
16 Ibid.
17 Simon Sebag Montefiore, *The Romanovs, 1613–1918*, London, Weidenfeld and Nicolson (2016), p. 435.
18 RA VIC/MAIN/QVJ/1880: 18 February.
19 Roger Fulford (ed.), *Beloved Mama: Private Correspondence of Queen Victoria and the German Crown Princess, 1879–1885*, London, Evans Brothers (1981), p. 97; QV to Vicky, 16 March 1881.
20 *Standard*, 15 March 1881.
21 *Morning Post*, 15 March 1881.
22 *Freiheit*, 19 March 1881.
23 Fulford (1981), p. 98; QV to Vicky, 30 March 1881.

24 RA VIC/MAIN/H/43/22, The Earl of Dufferin, 15 March 1881.
25 RA VIC/MAIN/QVJ/1839: 10, 14 and 15 October.
26 A. N. Wilson, *Victoria: A Life*, London, Atlantic Books (2014), p. 100.
27 Richard Hough (ed.), *Advice to a Granddaughter: Letters from Queen Victoria to Princess Victoria of Hesse*, Newton Abbot, Readers Union Ltd (1976), p. 19.
28 RA VIC/MAIN/H/43/85, The Earl of Dufferin, 25 March 1881.

CHAPTER ONE 'A GOOD SENSIBLE WIFE'

1 Arthur Ponsonby, *Henry Ponsonby, Queen Victoria's Private Secretary: His Life from his Letters*, London, Macmillan & Co (1942), p. 72.
2 Ibid., p. 79.
3 Elizabeth Longford, *Victoria R.I.*, Stroud, The History Press (1964; rev. edn 1999), p. 96.
4 RA VIC/MAIN/F/47/15, *A Sovereign's Worth*.
5 Ponsonby (1942), p. 79.
6 Hector Bolitho (ed.), *Further Letters of Queen Victoria, from the House of Brandenburg-Prussia*, London, Thornton Butterworth (1938), p. 185.
7 Norman Davies, *Europe: A History*, London, Pimlico (1996), pp. 837 and 807.
8 Ponsonby (1942), p. 69.
9 Ibid., p. 70.
10 RA VIC/MAIN/F/44–6.
11 RA VIC/MAIN/QVJ/1887: 20 June.
12 RA VIC/MAIN/QVJ/1887: 21 June.
13 RA VIC/MAIN/F/46/120, 21 June 1887.
14 Ibid.
15 RA VIC/MAIN/QVJ/1887: 21 June.
16 RA VIC/MAIN/F/47/28, Lord Rosebery to QV, 7 July 1887.
17 A. N. Wilson, *Victoria: A Life*, London, Atlantic Books (2014), p. 101.
18 *The Memoirs of Baron Stockmar*, vol. 1, p. 132.
19 Roger Fulford (ed.), *Dearest Mama: Private Correspondence of Queen Victoria and the Crown Princess of Prussia, 1861–1864*, London, Evans Brothers (1968), p. 30; 27 December 1861, QV to Vicky.
20 Jane Ridley, *Bertie: A Life of Edward VII*, London, Vintage (2012), p. 313.

21 Fulford (1968), p. 236, QV to Vicky, 27 June 1863.

22 R. D. Blumenfeld, *In the Days of Bicycles and Bustles*, New York, Brewer and Warren (1930), p. 2.

23 Georgina Battiscombe, *Queen Alexandra*, London, Constable (1969), p. 63.

24 Fulford (1968), p. 236, QV to Vicky, 27 June 1863.

25 Roger Fulford (ed.), *Your Dear Letter: Private Correspondence of Queen Victoria and the Crown Princess of Prussia, 1865–1871*, London, Evans Brothers (1971), p. 17, QV to Vicky, 27 January 1865.

26 RA VIC/ADDU/32: 17 March 1872.

27 Sir Harold Nicolson, *King George V: His Life and Reign*, London, Constable (1952), pp. 30–2.

28 Ibid., p. 39.

29 Michael Harrison, *Clarence: The Life of HRH the Duke of Clarence and Avondale*, London, W. H. Allen (1972), p. 68.

30 Sir Philip Magnus, *King Edward the Seventh*, London, John Murray (1964), p. 158.

31 RA VIC/MAIN/Z/92/5, QV to PAV, 19 December 1879.

32 RA VIC/MAIN/Z/92/21, QV to PAV, 6 January 1883.

33 RA VIC/MAIN/Z/92/31, PAV to QV, 9 January 1884.

34 RA VIC/MAIN/Z/92/10, 12 and 15, PAV to QV, 28 December 1880, 5 March 1882 and 19 May 1882.

35 RA VIC/MAIN/Z/474/15, Dalton to Bertie, 9 January 1882.

36 Magnus (1964), p. 169.

37 RA GV/PRIV/AA39/1, PAV to George, 15 June 1883.

38 RA GV/PRIV/AA39/2, PAV to George, 20 June 1883.

39 RA GV/PRIV/AA39/28, PAV to George, 26 February 1886.

40 RA VIC/MAIN/QVJ/1883: 3 September.

41 RA VIC/MAIN/Z/474/63, Stephen to Dalton, 30 August 1883.

42 Ibid.

43 RA VIC/MAIN/Z/92/29, PAV to QV, 23 December 1883.

44 RA VIC/MAIN/Z/474/15 and 17, Dalton to Bertie, 9 January 1882 and 20 October 1881.

45 Theo Aronson, *Grandmama of Europe: The Crowned Descendants of Queen Victoria*, London, Cassell & Co (1973, rev. edn 1994), p. 74.

46 RA VIC/MAIN/Z/92/38, PAV to QV, 17 November 1885.

47 James Pope-Hennessy, *Queen Mary, 1867–1953*, London, George Allen & Unwin (1959), p. 192.

48 David Newsome, *On the Edge of Paradise: A. C. Benson – The Diarist*, London, John Murray (1980), p. 327.

49 RA VIC/MAIN/Z/92/61, PAV to QV, 10 January 1888.
50 *International-Autograph-Auctions* /catalogue-id-in310035.
51 Andrew Cook, *Prince Eddy: The King Britain Never Had*, Stroud, The History Press (2008), p. 133.
52 RA VIC/MAIN/Z/92/68, George to QV, 1 January 1888.
53 RA GV/PRIV/AA39/50, PAV to George, 25 September 1888.
54 RA GV/PRIV/AA39/45, 46 and 52, PAV to George, 27 May 1888, 2 June 1888 and 27 October 1888.
55 Harrison (1972), p. 71.
56 Theo Aronson, *Prince Eddy and the Homosexual Underworld*, London, John Murray (1994), p. 117.
57 Bolitho (1938), p. 264.

CHAPTER TWO VICKY AND FREDERICK

1 Count Egon Caesar Corti, *The English Empress: A Study in the Relations between Queen Victoria and her Eldest Daughter, Empress Frederick of Germany*, London, Cassell & Co (1957), pp. 242–3.
2 Agatha Ramm (ed.), *Beloved and Darling Child: Last Letters between Queen Victoria and her Eldest Daughter, 1886–1901*, Stroud, Sutton Publishing (1990), p. 52, QV to Vicky, 27 May 1887.
3 R. D. Blumenfeld, *In the Days of Bicycles and Bustles*, New York, Brewer and Warren (1930), p. 2.
4 Ernst Alfred von Stockmar, *Memoirs of Baron Stockmar*, 2 vols, London, Longmans Green & Co (1873), pp. xv and xcviii.
5 RA VIC/MAIN/QVJ/1855: 14–29 September.
6 A. N. Wilson, *Victoria: A Life*, London, Atlantic Books (2014), pp. 101, 266–7, 272.
7 E. F. Benson, *The Kaiser and English Relations*, London, Longmans, Green & Co (1936), p. 8.
8 Frank Lorenz Muller, *Our Fritz: Emperor Frederick III and the Political Culture of Imperial Germany*, Cambridge, MA, Harvard University Press (2011), p. 67.
9 Corti (1957), p. 46.
10 Ibid., p. 78.
11 Stanley Weintraub, *Uncrowned King: The Life of Prince Albert*, New York, The Free Press (1997), p. 355.
12 Corti (1957), p. 78.

13 Roger Fulford (ed.), *Dearest Mama: Private Correspondence of Queen Victoria and the Crown Princess of Prussia, 1861–1864*, London, Evans Brothers (1968), p. 40, QV to Vicky, 15 January 1862.

14 Ibid., p. 29, Vicky to QV, 26 December 1861.

15 Corti (1957), pp. 81–2.

16 Weintraub (1997), p. 438.

17 Fulford (1968), p. 85, QV to Vicky, 2 July 1862.

18 Ibid., p. 172, QV to Vicky, 4 February 1863.

19 Corti (1957), p. 88.

20 Fulford (1968), p. 96, Vicky to QV, 19 July 1862.

21 Corti (1957), pp. 83–4.

22 *New York Times*, 1 July 1866.

23 Hector Bolitho (ed.), *Further Letters of Queen Victoria, from the House of Brandenburg-Prussia*, London, Thornton Butterworth (1938), p. 149.

24 Ibid., p. 177.

25 Corti (1957), p. 283.

26 Roger Fulford (ed.), *Beloved Mama: Private Correspondence of Queen Victoria and the German Crown Princess, 1879–1885*, London, Evans Brothers (1981), p. 49, Vicky to QV, 5 July 1879.

27 Ibid., p. 63, Vicky to QV, 29 January 1880.

28 John C. G. Röhl, *Young Wilhelm: The Kaiser's Early Life, 1859–1888*, Cambridge, Cambridge University Press (1993), p. 27, Vicky to QV, 25 February 1860.

29 Ibid., p. 28, Vicky to QV, 23 January 1861.

30 RA VIC/MAIN/QVJ/1861: 5 July.

31 Röhl (1993), p. 20.

32 Fulford (1968), p. 204, Vicky to QV, 28 April 1863.

33 Fulford (1981), p. 51, QV to Vicky, 20 August 1879.

34 Ibid., p. 57, 7 November 1879.

35 RA VIC/MAIN/Z/80/29, Wilhelm to QV, 23 May 1879.

36 Fulford (1981), p. 85, Vicky to QV, 5 August 1880.

37 Ibid., p. 88, QV to Vicky, 21 August 1880.

38 Richard Hough (ed.), *Advice to a Granddaughter: Letters from Queen Victoria to Princess Victoria of Hesse*, Newton Abbot, Readers Union Ltd (1976), p. 88.

39 Röhl (1993), p. 343.

40 RA VIC/MAIN/QVJ/1880: 14 March.

41 Fulford (1981), p. 70, QV to Vicky, 22 March 1880.

42 RA VIC/MAIN/Z/500/1, Wilhelm to QV, 28 December 1886.

43 Röhl (1993), p. 525.

44 John van der Kiste, *Kaiser Wilhelm II: Germany's Last Emperor*, Stroud, Sutton Publishing (1999, rev. edn 2014), p. 20.

45 Fulford (1981), p. 183, QV to Vicky, 13 February 1885.

46 Ibid., p. 183, QV to Vicky, 18 February 1885.

47 Corti (1957), p. 256.

48 RA VIC MAIN/Z/82/119, QV to Wilhelm, 13 December 1887.

49 RA VIC/MAIN/Z/83/6, Wilhelm to QV, 30 December 1887.

50 Corti (1957), p. 284.

51 Ibid., p. 259.

52 Ramm (1990), p. 64, QV to Vicky, 10 March 1888.

53 Corti (1957), p. 267.

54 Bolitho (1938), p. 266.

55 RA/VIC/ MAIN/ Z/68/34, Sir Arthur Ellis to Henry Ponsonby, 16 March 1888.

56 Corti (1957), p. 268.

57 Ramm (1990), p. 70, Vicky to QV, 12 May 1888.

58 RA VIC/MAIN/A/66/107, Salisbury to QV, 21 April 1888.

59 Röhl (1993), p. 807.

60 RA VIC/MAIN/QVJ/1888: 24 April.

61 Ibid.

62 Ramm (1990), p. 67, QV to Vicky, 27 April 1888.

63 RA VIC/MAIN/Z/500/2, Memorandum H. M., 25 April 1888.

64 *Daily Telegraph*, 15 June 1888.

65 *The Times*, 16 June 1888.

66 Ibid.

67 RA VIC/ADDU/173/143, QV to V of Hesse, 4 July 1888.

68 Corti (1957), p. 302.

69 Röhl (1993), p. 36.

70 Corti (1957), p. 303.

71 Bolitho (1938), pp. 259, 269, 273.

72 Röhl (1993), p. 813.

73 Ibid., p. 811.

74 Michael Balfour, *The Kaiser and His Times*, New York, Norton & Co (1972), p. 119.

75 Röhl (1993), p. 804.

76 Ramm (1990), p. 88, Vicky to QV, 30 May 1889.

77 RA VIC/MAIN/Z/68/191, QV to Vicky, 5 September 1888.

78 Ramm (1990), p. 77, QV to Vicky, 4 September 1888.

79 RA VIC/ADDU/173/143, QV to Victoria of Battenberg, 4 July 1888.
80 Van der Kiste (2014), p. 40.
81 Röhl (1993), pp. 813 and xviii.

CHAPTER THREE ELLA AND SERGEI

1 RA VIC/ADDU/173/133, QV to V of Hesse, 2 March 1887.
2 Marie, Queen of Romania, *The Story of My Life*, London, Cassell & Co (1934), vol. 1, pp. 74–5.
3 Baroness Sophie Buxhoeveden, *The Life and Tragedy of Alexandra Feodorovna, Empress of Russia*, London, Longmans, Green & Co (1928), p. 15.
4 Ibid., p. 12.
5 Ibid., p. 11.
6 RA VIC/ADDU/173/32, QV to V of Hesse, 5 July 1880.
7 RA VIC/MAIN/Z/86/53, Alix to QV, 6 June 1879.
8 RA VIC/MAIN/Z/87/43, Alix to QV, 18 July 1881.
9 MB 21/1/Vol. 1, Recollections of Victoria, Marchioness of Milford Haven, pp. 48 and 22.
10 Ibid., p. 17.
11 RA VIC/MAIN/Z/86/93, Alix to QV, 20 December 1879.
12 MB 21/1/Vol. 1, Recollections, p. 30.
13 RA VIC/MAIN/Z/87/42, V of Hesse to QV, 15 July 1881.
14 RA VIC/MAIN/Z/87/2, V of Hesse to QV, 30 October 1880.
15 RA VIC/MAIN/Z/89/63, Alix to QV, 8 June 1889.
16 MB 21/1/Vol. 1, Recollections, p. 39.
17 Buxhoeveden (1928), pp. 7–8.
18 RA VIC/ADDU/173/142, QV to V of Hesse, 14 June 1888.
19 RA VIC/ADDU/173/40, QV to V of Hesse, 8 December 1880.
20 Röhl (1993), p. 326.
21 Marie, Queen of Romania (1934), vol. 1, pp. 8 and 95.
22 Fulford (1981), p. 73, QV to Vicky, 5 April 1880.
23 E. M. Almedingen, *An Unbroken Unity: A Memoir of Grand-Duchess Serge of Russia*, London, Bodley Head (1964), p. 17.
24 RA VIC/MAIN/Z/86/62, Ella to QV, 28 July 1879.
25 Röhl (1993), p. 328.
26 Ibid., p. 333.
27 Fulford (1981), p. 73, QV to Vicky, 5 April 1880.
28 RA VIC/ADDU/173/69, QV to V of Hesse, 7 March 1880.
29 RA VIC/ADDU/173/24, QV to V of Hesse, 23 September 1879.

30 RA VIC/MAIN/Z/86/77, V of Hesse to QV, 3 October 1879.

31 RA VIC/ADDU/173/87, QV to V of Hesse, 21 October 1883.

32 'Russia and Turkey; or, Which is the Gobbler?', *Harper's Weekly*, 22 October 1870.

33 RA VIC/MAIN/QVJ/1854: 26 March.

34 RA VIC/MAIN/QVJ/1854: 12 March and 28 October.

35 George Earle Buckle (ed.), *The Letters of Queen Victoria: A Selection from her Majesty's Correspondence, 1862–1878*, London, John Murray (1926), vol. 2, p. 488.

36 Hannah Pakula, *The Last Romantic: The Life of the Legendary Marie, Queen of Romania*, New York, Simon & Schuster (1984), p. 34.

37 RA VIC/MAIN/QVJ/1876: 17 March.

38 Buckle (1926), p. 493.

39 Edvard Radzinsky, *Alexander II: The Last Great Tsar*, New York, Free Press (2005), p. 210.

40 RA VIC/MAIN/Z/87/30, Ella to QV, 23 March 1881.

41 RA VIC/MAIN/H/43/121, The Earl of Dufferin to QV, 31 March 1881.

42 RA VIC/MAIN/H/43/93, The Earl of Dufferin to Lord Granville, 25 March 1881.

43 RA VIC/MAIN/H/43/116, Sir Henry Eliot to QV, 15 April 1881.

44 RA VIC/MAIN/H/43/40 and 22, The Earl of Dufferin to FO, 15 and 16 March 1881.

45 RA VIC/MAIN/H/43/22, The Earl of Dufferin, 15 March 1881.

46 RA VIC/ADDU/173/69, QV to V of Hesse, 7 March 1883.

47 RA VIC/ADDU/173/66, QV to V of Hesse, 1 January 1883.

48 RA VIC/MAIN/Z/87/130, V of Hesse to QV, 9 January 1883.

49 RA VIC/MAIN/QVJ/1883: 22 May.

50 Lytton Strachey, *Queen Victoria*, London, Penguin, 1971, p. 217.

51 RA VIC/ADDU/173/74, QV to V of Hesse, 23 May 1883.

52 Fulford (1981), p. 178, QV to Vicky, 7 January 1885.

53 RA VIC/ADDU/173/75, QV to V of Hesse, 19 June 1883.

54 RA VIC/MAIN/QVJ/1883: 23 June.

55 RA VIC/MAIN/QVJ/1883: 16 August.

56 RA VIC/ADDU/173/80, QV to V of Hesse, 28 August 1883.

57 RA VIC/ADDU/173/81, QV to V of Hesse, 30 August 1883.

58 RA VIC/ADDU/173/82, QV to V of Hesse, 4 September 1883.

59 RA VIC/ADDU/173/83, QV to V of Hesse, 8 September 1883.

60 RA VIC/ADDU/173/84, QV to V of Hesse, 11 September 1883.

61 RA VIC/MAIN/Z/88/38, Ella to QV, 15 March 1884.

62 RA VIC/ADDU/173/85, QV to V of Hesse, 21 September 1883.

63 RA VIC/ADDU/173/87, QV to V of Hesse, 21 October 1883.

64 Ibid.

65 RA VIC/MAIN/Z/88/25, V of Hesse to QV, 23 December 1883.

66 RA VIC/MAIN/Z/88/36, Irene of Hesse to QV, 1 March 1884.

67 RA VIC/ADDU/173/91, QV to V of Hesse, 11 January 1884.

68 RA VIC/MAIN/Z/88/39, Ella to QV, 3 May 1884.

69 RA VIC/MAIN/QVJ/1884: 17 April.

70 RA VIC/ADDU/173/98, QV to V of Hesse, 26 April 1884.

71 RA VIC/MAIN/Z/88/47, Ella to QV, 31 May 1884.

72 Christopher Warwick, *Ella: Princess, Saint and Martyr*, Chichester, John Wiley (2006), p. 73.

73 Robert K. Massie, *The Romanovs: The Final Chapter*, London, Random House (1995), p. 9.

74 Buxhoeveden (1928), p. 18.

75 MB 21/1/Vol. 1, Recollections of Victoria, Marchioness of Milford Haven, p. 82.

76 Almedingen (1964), p. 23.

77 MB 21/1/Vol. 1, Recollections, p. 83.

78 RA VIC/MAIN/Z/88/57, Irene to QV, 2 July 1884.

79 Marie, Queen of Romania (1934), vol. 1, p. 93.

80 RA VIC/MAIN/Z/90/2, Ella to QV, 22 May 1890.

81 Andrei Maylunas and Sergei Mironenko (eds), *A Lifelong Passion: Nicholas & Alexandra, Their Own Story*, London, Phoenix (1997), pp. 6–7.

82 RA VIC/MAIN/Z/88, Alix to QV, 18 June 1884.

83 Maylunas and Mironenko (1997), pp. 5, 6 and 7.

84 Warwick (2006), p. 132.

85 Marie, Queen of Romania (1934), vol. 1, p. 94.

86 MB1/T95 (F1), Ella to L of Battenberg, 3 November [OS]/15 November 1886.

87 RA VIC/ADDU/173/132, QV to V of Hesse, 15 February 1887.

88 RA VIC/ADDU/173/133, QV to V of Hesse, 2 March 1887.

89 RA VIC/MAIN/Z/89/28, Ella to QV, 22 September [OS]/4 October 1887.

90 RA VIC/ADDU/173/131, QV to V of Hesse, 2 February 1887.

91 RA VIC/ADDU/173/133, QV to V of Hesse, 2 March 1887.

92 MB1/T77 (F2), PAV to L of Battenberg, 7 October 1888.

CHAPTER FOUR ALIX AND EDDY

1   RA VIC/MAIN/QVJ/1888: 31 July.
2   Marie, Queen of Romania, *The Story of My Life*, London, Cassell & Co (1934), vol. 1, pp. 74–5 and 19–20.
3   RA VIC/MAIN/QVJ/1888: 6 and 21 September.
4   RA VIC/MAIN/QVJ/1888: 23 July and 29 September.
5   RA VIC/MAIN/QVJ/1888: 7 September.
6   RA VIC/ADDU/173/144, QV to V of Battenberg, 8 September 1888.
7   RA VIC/MAIN/QVJ/1888: 10 September.
8   RA GV/PRIV/AA39/51, PAV to George, 12 October 1888.
9   RA VIC/MAIN/QVJ/1888: 25 September.
10 RA VIC/MAIN/QVJ/1888: 6 October.
11 MB1/T77 (F2) PAV to L of Battenberg, 7 October 1888.
12 RA VIC/MAIN/QVJ/1888: 10 October.
13 RA VIC/MAIN/Z/89/53, Alix to QV, 11 October 1888.
14 RA GV/PRIV/AA39/51, PAV to George, 12 October 1888.
15 MB1/T77 (F2) PAV to L of Battenberg, 6 September 1889.
16 E. M. Almedingen, *An Unbroken Unity: A Memoir of Grand-Duchess Serge of Russia*, London, Bodley Head (1964), pp. 33–4.
17 Christopher Warwick, *Ella: Princess, Saint and Martyr*, Chichester, John Wiley (2006), p. 148.
18 MB1/T95 (F1), Ella to L of Battenberg, 16 September [OS]/28 September 1889, and undated letter.
19 MB1/T95 (F1), Ella to L of Battenberg, 22 May [OS]/3 June 1890, and undated letter.
20 Andrei Maylunas and Sergei Mironenko (eds), *A Lifelong Passion: Nicholas & Alexandra, Their Own Story*, London, Phoenix (1997), p. 10.
21 Buxhoeveden, p. 22.
22 Maylunas and Mironenko (1997), p. 15.
23 Ibid., p. 11.
24 Ibid., pp. 12–13.
25 MB11/2/1 and MB11/2/2.
26 RA VIC/MAIN/Z/89/59, Ernie to QV, Tuesday, February 1889.
27 RA VIC/ADDU/173/150, QV to V of Battenberg, 31 March 1889.
28 MB1/T77 (F2), PAV to L of Battenberg, 6 September 1889.
29 L. Chester, D. Leitch and C. Simpson, *The Cleveland Street Affair*, London, Weidenfeld and Nicolson, 1976, pp. 15–17.

30 Ibid., pp. 7 and 23.
31 Andrew Roberts, *Salisbury: Victorian Titan*, London, Phoenix (2000), p. 841.
32 Theo Aronson, *Prince Eddy and the Homosexual Underworld*, London, John Murray, 1994, p. 34.
33 RA VIC/MAIN/Z/89/60 and 63, Alix to QV, 16 April and 8 June 1889.
34 RA VIC/MAIN/QVJ/1889: 27 August.
35 RA VIC/MAIN/QVJ/1889: 19 and 23 August.
36 RA VIC/MAIN/QVJ/1889: 9 September.
37 MB1/T77 (F2), PAV to L of Battenberg, 7 October 1889.
38 Ibid.
39 RA VIC/MAIN/QVJ/1889: 11 September.
40 MB1/T77 (F1), George to L of Battenberg, 15 September 1889.
41 RA VIC/MAIN/Z/89/65, Alix to QV, 4 October 1889.
42 MB1/T77 (F2), PAV to L of Battenberg, 7 October 1889.
43 RA VIC/ADDU/173/156, QV to V of Battenberg, 30 October 1889.
44 Ridley (2012), p. 273.
45 Andrew Cook, *Prince Eddy: The King Britain Never Had*, Stroud, The History Press (2008), p. 182.
46 Ridley (2012), pp. 116–17.
47 Chester, Leitch and Simpson, *The Cleveland Street Affair*, pp. 130 and 132.
48 *New York Times*, 10 November 1889.
49 *Cardiff Times*, 7 December 1889.
50 Cook (2008), p. 286.
51 Sir Philip Magnus, *King Edward the Seventh*, London, John Murray (1964), p. 219; Georgina Battiscombe, *Queen Alexandra*, London, Constable (1969), p. 185; and James Pope-Hennessy, *Queen Mary, 1867–1953*, London, George Allen & Unwin (1959), p. 192.
52 Battiscombe (1969), p. 185.
53 Aronson (1994), p. 120.
54 MB1/T77 (F2), PAV to L of Battenberg, 7 October 1889.
55 Maylunas and Mironenko (1997), p. 14.
56 RA VIC/MAIN/Z/92/75 and 76, PAV to QV, 29 November 1889 and 19 January 1890.
57 RA VIC/MAIN/Z/92/77, PAV to QV, 2 April 1890.
58 Count Egon Caesar Corti, *The English Empress: A Study in the Relations between Queen Victoria and her Eldest Daughter, Empress Frederick of Germany*, London, Cassell & Co (1957), p. 333.

59 RA VIC/MAIN/QVJ/1890: 23 April.
60 RA VIC/MAIN/QVJ/1890: 25 and 26 April.
61 Agatha Ramm (ed.), *Beloved and Darling Child: Last Letters between Queen Victoria and her Eldest Daughter, 1886–1901*, Stroud, Sutton Publishing (1990), p. 108, QV to Vicky, 7 May 1890.
62 RA VIC/ADDU/173/160, QV to V of Battenberg, 15 July 1890.

CHAPTER FIVE EDDY AND HÉLÈNE

1 RA VIC/MAIN/Z/475/3, QV to PAV, 19 May 1890.
2 RA VIC/MAIN/Z/83/60 and 64, Margaret to QV, 18 January and 28 June 1888.
3 RA VIC/MAIN/Z/84/52, Margaret to QV, 21 May 1891.
4 RA VIC/MAIN/Z/475/3, QV to PAV, 19 May 1890.
5 Ibid.
6 RA GV/PRIV/AA31/1, Princess A to George, 17 October 1888.
7 RA VIC/MAIN/QVJ/1848: 25 February.
8 RA VIC/MAIN/QVJ/1848: 4 March.
9 RA VIC/MAIN/QVJ/1871: 8 April.
10 RA VIC/MAIN/QVJ/1871: 30 April.
11 RA GV/PRIV/AA39/62, PAV to George, 13 September 1890.
12 RA VIC/MAIN/Z/475/3, QV to PAV, 19 May 1890.
13 Ibid.
14 Prince Michael of Greece, *Eddy and Hélène: An Impossible Match*, Falköping, Sweden, Rosvall Royal Books (2013), pp. 9–10.
15 RA GV/PRIV/AA39/62, PAV to George, 13 September 1890.
16 RA VIC/MAIN/Z/475/3, QV to PAV, 19 May 1890.
17 RA GV/PRIV/AA39/62, PAV to George, 13 September 1890.
18 Prince Michael of Greece (2013), pp. 11–12.
19 Ibid., pp. 13, 14 and 15.
20 RA VIC/ADDU/173/160, QV to V of Battenberg, 15 July 1890.
21 MB 21/1/Vol. 1, Recollections of Victoria, Marchioness of Milford Haven, p. 130.
22 Ibid., p. 131.
23 Baroness Sophie Buxhoeveden, *The Life and Tragedy of Alexandra Feodorovna, Empress of Russia*, London, Longmans, Green & Co (1928), p. 27.
24 RA VIC/ADDU/173/163, QV to V of Battenberg, 29 December 1890.

25 Ibid.

26 Louis Fischer, *The Life of Lenin*, London, Weidenfeld and Nicolson (1964), p. 10.

27 *London Evening Standard*, 3 October 1887, and *Hampshire Advertiser*, 31 October 1887.

28 John van der Kiste, *Kaiser Wilhelm II: Germany's Last Emperor*, Stroud, Sutton Publishing (1999, rev. edn 2014), p. 47.

29 John C. G. Röhl, *Wilhelm II, The Kaiser's Personal Monarchy, 1888–1900*, Cambridge, Cambridge University Press (2001), p. 342.

30 Prince Michael of Greece (2013), p. 65.

31 Aronson (1994), p. 199.

32 Cecil Roberts, *Alfred Fripp*, London, Hutchinson (1932), pp. 32–3.

33 *Aberdeen Evening Express*, 15 September 1890.

34 Roberts (1932), pp. 34–5.

35 *Yorkshire Post*, 28 August 1890.

36 *Sheffield Evening Telegraph*, 28 August, and *Huddersfield Chronicle*, 15 September 1890.

37 RA GV/PRIV/AA39/62, PAV to George, 13 September 1890.

38 Ibid.

39 Ibid.

40 RA GV/PRIV/AA31/13, Princess A to George, 30 August 1890.

41 RA VIC/MAIN/QVJ/1890: 26 August.

42 RA GV/PRIV/AA39/62, PAV to George, 13 September 1890.

43 Robin Harcourt Williams (ed.), *Salisbury-Balfour Correspondence*, Rickmansworth, Hertfordshire Record Society (1988), pp. 319–20, QV to Balfour, 29 August 1890.

44 RA GV/PRIV/AA39/62, PAV to George, 13 September 1890.

45 Williams (1988), p. 319, QV to Balfour, 29 August 1890.

46 Ibid., p. 322, Balfour to PM, 30 August 1890.

47 Ibid., pp. 321 and 318, Balfour to PM, 30 August 1890.

48 Ibid., pp. 321–2, Balfour to PM, 30 August 1890.

49 RA VIC/MAIN/L/3/27A, 30A, 36A, 36B, QV to Bertie, 7, 9, 19 and 20 September 1890.

50 Roberts (1932), pp. 58–9.

51 Patricia Cornwell, *Portrait of a Killer: Jack the Ripper – Case Closed*, London, Time Warner (2002), p. 135.

52 Andrew Cook, *Prince Eddy: The King Britain Never Had*, Stroud, The History Press (2008), p. 297.

53 Prince Michael of Greece (2013), p. 18.

54 Ibid., pp. 21–2.

55 Ibid., pp. 18–19.
56 Ibid., pp. 19–20.
57 RA GV/PRIV/AA39/62, PAV to George, 13 September 1890.
58 Prince Michael of Greece (2013), pp. 20 and 23.
59 Ibid., pp. 23–4.
60 Roberts (1932), pp. 46–7.
61 Prince Michael of Greece (2013), p. 37.
62 Ibid., p. 40.
63 Ibid., p. 67.
64 RA VIC/MAIN/L/3/41, Knollys to Ponsonby, 19 October 1890.
65 RA VIC/MAIN/L/3/45, Knollys to Ponsonby, 8 December 1890.
66 RA GV/PRIV/AA39/64, PAV to George, 10 February 1891.
67 Prince Michael of Greece (2013), p. 60.
68 Ibid., pp. 64 and 62.
69 Ibid., p. 68.

CHAPTER SIX EDDY AND MAY

1 MB1/T77 (F1), George to L of Battenberg, 15 March 1884.
2 RA GV/PRIV/AA10/19, QV to George, 2 June 1885.
3 MB1/T77 (F1), George to L of Battenberg, 20 May 1884 and 8 April 1885.
4 RA VIC/MAIN/Z/92/45, George to QV, 5 June 1896.
5 RA VIC/MAIN/Z/92/83, George to QV, 8 December 1890.
6 RA VIC/MAIN/Z/92/78, George to QV, 21 May 1890.
7 RA VIC/MAIN/Z/92/47, George to QV, 28 September 1886.
8 RA VIC/MAIN/Z/92/64 and 72, George to QV, 22 May 1888 and 6 April 1889.
9 MB1/T77 (F1), George to L of Battenberg, 13 June 1889.
10 RA GV/PRIV/AA31/16, Princess A to George, 16 January 1891.
11 RA GV/PRIV/AA31/23, Princess A to George, 3 October 1892.
12 Georgina Battiscombe, *Queen Alexandra*, London, Constable (1969), p. 143.
13 Ibid., pp. 141–2.
14 RA GV/PRIV/AA31/23, Princess A to George, 3 October 1892.
15 RA VIC/MAIN/Z/92/87, George to QV, 6 February 1891.
16 Ibid.
17 Ibid.
18 James Pope-Hennessy, *Queen Mary, 1867–1953*, London, George Allen & Unwin (1959), p. 200.

19 RA VIC/MAIN/Z/475/15, PAV to QV, 21 June 1891.

20 Ibid.

21 Sir Philip Magnus, *King Edward the Seventh*, London, John Murray (1964), p. 238.

22 RA VIC/MAIN/Z/475/17, QV to Bertie, 4 August 1891.

23 RA VIC/MAIN/Z/475/16, QV to PM, 4 August 1891.

24 RA VIC/MAIN/Z/475/19 and 17, QV to Bertie, 5 and 4 August 1891.

25 RA VIC/MAIN/Z/475/18, Bertie to QV, 5 August 1891.

26 RA VIC/MAIN/Z/475/16, QV to PM, 4 August 1891.

27 RA VIC/ADDA12/1797, Knollys to Ponsonby, 19 August 1891.

28 Pope-Hennessy (1959), p. 185.

29 Ibid.

30 Max Egremont, *Balfour: A Life of Arthur James Balfour*, London, Phoenix (1998), p. 103.

31 Ibid.

32 RA VIC/MAIN/Z/475/18, Bertie to QV, 5 August 1891.

33 RA VIC/ADDA12/1807, Knollys to Ponsonby, 10 October 1891.

34 RA VIC/MAIN/QVJ/1891: 5 November.

35 RA VIC/MAIN/QVJ/1891: 6 November.

36 Elizabeth Longford, *Victoria R.I.*, Stroud, The History Press (1964, rev. edn 1999), p. 89.

37 RA QM/PRIV/QMD/1891: 6 November.

38 RA QM/PRIV/QMD/1891: 12 November.

39 Agatha Ramm (ed.), *Beloved and Darling Child: Last Letters between Queen Victoria and her Eldest Daughter, 1886–1901*, Stroud, Sutton Publishing (1990), p. 134, QV to Vicky, 12 November 1891.

40 Pope-Hennessy (1959), p. 207.

41 RA VIC/MAIN/QVJ/1891: 8 and 10 November.

42 RA VIC/MAIN/QVJ/1891: 14 November.

43 *Edinburgh Evening News*, 16 November 1891.

44 *Derby Daily Telegraph*, 16 May 1891.

45 RA VIC/ADDC6/1891: 29 November.

46 Pope-Hennessy (1959), p. 193.

47 *Lloyd's Weekly Newspaper*, 11 October 1891, and *Manchester Courier*, 10 October 1891.

48 *New Zealand Herald*, 14 November 1891, and *Perth Daily News*, 6 October 1891.

49 'Adventures of a Gaiety Girl', *Auckland Star*, 7 April 1900.

50 RA VIC/MAIN/Z/475/23, Bertie to QV, 3 December 1891.

51 Ibid.

52   MB2 D14, Buxhoeveden's postcard album.

53   RA QM/PRIV/QMD/1891: 3 December.

54   Anne Edwards, *Matriarch: Queen Mary and the House of Windsor*, London, Rowman & Littlefield (1984), p. 40.

55   RA QM/PRIV/QMD/1891: 3 December.

56   RA VIC/MAIN/QVJ/1891: 5 December.

57   RA VIC/MAIN/QVJ/1891: 6 December.

58   Ramm (1990), p. 136, QV to Vicky, 6 December 1891.

59   RA VIC/ADDC6/1891: 5 December.

60   Ibid., 6 December 1891.

61   RA VIC/MAIN/Z/475/49, Princess A to QV, 6 December 1891.

62   RA VIC/MAIN/Z/475/34, L of Hesse to QV, 6 December 1891.

63   RA VIC/MAIN/Z/90/17, Alix of Hesse to QV, 12 December 1891.

64   RA VIC/MAIN/Z/475/57, Ella to QV, 7 December 1891.

65   *Leeds Mercury*, 8 December 1891.

66   Ibid.

67   E. M. Almedingen, *An Unbroken Unity: A Memoir of Grand-Duchess Serge of Russia*, London, Bodley Head (1964), p. 35.

68   Ibid., pp. 39–40.

69   Christopher Warwick, *Ella: Princess, Saint and Martyr*, Chichester, John Wiley (2006), p. 162.

70   RA VIC/ADDU/173/166, QV to V of Battenberg, 18 September 1891.

71   Greg King, *The Last Empress: The Life and Times of Alexandra Feodorovna*, London, Aurum Press (1995), p. 50.

72   Ramm (1990), p. 125, Vicky to QV, 29 March 1891.

73   E. F. Benson, *The Kaiser and English Relations*, London, Longmans, Green & Co (1936), p. 337.

74   Count Egon Caesar Corti, *The English Empress: A Study in the Relations between Queen Victoria and her Eldest Daughter, Empress Frederick of Germany*, London, Cassell & Co (1957), p. 339.

75   RA GV/PRIV/AA31/18, Princess A to George, 3 June 1891, and RA VIC/MAIN/Z/84/34, Margaret to QV, 27 December 1890.

76   Aronson (1973, rev. edn 1994), p. 71.

77   Ramm (1990), p. 126, QV to Vicky, 20 May 1891.

78   Benson (1936), p. 92.

79   Sebag Montefiore (2016), p. 473.

80   RA VIC/MAIN/QVJ/1891: 20 August.

81   Benson (1936), p. 94.

82   Ramm (1990), p. 135, Vicky to QV, 5 December 1891.

83 'Betrothal of the Duke of Clarence', *Manchester Weekly Times*, 11 December 1891.

84 *Exeter and Plymouth Gazette*, 7 December 1891.

85 *Manchester Guardian*, 12 December 1891.

86 *Dundee Evening Times*, 25 December 1891.

87 *Yorkshire Evening Post*, 7 December 1891.

88 RA VIC/ADDC6/1891: 7 December.

89 *Hampshire Advertiser*, 9 December 1891.

90 RA QM/PRIV/QMD/1891: 29 and 28 December.

91 Pope-Hennessy (1959), p. 213.

92 RA VIC/MAIN/QVJ/1891: 12 December.

93 RA QM/PRIV/QMD/1891: 12 December.

94 Ibid., 29 December 1891.

95 RA VIC/MAIN/Z/92/95, PAV to QV, 26 December 1891.

96 MB1/T77 (F2), PAV to L of Battenberg, 5 January 1892.

97 RA QM/PRIV/QMD/1891: 22 December.

98 RA VIC/MAIN/Z/475/138, Princess A to QV, 9 January 1892.

99 RA VIC/MAIN/Z/475/140, Bertie to QV, 10 January 1892.

100 RA QM/PRIV/QMD/1892: 12 and 13 January.

101 Ramm (1990), p. 138, QV to Vicky, 11 January 1892.

102 *West Australian*, 13 January 1892.

103 RA VIC/MAIN/QVJ/1892: 13 January.

104 RA VIC/MAIN/Z/95/6, Princess Mary Adelaide, 14 January 1892.

105 RA VIC/MAIN/QVJ/1892: 14 and 15 January.

106 *Daily Telegraph*, 15 January 1892.

107 *Edinburgh Evening News*, 14 January 1892.

108 Ponsonby (1942), p. 113.

109 Pope-Hennessy (1959), p. 225.

110 RA VIC/MAIN/QVJ/1892: 15 January.

111 RA VIC/MAIN/QVJ/1892: 19 January.

112 *Manchester Courier*, 20 January 1892.

113 RA VIC/MAIN/Z/475/192, QV to Bertie, 17 January 1892.

114 RA VIC/MAIN/Z/475/200, Princess A to QV, 18 January 1892.

115 *Daily Telegraph*, 21 January 1892.

116 RA QM/PRIV/QMD/1892: 20 January.

117 *Gloucester Citizen*, 21 January 1892.

118 RA VIC/MAIN/Z/95/9, Princess May to QV, 16 January 1892.

119 RA VIC/MAIN/Z/95/6, Princess Mary Adelaide to QV, 14 January 1892.

120 RA VIC/ADDU/173/170, QV to V of Battenberg, 3 February 1892.

121   RA VIC/MAIN/QVJ/1892: 14 January.

122   RA VIC/ADDU/173/170, QV to V of Battenberg, 3 February 1892.

123   RA VIC/ADDU/173/172, QV to V of Battenberg, 15 March 1892.

124   Ramm (1990), p. 139, QV to Vicky, 5 March 1892.

CHAPTER SEVEN GEORGE AND MISSY

1   RA GV/PRIV/AA69/15, Nicholas to George, January 1892.

2   RA VIC/MAIN/QVJ/1892: 2 and 6 February.

3   Agatha Ramm (ed.), *Beloved and Darling Child: Last Letters between Queen Victoria and her Eldest Daughter, 1886–1901*, Stroud, Sutton Publishing (1990), p. 142, QV to Vicky, 14 June 1892.

4   RA GV/PRIV/AA12/1, George to QV, 1 February 1892.

5   RA GV/PRIV/AA10/36, QV to George, 14 February 1892.

6   RA GV/PRIV/AA10/37, QV to George, 2 March 1892.

7   RA VIC/MAIN/QVJ/1892: 11 and 14 February.

8   James Pope-Hennessy, *Queen Mary, 1867–1953*, London, George Allen & Unwin (1959), p. 230.

9   RA QM/PRIV/QMD/1892: 27 February.

10   Marie, Queen of Romania, *The Story of my Life*, London, Cassell & Co (1934), vol. 1, p. 87.

11   RA VIC/MAIN/QVJ/1881: 17 March.

12   MB 21/1/Vol. 1, Recollections of Victoria, Marchioness of Milford Haven, p. 106.

13   Marie, Queen of Romania (1934), vol. 1, pp. 34–5.

14   Ibid., pp. 54, 72–3, 6, 7, 44, 42 and 36–7 *passim*.

15   Ibid., pp. 72, 75 and 19–20 *passim*.

16   Ibid., pp. 105–7, 137 and 140 *passim*.

17   MB 21/1/Vol. 1, Recollections, pp. 106 and 109.

18   Marie, Queen of Romania (1934), vol. 1, p. 137.

19   Hannah Pakula, *The Last Romantic: The Life of the Legendary Marie, Queen of Romania*, New York, Simon & Schuster (1984), p. 47.

20   Marie, Queen of Romania (1934), vol. 1, p. 20.

21   RA VIC/MAIN/Z/84/5, Missy to QV, May 1890.

22   Pakula (1984), p. 57, and https://tinyurl.com/zshy3rp.

23   RA GV/PRIV/AA31/17, Princess A to George, 18 April 1891.

24   Marie, Queen of Romania (1934), vol. 1, pp. 157–8.

25   RA GV/PRIV/AA31/17, Princess A to George, 18 April 1891.

26   RA GV/PRIV/AA10/33, Princess A to George, 31 July 1891.

27   Marie, Queen of Romania (1934), vol. 1, pp. 15, 28, 29 and 55.

28 RA GV/PRIV/AA69/78, Missy to George, 17 January 1892.
29 Pakula (1984), p. 57.
30 Pope-Hennessy (1959), p. 235.
31 Prince Michael of Greece, *Eddy and Hélène: An Impossible Match*, Falköping, Sweden, Rosvall Royal Books (2013), pp. 79 and 82.
32 Ibid., pp. 82, 85 and 87.
33 Vizetelly (1937), pp. 110 and 119.
34 *London Daily News*, 17 March 1892.
35 Pakula (1984), p. 57.
36 RA GV/PRIV/AA10/37, QV to George, 2 March 1892.
37 RA QM/PRIV/CC1/2, George to May, 29 March 1892.
38 *St James Gazette*, 5 April 1892, and *Yorkshire Evening Post*, 5 April 1892.
39 RA GV/PRIV/AA10/38 QV to George, 6 April 1892.
40 RA QM/PRIV/QMD/1892: 2 April.
41 RA GV/PRIV/AA12/2, George to QV, 8 April 1892.
42 RA GV/PRIV/AA10/38 QV to George, 6 April 1892.
43 *Manchester Times*, 29 April 1892.
44 RA QM/PRIV/QMD/1892: 5 May.
45 Ibid.
46 Edward Douglas Fawcett, *Hartmann, the Anarchist: The Doom of the Great City*, London, E. Arnold (1892), pp. 21, 84, 134, 138 and 140.
47 RA QM/PRIV/QMD/1892: 5 May.
48 Vizetelly (1937), pp. 124 and 126.

CHAPTER EIGHT MISSY AND FERDINAND

1 Marie, Queen of Romania, *The Story of my Life*, London, Cassell & Co (1934), vol. 1, p. 219.
2 Ibid., pp. 226–7, 219–22.
3 Ibid., pp. 228 and 244.
4 Hannah Pakula, *The Last Romantic: The Life of the Legendary Marie, Queen of Romania*, New York, Simon & Schuster, 1984, p. 85.
5 Marie, Queen of Romania, vol. 1, p. 204.
6 RA VIC/MAIN/Z/84/91, Missy to QV, 21 May 1892.
7 Marie, Queen of Romania, vol. 1, pp. 263 and 227.
8 Ibid., pp. 227–30.
9 RA/Queen Victoria's Journal, 2 and 4 June.
10 James Pope-Hennessy, *Queen Mary, 1867–1953*, London, George Allen & Unwin (1959), p. 251.

11 RA VIC/MAIN/Z/53/3, Vicky to QV, 7 June 1892.

12 RA/VIC/MAIN/Z/53/4, Vicky to QV, 9 June 1892.

13 RA VIC/MAIN/Z/53/3, Vicky to QV, 7 June 1892.

14 RA VIC/ADDU/173/175, QV to V of Battenberg, 2 June 1892.

15 RA VIC/ADDC6/1892: 3 June.

16 RA VIC/MAIN/Z/476/3, Ponsonby.

17 RA VIC/MAIN/Z/57/69, Bertie to QV, 6 May 1892.

18 RA VIC/MAIN/Z/457/70, QV to Bertie, 10 May 1892.

19 Nicholas's diary, 21 December 1891 [OS]/2 January 1892, cited in Andrei Maylunas and Sergei Mironenko (eds), *A Lifelong Passion: Nicholas & Alexandra, Their Own Story*, London, Phoenix (1997), p. 15.

20 Baroness Sophie Buxhoeveden, *The Life and Tragedy of Alexandra Feodorovna, Empress of Russia*, London, Longmans, Green & Co (1928), p. 21.

21 RA VIC/MAIN/Z/90/45, Alix to QV, 22 March 1893.

22 MB1/T95 (F2), Alix to L of Battenberg, 23 May and 10 June 1893.

23 RA VIC/MAIN/Z/90/28, Alix to QV, 16 August 1892.

24 RA VIC/MAIN/Z/90/40, Alix to QV, 22 December 1892.

25 Simon Sebag Montefiore, *The Romanovs, 1613–1918*, London, Weidenfeld and Nicolson (2016), p. 471.

26 Christopher Warwick, *Ella: Princess, Saint and Martyr*, Chichester, John Wiley (2006), p. 165.

27 Nicholas's diary, 29 January [OS]/10 February 1892, cited in Maylunas and Mironenko (1997), p. 16.

28 Mathilde Kschessinska, *Dancing in Petersburg: The Memoirs of Mathilde Kschessinska*, Arnold Haskell (trans.), Alton, Dance Books (2005), pp. 29 and 33.

29 Nicholas's diary, 1 April [OS]/13 April 1892, cited in Maylunas and Mironenko (1997), p. 16.

30 Kschessinska (2005), pp. 39 and 43.

31 RA GV/PRIV/AA19/35, Bertie to George, 24 August 1892.

32 RA QM/PRIV/CC5/2, May to George, 29 March 1892.

33 RA GV/PRIV/AA31/23, Princess A to George, 3 October 1892.

34 RA QM/PRIV/CC1/3, George to May, 9 June 1892.

35 *Derbyshire Times*, 30 July 1892.

36 RA VIC/MAIN/QVJ/1892: 10 June.

37 RA VIC/MAIN/QVJ/1892: 11 June.

38 *Daily Telegraph*, 18 June 1892.

39 RA GV/PRIV/AA12/5, George to QV, 20 September 1892.

40 RA GV/PRIV/AA10/44, QV to George, 14 October 1892.
41 RA GV/PRIV/AA31/26, Princess A to George, 3 October 1892.
42 RA VIC/MAIN/Z/476/21, George to QV, 2 November 1892.
43 RA GV/PRIV/AA12/5, George to QV, 20 September 1892.
44 Ibid.
45 MB 21/1/1, p. 146.
46 RA GV/PRIV/AA12/6, George to QV, 10 October 1892.
47 Marie, Queen of Romania (1934), vol. 1. p. 247.
48 RA VIC/MAIN/Z/84/106, Missy to QV, 1 November 1892.
49 RA VIC/MAIN/Z/84/107, Missy to QV, 21 November 1892.
50 Marie, Queen of Romania (1934), vol. 1, p. 247.
51 Ibid., p. 252.
52 Ramm (1990), p. 129, Vicky to QV, 25 July 1891.
53 Ibid.
54 RA VIC/MAIN/QVJ/1892: 10 December.
55 Marie, Queen of Romania (1934), vol. 1, pp. 247 and 249.
56 Ibid., pp. 266 and 291.
57 Hannah Pakula, *The Last Romantic: The Life of the Legendary Marie, Queen of Romania*, New York, Simon & Schuster (1984), p. 57.
58 Marie, Queen of Romania (1934), vol. 1, p. 288.
59 Ibid., p. 165.
60 Ramm (1990), pp. 153–4, QV to Vicky, 11 January 1893.

CHAPTER NINE GEORGE AND MAY

1 RA GV/PRIV/AA12/9, George to QV, 28 December 1892.
2 RA GV/PRIV/AA12/10, George to QV, 10 January 1893.
3 RA QM/PRIV/CC1/4, George to May, 25 December 1892.
4 RA QM/PRIV/CC5/3 and 4, May to George, 16 January 1893.
5 RA QM/PRIV/CC1/5, George to May, 15 January 1893.
6 RA GV/PRIV/AA31/28, Princess A to George, 7 February 1893.
7 *Pall Mall Gazette*, 19 January 1893.
8 RA GV/PRIV/AA10/46, QV to George, 9 January 1893.
9 RA GV/PRIV/AA31/27, Princess A to George, 1 February 1893.
10 Ibid.
11 RA GV/PRIV/AA31/29, Princess A to George, 13 February 1893.
12 RA QM/PRIV/CC1/6, George to May, 4 March 1893.
13 RA GV/PRIV/AA12/11, George to QV, 8 March 1893.
14 RA QM/PRIV/CC1/7, George to May, 17 March 1893.
15 RA QM/PRIV/CC5/6, May to George, 22 March 1893.

16 RA QM/PRIV/CC1/8, George to May, 31 March 1893.

17 RA GV/PRIV/AA12/14, George to QV, 11 April 1893.

18 RA VIC/MAIN/QVJ/1893: 1 February.

19 Ibid., 5 February 1893.

20 James Pope-Hennessy, *Queen Mary, 1867–1953*, London, George Allen & Unwin (1959), p. 259.

21 John C. G. Röhl, *Wilhelm II, The Kaiser's Personal Monarchy, 1888–1900*, Cambridge, Cambridge University Press (2001), p. 508.

22 RA VIC/MAIN/QVJ/1893: 14 March.

23 Ibid., 20 March 1893.

24 *Lincolnshire Echo*, 3 May 1893.

25 *Sheffield Evening Telegraph*, 3 May 1893.

26 *The Star*, 3 May 1893.

27 RA QM/PRIV/QMD/1893: 3 May.

28 Pope-Hennessy (1959), p. 259.

29 RA QM/PRIV/QMD/1893: 3 May.

30 RA VIC/MAIN/QVJ/1893: 3 and 4 May.

31 Agatha Ramm (ed.), *Beloved and Darling Child: Last Letters between Queen Victoria and her Eldest Daughter, 1886–1901*, Stroud, Sutton Publishing (1990), p. 158, QV to Vicky, 7 May 1893.

32 RA VIC/MAIN/Z/476/65, Princess Helena to QV, 4 May 1893.

33 *Telegraph, St James Gazette* and *The Times*, 4 May 1893.

34 RA VIC/MAIN/Z/476/28, annotations on *The Star*, 3 May 1893.

35 LPL/Benson 130/371, Pennington to Benson, 14 July 1893.

36 LPL/Benson 130/381, Bartlett to Benson, 4 June 1894.

37 LPL/Benson 130/383, Pelly to Benson, 30 June 1894.

38 RA QM/PRIV/CC1/16, George to May, 12 June 1893.

39 RA QM/PRIV/CC1/17, George to May, 13 June 1893.

40 RA QM/PRIV/CC1/18, George to May, 14 June 1893.

41 RA VIC/ADDC6/1893: 1 June.

42 Sir Harold Nicolson, *King George V: His Life and Reign*, London, Constable (1952), p. 84.

43 RA QM/PRIV/CC1/19, George to May, 19 June 1893.

44 RA QM/PRIV/CC5/15, May to George, 20 June 1893.

45 Ibid.

46 RA QM/PRIV/CC1/20, George to May, 20 June 1893.

47 RA QM/PRIV/CC1/23, George to May, 27 June 1893.

48 RA QM/PRIV/CC1/21, George to May, 24 June 1893.

49 RA QM/PRIV/CC1/25, George to May, 29 June 1893.

50 RA VIC/MAIN/Z/476/113 and 120, George to QV, 4 and 14 June 1893.

51 RA VIC/MAIN/Z/90/42, Alix to QV, 26 December 1892.

52 Nicholas's diary, 13 January [OS]/25 January 1893, and letter to Alix, 31 October [OS]/12 November 1893, cited in Andrei Maylunas and Sergei Mironenko (eds), *A Lifelong Passion: Nicholas & Alexandra, Their Own Story*, London, Phoenix (1997), pp. 18 and 23.

53 Nicholas's diary, 25 January [OS]/6 February 1893, cited in Maylunas and Mironenko (1997), p. 19.

54 Mathilde Kschessinska, *Dancing in Petersburg: The Memoirs of Mathilde Kschessinska*, Arnold Haskell (trans.), Alton, Dance Books (2005), p. 48.

55 Edward J. Bing (ed.), *The Letters of Tsar Nicholas and Empress Marie*, London, Ivor Nicholson & Watson (1937), pp. 70–2, 24 June [OS]/6 July 1893.

56 RA VIC/MAIN/QVJ/1893: 1 July.

57 Nicholas's diary, 19 June [OS] /1July 1893, cited in Maylunas and Mironenko (1997), p. 21.

58 RA VIC/MAIN/Z/90/49, Alix to QV, 2 June 1893.

59 Bing (1937), pp. 70–2, 24 June [OS]/6 July 1893.

60 RA VIC/ADDC6/1893: 5 July.

61 MB 21/1/Vol. 1, Recollections of Victoria, Marchioness of Milford Haven, p. 148.

62 RA VIC/MAIN/QVJ/1893: 5 July.

63 Bing (1937), pp. 70–2, 24 June [OS]/6 July 1893.

64 LPL/Benson 130/376, M. and E. Bourne to Benson, 8 October 1893.

65 LPL/Benson 130/383, Pelly to Benson, 30 June 1894.

66 LPL/Benson 130/378, A. Hayes to Benson, 13 October 1893.

67 *Chicago Daily Tribune*, 8 December 1936.

68 Nicolson (1952), p. 200.

69 RA QM/PRIV/CC1/26, George to May, 3 July 1893.

70 Ibid.

71 RA QM/PRIV/CC5/21, May to George, 6 July 1893.

72 *The Times*, 7 July 1893.

73 *New York Times*, 7 July 1893.

74 RA VIC/MAIN/QVJ/1893: 6 July.

75 RA VIC/ADDC6/1893: 6 July.

76 *The Times*, 7 July 1893.

77 *New York Times*, 7 July 1893.

78 Marie, Queen of Romania, *The Story of my Life*, London, Cassell & Co (1934), vol. 2, p. 60.

79 Ibid.

80 *New York Times*, 7 July 1893.

81 RA GV/PRIV/AA12/17, George to QV, 9 July 1893.

82 RA GV/PRIV/AA12/24, George to QV, 7 November 1893.

83 RA VIC/ADDU/173/182, QV to V of Battenberg, 24 September 1893.

84 Michael John Sullivan, *A Fatal Passion: The Story of the Uncrowned Last Empress of Russia*, New York, Random House (1997), p. 117.

85 Nicholas to Alix, 31 October [OS]/12 November 1893, cited in Maylunas and Mironenko (1997), p. 24.

86 Alix to Nicholas, 8 November [OS]/20 November 1893, cited in Maylunas and Mironenko (1997), pp. 24–5.

87 Simon Sebag Montefiore, *The Romanovs, 1613–1918*, London, Weidenfeld and Nicolson (2016), p. 479.

88 Nicholas's diary, 18 November [OS]/30 November 1893, cited in Maylunas and Mironenko (1997), pp. 24–5.

89 Nicholas to Alix, 17 December [OS]/29 December 1893, cited in Maylunas and Mironenko (1997), pp. 27–8.

90 RA VIC/MAIN/Z/90/56, Alix to QV, 14 October 1893.

91 *St James Gazette*, 8 November 1893.

92 G. R. Esenwein, *Anarchist Ideology and the Working Class Movement in Spain, 1868–1898*, Berkeley, CA: University of California Press, 1989.

93 RA VIC/MAIN/Z/90/62, Ella to QV, 8 November [OS]/20 November 1893.

94 Ibid.

95 RA VIC/MAIN/Z/90/64, Ernie to QV, 18 December 1893.

96 RA VIC/ADDU/173/184, QV to V of Battenberg, 15 February 1894.

CHAPTER TEN NICHOLAS AND ALIX

1 Alix to Xenia, 30 March [OS]/11 April 1894, cited in Andrei Maylunas and Sergei Mironenko (eds), *A Lifelong Passion: Nicholas & Alexandra, Their Own Story*, London, Phoenix (1997), p. 35.

2 Edward J. Bing (ed.), *The Letters of Tsar Nicholas and Empress Marie*, London, Ivor Nicholson & Watson (1937), p. 74, 10 April [OS]/22 April 1894.

3   Robert K. Massie, *Nicholas & Alexandra*, London, Victor Gollancz, 1968, p. 32.

4   RA QM/PRIV/CC52/201, Francis of Teck to Princess M. Adelaide, 14 September 1892.

5   RA VIC/MAIN/QVJ/1894: 3, 5, 10 and 14 April 1894.

6   Bing (1937), p. 75, 10 April [OS]/22 April 1894.

7   Ibid.

8   RA VIC/MAIN/QVJ/1894: 14 and 17 April.

9   Marie, Queen of Romania, *The Story of my Life*, London, Cassell & Co (1934), vol. 2, p. 60.

10 Nicholas's diary, 6 April [OS]/18 April 1894, cited in Maylunas and Mironenko (1997), p. 38.

11 Bing (1937), p. 75, 10 April [OS]/22 April 1894.

12 John C. G. Röhl, *Wilhelm II, The Kaiser's Personal Monarchy, 1888–1900*, Cambridge, Cambridge University Press (2001), p. 498.

13 MB 21/1/Vol. 1, Recollections of Victoria, Marchioness of Milford Haven, p. 154.

14 Bing (1937), p. 76, 10 April [OS]/22 April 1894.

15 RA VIC/MAIN/QVJ/1894: 14 and 17 April.

16 RA VIC/MAIN/Z/90/72, Alix to QV, 2 April 1894.

17 RA VIC/MAIN/QVJ/1894: 20 April.

18 Maylunas and Mironenko (1997), pp. 42–3, 45, 49.

19 *Morning Post*, 21 April 1894.

20 *Standard*, 21 April 1894.

21 Reuters, 20 April 1894.

22 RA VIC/MAIN/Z/274/9, Benson to QV, 21 April 1894.

23 RA VIC/MAIN/Z/274/10, PM to QV, 30 April 1894.

24 RA VIC/MAIN/QVJ/1894: 18 May.

25 Agatha Ramm (ed.), *Beloved and Darling Child: Last Letters between Queen Victoria and her Eldest Daughter, 1886–1901*, Stroud, Sutton Publishing (1990), pp. 167–8, Vicky to QV, 21 June 1894.

26 Ibid., pp. 179 and 183, Vicky to QV, 20 July 1895 and 14 November 1895.

27 RA VIC/MAIN/QVJ/1894: 4 May and Alix to Nicholas, 22 April [OS]/4 May 1894, cited in Maylunas and Mironenko (1997), p. 54.

28 RA VIC/MAIN/Z/90/74, Alix to QV, 9 June 1894.

29 MB 21/1/Vol. 1, Recollections of Victoria, Marchioness of Milford Haven, p. 155.

30 QV to Nicholas, 6 June 1894, cited in Maylunas and Mironenko (1997), p. 64.

31 RA VIC/ADDU/173/187, QV to V of Battenberg, 25 May 1894.
32 RA VIC/MAIN/QVJ/1894: 25 June.
33 Ibid., 29 June 1894.
34 Ibid., 17 and 31 July 1894.
35 RA VIC/ADDU/173/191, QV to V of Battenberg, 21 October 1894.
36 Alix to Nicholas, 11 September [OS]/23 September 1894, Nicholas to Alix, 1 and 11 September [OS]/13 and 23 September 1894, cited in Maylunas and Mironenko (1997), pp. 86, 87, 89.
37 RA VIC/MAIN/QVJ/1894: 22 October.
38 *Daily Telegraph*, 5 November 1894.
39 RA VIC/MAIN/QVJ/1894: 1 November.
40 Maylunas and Mironenko (1997), pp. 91, 97 and 99.
41 RA VIC/MAIN/QVJ/1894: 2 and 5 November.
42 Ramm (1990), p. 172, QV to Vicky, 5 November 1894.
43 RA VIC/MAIN/Z/275/25, Ella to QV, 5/17 November 1894.
44 RA VIC/MAIN/QVJ/1894, 13 and 15 November.
45 RA VIC/MAIN/Z/274/43, General Ellis, 26 November 1894.
46 Massie (1968), p. 44.
47 RA VIC/MAIN/QVJ/1894: 19 November.
48 Ramm (1990), p. 173, QV to Vicky, 25 November 1894.
49 Massie (1968), p. 44.
50 RA VIC/MAIN/QVJ/1894: 26 November.
51 RA VIC/MAIN/Z/274/55, Ella to QV, 19 November [OS]/1 December 1894.
52 RA VIC/MAIN/Z/90/78 and 81, Ella to QV, 26 March [OS]/7 April 1895 and 31 October [OS]/12 November 1895.
53 RA VIC/MAIN/Z/274/52, George to QV, 16 November 1894.
54 RA VIC/MAIN/Z/274/57, Alix to QV, 6 December 1894.
55 Nicholas's diary, 26 November [OS]/8 December 1894, cited in Maylunas and Mironenko (1997), p. 109.
56 Count Egon Caesar Corti, *The English Empress: A Study in the Relations between Queen Victoria and her Eldest Daughter, Empress Frederick of Germany*, London, Cassell & Co (1957), p. 349.
57 Massie (1968), p. 63.
58 Marie, Queen of Romania (1934), vol. 2, pp. 65–6.
59 Ibid., p. 66.
60 Ibid., pp. 68 and 71.
61 Ibid., p. 71.
62 MB 21/1/Vol. 1, Recollections, p. 172.

63 Simon Sebag Montefiore, *The Romanovs, 1613–1918*, London, Weidenfeld and Nicolson (2016), p. 499.

64 Marie, Queen of Romania (1934), vol. 2, p. 73.

65 Xenia's diary, 19 May [OS]/31 May 1896, cited in Maylunas and Mironenko (1997), p. 139.

66 RA VIC/MAIN/QVJ/1896: 3 and 4 June.

67 MB 21/1/Vol. 1, Recollections, p. 170.

68 MB 11/1/1, Victoria Battenberg's notes on her reading.

69 RA VIC/MAIN/QVJ/1896: 3, 6, 16 and 21 September.

70 Ramm (1990), p. 195, QV to Vicky, 26 September 1896.

71 RA VIC/MAIN/QVJ/1896: 22 and 23 September.

72 Bing (1937), p. 118, 13 September [OS]/25 September 1896.

73 MB 21/1/Vol. 1, Recollections, p. 243.

74 Röhl (2001), p. 789.

75 RA VIC/MAIN/QVJ/1896: 8 January.

76 RA VIC/MAIN/QVJ/1896: 5 January.

77 RA VIC/MAIN/Z/500/4, QV to Wilhelm, 4 January 1896.

78 E. F. Benson, *The Kaiser and English Relations*, London, Longmans, Green & Co (1936), p. 133.

79 RA VIC/MAIN/QVJ/1896: 10 January.

80 Christopher Hibbert (ed.), *Queen Victoria in her Letters and Journals*, New York, Viking (1984), p. 333, 11 January 1896.

81 Röhl (2001), pp. 969–70.

82 MB 1/T/95 (F2), Report of Conversation of Tsar, L of Battenberg and Prince Lobanoff, 10 June 1896.

83 Corti (1957), p. 352.

84 Maylunas and Mironenko (1997), p. 145, Nicholas to QV, 10 October [OS]/22 October 1896.

85 Ibid., p. 154, Konstantin's diary, 30 July [OS]/11 August.

86 RA VIC/MAIN/Z/90/86, Ella to QV, 3/15 February 1896.

87 Ibid.

CHAPTER ELEVEN ENA AND ALFONSO

1 RA VIC/MAIN/QVJ/1897: 22 June.

2 *St James Gazette*, 23 June 1897.

3 RA VIC/MAIN/QVJ/1897: 27 June.

4 RA VIC/MAIN/QVJ/1897: 20 and 21 June.

5 *St James Gazette*, 23 June 1897.

6 RA VIC/MAIN/QVJ/1897: 22 June.

7 *St James Gazette*, 23 June 1897.

8 MB 21/1/Vol. 1, Recollections of Victoria, Marchioness of Milford Haven, pp. 179 and 190.

9 *St James Gazette*, 23 June 1897.

10 RA GV/PRIV/AA12/46, George to QV, 24 October 1896.

11 RA GV/PRIV/AA12/43, George to QV, 17 February 1896.

12 RA VIC/MAIN/QVJ/1896: 22 July.

13 A. N. Wilson, *Victoria: A Life*, London, Atlantic Books (2014), p. 549.

14 Miranda Carter, *The Three Emperors*, London, Penguin (2009), p. 241.

15 John C. G. Röhl, *King Wilhelm II, 1859–1941: A Concise Life*, Cambridge, Cambridge University Press (2014), p. 67.

16 John C. G. Röhl, *Wilhelm II, The Kaiser's Personal Monarchy, 1888–1900*, Cambridge, Cambridge University Press (2001), pp. 925–6.

17 Agatha Ramm (ed.), *Beloved and Darling Child: Last Letters between Queen Victoria and her Eldest Daughter, 1886–1901*, Stroud, Sutton Publishing (1990), p. 206, QV to Vicky, 18 August 1897.

18 Ramm (1990), p. 210, Vicky to QV, 20 December 1897.

19 Christopher Hibbert (ed.), *Queen Victoria in Her Letters and Journals*, New York, Viking (1984), pp. 337–8, March 1899.

20 Catrine Clay, *King, Kaiser, Tsar: Three Royal Cousins who Led the World to War*, London, John Murray (2006), p. 193.

21 Röhl (2001), pp. 975–6.

22 Ramm (1990), p. 199, Vicky to QV, 19 February 1897.

23 Hibbert (1984), pp. 341–2.

24 Ibid., p. 344.

25 Ramm (1990), p. 221, QV to Vicky, 11 September 1898.

26 E. de Burgh, *Memoir of Empress Elizabeth*, London, Hutchinson & Co (1899), pp. 326–7.

27 Ramm (1990), p. 221, Vicky to QV, 12 September 1898.

28 Ibid., p. 215, QV to Vicky, 31 May 1898.

29 RA GV/PRIV/AA12/81, George to QV, 4 April 1900.

30 MB 21/1/Vol. 1, Recollections, p. 197.

31 Ramm (1990), p. 258, QV to Vicky, 27 December 1900 and 6 January 1901.

32 RA VIC/MAIN/QVJ/1901: 1 January.

33 Xenia's diary, 9 January [OS]/22 January 1901, cited in Andrei Maylunas and Sergei Mironenko (eds), *A Lifelong Passion: Nicholas & Alexandra, Their Own Story*, London, Phoenix (1997), p. 188.

34 MB 21/1/Vol. 1, Recollections, p. 196.

35 Wilson (2014), p. 569.

36 Count Egon Caesar Corti, *The English Empress: A Study in the Relations between Queen Victoria and her Eldest Daughter, Empress Frederick of Germany*, London, Cassell & Co (1957), p. 364.

37 Wilson (2014), p. 572.

38 Hibbert (1984), p. 500.

39 Boris Savinkov, *Memoirs*, cited in Maylunas and Mironenko (1997), p. 246.

40 Ibid., p. 240, Konstantin's diary, 12 September [OS]/25 September 1904.

41 MB 21/1/Vol. 1, Recollections, p. 228.

42 Prince Felix Yusupov, *Lost Splendour*, Ann Green and Nicolas Katkoff (trans.), London, Jonathan Cape (1953), p. 100.

43 Edvard Radzinsky, *Alexander II: The Last Great Tsar*, New York, Free Press (2005), p. 68.

44 MB 21/1/Vol. 1, Recollections, p. 233.

45 Savinkov, *Memoirs*, cited in Maylunas and Mironenko (1997), p. 247.

46 Konstantin's diary and M. Pavlovna's *Memoirs*, cited in Maylunas and Mironenko (1997), pp. 249–50, 254.

47 MB 21/1/Vol. 1, Recollections, p. 235.

48 Christopher Warwick, *Ella: Princess, Saint and Martyr*, Chichester, John Wiley (2006), p. 220.

49 Xenia's diary, 4 February [OS]/17 February 1905, cited in Maylunas and Mironenko (1997), p. 251.

50 MB 21/1/Vol. 1, Recollections, p. 236.

51 Ibid.

52 Ibid.

53 Radzinsky (2005), p. 74.

54 MB T75/F2, Bertie to Louis Battenberg, 15 July 1905.

55 Ibid.

56 Ibid.

57 Theo Aronson, *Grandmama of Europe: The Crowned Descendants of Queen Victoria*, London, Cassell & Co (1973, rev. edn 1994), p. 156.

58 Julia Gelardi, *Born to Rule: Granddaughters of Queen Victoria, Queens of Europe*, London, Headline (2004), p. 142.

59 *New York Times*, 31 May 1906.

60 RA QM/PRIV/QMD/1906: 31 May.

61 Ibid., letter attached from Mrs George Young.

62   James Pope-Hennessy, *Queen Mary, 1867–1953*, London, George Allen & Unwin (1959), p. 406.
63   Marie, Queen of Romania, *The Story of my Life*, London, Cassell & Co (1934), vol. 1, pp. 95–6.
64   E. M. Almedingen, *An Unbroken Unity: A Memoir of Grand-Duchess Serge of Russia*, London, Bodley Head (1964), p. 58.
65   Yusupov, *Lost Spendour*, p. 100.
66   MB 21/1/Vol. 1, Recollections, p. 244.
67   Warwick (2006), pp. 250–1.
68   MB 21/1/Vol. 1, Recollections, p. 247.
69   Ibid., p. 274.
70   Marie, Queen of Romania, *The Story of my Life*, London, Cassell & Co (1934), vol. 2, p. 205.
71   Röhl (2014), p. 254.
72   Ibid., p. 99.
73   MB T75/F2, Bertie to Louis of Battenberg, 15 July 1905.
74   Marie, Queen of Romania (1934), vol. 2, p. 303.
75   Ibid., p. 304.
76   MB 21/1/Vol. 2, Recollections of Victoria, Marchioness of Milford Haven, p. 303.
77   Ibid., pp. 304–5.
78   Michael Balfour, *The Kaiser and His Times*, New York, Norton & Co (1972), p. 355.
79   Robert K. Massie, *Nicholas & Alexandra*, London, Victor Gollancz (1968), p. 274.
80   MB 21/1/Vol. 2, Recollections, p. 306.
81   MB 11/3/1, Papers of Victoria Mountbatten, Marchioness of Milford Haven.

CHAPTER TWELVE THE FALL

1   Marie, Queen of Romania, *The Story of my Life*, London, Cassell & Co (1934), vol. 2, p. 352.
2   Ibid., p. 351.
3   Winston Churchill, *The World Crisis, 1916–18*, Part 1, London, Thornton Butterworth (1927), pp. 17–19.
4   Marie, Queen of Romania (1934), vol. 2, p. 353.
5   Ibid., vol. 3, p. 5.
6   Marie to GV, August 30/12 September 1916, cited in ibid., p. 57.

7 John C. G. Röhl, *Wilhelm II: Into the Abyss of War and Exile, 1900–1941*, Cambridge, Cambridge University Press (2014), pp. 1,108 and 1,122.

8 Marie to Nicholas, 24 September/7 October 1916, cited in Marie, Queen of Romania (1935), vol. 3, pp. 65–6.

9 Ibid., pp. 62, 95, and 100.

10 Ibid., p. 117.

11 Robert K. Massie, *Nicholas & Alexandra*, London, Victor Gollancz (1968), p. 297.

12 Michael T. Florinsky, *The End of the Russian Empire*, New York, Collier Books (1961), p. 63.

13 Ibid., p. 67.

14 Andrei Maylunas and Sergei Mironenko (eds), *A Lifelong Passion: Nicholas & Alexandra, Their Own Story*, London, Phoenix (1997), p. 427.

15 Simon Sebag Montefiore, *The Romanovs, 1613–1918*, London, Weidenfeld and Nicolson (2016), p. 595.

16 Prince Felix Yusupov, *Lost Splendour*, Ann Green and Nicolas Katkoff (trans.), London, Jonathan Cape (1953), p. 157.

17 Ibid., pp. 100 and 189.

18 Alix to Nicholas, 15 June [OS]/28 June 1915, and Ella's deposition, cited in Maylunas and Mironenko (1997), pp. 422 and 490.

19 Yusupov (1953), p. 157.

20 Sebag Montefiore (2016), p. 605.

21 Yusupov (1953), p. 195.

22 Sebag Montefiore (2016), pp. 604–9.

23 Alix to Nicholas, 22 February [OS]/7 March 1917, cited in Maylunas and Mironenko (1997), p. 544.

24 Massie (1968), p. 365.

25 Sandro (Grand Duke Alexander Mikhailovich), *Memoirs*, cited in Maylunas and Mironenko (1997), p. 537.

26 Theo Aronson, *Grandmama of Europe: The Crowned Descendants of Queen Victoria*, London, Cassell & Co (1973, rev. edn 1994), p. 222.

27 Sir Harold Nicolson, *King George V: His Life and Reign*, London, Constable (1952), p. 393.

28 Mabell, Countess of Airlie, *Thatched with Gold*, Jennifer Ellis (ed.), London, Hutchinson (1962), p. 132.

29 *Daily Mirror*, 16 and 17 March 1917.

30 Stamfordham to Balfour, 30 March 1917, cited in Kenneth Rose, *King George V*, London, Weidenfeld & Nicolson (1983), p. 211.

31 Stamfordham to Balfour, 6 April 1917, cited in Rose (1983), p. 212.

32 Ibid., p. 213.

33 Miranda Carter, *The Three Emperors*, London, Penguin (2009), p. 471.

34 *Daily Record*, 19 March 1917.

35 *Lancashire Evening Post*, 17 April and 1 June 1917.

36 *Liverpool Echo*, 22 June 1917.

37 Carter (2009), p. 473.

38 John C. G. Röhl, *Wilhelm II: Into the Abyss of War and Exile, 1900–1941*, Cambridge, Cambridge University Press (2014), p. 1,157.

39 Louis Fischer, *The Life of Lenin*, London, Weidenfeld and Nicolson (1964), p. 109.

40 Winston Churchill, *The World Crisis, 1916–1918*, Part 2, London, Thornton Butterworth (1927).

41 Röhl (2014), p. 1,157.

42 Julia Gelardi, *Born to Rule: Granddaughters of Queen Victoria, Queens of Europe*, London, Headline (2004), p. 214.

43 Theo Aronson, *Grandmama of Europe: The Crowned Descendants of Queen Victoria*, London, Cassell & Co (1973, rev. edn 1994), p. 211.

44 *The Greek White Book, Supplementary Diplomatic Documents, 1913–1917*, Forgotten Books, London (2015), p. 82, Sophie to Wilhelm, 13 December 1916 [OS]/26 December 1916.

45 Ibid., pp. 84 and 87, Sophie to Wilhelm, 20 December 1916 [OS] /2 January 1917 and 28 December 1916 [OS] /10 January 2017.

46 Marie, Queen of Romania (1935), vol. 3, pp. 181, 212 and 214.

47 Ibid., p. 186.

48 Ibid., pp. 249 and 431.

49 *The Scotsman*, 15 May 1917.

50 Rose (1983), p. 174.

51 *Nottingham Evening Post*, 17 July 1917.

52 Rose (1983), p. 222.

53 Nicholas to Xenia, 5 November [OS]/18 November 1917, cited in Maylunas and Mironenko (1997), p. 613.

54 Marie, Queen of Romania (1935), vol. 3, p. 319.

55 Nicholas's diary, 18 November [OS]/1 December 1917, cited in Maylunas and Mironenko (1997), p. 615.

56 Alix to A. Vyrubova, 15 December [OS]/28 December 1917, cited in ibid., p. 621.

57 Massie (1968), p. 470.

58 Yusupov (1953), p. 101.

59 Yurovsky's account, cited in Maylunas and Mironenko (1997), pp. 671–4.

60 Ryabov's account, cited in ibid., pp. 675–6.

61 Kaiser Wilhelm to General W. H. Waters, cited in Carter (2009), p. 480.

62 Röhl (2014), p. 1,176.

63 John Van der Kiste, *Kaiser Wilhelm II: Germany's Last Emperor*, Stroud, Sutton Publishing (1999, rev. edn 2014), p. 190.

64 Röhl (2014), pp. 1,177–8.

65 Decree of 30 September 1918, cited in Röhl (2014), p. 1,179.

66 Max von Baden, declaration 9 November 1918, cited in Röhl (2014), p. 1,186.

67 Carter (2009), p. 483.

68 E. F. Benson, *The Kaiser and English Relations*, London, Longmans, Green & Co (1936), p. 304.

69 John Gore, *King George V: A Personal Memoir*, London, John Murray (1941), p. 308.

70 Röhl (2014), p. 1,214.

71 Wilhelm II to General Mackensen, 2 December 1919, cited in ibid., p. 1,233.

72 Wilhelm II to Max von Mutius, 2 December 1920, cited in ibid., p. 1,234.

73 Wilhelm II to Poultney Bigelow, 15 August 1927, cited in ibid., p. 1,238.

74 Yuliy Osipovich Martov, *Down with the Death Penalty* (1918), original essay reprinted in S. V. Tyutyukin and O. V. Volobuev (eds), *Y. O. Martov*, Moscow, Izbrannoe (2000).

75 Michael John Sullivan, *A Fatal Passion: The Story of the Uncrowned Last Empress of Russia*, New York, Random House (1997), p. 358.

76 Frank Lorenz Muller, *Our Fritz: Emperor Frederick III and the Political Culture of Imperial Germany*, Cambridge, MA, Harvard University Press (2011), p. 274.

77 John McCrae, 'In Flanders Fields', *Punch*, 8 December 1915; Lieutenant-Colonel John McCrae, *In Flanders Fields and Other Poems*, London, Putnam's Sons (1919).

78 MB11/3/1, the Marchioness of Milford Haven's papers on her grandmother includes this adapted version of *Consolation*, by Theodor Storm.

Picture Credits

Queen Victoria, Prince Albert and five of their nine children. Franz Xaver Winterhalter, 1846 (*Royal Collection Trust/© Her Majesty Queen Elizabeth II 2017*)

Queen Victoria's family and guests (*The Royal Garden Party at Chiswick*). After Louis-William Desanges, c. 1876–9 (*Royal Collection Trust © Her Majesty Queen Elizabeth II 2017*)

Victoria, Princess Royal ('Vicky'). Thomas Richard Williams, 21 November 1856 (*Royal Collection Trust/© Her Majesty Queen Elizabeth II 2017*)

The assassination of Alexander II of Russia, 1881 (*Wikimedia Commons*)

Queen Victoria at the time of her Golden Jubilee. Alexander Bassano, 1882 (*Pictures from History/Alexander Bassano/ Bridgeman Images*)

Prince Albert Victor, known as 'Eddy'. British School, 1891–1910 (*Royal Collection Trust/© Her Majesty Queen Elizabeth II 2017*)

Princess Alix of Hesse. Carl Backofen, 1893 (*Royal Collection Trust/© Her Majesty Queen Elizabeth II 2017*)

Princess Elisabeth of Hesse. Hayman Selig Mendelssohn, 1887 (*Royal Collection Trust/© Her Majesty Queen Elizabeth II 2017*)

Prince George, Duke of York. Unknown photographer, c. 1890s
(*Getty Images/Popperfoto*)

Princess Marie of Edinburgh. Eduard Uhlenhuth, November 1890
(*Royal Collection Trust/© Her Majesty Queen Elizabeth II 2017*)

Nicholas, the Tsarevich of Russia, and Prince George, photographed together in 1893 when Nicholas came to Britain for
George's wedding (*Getty Images/Hulton Archive/Stringer*)

Princess Victoria Mary (May) of Teck. Byrne & Co., c. 1886
(*Royal Collection Trust/© Her Majesty Queen Elizabeth II 2017*)

Restaurant Véry, boulevard Magenta, Paris (Wikimedia Commons)

Cover of Le Petit Journal showing an explosion at the opera house
in Barcelona, 1893 (*World History Archive/Alamy Stock Photo*)

Cover of Le Petit Journal showing the assassination of the
French president, Carnot, by the Italian anarchist Sante Caserio
in Lyon, 1894 (*Chronicle/Alamy Stock Photo*)

Image from Hartmann the Anarchist, 1892 (*Paul Fearn/Alamy
Stock Photo*)

Queen Victoria's Diamond Jubilee celebrations, June 1897
(*Getty Images/Hulton Archive/Stringer*)

Queen Victoria's funeral, 2 February 1901 (*Getty Images/
Hulton Archive/Stringer*)

Bloody Sunday, St Petersburg, 22 January 1905 (*Getty Images/
Heritage Images*)

The remains of Grand Duke Sergei's carriage after his assassination in 1905 (*Wikimedia Commons*)

Princess Ena's wedding, Madrid, 1906 (*Getty Images/ullstein bild*)

First World War soldiers (*Getty Images/Frank Hurley/Hulton
Archive/Stringer*)

Index

Credit: Jerry Bauer

Deborah Cadbury is an award-winning documentary producer for the BBC. Her seven acclaimed books include *Seven Wonders of the Industrial World*, companion to the BAFTA-nominated BBC series; *The Feminization of Nature*; *The Dinosaur Hunters*; *The Lost King of France*; *Space Race*; and *Chocolate Wars*. Before turning to writing full time, she worked for thirty years as a BBC TV producer and executive producer and has won numerous international awards, including an Emmy Award. She lives in London.

A Note on the Type

The text of this book is set in Linotype Stempel Garamond, a version of Garamond adapted and first used by the Stempel foundry in 1924. It is one of several versions of Garamond based on the designs of Claude Garamond. It is thought that Garamond based his font on Bembo, cut in 1495 by Francesco Griffo in collaboration with the Italian printer Aldus Manutius. Garamond types were first used in books printed in Paris around 1532. Many of the present-day versions of this type are based on the *Typi Academiae* of Jean Jannon cut in Sedan in 1615.

Claude Garamond was born in Paris in 1480. He learned how to cut type from his father and by the age of fifteen he was able to fashion steel punches the size of a pica with great precision. At the age of sixty he was commissioned by King Francis I to design a Greek alphabet, and for this he was given the honourable title of royal type founder. He died in 1561.